# Instructor's Resource Guide

**Ellen G. Cohn**

**Florida International University**

# Criminology Today

## An Integrative Introduction

FOURTH EDITION

Frank Schmalleger

Professor Emeritius, The University of North Carolina at Pembroke

Upper Saddle River, New Jersey 07458

Pearson Education LTD.
Pearson Education Singapore, Pte. Ltd
Pearson Education, Canada, Ltd
Pearson Education–Japan
Pearson Education Australia PTY, Limited
Pearson Education North Asia Ltd
Pearson Educaçion de Mexico, S.A. de C.V.
Pearson Education Malaysia, Pte. Ltd

10 9 8 7 6 5 4 3 2 1

ISBN 0-13-170211-4

# Contents

# Introduction

The fourth edition of *Criminology Today* by Frank Schmalleger has been significantly revised and updated, and contains a considerable amount of new material. This *Instructor's Manual* is designed to accompany and to complement the textbook. It provides the instructor with a comprehensive overview and summary of the textbook to make teaching easier and more effective. The chapters of this manual directly correspond to those in the textbook. Each chapter of the *Instructor's Manual* contains the following information:

1. **Learning Objectives:** This section outlines the learning objectives for the chapter, as listed in the textbook at the start of the chapter. This list also appears in the *Student Study Guide*.

2. **Chapter Outline**: The chapter outline lists the major (first and second level) headings in the chapter, as shown in the textbook on the first page of the chapter. This outline also appears in the *Student Study Guide*.

3. **Chapter Summary:** The chapter summary is one to three pages in length and highlights the key points in the chapter. It also appears in the *Student Study Guide*. It is recommended that students read the chapter summary in the *Student Study Guide* both prior to and immediately after reading the textbook chapter.

4. **Lecture Outline:** This is a detailed outline of the material provided in the chapter and is intended to be used as a lecture guide. Each outline includes suggestions regarding when to show material from the Prentice Hall Video Library.

5. **Key Terms:** This section includes a list of the key terms for the chapter as well as the glossary definition for each term. This material also appears in the *Student Study Guide*.

6. **Additional Lecture Topics:** This section contains ideas for topics which are not contained in the textbook but which closely complement the material in each chapter. They may be used to expand upon the chapter and provide additional lecture material.

7. **Discussion Questions:** A list of discussion questions is provided at the end of each chapter in the textbook. This list is reproduced here and in the *Student Study Guide*. Instructors may which to focus on these questions after lecturing on the appropriate chapter.

8. **Student Activities:** This section includes several exercises that may be assigned to students. Some involve in-class group discussions, although many of these could also be conducted outside of class. Others involve take-home work and may be assigned for homework or extra credit. These exercises involve a wide variety of tasks, including searching the Internet, interviewing criminal justice system personnel, and examining crime-related data. Some of the assignments involve researching the criminal justice system of a city or state. The instructor may consider assigning each student a different area to research and then comparing their findings in class.

9. **Criminology Today on the Web:** This section, which is also found in the *Student Study Guide*, includes a list of sites on the World Wide Web that are related to the information in

the chapter. They may include links to criminal justice agencies, discussions of key criminological theories, or on-line articles on relevant topics.

10. **Student Study Guide Questions and Answers:** Each chapter of the *Student Study Guide* contains approximately 100 true/false, fill-in-the-blank, and multiple choice questions. This section in the *Instructor's Manual* includes all the questions that appear in the *Student Study Guide*, as well as the answers. An appendix in the *Student Study Guide* provides students with the answers to the odd-numbered questions only.

11. **Word Search and Crossword Puzzle Answers:** Each chapter in the *Student Study Guide* contains a word search puzzle and a crossword puzzle. The answer keys for these puzzles are provided in the *Instructor's Manual*.

On a personal note, I hope that you will find this *Instructor's Manual* both helpful and enjoyable. If you have any suggestions or ideas as to how this manual may be improved, please feel free to either contact Prentice Hall or to e-mail me directly.

Ellen G. Cohn, Ph.D.
Florida International University
cohne@fiu.edu

# 1 What Is Criminology?

## Learning Objectives

After reading this chapter, students should be able to:

1. Understand what criminology is and what criminologists do
2. Define *crime*
3. Recognize the difference between criminal and deviant acts and appreciate the complexity of this distinction
4. Understand the legalistic approach to the study of crime and know why it is limiting
5. Know what a theory is and explain the role of theorizing in the study of criminal behavior
6. Understand the distinction between the social problems and social responsibility perspectives on crime causation

## Chapter Outline

Introduction
What Is Crime?
Crime and Deviance
What Should Be Criminal?
What Do Criminologists Do?
What Is Criminology?
    *Theoretical Criminology*
Criminology and Social Policy
    *Social Policy and Public Crime Concerns*
The Theme of This Book
The Social Context of Crime
    *Making Sense of Crime: The Causes and Consequences of the Criminal Event*
The Primacy of Sociology?

# Chapter Summary

Chapter 1 provides an introduction to the textbook and to the field of criminology. It begins by discussing various perspectives for defining crime, including the legal, political, sociological, and psychological viewpoints. The definition used in the text is from the legal perspective, which sees crime as "human conduct in violation of the criminal laws of a state, the federal government, or a local jurisdiction that has the power to make such laws." This approach does have some limitations, however, some of which may be addressed by the other perspectives on crime.

While many crimes are forms of deviant behavior, behavior that violates social norms, not all crimes are deviant and not all deviant behavior is criminal. There is also a significant difference between what *is* criminal and what *should be* criminal. The consensus perspective holds that a law should be developed to criminalize a certain behavior when the members of a society generally agree that such a law is necessary. However, in a multicultural society, consensus may be difficult to achieve. The diversity of society is recognized in the pluralistic perspective which suggests that behaviors are typically criminalized through a political process after debate over the appropriate course of action. The issue of medical marijuana is an example of this process.

This chapter also discusses what a criminologist is, and considers the differences between a criminologist, a criminalist, and a criminal justice professional. Various professional opportunities for individuals with degrees in criminology are explored. The field of criminology itself is also discussed in detail, with various definitions considered. While criminology is primarily a social science, it is interdisciplinary. It contributes to, and overlaps, the field of criminal justice. One subfield is theoretical criminology, which posits explanations for criminal behavior. The chapter compares general and integrated theories of crime.

The development of social polices based on research findings may be of broader importance to society than theory testing. The chapter discusses how research into the effect of the media on teenage violence has been incorporated into federal reports and how it may eventually affect the development of new legislation regulating media programming. Concern over crime is one of the key issues in the country, making it an important determinant of public policy.

The social policy theme of the text is expanded through a contrast of the two main perspectives popular in today's society: the social problems perspective and the social responsibility perspective. The case of Jesse Timmendequas is discussed as an example of the contrast between these two perspectives. Recently, the social responsibility perspective has had a substantial influence on national crime control policy.

Crime is seen as a social event rather than as an isolated individual activity. The criminal event is the result of the coming together of inputs provided by the offender, the victim, the criminal justice system, and the general public (society). Background and foreground features or inputs provided by each contributor are discussed. In addition, each crime has consequences, or outputs, which affect not only the victim and offender but also society and the criminal justice system. These consequences may be immediate or more long-term.

This text recognizes the primacy of sociology: the belief that the primary perspective from which many contemporary criminologists operate is a sociological one. However, not all criminologists agree with this perspective and new and emerging perspectives are being developed.

# Lecture Outline

I. Introduction
   A. Discuss the Michael Jackson case
   B. Review the reaction of Jackson's family and friends (see *Crime in the News* on p. 6)

II. What Is Crime?
   A. Explain that various definitional perspectives exist when one attempts to define crime
      1. The four perspectives are legal, political, sociological, and psychological
      2. Perspective is important because it determines what assumptions are made about how crime should be studied: what questions are asked, what research is conducted, what type of answers are expected, and what conclusions are drawn
   B. Discuss the legalistic perspective
      1. Crime is defined as "human conduct in violation of the criminal laws of a state, the federal government, or a local jurisdiction that has the power to make such laws"
      2. Emphasize that this is the definition and the perspective used in this text
      3. Discuss the limitations of the legalistic approach to crime
         a. Immoral forms of behavior, which are not contravened by state statute, are not recognized by this approach
         b. It insists that the nature of crime and the nature of law cannot be separated
         c. Powerful individuals may use their power to ensure that their immoral behaviors are not criminalized
         d. Formalized criminal laws did not always exist
      4. Laws are constantly changing, creating new crimes or legalizing behaviors: discuss issues such as same-sex marriages and biomedical research
   C. Discuss the remaining three perspectives
      1. The political perspective sees crime as behavior that in some way threatens the interests of those with political power
      2. The sociological perspective considers crime as behavior that offends against human relationship or in some way injures the existing social system
      3. The psychological perspective sees crime as maladaptive behavior that prevents persons from living within the existing social framework
   D. Summary
      1. It is difficult to come up with one simple definition of crime that is acceptable to everyone
      2. Consider the four perspectives as points on a continuum, with strict legalistic definitions at one end and more fluid behavioral and moralistic definitions at the other

**Show the ABC News program *Mercy or Murder* from the video library.**

III. Crime and Deviance
   A. Deviant behavior is defined as "human activity that violates social norms"
   B. Discuss the relationship between crime and deviance
      1. Deviance and crime overlap but are not identical
         a. Not all deviant behavior is criminal
         b. Not all criminal behavior is deviant
      2. Discuss examples of deviant but noncriminal behavior (e.g., unusual dress styles)
      3. Discuss examples of criminal but common (and often socially acceptable) behavior (e.g., speeding)

IV. What Should Be Criminal?
   A. Discuss the difference between the questions "What is crime?" and "What should be criminal?"
   B. Two contrasting perspectives are used to answer the question "What should be criminal?"
      1. The consensus perspective emphasizes agreement among members of society as to what behaviors should be considered criminal and suggests that laws should be made to criminalize behaviors when members of society agree that the laws are necessary
      2. The pluralistic perspective suggests that societies are diverse and behaviors become criminalized through a political process involving considerable debate as to the appropriate course of action
   C. Discuss the issue of medical marijuana

V. What Do Criminologists Do?
   A. Explain the difference between a criminologist and a criminalist
      1. A criminologist is defined as "one who studies crime, criminals, and criminal behavior"
      2. A criminalist is "a specialist in the collection and examination of the physical evidence of crime"
      3. Criminal justice professionals include police and correctional officers, probation and parole officers, judges, defense attorneys and prosecutors, and others who do the day-to-day work of the criminal justice system
   B. Discuss the characteristics of academic and research criminologists
      1. They generally have a Ph.D. in criminology or criminal justice from an accredited university (or have a degree in a related field such as sociology with a specialization in the study of crime and deviance)
      2. They generally teach in universities and in two- and four-year colleges
      3. They generally conduct research and write for publication in journals published in the United States and abroad
      4. Discuss other options for people with degrees in criminology and/or criminal justice

VI. What Is Criminology?
   A. Discuss the definition of criminology
      1. Review the wide variety of definitions presented in the text
      2. The text concludes that criminology may be defined as "an interdisciplinary profession built around the scientific study of crime and criminal behavior, including their manifestations, causes, legal aspects, and control"

3. Criminology is mainly a social science but is interdisciplinary, drawing on other disciplines, such as anthropology, biology, sociology, political science, psychology, psychiatry, economics, ethology, medicine, law, philosophy, and ethics

B. Criminology also contributes to the field of criminal justice
   1. Criminal justice focuses on the application of the criminal law and the study of the components of the justice system, especially the police, courts and corrections
   2. Essentially, criminology focuses on the causes of criminality whereas criminal justice focuses on the control of crime

C. Theoretical criminology
   1. Theoretical criminology is a subfield of criminology that attempts to develop explanations for criminal behavior
   2. Criminologists have developed many theories to explain and understand crime
      a. A theory is "a series of interrelated propositions that attempt to describe, explain, predict, and ultimately control some class of events"
      b. A general theory is one that attempts to explain all or most types of criminal behavior through one basic overarching approach
      c. Unicausal theories suggest only once source for all serious deviant and criminal behavior
      d. Integrated theories do not attempt to explain all criminality but attempt to merge concepts drawn from different sources

VII. Criminology and Social Policy

A. Social policy based on research findings may have broader importance than theory testing
   1. Social policy includes government initiatives, programs, and plans intended to address problems in society
   2. Discuss the possible link between media violence and violent behavior in juveniles

B. Discuss social policy and public crime concerns
   1. Crime, terrorism, and national security are major concerns in the United States today, despite the fact that crime rates have been declining steadily for over 10 years
   2. A 2001 Gallup poll ranked crime as the fourth most important problem facing the United States today following terrorism, the economy, and fear (including fear of war)
   3. Concern about crime is not necessarily related to the actual incidence of crime
   4. Concern about crime is an important factor in determining public policy, so that political agendas focusing on reducing crime or changing criminogenic conditions tend to be favorably received

VIII. The Theme of This Book

A. This text builds on a social policy theme by contrasting two perspectives which are popular in the United States and the rest of the world
   1. The social problems perspective holds that crime is a manifestation of underlying social problems (poverty, discrimination, inequality of opportunity, the poor quality of education in some parts of the country, etc.)

    a. This perspective suggests that we need to deal with crime the same way we deal with public health concerns
    b. Solutions to the crime problem are seen as coming from large-scale government expenditures supporting social programs that address the macro-level issues that are at the root of crime
  2. The social responsibility perspective holds that people are fundamentally responsible for their own behavior and that they choose crime over other, more law-abiding courses of action
    a. This perspective suggests that we need to focus on crime-prone individuals rather than developing social programs
    b. Crime-reduction strategies include firm punishments, imprisonment, individualized rehabilitation, and increased security
B. While both viewpoints are popular, the social responsibility perspective recently has been significantly influencing national crime control policy
  1. Discuss federal examples such as the expanded number of capital crimes under federal laws, increased funding for prison construction, federal "Three Strikes" laws, and increased penalties for many federal offenses
  2. Consider discussing appropriate examples of how the criminal justice system of your state has been influenced by the social responsibility perspective

IX. The Social Context of Crime
  A. Every crime has a unique set of causes, consequences, and participants
    1. Crime provokes reactions from victims, concerned citizens, the criminal justice system, and society as a whole
    2. These reactions may contribute to the creation of new social policy
  B. The text attempts to identify and examine some of the causes of crime and discusses the various different perspectives that have been proposed to explain crime and criminality
  C. Making sense of crime: the causes and consequences of the criminal event
    1. This text sees crime as a social event rather than an isolated individual activity
    2. The text applies the concept of social relativity to the study of crime, focusing on how social events are differently interpreted based on an individual's experiences and interests
    3. Thus, crime means different things to the offender, the victim, the investigating officer, and the criminologist who studies the crime
    4. Discuss the causes and consequences of crime and explain how the criminal event results from inputs provided by the offender, the victim, society, and the criminal justice system

**Show the ABC News program *Bored to Death* from the video library.**

X. The Primacy of Sociology?
  A. Although many disciplines contribute to criminology, many criminologists operate primarily from a sociological perspective
    1. This means that many theories of criminal behavior are based in sociology
    2. The social problems/social responsibility dichotomy used in the text is an example of this

B. Advantages of the primacy of sociology include:
 1. Crime is a social phenomenon
 2. Much of contemporary criminology rests on a tradition of social scientific investigation into the nature of crime and criminal behavior

C. Problems with the primacy of sociology include:
 1. Sociology's apparent reluctance to accept the significance of findings from other disciplines
 2. Its frequent inability to integrate these findings into existing sociological understanding of crime
 3. Its seeming inability to demonstrate effective means of controlling crime

D. Discuss new and emerging perspectives in criminology, such as the increasing emphasis on integrated theories

E. The sociological perspective is likely to continue to dominate criminology for some time

# Key Concepts

**Crime**: Human conduct in violation of the criminal laws of a state, the federal government, or a local jurisdiction that has the power to make such laws.

**Criminalist**: A specialist in the collection and examination of the physical evidence of crime.

**Criminality**: A behavioral predisposition that disproportionately favors criminal activity.

**Criminalize**: To make illegal.

**Criminal justice**: The scientific study of crime, the criminal law, and components of the criminal justice system, including the police, courts, and corrections.

**Criminal justice system**: The various agencies of justice, especially the police, courts, and corrections, whose goal it is to apprehend, convict, punish, and rehabilitate law violators.

**Criminologist**: One who is trained in the field of criminology. Also, one who studies crime, criminals, and criminal behavior.

**Criminology**: An interdisciplinary profession built around the scientific study of crime and criminal behavior, including their forms, causes, legal aspects, and control.

**Deviant behavior**: Human activity that violates social norms.

**General theory**: One that attempts to explain all (or at least most) forms of criminal conduct through a single, overarching approach.

**Integrated theory**: An explanatory perspective that merges (or attempts to merge) concepts drawn from different sources.

**Socialization**: The lifelong process of social experience whereby individuals acquire the cultural patterns of their society.

**Social policy**: A government initiative, program, or plan intended to address problems in society. The "war on crime," for example, is a kind of generic (large-scale) social policy—one consisting of many smaller programs.

**Social problems perspective**: The belief that crime is a manifestation of underlying social problems, such as poverty, discrimination, pervasive family violence, inadequate socialization practices, and the breakdown of traditional social institutions.

**Social relativity**: The notion that social events are differently interpreted according to the cultural experiences and personal interests of the initiator, the observer, or the recipient of that behavior.

**Social responsibility perspective**: The belief that individuals are fundamentally responsible for their own behavior and that they choose crime over other, more law-abiding courses of action.

**Statute**: A formal written enactment of a legislative body.

**Statutory law**: Law in the form of statutes or formal, written strictures made by a legislature or governing body with the power to make law.

**Theory**: A series of interrelated propositions that attempt to describe, explain, predict, and ultimately to control some class of events. A theory gains explanatory power from inherent logical consistency and is "tested" by how well it describes and predicts reality.

**Unicausal**: Having one cause. Unicausal theories posit only one source for all that they attempt to explain.

# Additional Lecture Topics

One topic for discussion during this chapter is the impact of the mass media on crime. The mass media includes not only television news but also television reality programs, nonreality-based television programs, movies, radio news, and newspapers. This lecture segment could include:

- What are the typical images of crime that are presented by the mass media (a focus on unusual circumstances or elements)?
- How are these images and information influenced or even distorted by the needs of the media?
- What types of crime are most commonly featured by the media (a focus on violent crime)?
- How "real" are reality-based TV shows (*Cops*, *America's Most Wanted*, etc.)?

- Do the large number of crime-related shows and information presented by the media leave viewers with a mistaken impression concerning the true amount and seriousness of crime in society?
- Are certain types of media more likely to sensationalize crime than other types?
- In what ways might the media improve its coverage of crime?

Another lecture topic would involve discussing the various fields or areas within the discipline of criminology, in addition to theoretical criminology. These might include:

- Penology
- Victimology
- The sociology of law
- Criminal statistics
- Criminal behavior systems

# Discussion Questions

These discussion questions are found in the textbook at the end of the chapter. The instructor may want to focus on these questions during the coverage of Chapter 1.

1. This book emphasizes a social problems versus social responsibility theme. Describe both perspectives. How might social policy decisions based on these perspectives vary?

2. What is crime? What is the difference between crime and deviance? How might the notion of crime change over time? What impact does the changing nature of crime hold for criminology?

3. Do you believe that doctor-assisted suicide should be legalized? Why? What do such crimes as doctor-assisted suicide have to tell us about the nature of the law and about crime in general?

4. Do you think that policymakers should address crime as a matter of individual responsibility and accountability, or do you think that crime is truly a symptom of a dysfunctional society? Why?

5. Describe the various participants in a criminal event. How does each contribute to an understanding of the event?

6. What do criminologists do? Do you think you might want to become a criminologist? Why?

7. Why is the sociological perspective especially important in studying crime? What other perspectives might be relevant? Why?

# Student Exercises

## Activity #1

Watch a number of reality-based television shows such as *Cops* and keep a record of the following information for each crime/event:

1. The gender and race of the suspects
2. The gender and race of the police officers
3. The type of crime
4. The products being advertised during these programs

Questions to consider:

1. What is the predominant race of the suspects? The police officers?
2. Do you notice any difference in the behavior of the suspects and police officers when they are both of the same race? Of different races? Of different genders?
3. What types of crimes are featured? Does one type of crime predominate?
4. Are the products advertised during these programs directed toward any specific subgroup of the population? Are they age- or gender-based?

## Activity #2

First, identify five behaviors that are against the law but which you do not consider to be deviant as well as five legal behaviors which you do consider to be deviant. Your instructor will divide the class into groups. Within each group, compare and contrast the items on your lists. Focus on the wide range of opinions present among a fairly homogenous group (university students studying criminal justice). Discuss possible reasons for differing opinions (e.g., religious beliefs, profession, prior experiences with the criminal justice system).

# Criminology Today on the Web

### http://www.talkjustice.com/cybrary.asp

This site is maintained by the author of your textbook, Dr. Frank Schmalleger, and includes an extensive collection of links to criminal justice and criminology web sites.

### http://www.criminology.fsu.edu/cjlinks

This is Dr. Cecil Greek's Criminal Justice Links, which includes a huge number of links to all sorts of criminology- and criminal justice-related web sites.

### http://faculty.ncwc.edu/toconnor/linklist.htm

This is the Criminal Justice Mega-Sites web page, which includes an annotated list of criminology and criminal justice sites.

# Student Study Guide Questions and Answers

## True/False

1. The legalistic perspective defines crime as conduct in violation of the criminal law. **(True, p. 5)**

2. Formalized laws have always existed. **(False, p. 7)**

3. The political perspective defines crime in terms of popular notions of right and wrong. **(False, p. 7)**

4. The sociological perspective sees crime as encompassing any harmful acts. **(True, p. 8)**

5. A unified definition of crime is simple to achieve. **(False, p. 9)**

6. All criminal behavior is deviant. **(False, p. 9)**

7. The pluralistic perspective is most applicable to societies characterized by a shared belief system. **(False, p. 12)**

8. A shared consensus is easy to achieve in the United States. **(False, p. 12)**

9. There is a growing tendency to apply the term *criminologist* to anyone who works in the criminal justice field. **(False, p. 12)**

10. Criminology is an interdisciplinary field. **(True, p. 15)**

11. Theoretical criminology focuses on describing crime and its occurrence. **(False, p. 17)**

12. Concern over crime is no longer a serious issue in the United States. **(False, p. 19)**

13. Concern over crime is not necessarily related to the actual incidence of crime. **(True, p. 20)**

14. The social problems perspective is also known as the individual responsibility perspective. **(False, p. 21)**

15. According to the text, crime is an isolated individual activity. **(False, p. 22)**

16. Inputs are the background causes of crime. **(False, p. 23)**

17. Background contributions to crime are generally not very important. **(False, p. 24)**

18. Proper system response may increase crime. **(False, p. 24)**

## Fill in the Blank

19. Michael Jackson was charged with __________. **(child molestation, p. 6)**

20. To criminalize a behavior involves making it __________. **(illegal, p. 7)**

21. Societies with shared values, norms and belief systems are best described by the __________ perspective. **(consensus, p. 12)**

22. The psychological perspective is also known as the __________ perspective. **(maladaptive, p. 9)**

23. __________ is human behavior that violates social norms. **(Deviant behavior, p. 9)**

24. A __________ specializes in the collection and examination of the physical evidence of crime. **(criminalist, p. 12)**

25. The term *criminology* was coined by __________. **(Paul Topinard, p. 14)**

26. Criminology contributes to the discipline of __________. **(criminal justice, p. 17)**

27. __________ has been attributed to films and television. **(Copycat violence, p. 18)**

28. The social problems perspective is characteristic of what social scientists term a __________ approach. **(macro, p. 20)**

29. The immediate results or consequences of crime are known as __________. **(outputs, p. 23)**

30. A specific intent is an example of a __________ contribution to crime. **(foreground, p. 24)**

31. The primacy of sociology emphasizes that crime is a __________. **(social phenomenon, p. 28)**

## Multiple Choice

32. "Human conduct that is in violation of the criminal laws of a state, the federal government, or a local jurisdiction that has the power to make such laws" is a definition of
    a. criminology.
    b. **crime. (p. 5)**
    c. criminal.
    d. deviance.

33. The legalistic approach would suggest that crime is socially relative in the sense that is created by
    a. **legislative activity. (p. 7)**
    b. social mores.
    c. the democratic process.
    d. human conduct.

34. The concept that crime is defined in terms of the power structures that exist in society exemplifies the __________ perspective.
    a. sociological
    b. mainstream
    c. **political (p. 7)**
    d. psychological

35. The belief that crime is an antisocial act of such a nature that repression is necessary to preserve the existing system of society is the basis of the __________ perspective on crime.
    a. legal
    b. political
    c. **sociological (p. 8)**
    d. psychological

36. The psychological perspective sees crime primarily as
    a. a violation of a law.
    b. an offense against human relationships.
    c. a form of social maladjustment.
    d. **problem behavior. (p. 9)**

37. Because you were late for this exam, you exceeded the speed limit by about 10 to 15 miles per hour while driving to class. This is an example of behavior that is
    a. deviant but not criminal.
    b. **criminal but not deviant. (p. 10)**
    c. both deviant and criminal.
    d. neither deviant nor criminal.

38. Taiwan is expected to become the first country in Asia to legalize
    a. gambling.
    b. female prostitution.
    c. adult pornography.
    d. **some form of gay marriage. (p. 10)**

39. The medical marijuana debate is an example of the __________ perspective.
    a. consensus
    b. psychological
    c. sociological
    d. **pluralistic (p. 12)**

40. One who studies crime, criminals, and criminal behavior is called a
    a. scientist.
    b. criminal justice professional.
    c. **criminologist. (p. 12)**
    d. criminalism.

41. The official publication of the American Society of Criminology is
    a. ***Criminology*. (p. 12)**
    b. *Justice Quarterly*.
    c. *The Journal of Quantitative Criminology*.
    d. *Crime and Delinquency*.

42. The __________ definition of criminology literally defines the term as "the study of crime."
    a. **linguistic (p. 14)**
    b. disciplinary
    c. causative
    d. scientific

43. Which of the following is *not* one of the three principle components of criminology proposed by Clarence Ray Jeffery?
    a. Detection of the offender
    b. **The control of crime (p. 14)**
    c. Treatment
    d. Explanation of crime and criminal behavior

44. Which of the following is a disciplinary definition of criminology?
    a. **Criminology is the body of knowledge regarding the social problem of crime. (p. 16)**
    b. Criminology is the scientific study of crime.
    c. Criminology is the study of the causes of crime.
    d. Criminology is the scientific study of crime, criminals, and criminal behavior.

45. The field of study that is concerned primarily with the causes and consequences of crime is
    a. **criminology. (p. 17)**
    b. criminal justice.
    c. criminality.
    d. criminalistics.

46. A(n) __________ theory does not necessarily attempt to explain all criminality.
    a. general
    b. **integrated (p. 18)**
    c. uncausal
    d. complete

47. According to a recent Gallup poll, which of the following social problems was of greater concern than crime?
    a. Racial integration
    b. **Terrorism (p. 19)**

c. Education
d. Health-related issues

48. Workplace homicide is
a. the fastest-growing type of murder in the United States.
b. the leading cause of workplace death for women.
c. **both a and b (p. 19)**
d. none of the above

49. The social problems perspective holds that crime is
a. **a manifestation of underlying social problems. (p. 20)**
b. chosen by individual perpetrators.
c. not going to be solved by social programs.
d. none of the above

50. Which of the following crime reduction or prevention strategies is most characteristic of the social problems perspective?
a. **A government-funded initiative to enhance educational opportunities among low-income individuals (p. 20)**
b. A move to broaden police powers by increasing the number of exceptions to the Exclusionary Rule
c. Rewriting state statutes to increase the severity of punishment for violent offenders, such as three-strikes laws
d. All of the above

51. Which of the following is not a foreground contribution by an offender?
a. A particular motivation
b. **A peculiar biology (p. 23-24)**
c. A specific intent
d. A drug-induced state of mind

52. A victim may actively contribute to his/her own victimization through the appearance of
a. defensiveness.
b. exposure.
c. **defenselessness. (p. 24)**
d. precipitation.

# Word Search Puzzle

```
B P I T K B A Z Q V E D O T Z Z Y F J K F F M W M L Q I P
P P L J A P U T S B X U A U H R C H J H A S Z A T P T H B
S C S W Z C N Y M R G K B B O E R P E R F K B T V R B G C
U K U U V C G Y O U U E Z T E Y O N F A A J F V D N Z R G
R Y N J B W H V K I R Z E I C F Q R Y D Z K B N P L R O U
H V T O T D T Y S M V I A W Z J R Y Y K M G M Z B F Z G B
X W Y N G B I R D C I O A L U I R O T J V X A I G X W Q K
M A O P F Z Q L C Z W H I Y J C R I M I N O L O G I S T I
B N S T X C H P S I L D P R U K K F C Q E B K R L W X O F
R O U W P I S K N H E Q W N T Z M T R Y V A W N B A E D Z
T X C R I M I N A L I T Y W V E E L I K A R W P L Z I S X
I I B N S J W L Y O O T Z Z F K A X M D B T H N Q S I N I
H Z F E O K A S G F R Y D T X K N L I X X M Z L Z O V Z Y
L I C D C I N T E G R A T E D G O C N Y U Z K K H C P L Q
F V R M I U Z D C T R K R C B U V I A D J H W U P D G E K
O U I C A N L B R Q B Z P C O L U W L X R X S O Y A L B L
J E M H L S L D I R Y K J Z M U F G I E R K C J F M Y O U
A S E F I J O E M L N R B P X N S K S P E L S X J C U Z J
S N M D Z Q H N I X B G E K K I G T T M I T O X K R B H J
G E O B A R I O N C B J L O C C P Z U W J J N O X I T C H
Z X H A T Z P Q A E R Y F D O A B M S U C P B N D M R G C
M O X O I U A P L N F W W E O U S Z E R L G E X H I E P F
Z R P W O O X O I X S W A V Q S C T R R Y Y L J E N L X M
I P E C N Q V X Z K C Q V I U A H K A J K N Y U H O A L Q
U X W Y I W G T E C T P H A J L T O B T Y U Y L Z L T S K
B K B D D I K W O F A D E N W F M K O O U V P P D O I G R
Q Q I P R S E R M K F N L T A R N L B E D T V S C G V O V
D D C R V A S Z S W Z Q D D F N T H K S I Q E A E Y I L G
T V P Q B W E V G E A O L Y I O B A I A R Y J Z S T T O X
Y D B C G G O L V Z C C P I P G O S B Q J G Z S E Q Y R G
```

Criminalist
Criminality
Criminalize
Criminologist
Criminology
Deviant

Integrated
Relativity
Socialization
Statute
Theory
Unicausal

# Crossword Puzzle

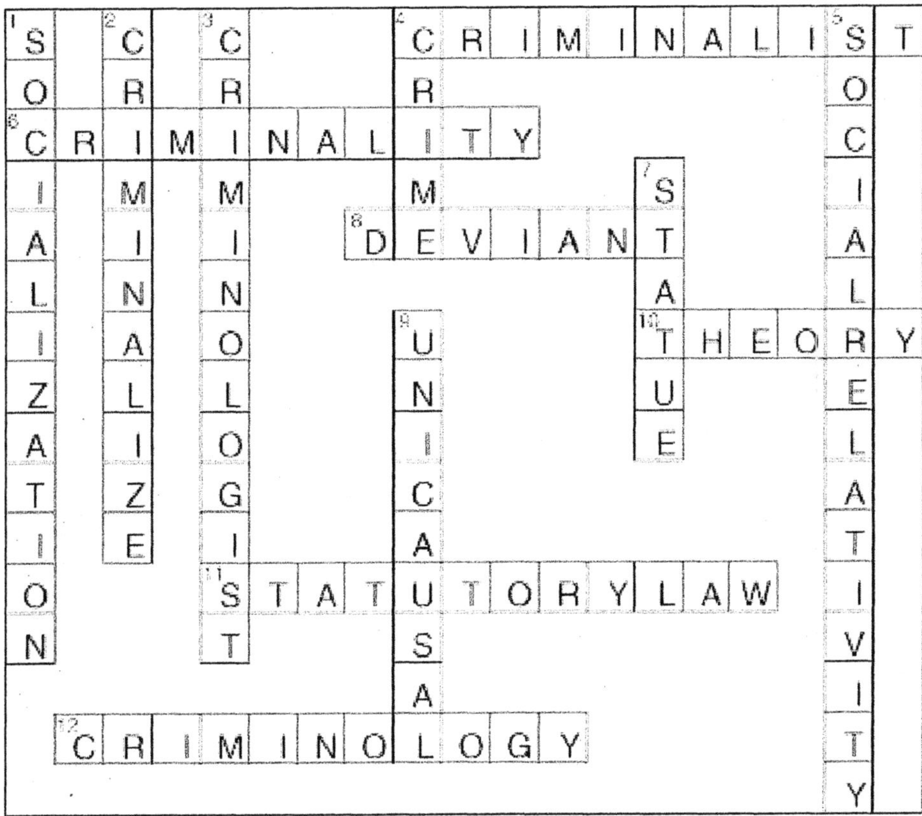

## Across

4. Someone who collects and examines the physical evidence of crime.
6. A behavioral predisposition that disproportionately favors criminal activity.
8. Behavior that violates social norms.
10. A series of interrelated propositions that describe, explain, predict, and control events.
11. Law in the form of formal written strictures. (2 words)
12. An interdisciplinary profession built around the scientific study of crime.

## Down

1. The process of social experience by which individuals acquire cultural patterns.
2. To make illegal.
3. Someone who studies crime and criminals.
4. Human conduct in violation of the criminal laws of a state or the federal government.
5. The notion that social events are differently interpreted according to the cultural experiences and personal interests of the initiator, the observer, or the recipient of that behavior.
7. A formal written enactment of a legislative body.
9. Having one cause.

# Patterns of Crime

## Learning Objectives

After reading this chapter, students should be able to:

1. Explain the history of statistical crime data collection and analysis, and understand the usefulness and limitations of crime data
2. Recognize the various methods currently in use to collect and disseminate crime data
3. Describe and explain the major sources of crime data in the United States, including the UCR, NIBRS, and NCVS
4. Define and discuss the social dimensions of crime, including key demographic factors

## Chapter Outline

Introduction
A History of Crime Statistics
- *Adolphe Quételet and André Michel Guerry*

Crime Statistics Today
- *Programmatic Problems with Available Data*
- *The UCR Program*
- *NIBRS: The New UCR*
- *Hate Crimes*
- *Data Gathering Under the NCVS*

Patterns of Change
The Crime Problem
- *Crime in World Context*

Major Crimes
- *Criminal Homicide*
- *Forcible Rape*
- *Robbery*
- *Aggravated Assault*
- *Burglary*
- *Larceny*
- *Motor Vehicle Theft*
- *Arson*

Part II Offenses

# Chapter Summary

This chapter describes various sources of crime statistics. It begins with a brief history of crime statistics, focusing on Thomas Robert Malthus, Adolphe Quételet, and André Michel Guerry, and reviewing the developing of the statistical school of criminology.

The two primary sources of information on crime in the United States today are official statistics and victimization statistics. Official statistics are found in the FBI's ***Uniform Crime Reports*** (UCR) and National Incident-Based Reporting System (NIBRS). Both are compiled annually by the FBI and contain data provided by police departments around the country. However, official statistics only include information on crimes known to the police and provide no insight into the dark figure of unreported crime. Victimization statistics, as provided by the National Crime Victimization Survey (NCVS), seek to obtain information on unreported crime. Subjects in the survey are asked about their victimization experiences; information is collected on the crime, the offender, and the specific incident, including whether or not the victim reported the criminal event to the police. Both sources of information have limitations. The differences among the three sources are reviewed.

The text also discusses the eight Part I or index offenses defined by the UCR. These include criminal homicide, forcible rape, robbery, aggravated assault, burglary, larceny, motor vehicle theft, and arson. Information about these crimes obtained from the UCR and the NCVS is presented. Hate crimes and Part II crimes are also discussed.

Information on unreported crime, known as the "dark figure of crime," may also be obtained from self-report surveys, in which anonymous respondents are asked to report confidentially any crimes they may have committed. The best known such surveys include the National Youth Survey, which surveys juveniles between the ages of 11 and 17, and the *Monitoring the Future* study, which focuses on the behaviors, attitudes, and values of students and young adults in the United States.

The social dimensions of crime are aspects of crime and victimization that relate to socially significant attributes by which groups are defined. These include age, gender, ethnicity, and social class. Criminal activity is associated more with youth, and most forms of criminality decrease with age (the desistance phenomenon). Elderly offenders are more likely to commit crimes requiring special skills and knowledge. The elderly are less likely to be victimized than any other group. Gender may be the best single predictor of criminality, with males being much more likely than women to commit most crimes. Women are also victimized less frequently than men in most crime categories (with the exceptions of the crimes of rape and spouse abuse).

Race may also be related to crime; arrest rates of blacks are significantly higher than their proportion in the population. The question of whether the criminal justice system is racist is discussed. Blacks are also more likely to be victimized than whites; the high rates of both crime and criminal victimization within the black community have led to a heightened fear of crime among blacks in the United States. The relationship of social class to crime originally assumed to exist began to be questioned in the 1960s. Recent data from the National Youth Survey does suggest that a fairly significant correlation between criminality and social class exists, with members of lower social classes being more likely to be involved in serious street crimes.

# Lecture Outline

I. Introduction: Discuss the Wesley "Pop" Honeywood case and why it is unusual

II. A History of Crime Statistics
  A. Population statistics have been gathered periodically since pre-Roman times
    1. Making inferences based on statistical demographics is a more recent development (in the last 200 years)
    2. Thomas Robert Malthus predicted exponential population growth, which would lead to a shortage of essential resources and increased conflict
  B. Adolph Quételet and André Michel Guerry
    1. André Michel Guerry (1802—1866), who calculated per capita crime rates in French provinces in the early 1800s, was one of the first to gather crime statistics systematically
    2. Adolphe Quételet (1796—1864) looked at the degree to which crime rates vary with climate, gender, and age
      a. Quételet developed the thermic law, which suggests that crime varies by season
      b. Violent crimes increase during hot summer months, and property crimes increase during colder periods of the year
    3. This type of work led to the development of the statistical school, a criminological perspective that seeks to uncover correlations between crime rates and other types of demographic data

III. Crime Statistics Today
  A. The main sources of crime statistics
    1. The National Crime Victimization Survey (NCVS) conducted annually by the Bureau of Justice Statistics (BJS)
    2. The FBI's Uniform Crime Reporting Program (UCR) and National Incident-Based Reporting Program (NIBRS)
    3. Briefly mention other sources of crime-related and criminal justice information such as the ICPSR
  B. Programmatic problems with available data (data sources are not strictly comparable)
    1. Each source uses specialized definitions which may not be based strictly on statutory crime classifications
    2. Compare the different definitions of rape found in the UCR, the NIBRS, the NCVS, and the U.S. Code

C. The UCR program
   1. Discuss the history and development of the UCR program
      a. It was begun by the FBI in 1929
      b. It was originally structured in terms of seven major offense categories; an eighth, arson, was added in 1979 – these are known as Part I or index crimes
      c. The crime index averages these crimes together and compares them with the population of the United States, providing a crime rate that can be compared over time and among geographic locations
   2. UCR Part I offenses
      a. Violent crimes: murder, rape, robbery, aggravated assault
      b. Property crimes: burglary, larceny, motor vehicle theft, arson
      c. Information provided for Part I crimes includes
         (1) Number of crimes reported to the police
         (2) Clearance rate: the proportion of crimes reported or discovered within a given offense category that are solved
      d. According to the UCR, a Part I offense is cleared when either:
         (1) "A law enforcement officer has charged at least one person with the offense" or
         (2) "A suspect has been identified and located and an arrest is justified, but action is prevented by circumstances outside law enforcement control"
   3. Define the "dark figure of crime" and explain why the UCR may seriously underestimate the incidence of crime in the United States

D. NIBRS: The new UCR
   1. NIBRS is a new incident-based crime reporting program that involves significant changes in the UCR
   2. Its key feature is that it is incident-driven: it includes data on the circumstances surrounding each serious criminal incident, focusing on single incidents and arrests within 22 crime categories (46 specific "Group A offenses")
   3. Information is collected on the incident, victim, property, offender, and arrestee
   4. The goal of NIBRS is to make data on reported crime more useful by relating it more completely to other available information such as victim and offender characteristics
   5. Compare the information that a police department must collect under NIBRS and under the summary-based UCR program
   6. Discuss the advantages of incident-based crime reporting
   7. NIBRS still includes only those crimes reported to the police

E. Hate crimes (also known as bias crimes)
   1. A hate crime is "a criminal offense in which the motive was hatred, bias, or prejudice based on the actual or perceived race, color, religion, national origin, ethnicity, gender, or sexual orientation of another individual or group of individuals"
   2. Congress passed the Hate Crime Statistics Act in 1990, requiring the FBI to collect and report data on hate crimes - the UCR began reporting hate crime information in 1997
   3. Compare and contrast the UCR and Bureau of Justice Statistics' definitions of hate crimes
   4. The role of hate groups

    a. Discuss the concept of hate groups such as the Ku Klux Klan and the Aryan Nations
    b. The majority of reported hate crimes are not committed by members of organized hate groups but by teenagers (mainly young white males), acting alone or in a group

F. Data gathering under the NCVS
1. The NCVS began in 1972 and differs from the UCR in that it obtains information through interviews with members of randomly selected households throughout the United States
2. The NCVS obtains information on crimes that were not reported to the police and therefore do not appear in the UCR or NIBRS
3. Discuss the process of collecting NCVS data
4. Crimes studied by the NCVS include rape, personal robbery, aggravated and simple assault, household burglary, personal and household theft, and motor vehicle theft
5. Discuss some of the findings obtained from NCVS reports
6. Critique of the NCVS
    a. There is possible overreporting: no attempt is made to verify whether crimes reported to the NCVS actually occurred
    b. Definitions of crimes do not necessarily correspond to federal or state statutes or definitions used by other programs
    c. Recent changes in the NCVS make it difficult to easily compare even recent findings with current data

IV. Patterns of Change – there have been three major shifts in crime rates since 1930

A. A sharp decline in crime in the early 1940s because many young men entered military service

B. An increase in crime beginning in the 1960s and ending in the 1990s; possible causes include:
1. "Baby boomers" becoming teenagers
2. Victims becoming sensitized to the importance of reporting crimes
3. More accurate and increased data collection by police departments
4. The disruption and tumult of the 1960s

C. A decrease in most major crimes since 1991; possible causes include:
1. The aging out of the baby-boomer generation
2. New strict laws
3. An expanded justice system and an increase in police funding
4. Changes in crime fighting technologies
5. The development and implementation of family planning practices
6. Economic expansion
7. Changes in the demographics caused by an aging of the population

V. The Crime Problem

A. Discuss whether crime rates provide an accurate measure of the extent of the crime problem in the United States
1. Official rates suggest crime is decreasing, but they are based only on a specific group of crimes and do not include drug offenses (for which arrests are still increasing)
2. Discuss whether the size of the correctional population might provide more accurate information on the crime problem in the United States

B. Crime rates may not provide an accurate assessment of the actual extent of the crime problem in any society if the rates are computed without regard to an international context
   1. Elliott Currie states that the rate of violent crime in the United States is much higher than in other industrial democracies
   2. He argues that the drop in crime is a "falling-off from an extraordinary peak" and that levels of violence in the United States are still unreasonably high
   3. Discuss Currie's criminality index and explain the concept of latent crime rate: a rate of crime calculated on the basis of crimes likely to be committed by those who are incapacitated by the criminal justice system

VI. Major Crimes in the United States
   A. Criminal homicide
      1. Homicide versus murder
         a. Homicide: the willful killing of one human being by another (this includes legal killings such as self-defense)
         b. Murder/criminal homicide: unlawful homicide, causing the death of another person without legal justification or excuse
      2. Types of murder
         a. First-degree murder is planned or premeditated and involves malice aforethought or any activity in preparation to kill that shows the passage of time between the formation of the intent to kill and the act of killing
         b. Second-degree murder is a crime of passion; the intent to kill and the actual killing are almost simultaneous
         c. Some jurisdictions use the term third-degree murder to refer to a homicide that is the result of some other unlawful or negligent action (also known as manslaughter, involuntary manslaughter, negligent manslaughter, or negligent homicide)
      3. Some jurisdictions classify felony murder (killing that occurs during the commission of another felony) as first-degree murder despite the lack of intent to kill
      4. Discuss statistics on murder derived from the UCR
   B. Forcible rape
      1. The UCR recognizes three categories of rape: forcible rape, statutory rape, and attempted forcible rape
      2. Other types of rape include:
         a. Spousal rape: a relatively new concept as most states have only recently revised statutes to allow a woman to prosecute her spouse under rape statutes if he forces her to have nonconsensual intercourse
         b. Gang rape
         c. Date rape: unlawful forced sexual intercourse with a woman against her will occurring within the context of a dating relationship
         d. Same-sex rape: not punishable as rape in all jurisdictions but becoming more widely recognized
      3. Discuss the existence of gender bias in many rape statutes
      4. Rape is generally considered a crime of power although some scholars have begun to return to the idea of sexual gratification as the underlying cause of rape
      5. Discuss UCR and NCVS rape statistics and how they differ

**Show the ABC News program *Watch What You Drink* from the video library**

C. Robbery
  1. The UCR/NIBRS defines robbery as "the unlawful taking or attempted taking of property that is in the immediate possession of another force or threat of force and/or by putting the victim in fear" (the NCVS definition is similar and also involves attempts)
  2. Distinguish between the terms "robbery" and "burglary" and explain that individuals are victims of robbery while houses (or other structures) are burglarized
  3. Types of robbery
     a. Highway/street robbery involves robbery that occurs in a public place (usually outdoors)
     b. Strong-arm robbery involves robbers who are unarmed and use intimidation or brute physical force to obtain the victim's possessions
     c. Armed robbery involves a weapon (usually a gun) and usually target commercial establishments (banks, convenience stores, service stations, etc.)
  4. Discuss UCR and NCVS robbery statistics

D. Aggravated assault
  1. The UCR defines aggravated assault as "the unlawful attack by one person upon another for the purpose of inflicting severe or aggravated bodily injury" (the NCVS definition is essentially the same)
     a. Generally, this means that a weapon is used or serious bodily injury involving hospitalization results
     b. The NCVS also reports statistics on the crime of simple assault, which does not involve a weapon and results in no injury or minor injury involving limited hospitalization
  2. Discuss UCR and NCVS assault statistics

E. Burglary
  1. The UCR defines burglary as "the unlawful entry of a structure to commit a felony or a theft"
  2. The NCVS and UCR/NIBRS generally recognize three subclassifications of burglary:
     a. Forcible entry: burglary involving some evidence of forcible entry (such as breakage or prying)
     b. Attempted forcible entry: evidence of force exists but the offender may not actually have entered
     c. Unlawful entry where no force is used: entry without force (such as through an unlocked door)
  3. Some jurisdictions punish nighttime home burglaries more harshly because of the increased likelihood for a violent confrontation between the offender and the homeowner
  4. Discuss UCR and NCVS statistics on burglary

F. Larceny (sometimes known as larceny/theft)
  1. The UCR/NIBRS defines larceny/theft as "the unlawful taking, carrying, leading, or riding away by stealth of property, other than a motor vehicle, from the possession or constructive possession of another"
  2. Larceny does not involve force or intentionally putting the victim in fear

3. Discuss differences between how the UCR and NCVS categorize subtypes of larceny
4. Discuss UCR and NCVS data on larceny

G. Motor vehicle theft
1. The UCR defines this crime as "the theft or attempted theft of a motor vehicle," including automobiles, trucks, buses, motorcycles, motorscooters, and snowmobiles, but not planes, boats, trains, and spacecraft
2. Carjacking
   a. A significantly more serious crime that involves stealing a car while it is occupied; it usually involves a weapon and the victim is frequently injured or killed
   b. Although it involves elements of theft, it is more closely related to robbery and/or kidnapping
3. Discuss UCR and NCVS statistics on motor vehicle theft

H. Arson
1. Arson involves "the willful or malicious burning or attempt to burn, with or without attempt to defraud, of a dwelling house, public building, motor vehicle or aircraft, personal property of another, etc."
2. Discuss the various motivations for the commission of arson
   a. Thrill-seekers set fires for excitement
   b. Vandals seek random destruction
   c. Pyromaniacs may suffer from psychological problems that contribute to their fire-setting activities
   d. Arson for vengeance involves an attempt to "strike back" at another person (employer, former spouse, etc.)
   e. Vanity pyromaniacs set fires so that they can take credit for putting them out
   f. Some offenders use arson to conceal other felonies (murder, burglary, etc.)
   g. Arson to defraud insurance companies is the most common motivation
3. Discuss UCR arson statistics

VII. Part II Offenses

A. In addition to the eight Part I crimes, the UCR also collects data on arrests made by police for a number of less serious offenses known as Part II offenses

B. Only arrests are recorded because many Part II offenses are less serious or are considered victimless crimes and are discovered only when an arrest occurs

VIII. Other Sources of Data

A. The Crime Awareness and Campus Security Act of 1990 requires all colleges and universities that receive any form of federal funding to report campus crime statistics to the Department of Education

B. The 1990 Act was amended in 1992 by the Campus Sexual Assault Victims' Bill of Rights to require schools to develop policies to deal with sexual assault on campus and provide certain assurances to victims

C. A 1998 amendment created the Campus Security Statistics Web site, which provides a direct link to criminal offenses reported at over 6,700 colleges and universities in the United States

IX. Unreported Crime
   A. Self-report surveys
      1. Involves interviewing subjects regarding crimes they have committed as a way of learning more about unreported crime
      2. Subjects are generally anonymous so there is no fear of disclosure or arrest and the individual responses are confidential
      3. Discuss the limitations of self-report studies of crime
         a. Subjects are usually young people (high school or college students)
         b. Studies frequently are limited to questions about petty offenses such as shoplifting and simple theft
         c. They typically focus on juvenile delinquency, not adult criminality
         d. There is no guarantee of respondent accuracy
      4. Recent self-report surveys include the National Youth Survey and the Monitoring the Future study
   B. NCVS data can also be used to partially estimate the dark figure of crime
   C. Discuss reasons why victims may not report crimes to the police

X. The Social Dimensions of Crime
   A. What are "social dimensions"?
      1. Social dimensions are social factors and characteristics that are related to crime (gender, ethnicity/race, age, income, profession, social class)
      2. These social dimensions are related or correlated with crime and victimization
         a. Discuss positive and negative correlations
         b. Correlation does not imply causation
         c. Discuss the concept of spurious correlations
   B. Age and crime
      1. Age is negatively related to crime: young persons (late teens to mid-20s) commit the majority of street, property, and predatory crime reported in the United States
         a. Juveniles aged 13—18 constitute about 6% of the population but account for about 30% of all arrests for major crimes and 18% of total arrests in the United States
         b. Discuss the possible relationship between the size of the teenage population and the crime rate
      2. The desistance phenomenon suggests that most forms of criminality decrease with age
      3. Discuss the involvement of the elderly in crime as offenders (geriatric criminality) and as victims
      4. Elder abuse is the physical and emotional abuse of elderly persons by family members, caregivers, and others affects 1 out of 25 Americans over the age of 65
   C. Gender and crime
      1. Gender may be the "best single predictor of criminality"
      2. Discuss possible explanations for the apparently low rate of female criminality
         a. Early socialization
         b. Role expectations
         c. Gender bias in the criminal justice system resulting in a reluctance to arrest and prosecute women

3. Women are also victimized much less frequently than men in most crime categories (with the exception of rape and spousal abuse)

D. Race and crime
   1. There does appear to be a link between crime (especially violent, street, and predatory crimes) and race
      a. African-Americans make up approximately 12% of the U.S. population and account for over 50% of all violent crime arrests
      b. The arrest rate for African-Americans is six times that of whites
      c. Approximately 30% of all young African-American men in the country are under correctional supervision on any given day
   2. Discuss the possibility of differential treatment of minorities by a discriminatory criminal justice system
      a. Discuss William Wilbanks' claim that the system is basically objective today in processing criminal defendants
      b. Review critiques of Wilbanks' claim by Coramae Richey Mann
   3. High rates of crime and victimization within the African-American community have led to a heightened fear of crime among African-Americans
   4. Review the issue of racial identity and why categorizing offenders on the basis of race may become far less meaningful for analytical purposes

E. Social class and crime
   1. Prior to 1960, criminologists assumed the existence of a correlation between social class and crime, with members of lower social classes more prone to commit crime
      a. In the early 1960s, results of self-report studies found that rates of self-reported delinquency and criminality were fairly consistent across social classes
      b. These results suggested that the relationship between social class and crime was the result of discretionary practices within the criminal justice system
   2. Many of the problems surrounding research into the relationship between social class an crime may result from a lack of definitional clarity (e.g., how is "class" defined)
   3. Recent research has found a significant correlation between certain forms of criminality and social class, with street crimes more likely to be committed by people of low socioeconomic status

# Key Concepts

**Aggravated assault**: An unlawful attack by one person upon another for the purpose of inflicting severe or aggravated bodily injury. (UCR definition).

**Arson**: Any willful or malicious burning or attempt to burn, with or without intent to defraud, a dwelling house, public building, motor vehicle or aircraft, personal property of another, and so on.

**Burglary**: By the narrowest and oldest definition: the trespassory breaking and entering of the dwelling house of another in the nighttime with the intent to commit a felony. Also, the unlawful entry of a structure to commit a felony or a theft. The

UCR definition of burglary is the unlawful entry of any fixed structure, vehicle, or vessel used for regular residence, industry, or business, with or without force, with intent to commit a felony or larceny.

**Carjacking**: The stealing of a car while it is occupied.

**Clearance rate**: The proportion of reported or discovered crimes within a given offense category that are solved.

**Cohort**: A group of individuals having certain significant social characteristics in common, such as gender and date and place of birth.

**Correlation**: A causal, complementary, or reciprocal relationship between two measurable variables.

**Criminal homicide:** The illegal killing of one human being by another. Also, the UCR category which includes and is limited to all offenses of causing the death of another person without justification or excuse.

**Criminality index:** The actual extent of the crime problem in a society. The criminality index is computed by adding the actual crime rate and the latent crime rate.

**Dark figure of crime:** The numerical total of unreported crimes that are not reflected in official crime statistics.

**Date rape**: Unlawful forced sexual intercourse with a woman against her will which occurs within the context of a dating relationship.

**Demographics**: The characteristics of population groups, usually expressed in statistical fashion.

**Desistance phenomenon**: The observable decrease in crime rates that is invariably associated with age.

**Felony murder**: A special class of criminal homicide in which an offender may be charged with first-degree murder when that person's criminal activity results in another person's death.

**First-degree murder**: Criminal homicide that is planned or involves premeditation.

**Forcible rape**: The carnal knowledge of a female forcibly and against her will. Assaults or attempts to commit rape by force or threat of force are also included in the UCR definition; however, statutory rape (without force) and other sex offenses are excluded.

**Hate crime**: A criminal offense in which the motive is hatred, bias, or prejudice, based on the actual or perceived race, color, religion, national origin, ethnicity, gender, or sexual orientation of another individual or group of individuals. Also called *bias crime*.

**Larceny-theft:** Larceny is defined as the unlawful taking or attempted taking of property (other than a motor vehicle) from the possession of another, by stealth, without force or deceit, with intent to permanently deprive the owner of the property. The UCR definition of larceny-theft is the unlawful taking, carrying, leading, or riding away of property (other than a motor vehicle) from the possession or constructive possession of another. Attempts are included.

**Latent crime rate**: A rate of crime calculated on the basis of crimes that would likely be committed by those who are in prison or jail or who are otherwise incapacitated by the justice system.

**Monitoring the Future:** A national self-report survey on drug use that has been conducted since 1975.

**Motor vehicle theft:** As defined by the UCR, the theft or attempted theft of a motor vehicle. According to the Federal Bureau of Investigation, this offense category includes the stealing of automobiles, trucks, buses, motorcycles, motorscooters, and snowmobiles.

**National Crime Victimization Survey (NCVS)**: A survey conducted annually by the Bureau of Justice Statistics that provides data on surveyed households that report they were affected by crime.

**National Incident-Based Reporting System (NIBRS)**: A new and enhanced statistical reporting system that will collect data on each single incident and arrest within 22 crime categories.

**National Youth Survey (NYS)**: A longitudinal panel study of a national sample of 1,725 individuals that measured self-reports of delinquency and other types of behavior.

**Negligent homicide**: The act of causing the death of another person by recklessness or gross negligence.

**Part I offenses**: The crimes of murder, rape, robbery, aggravated assault, burglary, larceny, and motor vehicle theft, as defined under the FBI's Uniform Crime Reporting Program. Also called *major crimes*.

**Part II offenses**: Less serious offenses as identified by the FBI for the purpose of reporting arrest data.

**Rape:** As defined by the NCVS, carnal knowledge through the use of force or the threat of force, including attempts. Statutory rape (without force) is excluded. Both heterosexual and homosexual rape are included. For the UCR definition, see **forcible rape.**

**Robbery:** The taking or attempting to take anything of value from the care, custody, or control of a person or persons by force or threat of force or violence or by putting the victim in fear. (UCR definition)

**Second-degree murder**: Criminal homicide that is unplanned and is often described as a "crime of passion."

**Self-report surveys**: A survey in which anonymous respondents, without fear of disclosure or arrest, are asked to confidentially report any violations of the criminal law that they have committed.

**Simple assault:** An attack without a weapon, resulting either in minor injury or in undetermined injury requiring less than two days of hospitalization. (NCVS definition).

**Statistical school**: A criminological perspective with roots in the early 1800s which seeks to uncover correlations between crime rates and other types of demographic data.

**Uniform Crime Reporting (UCR) Program**: A Federal Bureau of Investigation summation of crime statistics tallied annually and consisting primarily of data on crimes reported to the police and of arrests.

# Additional Lecture Topics

One lecture topic is to discuss the possible problems that might occur when comparing crimes rates across locations during the same year. For example, discuss how the presence of seasonal residents in southern states such as Florida might affect the accuracy of the crime rates as reported in the *Uniform Crime Reports*. Because these individuals are not residents of the state, they do not appear in the denominator of the crime rate equation (the population). However, if they are victimized they may appear in the numerator of the equation (reported crimes). Thus, crime rates could be overestimated. Other groups that are not counted in the population but who are potential crime victims include out-of-state students, tourists, and illegal immigrants. Cities in which the crime rate may be inflated due to errors in population estimates include Miami, Fort Lauderdale, Los Angeles, San Diego, and New York.

Another topic for discussion is the importance of the police role in producing official crime statistics. Explain the importance of "founding," which gives the police the final decision as to whether an incident will be treated as a crime and thus appear in the official statistics. Discuss various legitimate and illegitimate reasons why the police might choose to unfound a crime, which include:

- The police considered the incident to be too trivial
- The victim was unlikely to prosecute the offender
- The incident was not a "real" crime (prostitution, marijuana use, gambling, etc.)

Discuss the impact of citizen behavior on the founding decision, such as the demeanor of the victim, the demeanor of the suspect, and the relationship between the victim and the suspect.

# Discussion Questions

These discussion questions are found in the textbook at the end of the chapter. The instructor may want to focus on these questions during the coverage of Chapter 2.

1. This book emphasizes a social problems versus a social responsibility theme. Which perspective is best supported by a realistic appraisal of the "social dimensions" of crime discussed in this chapter? Explain.

2. What are the major differences among the NCVS, UCR, and NIBRS? Can useful comparisons be made among these programs? If so, what comparisons?

3. What does it mean to say that the UCR is summary-based, while NIBRS is incident-based? When NIBRS is fully operational, what kinds of data will it contribute to the UCR Program? How will this information be useful?

4. What is a *crime rate*? How are rates useful? How might the NCVS, UCR, and NIBRS make better use of rates?

5. Why don't victims report crimes to the police? Which crimes appear to be the most underreported? Why are those crimes so infrequently reported? Which crimes appear to be the most frequently reported? Why are they so often reported?

6. Is the extent of the crime problem in this country accurately assessed by the statistical data available through the UCR/NIBRS and the NCVS? Why?

7. This chapter says that African-Americans appear to be overepresented in many categories of criminal activity. Do you believe that the statistics cited in this chapter accurately reflect the degree of African-American–white involvement in crime? Why? How might they be inaccurate?

# Student Exercises

## Activity #1

This activity involves comparing the definitions used by the FBI with those used by state criminal codes.

1. Obtain the definitions used by the FBI for each of the eight Part I offenses. This information is available on the World Wide Web at the FBI's web site (http://www.fbi.gov/ucr/ucr.htm).

2. Obtain the definitions of the same eight crimes for your state. One way to locate state statutes on the Web is to access the Cornell University School of Law's Legal Information Institute Web site at http://www.law.cornell.edu/states/listing.html. (**Note**: Your instructor may choose to assign you a different state.)

3. Compare and contrast the definitions used by the FBI with those of your state. What differences do you see?

**Note to instructor:** Rather than assigning all students in the class the same state, you may consider assigning each student a different state and then comparing the results in class.

## Activity #2

Your instructor will assign you two large cities in the United States and one index offense (for example, burglary). Go to the FBI's web site and access the most recent UCR data for these two cities. Answer the following questions:

1. Print out the number of burglaries known to the police for each of the two cities.

2. Which city had more reported burglaries?

3. What were the burglary rates for each of the two cities?

4. Did the burglary rates change over time in either city?

5. What factors might explain the differences in the burglary rates?

# Criminology Today on the Web

### http://www.fbi.gov/ucr/ucr.htm

This Web site will provide you with access to recent issues of the *Uniform Crime Reports* as well as information on the National Incident-Based Reporting System and other statistics collected by the FBI.

### http://www.ojp.usdoj.gov/bjs/

This is the home page for the Bureau of Justice Statistics. From here you can access recent issues of the *National Crime Victimization Survey* as well as data from many other sources.

### http://www.albany.edu/sourcebook/

This Web site provides a link to the *Sourcebook of Criminal Justice Statistics*, which is published by the Bureau of Justice Statistics and includes data from many sources covering many aspects of the U.S. criminal justice system.

### http://www.law.cornell.edu/

This is the site of the Legal Information Institute of the Cornell University School of Law. It includes links to federal and state constitutions, statutes, and codes of law.

# Student Study Guide Questions and Answers

## True/False

1. The likelihood of crime commission declines with age. **(True, p. 35)**

2. The collection of population statistics is a relatively new phenomenon. **(False, p. 35)**

3. The UCR program was begun by the FBI in 1929. **(True, p. 37)**

4. Kidnapping was added to the list of index offenses in 1979. **(False, p. 38)**

5. If an offender is deceased, the crime cannot be cleared. **(False, p. 38)**

6. The UCR program may seriously overestimate the true incidence of crime in the United States. **(False, p. 38)**

7. For NIBRS Group B offenses, only arrest data are reported. **(True, p. 39)**

8. NIBRS is fully implemented. **(False, p. 41)**

9. The most common type of hate crime is a crime against property. **(False, p. 41)**

10. Hate crimes are most commonly perpetrated against an individual. **(True, p. 41)**

11. The NCVS began collecting data in 1929. **(False, p. 44)**

12. Households remain in the NCVS sample for as long as they wish to participate. **(False, p. 45)**

13. According to the NCVS, young people are more likely to be victimized than older people. **(True, p. 46)**

14. The actual occurrence of all crimes that are reported to NCVS interviewers is verified before they are included in the data. **(False, p. 46)**

15. Second-degree murder involves the concept of malice aforethought. **(False, p. 50)**

16. If an offender commits a crime during which someone dies, but the offender had no intention of killing, the offender cannot be convicted of first-degree murder. **(False, p. 50)**

17. Most murder offenders are male. **(True, p. 51)**

18. Murder is primarily an interracial crime. **(False, p. 51)**

19. The rape laws of most states have eliminated gender bias. **(False, p. 51)**

20. According to the NCVS, stranger rapes are more common than rapes by nonstrangers. **(True, p. 54)**

21. A recent study of rape found that rape of young girls is rare. **(False, p. 54)**

22. Higher income families are more likely to be robbed. **(False, p. 55)**

23. According to the UCR, aggravated assaults are more common in the summer months. **(True, p. 56)**

24. According to the UCR, the number of reported aggravated assaults is decreasing. **(True, p. 56)**

25. According to the UCR definition, the use of force to gain entry is essential to classify an offense as burglary. **(False, p. 56)**

26. Burglary offenders are primarily male. **(True, p. 57)**

27. Self-report surveys provide information on the dark figure of crime. **(True, p. 60)**

28. According to recent self-report studies, females appear to be involved in a much higher proportion of crime than previously thought. **(True, p. 61)**

29. Fear of future victimization is one of the most common reasons for not reporting a violent victimization to the police. **(False, p. 62)**

30. When one variable increases in value as another decreases, a negative correlation exists. **(True, p. 62)**

31. Correlation does not imply causation. **(True, p. 62)**

32. Criminal activity is more associated with youth than with any other stage of life. **(True, p. 62)**

33. Proportionate differences in offense rates remain stable throughout the life course. **(True, p. 63)**

34. The elderly are more likely to be victimized than other groups. **(False, p. 65)**

35. When women commit crimes, they are generally the instigators and leaders. **(False, p. 66)**

36. According to the NCVS, black women aged 65 or older have the lowest violent crime victimization rates. **(False, p. 67)**

37. It appears that members of all social classes have nearly equal tendencies toward criminality. **(True, p. 70)**

## Fill in the Blank

38. Inferences based on statistical __________ appear to be a product of the last 200 years. **(demographics, p. 35)**

39. The English economist __________ described a worldwide future of warfare, crime, and starvation. **(Thomas Robert Malthus, p. 35)**

40. According to Adolphe Quételet, property crime rates __________ during the colder months of the year. **(decrease, p. 35)**

41. A crime is considered to be __________ when an arrest has been made or when the perpetrator is known but an arrest is not possible. **(cleared, p. 38)**

42. Unreported criminal activity is known as the __________. **(dark figure of crime, p. 38)**

43. The Hate Crime Statistics Act of 1990 requires the __________ to collect and report data on hate crimes. **(FBI, p. 41)**

44. According to the NCVS, approximately __________ of all violent crimes are reported to the police. **(one-half, p. 46)**

45. The criminality index includes the actual crime rate and the __________ crime rate. **(latent, p. 49)**

46. __________ is the wilful killing of one human being by another. **(Homicide, p. 50)**

47. __________ has the highest clearance rate of any index offense. **(Criminal homicide, p. 51)**

48. Homosexual rape is also known as __________ rape. **(same-sex, p. 51)**

49. Scholars such as A. Nicholas Groth consider rape to be a crime of ________. **(power, p. 51)**

50. According to the UCR, in 2003, the month of __________ showed the largest number of reported forcible rapes. **(July, p. 54)**

51. A __________ robbery refers to a robbery where the offender was unarmed. **(strong-arm, p. 54)**

52. According to the UCR, the rate of burglary has been ________ during the 1990s. **(decreasing steadily, p. 57)**

53. The __________ established campus crime statistic reporting requirements for universities receiving any form of federal funding. **(Crime Awareness and Campus Security Act, p. 59)**

54. According to the NCVS, as the value of property loss increases, the likelihood that a household crime will be reported __________. **(increases, p. 61)**

55. ________ are more likely to report violent victimizations to the police. **(Women, p. 61)**

56. Race and income are examples of __________ attributes. **(socially significant, p. 62)**

57. A(n) __________ is a connection or association observed to exist between two measurable variables. **(correlation, p. 62)**

58. Geriatric criminality refers to crimes committed by the __________. **(elderly, p. 64)**

59. The arrest rate for murder among African-Americans is __________ times that for whites. **(six, p. 68)**

60. Prior to 1960, criminologists assumed that a __________ existed between social class and crime. **(correlation, p. 70)**

## Multiple Choice

61. The thermic law of crime was developed by
    a. André Michel Guerry.
    b. Cesare Beccaria.
    c. **Adolphe Quételet. (p. 35)**
    d. Thomas Robert Malthus.

62. The *Sourcebook of Criminal Justice Statistics* contains data from the
    a. Uniform Crime Reporting Program.
    b. **National Crime Victimization Survey. (p. 36)**
    c. National Incident-Based Reporting System.
    d. all of the above

63. Which of the following is *not* a UCR Part I offense?
    a. Arson
    b. **Fraud (p. 38)**
    c. Burglary
    d. Theft of a motor vehicle

64. The __________ definition of rape excludes homosexual rape.
    a. **Uniform Crime Reports (p. 37)**
    b. National Incident-Based Reporting System
    c. National Crime Victimization Survey
    d. U.S. Code

65. UCR Part I offenses are subdivided into two categories:
    a. felonies and misdemeanors.
    b. violent crimes and personal crimes.
    c. **violent personal crimes and property crimes. (p. 38)**
    d. violent personal crimes and index crimes.

66. The proportion of reported or discovered crime within a given offense category which is solved by the police is known as the __________ rate.
    a. arrest
    b. index
    c. **clearance (p. 38)**
    d. indictment

67. Which of the following is not a NIBRS Group A offense?
    a. Pornography
    b. Kidnapping
    c. Gambling offenses
    d. **Disorderly conduct (p. 39)**

68. Hate crimes are most commonly committed by
    a. black males.
    b. black females.
    c. **white males. (p. 44)**
    d. white females.

69. According to the NCVS, members of which racial group experience the highest rates of violent victimization?
    a. Whites
    b. **African-Americans (p. 45)**
    c. Hispanics
    d. Asians

70. According to the NCVS, members of _________ families are more likely to become victims of violent crime.
    a. **lower income (p. 46)**
    b. middle-income
    c. upper-income
    d. they are all equally likely to be victimized

71. Based on NCVS findings, which of the following individuals would be most likely to be the victim of a violent crime?
    a. **A young black male (p. 46)**
    b. A young black female
    c. A young white male
    d. A young white female

72. Which of the following was *not* a possible cause of the increase in reported crime between the 1960s and the 1990s?
    a. Victims becoming sensitized to the importance of reporting crimes
    b. More accurate and increased data collection by police departments
    c. The disruption and tumult of the 1960s
    d. **The aging out of the baby-boomer generation (p. 47)**

73. Which of the following was *not* a possible cause of the decrease in reported crime since the mid-1990s?
    a. New strict laws, an expanded justice system, and an increase in police funding
    b. Changes in crime-fighting technologies
    c. **Social upheaval (pp. 47-48)**
    d. Economic expansion

74. Official crime rates in the United States are __________; correctional populations are __________.
    a. **decreasing; increasing (p. 48)**
    b. decreasing; decreasing
    c. increasing, decreasing
    d. increasing; increasing

75. Premeditated murder is
    a. **first-degree murder. (p. 50)**
    b. second-degree murder.
    c. third-degree murder.
    d. negligent homicide.

76. __________ is legally seen as a true crime of passion.
    a. First-degree murder
    b. **Second-degree murder (p. 50)**
    c. Third-degree murder
    d. Negligent homicide

77. Which of the following terms is *not* used to refer to third-degree murder?
    a. **Voluntary manslaughter (p. 50)**
    b. Negligent homicide
    c. Involuntary manslaughter
    d. Negligent manslaughter

78. Which of the following is the weapon of choice in most murders?
    a. **A handgun (p. 51)**
    b. A shotgun
    c. A knife or other sharp instrument
    d. A blunt instrument

79. According to the UCR, the rate of reported forcible rape is highest in the __________ months.
    a. **summer (p. 54)**
    b. spring
    c. winter
    d. fall

80. Robbery that occurs in a public place, generally out of doors, is known as ______ robbery.
    a. strong-arm
    b. armed
    c. **highway (p. 54)**
    d. simple

81. According to the UCR, the most common month for robbery is
    a. January.
    b. July.
    c. September.
    d. **December. (p. 55)**

82. If you unlawfully enter a structure to commit a felony, you have probably committed the crime of
    a. theft.
    b. robbery.
    c. **burglary. (p. 56)**
    d. breaking and entering.

83. According to UCR larceny statistics, most items reported stolen were taken from
    a. buildings.
    b. coin-operated machines.
    c. **motor vehicles. (p. 58)**
    d. private residences.

84. According to the UCR, most motor-vehicle thefts occur in
    a. **large cities. (p. 58)**
    b. small cities.
    c. suburbs.
    d. rural areas.

85. Vanity pyromaniacs commit arson because they
    a. suffer from psychological problems.
    b. **are trying to take credit for putting out the fire they originally started. (pp. 58-59)**
    c. are trying to defraud an insurance company.
    d. are attempting to disguise another felony, such as burglary or murder.

86. Which of the following is *not* a UCR Part II offense?
    a. Simple assault
    b. **Aggravated assault (p. 59)**
    c. Fraud
    d. Gambling

87. Which of the following is *not* a finding of the National Youth Survey?
    a. **Females are involved in a smaller proportion of crime than previously thought. (p. 61)**
    b. Violent offenders begin lives of crime earlier than originally believed.
    c. Race differentials in crime are smaller than traditional data sources indicated.
    d. There is a consistent progression from less serious to more serious acts of delinquency over time.

88. One of the two most common reasons for not reporting violent crime is that the victim
    a. fears future victimization by the same offender.
    b. believes the police will be ineffective in solving the crime.
    c. is embarrassed over the type of victimization.
    d. **considers the crime to be a private matter. (p. 62)**

89. Older offenders are more likely to commit
    a. assault.
    b. theft.
    c. street crimes.
    d. **fraud. (p. 65)**

90. *The Myth of a Racist Criminal Justice System* was written by
    a. Marvin D. Free, Jr.
    b. **William Wilbanks. (p. 68)**
    c. James Fox.
    d. Coramae Richey Mann.

# Word Search Puzzle

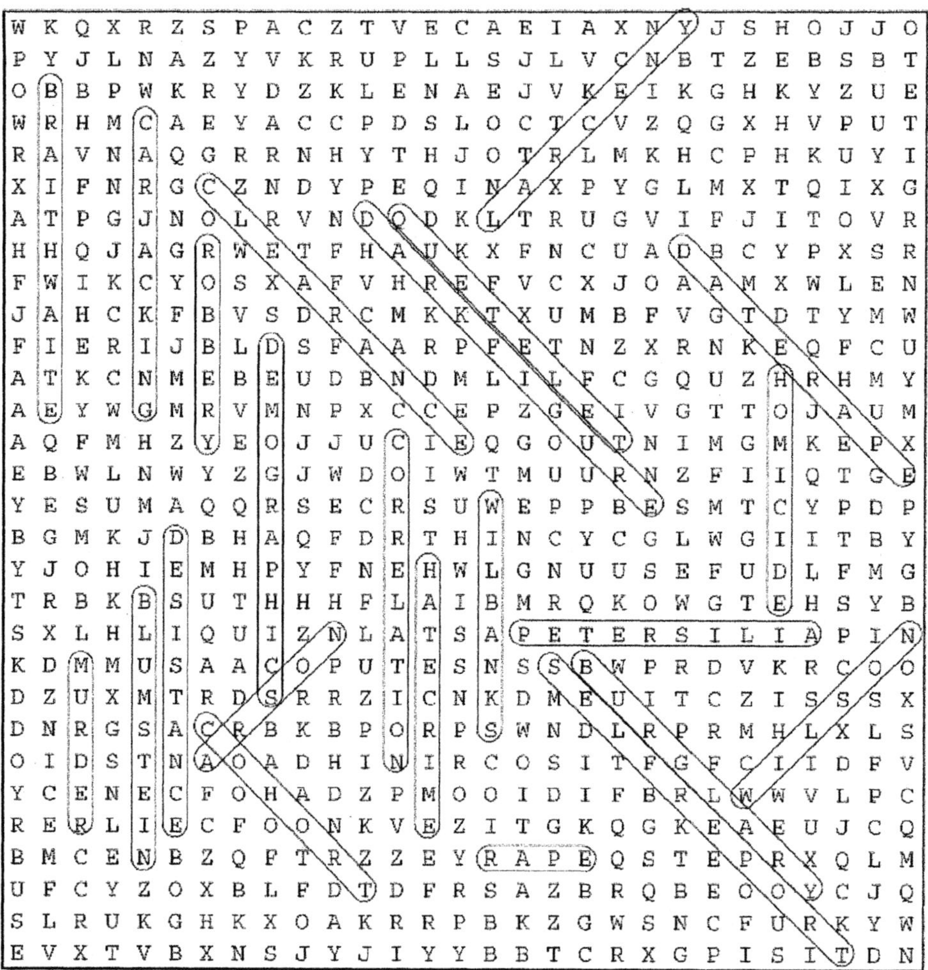

Arson
Blumstein
Braithwaite
Burglary
Carjacking
Clearance
Cohort
Correlation
Dark figure
Date rape
Demographics
Desistance
Hate crime
Homicide
Larceny
Murder
Petersilia
Quételet
Rape
Robbery
Self report
Wilbanks
Wilson

# Crossword Puzzle

| | | | | | | | | | | | | | | | | | | | |
|---|---|---|---|---|---|---|---|---|---|---|---|---|---|---|---|---|---|---|---|
| A | R | S | O | N | | | | | | | | D | | | N | | | | |
| | | E | | | | | | | | | H | A | T | E | C | R | I | M | E |
| C | A | R | J | A | C | K | I | N | G | | | R | | | V | | | | |
| L | | I | | | O | | | | | | | K | | | S | | | | |
| E | | A | | | H | | | D | | R | | F | | | | | | | |
| A | | L | | C | O | R | R | E | L | A | T | I | O | N | | | | | |
| R | | | L | | R | | | M | | P | | G | | | | | B | | |
| A | | | A | | T | | | O | | E | | U | | | | | U | | |
| N | | | R | | | | | G | | | | R | O | B | B | E | R | Y | |
| C | | | C | | | | | R | | | | E | | | | | G | | |
| E | | D | E | S | I | S | T | A | N | C | E | | | | | | L | | |
| R | | | N | | | | | P | | | | | | | | | A | | |
| A | | | Y | | | | | H | | | | | | | | | R | | |
| T | | | | | | | | I | | | | | | | | | Y | | |
| E | | | | | | | | C | | | | | | | | | | | |
| | | | | | | | | S | | | | | | | | | | | |

## Across

1. The willful or malicious burning of a building or personal property of another.
5. A crime motivated by bias based on the victim's perceived race, color, religion, sexual orientation, etc. (2 words)
6. Stealing a car while it is occupied.
10. A relationship between two measurable variables.
13. Taking something of value from another person by force.
14. The observable decrease in crime rates that is associated with age.

## Down

2. ________ murder involves the killing of several victims in three or more events.
3. The number of unreported crimes that are not reflected in official crime statistics. (2 words)
4. A victim survey conducted annually by the Bureau of Justice Statistics.
6. The proportion of reported or discovered crimes that are solved. (2 words)
7. A group of individuals having certain significant social characteristics in common.
8. The characteristics of population groups, usually expressed in statistical fashion.
9. Carnal knowledge through the use of force or the threat of force.
11. Illegally taking property of another without force.
12. The unlawful entry of a structure with intent to commit a felony or theft.

# 3 Research Methods and Theory Development

## Learning Objectives

After reading this chapter, students should be able to:

- Appreciate the relevance of criminological theory to the study of crime and criminals
- Recognize the role of criminological research in theory development and display an understanding of various types of research designs
- Identify research limitations, including problems in data collection and analysis
- Recognize the ethical considerations involved in conducting criminological research
- Describe the process of writing the research report and identify common sources for publishing research findings
- Identify the impact of criminological research on the creation of social policy

## Chapter Outline

Introduction
The Science of Criminology
Theory Building
The Role of Research
*Problem Identification*
*Research Designs*
*Techniques of Data Collection*
*Data Analysis*
Quantitative versus Qualitative Methods
Values and Ethics in the Conduct of Research
Social Policy and Criminological Research
Writing the Research Report
*Writing for Publication*

# Chapter Summary

Criminological theory cannot be fully appreciated unless one understands its fundamental assumptions. This chapter examines how social scientific research methods are used in the development of criminological theories. A theory is a series of interrelated propositions which attempt to describe, explain, predict, and ultimately control some class of events, such as criminal behavior. Theories serve a variety of purposes and are tested through research, the use of standardized, systematic procedures in the search for knowledge. Research can be pure or applied, and can be primary or secondary. Research is conducted in four stages: problem solving, research design development, the selection of data-gathering techniques, and a review of the findings.

Problem identification involves choosing a problem or issue to be studied. Much contemporary criminological research involves hypothesis testing. Research designs structure the research process. One basic design is the one-group pretest–posttest. However, this type of design does not eliminate the possibility of confounding effects, or rival explanations, which may affect both the internal and external validity of the research. The chapter lists a number of factors that may threaten the internal or external validity of a research design. The use of a controlled experiment or a quasi-experimental design may increase the validity of the results by eliminating some rival explanations. These designs require the use of randomization when assigning research subjects to experimental and control groups.

There are five main data-gathering strategies commonly used in criminology: survey research, case studies, participant observation, self-reporting, and secondary analysis. The strategy selected must produce information in a form usable to the researcher and thus depends on the questions to be answered. Data collection involves scientific observation, which must meet the criteria of intersubjectivity and replicability. Even so, some observations may lead to unwarranted conclusions. Once the data have been collected, they are usually analyzed in some way, generally using statistical techniques. Descriptive statistics, such as the mean, median, mode, and standard deviation, describe, summarize, and highlight the relationships within the data. Inferential statistics, including tests of significance, attempt to generalize findings by specifying how likely they are to be true for other populations or locations.

Research methods can be quantitative or qualitative. Both are useful and provide important information. Some criminologists believe that qualitative data-gathering strategies represent the future of criminological research.

Research is not conducted in a vacuum and cannot be free of biases and preconceptions. The best way to control biases is to be aware of them at the start of the research. Ethical issues are also extremely important; although they may not affect the validity of the results, they may have a significant impact upon the lives of researchers and subjects. Key ethical issues include protection of subjects from harm, privacy, disclosure, and data confidentiality. One way to overcome many of these ethical issues is through the use of informed consent. Criminological research may also have an impact on social policy, although many publicly elected officials may prefer to create politically expedient policies rather than consider current research.

After a research study has been conducted, the results are presented in the form of a research report or paper. There is a standard format which is generally followed. Most criminologists seek to publish their research results. The primary medium for such publication is refereed professional journals, which use peer reviewers to determine the quality of submitted manuscripts.

# Lecture Outline

I. Introduction:
   A. Explain why an understanding of the fundamental assumptions underlying criminological theory is essential if students are to fully appreciate the value of criminological theory
   B. Relate the topic of research methods to the applicability of criminology to the modern world

II. The Science of Criminology
   A. Review John Laub's eras of criminology as a field of study
      1. The Golden Age of Research (1990—1930) – a period when data on crime and criminal behavior were largely gathered and evaluated independent of any particular ideological framework
      2. The Golden Age of Theory (1930—1960) – a focus on intellectual theorizing but no systematic attempt to link criminological research to theory
      3. Era three (1960—2000) – empirical testing of the accuracy of dominant theories
      4. Laub suggests that 21st century criminology contains "all possible offspring" of what came before
   B. Explain the difference between armchair and scientific criminologists and discuss the criterial that may be necessary for declaring an endeavor "scientific"
      1. The systematic collection of related facts
      2. An emphasis on the availability and application of the scientific method
      3. The existence of general laws, a field for experiment or observation, and control of academic discourse by practical application
      4. Acceptance into the scientific tradition
      5. An emphasis on a worthwhile subject in need of independent study even if adequate techniques of study are not yet available
   C. Gathering facts is part of criminology but does not offer explanations for crime
      1. Contemporary criminologists are concerned with identifying relationships among observed facts and attempting to understand the causes of crime
      2. Emphasis on measurement and objectivity gives criminology its scientific flavor

III. Theory Building
   A. The ultimate goal of criminological research is to construct theories or models that improve our understanding of criminal behavior and help us create effective strategies to deal with the crime problem
      1. A theory is a series of interrelated propositions which attempt to describe, explain, predict, and ultimately control some class of events
      2. A theory gains explanatory power from inherent logical consistency
      3. A theory is tested by how well it describes and predicts reality

4. Theories are improved through hypothesis testing, examining evidence from observations, and revising the theory based on the evidence
5. Theories give meaning to observations, explaining what we see in a particular setting by relating these observations to other things already understood

B. Discuss Kenneth Hoover's four uses of theory in social scientific thinking
1. Theories provide patterns for the interpretation of data
2. Theories link studies together
3. Theories supply frameworks within which concepts and variables acquire special significance
4. Theories allow us to interpret the larger meaning of our findings for ourselves and for others

IV. The Role of Research

A. Research is defined as the use of standardized, systematic procedures in the search for knowledge
1. Because knowledge is built on experience and observation, the crux of scientific research is data collection
2. Some researchers distinguish between pure and applied research
   a. Applied research is conducted with practical applications in mind so that the researcher is working toward a practical goal (reducing crime, evaluating police effectiveness, etc.)
   b. Pure research is conducted solely to advance knowledge; it may not produce anything of immediate relevance or application
3. There is also a distinction between primary and secondary research
   a. Primary research is original and direct investigation
   b. Secondary research involves a new evaluation or examination of existing information which has already been collected by other researchers
4. Scientific research generally involves four stages
   a. Problem identification
   b. Research design development
   c. Choice of data-gathering techniques
   d. Review of findings

B. Problem identification
1. The first step in research involves choosing a problem or issue to be studied or a question to be answered
2. Much criminological research is intended to explore the claims made by theories which purport to explain criminal behavior
3. Discuss the concept of hypothesis testing

C. Research designs
1. Research designs consist of the logic and structure inherent in any particular approach to data gathering – they act as a guide to the systematic collection of data
2. Discuss a simple study using a one-group pretest—posttest design
   a. Notation: $O_1$ X $O_2$
      (1) $O_1$: pretest (information gathered prior to the introduction of the treatment)
      (2) X: treatment or experimental intervention
      (3) $O_2$: posttest (observations after the treatment has been administered)

b. The procedure involves measuring subjects on some variable (e.g., aggressiveness), administering some treatment (e.g., dietary changes), and measuring subjects on the same variable again
c. The problem with this design is that it does not eliminate other possible explanations for behavioral changes (confounding effects/competing hypotheses)

3. Achieving validity in research designs
   a. Confounding effects may invalidate the results of research by affecting either the internal or external validity of the research
      (1) Internal validity asks whether something other than the treatment could have produced the behavioral change
      (2) External validity is the ability of researchers to generalize research results to other settings (such as outside a laboratory)
      (3) Most researchers consider interval validity the most vital component of any planned research
   b. Threats to internal validity include
      (1) History: events occurring between the first and second observations that could affect measurement
      (2) Maturation: processes occurring within the subjects as a result of the passage of time (e.g., fatigue)
      (3) Testing: the effect of taking a test upon the scores of a later testing
      (4) Instrumentation: changes in measuring instruments or survey takers which occur as a result of time
      (5) Statistical regression: subjects selected for testing based on extreme scores will show regression toward the mean in later testing
      (6) Differential selection: built-in biases result when several groups of subjects are involved in a study and the groups are not equivalent (this problem can be reduced by the use of random assignment of subjects to test groups)
      (7) Experimental mortality: a differential loss of subjects from comparison groups
   c. Threats to external validity include
      (1) Reactive effects of testing: a pretest may sensitize subjects so they will respond differently to the introduction of the treatment
      (2) Self-selection: if subjects choose whether or not to participate in the study, they may be more interested in participation or more responsive to the treatment
      (3) Reactive effects of experimental arrangements: subjects who know they are being tested may react differently than if they were in a more natural setting
      (4) Multiple-treatment interference: if the same set of subjects is used for several studies, treatments may interact and affect results
4. Experimental and quasi-experimental research designs
   a. To be reasonably certain that the observed variations result from the treatment, it is necessary to have employ a research design that provides some control over factors that threaten internal validity
      (1) Controlled experiments attempt to hold conditions (other than the experimental intervention) constant
      (2) Quasi-experimental designs are approaches to research which, although less powerful than experimental designs, are deemed worthy of use when better designs are not feasible

(3) These strategies attempt to eliminate rival explanations for observed effects

b. Show a diagram of research design for the pretest—posttest control group design, which involves a second (control) group that is not exposed to the experimental intervention:

| | | | |
|---|---|---|---|
| Experimental group: | $O_1$ | X | $O_2$ |
| Control group: | $O_3$ | | $O_4$ |

(1) $O_1$ and $O_3$: pretests (information gathered prior to the introduction of the treatment)

(2) X: treatment or experimental intervention

(3) $O_2$ and $O_4$: posttests (observations after the treatment has been administered)

c. These strategies rely on randomization in the assignment of subjects to both groups

(1) People are assigned to study groups without biases or differences resulting from selection

(2) Self-selection is not allowed. nor are researchers allowed to use personal judgment in assigning subjects to groups

(3) Because randomization assumes that both groups are essentially the same at the start, it provides control over threats to internal validity because such threats will affect both groups equally

D. Techniques of data collection

1. Data-gathering strategies provide approaches to the accumulation of information needed for analysis
2. The key issue in selecting a strategy is whether it will produce information in a form usable to the researcher
3. The five main strategies used in criminology are:

a. Survey research involves using questionnaires to gather information, known as "survey data"

b. Case studies involve the in-depth study of individual cases

c. Participant observation involves strategies in which the researcher observes a group by participating in the group's activities

(1) Participant as observer: the researcher makes his/her presence known to the group but does not attempt to influence the group's activities

(2) Observer as complete participant: the researcher participates in the group's activities, thus potentially influencing the group's direction

d. Self-reporting involves asking subjects to record and report rates of some type of behavior (often considered another form of survey research)

e. Secondary analysis obtains preexisting information from data that have already been gathered and examines the data in new ways

4. Problems in data collection

a. Scientific observation must meet two key criteria:

(1) Intersubjectivity requires that for observations to be valid, independent observers must report seeing the same thing under the same circumstances

(2) Replicability of observations means that when the same conditions exist, the same results can be expected to follow

   b. Observations that meet these criteria may still lead to unwarranted conclusions

E. Data analysis

   1. Most data are subjected to some form of analysis, usually involving mathematical techniques intended to locate correlations between variables and determine if research findings can be generalized to other settings
   2. There are two main types of statistical methods:
      a. Descriptive statistics describe, summarize, or highlight relationships within data (measures include the mean, median, mode, standard deviation, degree of correlation)
      b. Inferential statistics attempt to generalize findings by specifying how likely they are to be true for other populations or in other locales (tests of significance)

V. Quantitative versus Qualitative Methods

A. Quantitative methods

   1. Techniques that produce measurable results that can be analyzed statistically (surveys, self-report studies, etc.)
   2. American criminology has had a tendency to overemphasize quantitative techniques
   3. The mystique of quantity is the delusion that everything can and must be quantified

B. Qualitative methods

   1. Techniques that produce subjective results or results which are difficult to quantify (life histories, case studies, participant observation, etc.)
   2. Findings are not expressed numerically
   3. Verstehen is a term used to describe the type of subjective understanding that can be achieved by criminologists who immerse themselves in the world of the criminals they study

VI. Values and Ethics in the Conduct of Research

A. Research does not occur in a vacuum; values affect all stages of the research process

   1. Research is never free from preconceptions and biases, but it is necessary to limit the impact of biases on research
   2. The most effective way to control the effect of biases is to be aware of them at the beginning of the research

B. Ethical issues may not affect the validity of results but may affect the lives of researchers and research subjects:

   1. Protection of human subjects from harm
   2. Privacy
   3. The need for disclosure of research methods
   4. Data confidentiality

C. Both the American Society of Criminology and the Academy of Criminal Justice Sciences have adopted official Codes of Ethics which address a variety of ethical issues

D. Informed consent

   1. This is a strategy used by researchers to overcome many ethical issues inherent in criminological research
   2. It involves informing research subjects as to the nature of the research, their anticipated role in it, and the uses to be made of the data they provide

VII. Social Policy and Criminological Research
   A. Criminological research has affected social policy significantly in many ways, but publically elected officials are often ignorant of current research or do not take the advice of criminologists
      1. Research findings may be ignored because they conflict with public sentiment, is not politically expedient, or does not serve the dominant ideology
      2. Policy makers rarely consult criminologists when debating crime legislation or considering the effectiveness of past policy
   B. Discuss the three-strikes laws as an example of the dilemma facing criminologists who want to influence social policy on the basis of statistical evidence

VIII. Writing the Research Report
   A. Most research reports follow a traditional format with a number of key components:
      1. Title page
      2. Acknowledgments
      3. Table of contents
      4. Preface (if desired)
      5. Abstract
      6. Introduction
      7. Review of existing literature
      8. Description of existing situation
      9. Statement of the hypotheses
      10. Description of the research plan
      11. Disclaimers and limitations
      12. Findings or results
      13. Analysis and discussion
      14. Summary and conclusions
      15. Appendixes
      16. List of references
      17. Endnotes
   B. Writing for publication
      1. Refereed journals, journals that use peer reviewers to gauge the quality of submitted manuscripts, are the primary medium for publication
      2. Discuss some of the best-known professional journals in the field of criminology
      3. Most journals require that manuscripts may be submitted to only one journal at a time

# Key Concepts

**Applied research**: Scientific inquiry that is designed and carried out with practical applications in mind.

**Confounding effects**: A rival explanation, or competing hypothesis, which is a threat to the internal or external validity of a research design.

**Control group**: A group of experimental subjects which, although the subject of measurement and observation, is not exposed to the experimental intervention.

**Controlled experiment**: An experiment that attempts to hold conditions (other than the intentionally introduced experimental intervention) constant.

**Data confidentiality**: The ethical requirement of social scientific research to protect the confidentiality of individual research participants, while simultaneously preserving justified research access to the information participants provide.

**Descriptive statistics**: Statistics that describe, summarize, or highlight the relationships within data which have been gathered.

**External validity**: The ability to generalize research findings to other settings.

**Hypothesis**: An explanation that accounts for a set of facts and that can be tested by further investigation. Also, something that is taken to be true for the purpose of argument or investigation.

**Inferential statistics**: Statistics specify how likely findings are to be true for other populations or in other locales.

**Informed consent**: The ethical requirement of social scientific research that research subjects be informed as to the nature of the research about to be conducted, their anticipated role in it, and the uses to which the data they provide will be put.

**Internal validity**: The certainty that experimental interventions did indeed cause the changes observed in the study group. Also, the control over confounding factors which tend to invalidate the results of an experiment.

**Intersubjectivity**: A scientific principle which requires that independent observers see the same thing under the same circumstances for observations to be regarded as valid.

**Meta-analysis**: A study of other studies about a particular topic of interest.

**Operationalization**: The process by which concepts are made measurable.

**Participant observation**: A strategy in data gathering in which the researcher observes a group by participating, to varying degrees, in the activities of the group.

**Primary research**: Research characterized by original and direct investigation.

**Pure research**: Research undertaken simply for the sake of advancing scientific knowledge.

**Qualitative method**: A research technique that produces subjective results, or results that are difficult to quantify.

**Quantitative method**: A research technique that produces measurable results.

**Quasi-experimental design**: An approach to research which, although less powerful than experimental designs, is deemed worthy of use when better designs are not feasible.

**Randomization**: The process whereby individuals are assigned to study groups without biases or differences resulting from selection.

**Replicability:** A scientific principle which holds that valid observations made at one time can be made again at a later time if all other conditions are the same.

**Research**: The use of standardized, systematic procedures in the search for knowledge.

**Research design**: The logic and structure inherent in an approach to data gathering.

**Secondary research**: New evaluations of existing information which had been collected by other researchers.

**Survey research**: A social science data-gathering technique that involves the use of questionnaires.

**Test of significance**: A statistical technique intended to provide researchers with confidence that their results are, in fact, true and not the result of sampling error.

**Theory**: A series of interrelated propositions that attempt to describe, explain, predict, and ultimately to control some class of events. A theory gains explanatory power from inherent logical consistency and is "tested" by how well it describes and predicts reality.

**Variable**: A concept that can undergo measurable changes.

***Verstehen***: The kind of subjective understanding that can be achieved by criminologists who immerse themselves in the everyday world of the criminals they study.

# Additional Lecture Topics

One lecture topic is to discuss specific ways in which criminological research has affected social policy. An example would be the impact of the Minneapolis Domestic Violence Experiment and the replications on police policy and state law:

- Many states changed their laws regarding the requirements for misdemeanor arrest in cases of domestic assault

- Many police departments moved to a policy emphasizing arrest in domestic cases; some developed a policy of mandatory arrest

- Most states mandate a minimum number of hours of pre-service and in-service training on domestic violence for police officers

Another topic for discussion is to cover specific types of criminological research methods in more detail. Possible subjects include:

- A discussion of cohort research, including both longitudinal and retrospective cohort studies
- A discussion of time-series analysis
- A discussion of some of the key criminological experiments (e.g., the Kansas City Preventive Patrol Experiment, the Newark Foot Patrol Experiment, the Minneapolis Domestic Violence Experiment and the five follow-up experiments)
- A discussion of random and nonrandom sampling techniques and how the method used to select the sample can affect external validity

# Discussion Questions

These discussion questions are found in the textbook at the end of the chapter. The instructor may want to focus on these questions during the coverage of Chapter 3.

1. This book emphasizes a social problems versus social responsibility theme. How might a thorough research agenda allow us to decide which perspective is most fruitful in combating crime?

2. What is a hypothesis? What does it mean to operationalize a hypothesis? Why is operationalization necessary?

3. What is a theory? Why is the task of criminological theory construction so demanding? How do we know if a theory is any good?

4. Explain experimental research. How might a good research design be diagrammed? What kinds of threats to the validity of research designs can you identify? How can such threats be controlled or eliminated?

5. List and describe the various types of data-gathering strategies discussed in this chapter. Is any one technique “better” than another? Why? Under what kinds of conditions might certain types of data-gathering strategies be most appropriate?

6. What is the difference between qualitative and quantitative research? What are the advantages and disadvantages of each?

# Student Exercises

## Activity #1

Many social science organizations have adopted official codes of ethics. This exercise deals with the similarities and differences found in the ethical codes of various fields.

1. First, go to the Academy of Criminal Justice Sciences (ACJS) home page at http://www.acjs.org and access the code of ethics. What (if anything) does the ACJS code of ethics have to say about each of the following?
    - Informed consent
    - Confidentiality
    - Reporting of research
    - Protection of subjects from harm
    - Plagiarism

2. Then go to the home page of the American Society of Criminology (ASC) at http://www.asc41.com and access the ASC code of ethics. What does this code have to say about the subjects above?

3. Finally, go to the home page of the American Sociological Association (ASA) at http://www.asanet.org and locate the ASA code of ethics. What does this code have to say about the subjects above?

4. Which of the three codes do you prefer, and why?

## Activity #2

Aprilville, a small town outside Bigcity, plans to implement a Neighborhood Watch program. The town mayor has asked you to find out if the program, once implemented, will have any effect on the town's crime rate. Design a research study to answer this question:

1. Formulate one or more hypotheses and operationalize the concepts.

2. Choose a research design from those discussed in the chapter and explain why you selected this design.

3. Select a data-gathering strategy and explain why you chose this technique.

# Criminology Today on the Web

### http://www.acjs.org

This is the home page for the Academy of Criminal Justice Sciences, an international organization that promotes scholarly and professional activities in criminal justice.

### http://www.asc41.com

This is the home page for the American Society of Criminology, an international organization that promotes research, study, and educational activities in the field of criminology.

### http://www.britsoccrim.org/

This is the home page for the British Society of Criminology, the major criminological society of Great Britain. It includes the BSC code of ethics for researchers in the field of criminology.

### http://arapaho.nsuok.edu/~dreveskr/CJRR.html-ssi

This site contains links to information about research methods and statistics in criminology.

# Student Study Guide Questions and Answers

## True/False

1. Armchair criminologists emphasize the use of research methods. **(False, p. 80)**

2. Research involves the use of standardized, systematic procedures in the search for knowledge. **(True, p. 82)**

3. A researcher who is attempting to evaluate the effectiveness of a new policy is engaged in pure research. **(False, p. 82)**

4. Primary research is characterized by original and direct investigation. **(True, p. 82)**

5. Problem identification often includes statistical analysis. **(False, p. 82)**

6. A hypothesis cannot be tested until the concepts are operationalized. **(True, p. 82)**

7. The task of theory testing predominantly involves rejecting inadequate hypotheses. **(True, p. 83)**

8. In a one-group pre-test-posttest design, the posttest involves observations made prior to the experimental intervention. **(False, p. 83)**

9. A one-group pretest–posttest design eliminates all other possible explanations of behavioral change. **(False, p. 83)**

10. Confounding effects increase the certainty of results of any single series of observations. **(False, p. 84)**

11. Instrumentation involves the effects of taking a test upon the scores of later testing. **(False, p. 84)**

12. Interviewer fatigue is an example of experimental mortality. **(False, p. 84)**

13. Multiple-treatment interference is a threat to internal validity. **(False, p. 84)**

14. The reactive effects of testing are a threat to external validity. **(True, p. 84)**

15. A controlled experiment provides some control over factors that threaten external validity. **(False, p. 85)**

16. The group that is exposed to the treatment is known as the experimental group. **(True, p. 85)**

17. During randomization, a researcher may not use his or her personal judgment when assigning subjects to groups. **(True, p. 85)**

18. In a controlled experiment, observable net effects are assumed to be attributable to experimental intervention. **(True, p. 85)**

19. Data-gathering is necessary before analysis can occur. **(True, p. 86)**

20. Reports generated out of the NCVS are the result of survey data. **(True, p. 86)**

21. Life histories may only be gathered on single subjects, not on groups of individuals. **(False, p. 86)**

22. A concern with the observer as complete participant strategy is that the researcher may influence the group's direction. **(True, p. 86)**

23. A researcher using the participant as observer strategy does not have to be concerned about influencing the behavior of the group being observed. **(False, p. 87)**

24. Participant observation is a good example of nonreactive research. **(False, p. 87)**

25. Self-report studies are often a form of survey research. **(True, p. 87)**

26. Valid experiments can be replicated. **(True, p. 88)**

27. The mode defines the midpoint of a data series. **(False, p. 89)**

28. If one variable increases whenever another does the same, a positive correlation exists. **(True, p. 89)**

29. Tests of significance measure the likelihood that a study's findings are the result of chance. **(True, p. 89)**

30. A statistical test of significance involves testing all members of a given population. **(False, p. 89)**

31. The findings of qualitative methods are expressed numerically. **(False, p. 90)**

32. *Verstehen* relates to quantitative methodology. **(False, p. 90)**

33. The American Society of Criminology has an official Code of Ethics. **(True, p. 91)**

34. Informed consent requires that research subjects remain anonymous. **(False, p. 92)**

35. Criminological research findings are frequently at odds with public sentiment. **(True, p. 93)**

36. The primary medium for the publication of criminological research results is the refereed professional journal. **(True, p. 98)**

37. A researcher may submit an article to several journals at the same time. **(False, p. 99)**

## Fill in the Blank

38. One of the criteria for declaring an endeavor scientific is an emphasis on the availability and applicability of the __________. **(scientific method, p. 80)**

39. A __________ is a set of interrelated propositions that provide a relatively complete form of understanding. **(theory, p. 80)**

40. A theory can be improved through __________ testing. **(hypothesis, p. 80)**

41. Theories provide __________ for the interpretation of data. **(patterns, p. 81)**

42. Theories supply __________ within which concepts and variables acquire special significance. **(frameworks, p. 81)**

43. In __________ research, the research is working toward some practical goal. **(applied, p. 82)**

44. Research that involves an evaluation of existing data is known as __________ research. **(secondary, p. 82)**

45. A(n) __________ is something that is taken to be true for the purpose of argument or investigation. **(hypothesis, p. 82)**

46. An __________ hypothesis is stated in such a way as to facilitate measurement. **(operationalized, p. 82)**

47. Rival explanations or competing hypotheses are known as __________. **(confounding effects, p. 84)**

48. A threat to __________ validity reduces the researcher's confidence that the intervention will be as effective in the field as under laboratory-like conditions. **(external, p. 84)**

49. __________ involves events that occur between the first and second observations and which may affect measurement. **(History, p. 84)**

50. When respondents in a study are selected on the bases of extreme scores, later testing will tend to show a __________ toward the mean. **(regression, p. 84)**

51. __________ occurs when there is a differential loss of respondents from comparison groups. **(Experimental mortality, p. 84)**

52. The problem of __________ occurs when subjects are allowed to decide whether they want to participate in a study. **(self-selection, p. 84)**

53. __________ is the process by which individuals are assigned to the control or experimental group without any biases or differences resulting from the selection. **(Randomization, p. 85)**

54. The use of randomization controls potential threats to __________ validity. **(internal, p. 85)**

55. A case study focusing on a single subject is known as a __________. **(life history, p. 86)**

56. __________ involves the analysis of existing data. **(Secondary analysis, p. 87)**

57. If replicability cannot be achieved, the __________ of the observation is cast into doubt. **(validity, p. 88)**

58. Most data are not merely stored but are subject to some form of __________. **(analysis, p. 88)**

59. The midpoint of a data series is the __________. **(median, p. 89)**

60. A correlation provides information on the degree of __________ between variables. **(interdependence, p. 89)**

61. When one variable decreases in value as another rises, a __________ correlation exists. **(negative or inverse, p. 89)**

62. The likelihood of faulty findings in a test of significance increases as sample size __________. **(decreases, p. 89)**

63. In a research report, information about the authors of the report and their professional affiliations is usually found on the __________. **(title page, p. 95)**

## Multiple Choice

64. __________ is defined as the use of standardized, systematic procedures in the search for knowledge.
    1. A theory
    2. A hypothesis
    3. **Research (p. 82)**
    4. Geographic profiling

65. __________ research is undertaken for the sake of advancing scientific knowledge.
    1. **Pure (p. 82)**
    2. Applied
    3. Secondary
    4. Primary

66. The second stage of the research process is to
    1. **develop a research design. (p. 82)**
    2. review the findings.
    3. choose a data collection technique.
    4. identify a problem.

67. __________ is the process of turning a simple hypothesis into one that is testable.
    1. Theory building
    2. Variable development
    3. **Operationalization (p. 82)**
    4. Hypothesis testing

68. Given the following research design diagram, what does the "X" stand for?
    $O_1$ X $O_2$
    1. The pretest
    2. The posttest
    3. **The experimental intervention (p. 83)**
    4. None of the above

69. __________ refer(s) to a researcher's ability to generalize research findings to other settings.
    1. Internal validity
    2. Randomization
    3. Confounding effects
    4. **External validity (p. 84)**

70. The problem of differential selection can be reduced through the use of
    1. statistical regression.
    2. **random assignment. (p. 84)**
    3. maturation.
    4. experimental mortality.

71. Which of the following factors is *not* a threat to external validity?
    1. Self-selection
    2. Multiple treatment interference
    3. **Differential selection (p. 84)**
    4. Reactive effects of testing

72. A __________ is especially valuable when aspects of the social setting are beyond the control of the researcher.
    1. controlled experiment
    2. one-group pretest–posttest design
    3. **quasi-experimental design (p. 85)**
    4. case study

73. Which of the following is *not* a data-gathering strategy?
    1. **Controlled experiment (p. 86)**
    2. Participant observation
    3. Life history
    4. Secondary analysis

74. William Foote Whyte's study of Cornerville utilized the __________ strategy.
    1. **participant observation (p. 86)**
    2. life history
    3. survey
    4. case study

75. The data-gathering technique that does not produce new data is
    1. survey research.
    2. case study.
    3. participant observation.
    4. **secondary analysis. (p. 87)**

76. __________ means that when the same conditions exist, the same results can be expected to follow.
    1. Intersubjectivity
    2. Internal validity
    3. **Replicability (pp. 87-88)**
    4. Randomization

77. __________ statistics attempt to generalize findings by specifying how likely they are to be true for other populations.
    1. Descriptive
    2. Theoretical
    3. **Inferential (p. 89)**
    4. Hypothetical

78. Which of the following statistical techniques is an example of inferential statistics?
    1. The standard deviation
    2. **A test of significance (p. 89)**
    3. A degree of correlation
    4. The mean

79. Adding together all scores and dividing by the total number of observations yields the
    1. **mean. (p. 89)**
    2. median.
    3. mode.
    4. standard deviation.

80. A __________ correlation exists between sample size and the degree of confidence we can have in our results.
    1. curvilinear
    2. **positive (p. 89)**
    3. negative
    4. inverse

81. Techniques that produce measurable results which can be analyzed statistically are
    1. tests of significance.
    2. qualitative methods.
    3. intersubjectivity.
    4. **quantitative methods. (p. 89)**

82. Which of the following research methods produces quantitative data?
    1. Participant observation
    2. Life histories
    3. Case studies
    4. **Controlled experiments (p. 90)**

83. Which of the following is *not* a critical ethical issue to researchers?
    1. Data confidentiality
    2. The protection of human subjects
    3. Disclosure of research methods
    4. **Application of results to social policy (p. 91)**

84. The principle of __________ means that research data are not shared outside the research environment.
    1. informed consent
    2. disclosure
    3. **data confidentiality (p. 91)**
    4. anonymity

85. In which of the following areas has research funded by the National Institute of Justice affected social policy?
    1. It has shaped the way that police are deployed.
    2. It has helped to identify career criminals.
    3. It has shown that rehabilitation does not necessarily reduce recidivism.
    4. **All of the above (p. 94)**

86. In a research report, the purpose of the __________ is to allow the author to make personal observations that may not be appropriate in the body of the report.
    1. abstract
    2. analysis
    3. introduction
    4. **preface (p. 95)**

# Word Search Puzzle

```
Q S K K I X R E D T G L F O L V B V U S I C S P S E G A Z
F S B N O O J G U M Y T N V P F G P V T X F L P R U D P S
K E I N P R F K N E K L Z Z U K Z U E A S T W T E Q E V K
L E F Z N W H R H T H L E S Y P K R K T S X R N H G S B M
Y W C T V H Z U L A Z P M I L N Y M F I C K B S J T M S P
D D O D S F B M T A W E Y K I V F L F S U C S S Y O O B Q
F U M B T N Y M Y N W X Z J D E L H T T W B J C Z Y Y N N
M H R I P N P E B A I P F K Z R B A J I D J X A W T F V K
R H Y O S J Y F F L T E Z L J S R S X C Q P H K I W Z J V
V A I P L H C U U Y S R M Q C T J B O S A Y G L Y L J O A
X K H E O N Q A S S O I M L V E H S F L Q N I B R R I L D
W I T R H T L N I I R M Z G A H L W U N S B T T W E E Q O
E R D A Z J H W R S Y E A N W E H X S R A E O K C X H B J
U F P T T M V E X T F N M H W N W F Z C V D B L T Q D F N
O Q K I Q L A N S M S T X J T X C G I Y I E I S L M E O Y
P N R O U O R B G I G D I B C X V L Y M Z V Y H X P I Y K
E I P N A A I T R C S E N G U L P R Y N P J M V H T A U H
W N Q A N J A S A R Y S F V U E O K U A T K W S A W F C Z
I E W L T Z B I O W V C E X R E M H B Z P F I Z L H R A P
Z Q E I I S L X G P A R R S H T B P K U T X I Q M A I L V
Y M L Z T C E J N H L I E T G U W V F W O M G C E B Y P Z
V M X A A F W T T I I P N N A D D H A N O I F S P X I Z Z
L B K T T P D B C O D T T K U O K B Y D R O E F T B Y B L
D N A I I A G V T L I I I R L M J O N X P R B Q T Z P F X
Z X Y O V P B V M P T V A W J G U A P W F N B Z L R N X L
Q P Z N E P U P E T Y E L Y Y Y R V Z R G Q J B U R M Q M
C J M N T L K L Z H Y D I N T E R S U B J E C T I V I T Y
L Z Q S C I C B O E M A B P T L B P G M E M H X H R Z A N
E G S H D E V M S Q J Q J L K A Z Q B V K N T M J M Q W I
S Z B H U D B V U R W I I H G Z G S M N B A B Y H J Y H P
```

Applied
Descriptive
Experiment
Hypothesis
Inferential
Intersubjectivity
Metaanalysis
Operationalization
Quantitative
Randomization
Replicability
Research
Statistics
Survey
Theory
Validity
Variable
*Verstehen*

# Crossword Puzzle

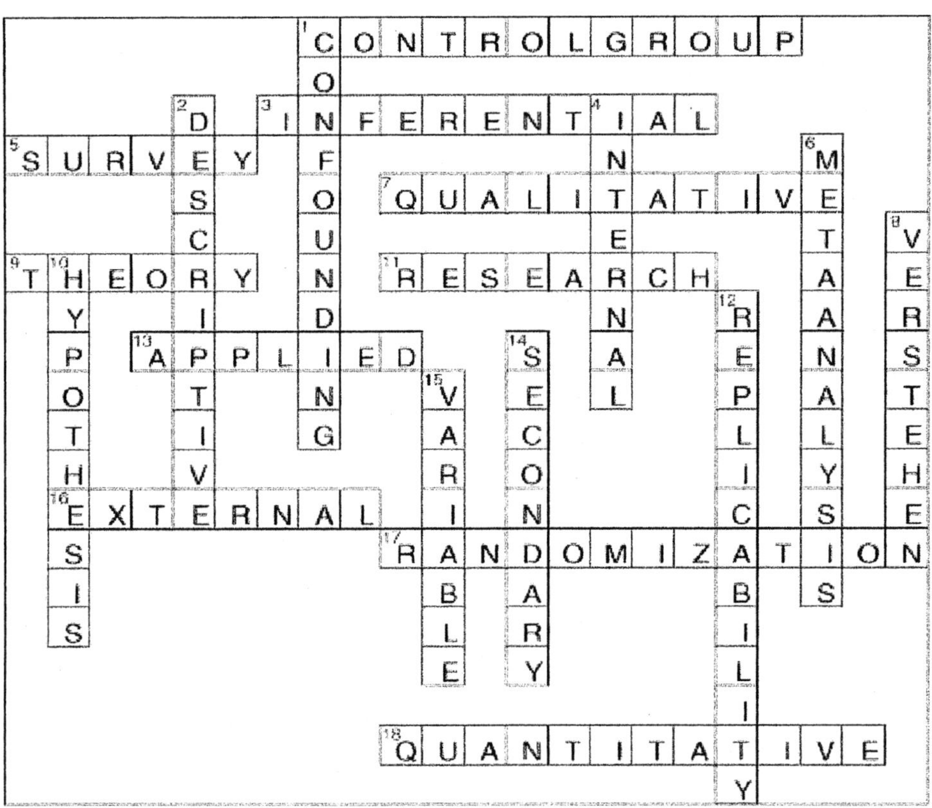

## Across

1. Subjects who are not exposed to the experimental intervention. (2 words)
3. _______ statistics specify how likely findings are to be true for other populations.
5. _______ research gathers data through the use of questionnaires.
7. Research methods that produce subjective results.
9. A series of interrelated propositions that attempt to describe, explain, predict, and control events.
11. The use of standardized, systematic procedures in the search for knowledge.
13. ______ research is designed and carried out with practical applications in mind.
16. ________ validity is the ability to generalize research findings to other settings.
17. The process by which individuals are assigned to study groups without biases resulting from selection.
18. Research methods that produce measurable results.

## Down

1. ________ effects are rival explanations that threaten the internal or external validity of a research design.
2. ________ statistics summarize relationships within data.
4. _______ validity is the certainty that the experimental interventions caused the changes observed in the study group.
6. A study of other studies.
8. The kind of subjective understanding achieved by criminologists who immerse themselves into the everyday world of the criminals they study.
10. An explanation that accounts for a set of facts and that can be tested by further investigation.
12. Valid observations made at one time can be made again at a later time if all other conditions are the same.
14. _______ analysis is the reanalysis of existing data.
15. A concept that can undergo measurable changes.

# 4 Classical and Neoclassical Thought

## Learning Objectives

After reading this chapter, students should be able to:

1. Recognize the major principles of the Classical School of criminological thought
2. Explain the philosophical bases of classical thought
3. Discuss the Enlightenment and describe its impact on criminological theorizing
4. Identify modern-day practices that embody principles of the Classical School
5. Discuss the policy implications of the Classical School
6. Assess the shortcomings of the classical approach

## Chapter Outline

Introduction
Major Principles of the Classical School
Forerunners of Classical Thought
- *The Demonic Era*
- *Early Sources of the Criminal Law*
- *The Enlightenment*

The Classical School
- *Cesare Beccaria (1738–1794)*
- *Jeremy Bentham (1748–1832)*
- *Heritage of the Classical School*

Neoclassical Criminology
- *Rational Choice Theory*
- *The Seductions of Crime*
- *Situational Crime Control Policy*
- *Critique of Rational Choice Theory*

Punishment and Neoclassical Thought
- *Just Deserts*
- *Deterrence*
- *The Death Penalty*

Policy Implications of the Classical School
A Critique of Classical Theories

# Chapter Summary

This chapter introduces the Classical School of Criminology, which grew out of concepts and ideas developed by Enlightenment thinkers in the late seventeenth and early eighteenth centuries. It discusses the forerunners of classical thought, including the concepts of morality known as folkways and mores and the method of dividing crimes into the categories of *mala in se* (acts that are fundamentally wrong) and *mala prohibita* (acts that are wrong because they are prohibited). Early sources of the criminal law include the Code of Hammurabi, the Twelve Tables (the basis for early Roman law), English common law, and the Magna Carta, which was eventually expanded into the concept of due process.

The Enlightenment was a social movement that emphasized reason and rational thought. Key intellectual figures included Thomas Hobbes, John Locke, Montesquieu, Jean-Jacques Rousseau, and Thomas Paine. The Enlightenment conceptualized humans as rational beings possessing freedom of choice and led to the development of the Classical School of criminological thought, viewing crime and deviance as products of the exercise of free will. Cesare Beccaria, a key Enlightenment philosopher, published his *Essay on Crimes and Punishments* in 1764, setting forth his philosophy of punishment. Beccaria emphasized punishment based on the degree injury caused, felt that the purpose of punishment should be deterrence (rather than retribution), and saw punishment as a tool to an end (crime prevention), rather than an end in itself. He emphasized the need for adjudication and punishment to be swift and for punishment, once decreed, to be certain. He also felt that punishment should only be severe enough to outweigh the personal benefits to be derived from crime. He opposed the use of torture and accepted the death penalty only for serious crimes against the state.

Jeremy Bentham, another founder of the Classical School, developed an approach known as utilitarianism or hedonistic calculus. Bentham believed that humans are rational and weigh the consequences of their behavior, considering pleasure versus pain. Therefore, he emphasized that to prevent crime, the pain of punishment must outweigh the pleasure derived from the crime. Like Beccaria, Bentham considered punishment to be a deterrent for those considering criminal activity.

The Classical School emphasized five basic principles, which are fundamental constituents of modern perspectives on crime and human behavior: rationality, hedonism, punishment, human rights, and due process.

By the start of the $20^{th}$ century, classical criminology was being replaced by positivism, which rejected the notion of free will and emphasized the concept of hard determinism: the belief that crime results from forces beyond the individual's control. However, by the 1970s, studies suggesting the failure of rehabilitation, combined with an increasing fear of crime, led to a resurgence of classical ideals known as neoclassical criminology.

Rational choice theory was developed out of the neoclassical school of criminology and is based on the belief that criminals make a conscious, rational, and at least partially informed choice to commit crime after weighing the costs and benefits of available alternatives. The two main varieties of choice theory are routine activities theory and situational choice theory. Routine activities theory suggests that crime is likely to occur when a motivated offender and suitable target come together in the absence of a capable guardian and focuses on how lifestyle can contribute to potential victimization. Situational choice theory revolves around the need for criminal opportunity and emphasizes the use of situational crime prevention strategies such as defensible space, improved lighting, controlling alcohol sales at sporting events, etc. These theories have been criticized for overemphasizing individual choice, disregarding the role of social factors (poverty, poor home environment, inadequate socialization, etc.) on crime causation, and assuming that everyone is equally capable of making rational decisions. Their emphasis on situational crime prevention strategies may also result in displacement rather than true prevention.

Both classical and neoclassical thought emphasize punishment. However, the Classical School sees deterrence as the purpose of punishment while the neoclassical view also incorporates retribution: if an individual chooses to violate the law, s/he deserves punishment and must be punished. Just deserts is the sentencing model that refers to the notion that the offender deserves the punishment s/he receives at the hands of the law. Neoclassical thinkers distinguish between specific and general deterrence. For punishment to be an effective deterrent, it must be swift, certain, and severe enough to outweigh the rewards of the crime. However, these requirements are rarely met by the modern criminal justice system, which may explain the extremely high rates of recidivism in the United States.

The death penalty is probably the most controversial punishment. Research suggests it may not be an effective general deterrent and that it is applied inequitably. Many capital cases appear to be seriously flawed, resulting in the conviction of innocent individuals. There is also much concern over the disproportionate imposition of the death penalty on racial minorities. There is a large number of arguments both for and against the use of capital punishment in the United States.

There is a number of policy implications to come out of the Classical School, including the concepts of determinate sentencing, truth-in-sentencing laws, and incapacitation. Overall, the classical and neoclassical schools are more a philosophy of justice than a theory of crime causation. They do not explain how a choice for or against criminal activity is made nor do they take into account personal motivations. There is no scientific basis for the claims made by the Classical School and many neoclassical thinkers also emphasize philosophical ideals over scientific research.

# Lecture Outline

I. Major Principles of the Classical School
   A. Outline the basic assumptions made by most classical theories of crime causation:
      1. Human beings are fundamentally rational, and most human behavior is the result of free will coupled with rational choice
      2. Pain and pleasure are the two central determinants of human behavior
      3. Punishment, a necessary evil, is sometimes required to deter law violators and to serve as an example to others who would also violate the law
      4. Root principles of right and wrong are inherent in the nature of things, and cannot be denied
      5. Society exists to provide benefits to individuals that they would not receive in isolation
      6. When men and women band together for the protection offered by society, they forfeit some of the benefits that accrue from living in isolation

7. Certain key rights of individuals are inherent in the nature of things, and governments that contravene those rights should be disbanded
8. Crime disparages the quality of the bond that exists between individuals and society and is therefore an immoral form of behavior

B. Stress that this is an overview and introductory guide to the chapter and that these assumptions are discussed in greater detail later in the chapter

II. Forerunners of Classical Thought

A. Primitive societies did not have the concept of crime as a violation of established law because of the absence of formal written laws or lawmaking bodies

1. All human societies had concepts of right and wrong — these concepts of morality and propriety are known as mores and folkways
2. William Graham Sumner
   a. Used the terms mores, folkways, and laws to describe the basic forms of behavioral strictures imposed by social groups upon their members
      (1) Small primitive societies use folkways and mores to govern behavior
      (2) Large complex societies use written laws
   b. Mores: proscriptions covering potentially serious violations of a group's values (e.g., murder, rape, robbery)
   c. Folkways: customs which have the force of tradition but whose violation is less likely to threaten the survival of the social group (e.g., dress codes, social manners)
   d. Only laws have been codified into formal structures created specifically for enforcement purposes
3. Another way some criminologists categorize socially proscriptive behavior is by dividing crimes into two categories:
   a. *Mala in se* acts are said to be fundamentally or inherently wrong regardless of time or place (e.g., rape, murder)
   b. *Mala prohibita* acts are said to be wrong only because they are prohibited and their status varies among jurisdictions (e.g., prostitution, gambling, drug use)

B. The demonic era

1. Early explanations of evil included demonic possession, spiritual influences, and divine punishment
2. Some early human societies believed that outlandish behavior was the result of spirit possession
3. Archeological evidence suggests that trephination was practiced to release evil spirits believed to be residing in the heads of offenders

C. Early sources of the criminal law

1. The Code of Hammurabi: one of the first known written bodies of law, emphasized retribution
2. Early Roman law: derived from the Twelve Tables (450 B.C.), a collection of basic rules regulating family, religious, and economic life
3. Common law: a traditional body of unwritten legal precedents created through everyday practice and supported by court decisions during the Middle Ages in England
4. The Magna Carta: a document in which King John of England pledged to respect the individual rights and privileges of landowners and which eventually was expanded into the concept of "due process of law"

D. The Enlightenment (the Age of Reason)
  1. The Enlightenment was a very important social movement in the seventeenth and eighteenth centuries
  2. Discuss some of the key thinkers whose ideas were the foundation for the Enlightenment:
    a. Thomas Hobbes
    b. John Locke
    c. Jean-Jacques Rousseau
    d. Thomas Paine
  3. Discuss the concepts of social contract, natural law, and natural rights
    a. Social contract: humans abandon their natural state of individual freedom to join together and form a society, surrendering some freedoms but forming a government which is obligated to assume certain responsibilities toward citizens and to provide for their protection and welfare
    b. Natural law: the concept that certain immutable laws are fundamental to human nature and can be determined through reason
    c. Natural rights: rights that individuals retain in the face of government action and interests
  4. Discuss the abortion debate as an example of the use of natural law arguments to support both sides of a dispute

III. The Classical School
A. Discuss the effect of the Enlightenment on society and on criminology
  1. The Enlightenment contributed to the French and American Revolutions and to the U.S. Constitution
  2. It emphasized free will and rational thought as the basis for human activity
  3. It led to the development of the Classical School of criminology, which saw crime as a product of the exercise of free will and personal choice
B. Cesare Beccaria (1738–1794)
  1. Cesare Bonesara, Marquis di Beccaria, born in Milan, Italy, earned a doctor of laws degree by age 20
  2. *Essay on Crimes and Punishments*, published in 1764, contained Beccaria's observations on the laws and justice system of the time
  3. In his *Essay*, Beccaria presented a philosophy of punishment
    a. Punishment should be based on the degree of injury caused rather than on criminal intent
    b. The purpose of punishment should be deterrence rather than retribution: punishment was a tool to prevent crime
    c. To prevent crime, adjudication and punishment should be swift and certain
    d. Punishment should be just severe enough to outweigh the personal benefits from crime commission
    e. Beccaria recognized three types of crimes and said the punishment should fit the crime
      (1) Property crimes should be punished with fines
      (2) Personal injury crimes should be punished with corporal punishment
      (3) Serious crimes against the state should be punished by death
    f. Beccaria was opposed to the death penalty except for crimes against the state and condemned the use of torture
  4. Other topics discussed by Beccaria in his *Essay*:

- a. Distinguished between two types of proof: perfect and imperfect
- b. Discussed the composition of the jury
- c. Discussed the efficacy of oaths in a court of law

5. Discuss the impact of Beccaria
   - a. His principles were incorporated into the French penal code of 1791 as well as influencing various European leaders
   - b. His *Essay* influenced the framers of the U.S. Constitution

C. Jeremy Bentham (1748–1832)

1. *An Introduction to the Principles of Moral Legislation*, published in 1789, outlined Bentham's approach to crime prevention (utilitarianism/hedonistic calculus)
   - a. To reduce crime, the pain of the crime commission must outweigh the pleasure to be derived from criminal activity
   - b. People are rational and will weigh the pain of punishment against the pleasure to be gained from the crime
   - c. Bentham did not favor extreme or cruel punishment but suggested that the pain of the punishment should just outweigh the pleasure of the crime
   - d. He also stated that for punishment to be effective, it must be swift and certain
2. Bentham focused on how punishment could prevent crime and act as a deterrent for those considering criminal activity—he distinguished betwen 11 different types of punishment
3. Bentham also designed a model prison, the Panopticon House

D. The heritage of the Classical School involves five key principles:

1. Rationality: humans have free will and choose their actions
2. Hedonism: pleasure and pain, reward and punishment are the major determinates of choice
3. Punishment: criminal punishment is a deterrent to crime, and deterrence is the best justification for punishment
4. Human rights: because society exists due to the cooperation of individuals, society owes citizens respect for their rights and their autonomy, at least as far as that autonomy can be secured without endangering other individuals or the greater good
5. Due process: an accused is presumed innocent until proven otherwise and should not be subjected to punishment before guilt has been lawfully established

IV. Neoclassical Criminology

A. Discuss the development of the neoclassical school

1. In the late 1800s, classical criminology gave way to the approach known as positivism
   - a. Positivism uses the scientific method to study criminality
   - b. Positivism is based on hard determinism, the belief that crime results from forces beyond one's control, and rejects the idea of free will
2. In the 1970s, many assumptions of positivism were undermined and a resurgence of classical ideals led to the development of neoclassical criminology
   - a. Neoclassical criminology focused on the importance of character, the dynamics of character development, and the rational choices that people make when faced with opportunities for crime
   - b. Contributors to the neoclassical movement include:

(1) Robert Martinson's study of rehabilitation, which led to the nothing-works doctrine
(2) James Q. Wilson's argument that crime was not the result of social conditions and could not be affected by social programs
(3) David Fogel's justice model, which suggested that offenders must be treated as responsible as well as accountable

B. Rational choice theory
1. Developed in the 1970s and 1980s, rational choice theory includes many of the principles of classical criminology
a. It is based on the belief that criminals make a conscious, rational, and at least partially informed choice to commit crime
b. There are two main varieties of choice theory: routine activities theory and situational choice theory
2. Routine activities theory/lifestyle theory was proposed by Lawrence Cohen and Marcus Felson in 1979 and builds on an emerging emphasis on victimization
a. They suggested that changes in the nature of society in the 1970s (increased personal wealth, decline in home-based activities) contributed to increased rates of household theft and personal victimization outside the home
b. The approach claims that crime is likely to occur when a motivated offender and a suitable target come together in the absence of a capable guardian (someone who effectively discourages crime)
(1) Lifestyles that contribute to criminal opportunities are likely to result in crime because they increase the risk of potential victimization
(2) Choices made by victims and criminals contribute to the frequency and type of crime in society
3. Situational choice theory was developed by Ronald V. Clarke and Derek Cornish and is an extension of the rational choice perspective
a. An example of soft determinism, seeing crime as a matter of both motivation and opportunity
b. Focuses on the choice-structuring properties of a potentially criminal situation, the opportunities, costs, and benefits attached to particular types of crime
c. Suggests the use of situational strategies to prevent crime and lower the likelihood of criminal victimization
4. Rational choice theorists concentrate on the decision-making process of offenders confronted with specific contexts and have shifted the focus of crime prevention to specific strategies that would dissuade a motivated offender
5. Discuss the four objectives of situational prevention and the sixteen techniques of situational crime control that may be used to meet these objectives
6. Rational choice theory is similar to classical theory but puts more emphasis on rationality and cognition and less emphasis on pleasure and emotionality

C. The seductions of crime
1. Jack Katz's book *Seductions of Crime* explains crime as the result of the pleasure experienced by the offender

2. Katz emphasizes the pleasure derived from crime as the major motivation behind crime: crime is rewarding to offenders because it is exciting and feels good
3. His approach stresses the sensual dynamics of criminality and says that for many people crime is sensually compelling

D. Situational crime control policy
1. Situational crime prevention shifts the focus of crime prevention away from the offender and onto the context in which crime occurs
   a. Instead of focusing on why people commit crime, it looks primarily at why crime occurs in specific settings
   b. It emphasizes the concept of opportunity – reduce opportunities for crime in specific situations to prevent crime
2. Discuss the twelve methods suggested by situational crime control policy as ways to alter environments and situations to reduce crime

E. Critique of rational choice theory
1. There is an overemphasis on individual choice and a relative disregard for the role of social factors in crime causation
2. There is an assumption that everyone is equally capable of making rational decisions
3. The issue of displacement – situational crime prevention strategies may cause criminals to find new targets of opportunities in other areas

V. Punishment and Neoclassical Thought

A. Both classical and neoclassical thought emphasize punishment
1. The Classical School sees deterrence as the purpose of punishment
2. The neoclassical view also incorporates retribution – if an individual chooses to violate the law, s/he deserves to be punished and must be punished to curtail future criminal behavior
3. Discuss the 1994 caning of Michael Fay in Singapore as an example of the neoclassical viewpoint

B. Just deserts
1. The just deserts model of criminal sentencing refers to the idea that criminal offenders deserve their punishment, which should be appropriate to the type and severity of the crime committed
2. Neoclassical thought states that justice is what the individual deserves when all the circumstances surrounding that person's situation and behavior are considered

C. Deterrence

**Show the ABC News program *Intro/Solitary Confinement* from the video library.**

1. Modern neoclassical thinkers distinguish between two types of deterrence:
   a. Specific deterrence: a goal of criminal sentencing that seeks to prevent an offender from committing further crimes
   b. General deterrence: works by example and seeks to prevent others from committing crimes similar to the one for which a particular offender is being sentenced

2. Modern-day advocates of general deterrence stress that to be an effective impediment to crime, punishment must be swift, certain, and severe; this is difficult to achieve in the modern criminal justice system
3. Define recidivism and explain the concept of a recidivism rate
4. Recidivism rates suggest that punishment does not prevent repeat crime
   a. Studies suggest recidivism rates reach levels of 80 to 90% in some cases
      (1) This means that 8 or 9 of every 10 offenders are rearrested for new crimes within five years of release from confinement
      (2) This rate is probably higher as these figures do not include offenders who are not caught or who recidivate more than five years after release from prison
5. Discuss the concept of the crime funnel as a possible reason why the criminal justice system is not very effective in preventing crime and reducing recidivism

D. The death penalty
1. There is a lot of disagreement over the use of capital punishment as a criminal sanction
2. Discuss the claims made by opponents of capital punishment:
   a. It does not deter crime
   b. It has at times been imposed upon innocent people
   c. Human life is sacred
   d. State-imposed death lowers society to the same level as the murderer
   e. It has been imposed in a haphazard and seemingly random fashion
   f. It is imposed disproportionately upon ethnic minorities
   g. It goes against the fundamental precepts of almost every organized religion
   h. It is more expensive than imprisonment
   i. Internationally, it is widely viewed as inhumane and barbaric
   j. There is a better alternative (life in prison without the possibility of parole)
3. Advocates of capital punishment generally discount these claims, and propose that death is deserved by those who commit especially heinous acts and that any lesser punishment would itself be an injustice
4. There has been considerable research into the extent to which the death penalty acts as a general deterrent
   a. Comparisons between states that have eliminated the death penalty and those that still have it find little variation in the murder rate
   b. Similar results have been found in studies looking at variations in murder rates over time in jurisdictions that have eliminated capital punishment
5. Advocates claim that the death penalty could be an effective deterrent if it is swift and certain but modern-day capital punishment rarely meets these requirements
6. Capital punishment and race
   a. Discuss research suggesting that the death penalty has been imposed disproportionately on racial minorities
      (1) Currently approximately 50 percent of offenders on death row are minorities, although only approximately 20 percent of the population of the United States is made up of minorities

(2) Blacks constitute approximately 12 percent of the population of the U.S. but almost 40 percent of offenders executed since 1976 have been black

(3) In almost every death penalty case, the race of the victim is white, even though approximately 50 percent of homicides have black victims

b. Advocates of capital punishments are more concerned with whether the death penalty is fairly imposed than whether there are ethnic differences in the rates of imposition

(1) If 50 percent of all crimes eligible for capital punishment are committed by members of one ethnic group, then one would expect to see 50 percent of death row inmates to be members of that ethnic group

(2) They say that the focus should be on sentencing those who commit capital crimes to death, regardless of any social characteristic (race, ethnicity, gender, etc.)

7. Is the system flawed?

a. A recent National Institute of Justice-funded study, *Convicted by Juries, Exonerated by Science*, reviewed 28 cases in which postconviction DNA evidence was used to prove the innocence of 28 convicted offenders, showing the fallibility of the justice process (these cases did not involve the death penalty)

b. Recent studies on the imposition of the death penalty have focused on injustices inherent in the sentencing process and on the apparently inequitable application of capital punishment

(1) A 2000 study in Texas looked at capital trials and appeals and found that

(a) Poor clients received bad representation by court-appointed attorneys

(b) Prosecutors are more likely to ask for the death penalty in cases where the victim is white

(c) Blacks and Hispanics are often excluded from capital juries

(2) A year-2000 study by the U.S. Department of Justice found significant racial and geographic disparities in the imposition of federal death sentences

(3) Research of death penalty appeals between 1973 and 1995 found serious flaws in many death penalty cases, so that the conviction or sentence was thrown out in 68 percent of the cases studied

c. Recently, some jurisdictions have begun to rethink the use of capital punishment

**Show the ABC News program *Fatal Flaws* from the video library.**

(1) Illinois suspended executions in January 2000 after DNA results showed that 13 death row prisoners were not guilty

(2) Maryland declared a moratorium on executions in 2002

d. Other states are not in favor of abolishing capital punishment; for example, the governor of Massachusetts has made efforts to revive capital punishment

VI. Policy Implications of the Classical School
- A. Lawrence W. Sherman described four paradigms of justice, which can be depicted in a two-by-two table based on the rationality or emotionality of the offender and the rationality or emotionality of justice
  1. The paradigm that best describes current practice is that of expressive economics
     a. This assumes that the offender is rational but that justice is emotional and uses the law and the justice system to express society's anger and outrage and to inflict retribution on the offender
     b. This paradigm does not satisfy most participants because while the offender rationally calculates costs and benefits, the system is expressing irrational emotion
  2. The rational economics paradigm best exemplifies the principles of classical and neoclassical thought discussed in this chapter
     a. This assumes that both the offender and the justice system are rational and favors deterrence
     b. Punishment is used to make the economics of crime more favorable to obeying the law than to breaking the law
- B. During the past 30 years, the philosophy of the American justice system has mixed both expressive and rational economics, resulting in the advent of a number of sentencing practices
  1. Determinate sentencing: a strategy that mandates a specific and fixed amount of time to be served for each offense category
  2. Truth in sentencing
     a. Requires judges to assess and make public the actual time an offender is likely to serve once sentenced to prison
     b. Many truth in sentencing laws also require offenders to serve a large portion of their sentence (usually 80 percent) before becoming eligible for release
  3. Incapacitation
     a. The use of imprisonment or other means to reduce the likelihood that an offender will be capable of committing future offenses
        (1) Selective incapacitation controls crime by imprisoning specific individuals
        (2) Collective incapacitation uses changes in legislation or sentencing patterns to remove from society entire groups of individuals judged to be dangerous
        (3) Discuss research by Marvin Wolfgang and others showing that the majority of crimes are committed by a small number of hard-core repeat offenders
  4. Review Sherman's other two paradigms, which are based on an emotional rather than a rational offender
     a. The expression paradigm combines an emotional offender and an emotional justice system
     b. The emotional intelligence paradigm involves an emotional offender and a rational justice system
        (1) This is the paradigm Sherman advocates as the best hope for the future
        (2) Actors in the criminal justice system would control their emotions and work with offenders and victims to bring about a reasonable resolution of the situation to repair the harm caused by the crime

VII. A Critique of Classical Theories
   A. Proponents of the neoclassical school take credit for the recent decline in crime rates
      1. They claim that following the implementation of get-tough-on-crime policies, official rates of crime have decreased substantially
      2. This decline may also be an artifact of the measuring process or be due to demographic changes in the U.S. population
   B. Critics claim that classical and neoclassical thought does not really explain criminal motivation
      1. It suggests that crime is the result of free will and individual choice but does not explain how a choice for or against criminal activity is made
      2. There is little scientific basis for the claims made by the Classical School

# Key Concepts

**Capable guardian**: One who effectively discourages crime.

**Capital punishment**: The legal imposition of a sentence of death upon a convicted offender. Also called *death penalty*.

**Classical School**: A criminological perspective of the late 1700s and early 1800s that had its roots in the Enlightenment and that held that humans are rational beings, that crime is the result of the exercise of free will, and that punishment can be effective in reducing the incidence of crime, as it negates the pleasure to be derived from crime commission.

**Code of Hammurabi**: An early set of laws established by the Babylonian King Hammurabi, who ruled the ancient city from 1792 to 1750 B.C.

**Common law**: Law originating from usage and custom rather than from written statutes. The term refers to nonstatutory customs, traditions, and precedents that help guide judicial decision making.

**Dangerousness**: The likelihood that a given individual will later harm society or others. Dangerousness is often measured in terms of recidivism, or the likelihood of new crime commission or rearrest for a new crime within a five-year period following arrest or release from confinement.

**Determinate sentencing**: A criminal punishment strategy that mandates a specified and fixed amount of time to be served for every offense category. Under the strategy, for example, all offenders convicted of the same degree of burglary would be sentenced to the same length of time behind bars. Also called *fixed sentencing*.

**Deterrence**: The prevention of crime. See also **general deterrence**; **specific deterrence.**

**Displacement**: A shift of criminal activity from one location to another.

**Enlightenment**: A social movement that arose during the eighteenth century and that built upon ideas such as empiricism, rationality, free will, humanism, and natural law. Also called *Age of Reason*.

**Folkways**: Time-honored customs. Although folkways carry the force of tradition, their violation is unlikely to threaten the survival of the group. See also **mores**.

**General deterrence**: A goal of criminal sentencing which seeks to prevent others from committing crimes similar to the one for which a particular offender is being sentenced.

**Hard determinism**: The belief that crime results from forces that are beyond the control of the individual.

**Hedonistic calculus:** The belief, first proposed by Jeremy Bentham, that behavior holds value to any individual undertaking it according to the amount of pleasure or pain that it can be expected to produce for that person. Also called *utilitarianism*.

**Incapacitation**: The use of imprisonment or other means to reduce the likelihood that an offender will be capable of committing future offenses.

**Just deserts model**: The notion that criminal offenders deserve the punishment they receive at the hands of the law and that punishments should be appropriate to the type and severity of crime committed.

**Justice model**: A contemporary model of imprisonment in which the principle of just deserts forms the underlying social philosophy.

**Lifestyle theory**: See **routine activities theory.**

***Mala in se***: Acts that are thought to be wrong in and of themselves.

***Mala prohibita***: Acts that are wrong only because they are prohibited.

**Mores**: Behavioral proscriptions covering potentially serious violations of a group's values. Examples include strictures against murder, rape, and robbery. See also **folkways**.

**Natural law**: The philosophical perspective that certain immutable laws are fundamental to human nature and can be readily ascertained through reason. Human-made laws, in contrast, are said to derive from human experience and history—both of which are subject to continual change.

**Natural rights**: The rights which, according to natural law theorists, individuals retain in the face of government action and interests.

**Neoclassical criminology**: A contemporary version of classical criminology which emphasizes deterrence and retribution, with reduced emphasis on rehabilitation.

**Nothing-works doctrine:** The belief, popularized by Robert Martinson in the 1970s, that correctional treatment programs have little success in rehabilitating offenders.

**Panopticon**: A prison designed by Jeremy Bentham which was to be a circular building with cells along the circumference, each clearly visible from a central location staffed by guards.

**Positivism**: The application of scientific techniques to the study of crime and criminals.

**Rational choice theory**: A perspective which holds that criminality is the result of conscious choice and which predicts that individuals choose to commit crime when the benefits outweigh the costs of disobeying the law.

**Recidivism**: The repetition of criminal behavior.

**Recidivism rate**: The percentage of convicted offenders who have been released from prison and who are later rearrested for a new crime, generally within five years following release. Also see **dangerousness.**

**Retribution**: The act of taking revenge upon a criminal perpetrator.

**Routine activities theory:** A brand of rational choice theory that suggests that lifestyles contribute significantly to both the volume and type of crime found in any society. Also called *lifestyle theory*.

**Situational choice theory**: A brand of rational choice theory which views criminal behavior "as a function of choices and decisions made within a context of situational constraints and opportunities."

**Situational crime prevention:** A social policy approach that looks to develop greater understanding of crime and more effective crime prevention strategies through concern with the physical, organizational, and social environments that make crime possible.

**Social contract**: The Enlightenment-era concept that human beings abandon their natural state of individual freedom to join together and form a society. In the process of forming a social contract, individuals surrender some freedoms to society as a whole, and government, once formed, is obligated to assume responsibilities toward its citizens and to provide for their protection and welfare.

**Soft determinism**: The belief that human behavior is the result of choices and decisions made within a context of situational constraints and opportunities.

**Specific deterrence**: A goal of criminal sentencing which seeks to prevent a particular offender from engaging in repeat criminality.

**Target hardening**: The reduction in criminal opportunity for a particular location, generally through the use of physical barriers, architectural design, and enhanced security measures.

**Trephination**: A form of surgery typically involving bone, especially the skull. Early instances of cranial trephination have been taken as evidence for primitive beliefs in spirit possession.

**Truth in sentencing:** A close correspondence between the sentence imposed upon those sent to prison and the time actually served prior to prison release.

**Twelve Tables**: Early Roman laws written circa 450 B.C. which regulated family, religious, and economic life.

**Utilitarianism**: See **hedonistic calculus.**

# Additional Lecture Topics

Consider discussing the issue of shaming as a form of deterrence, including both stigmatic and reintegrative shaming. Topics to discuss could include:

- The use of stigmatic shaming or degradation throughout U.S. history (e.g., branding, stocks, public punishments)
- The recent revival of stigmatic shaming (e.g., publishing the names of offenders in newspapers, posting them on billboards, televising criminal trials)
- John Braithwaite's concept of reintegrative shaming

Another option is to discuss various ways in which the Classical School has affected the criminal justice system. Topics for discussion include:

- The reform of criminal codes to eliminate torture, develop more consistent and certain punishments, and reduce the use of capital and corporal punishment
- The increased use of incarceration as a punishment as well as for short-term detention of those awaiting trial, execution, or corporal punishment
- The reform of law enforcement, including the development of the modern full-time police force with the goal of deterring and preventing crime

# Discussion Questions

These discussion questions are found in the textbook at the end of the chapter. The instructor may want to focus on these questions during the coverage of Chapter 4.

1. This book emphasizes a social problems versus social responsibility theme. Which perspective is most clearly supported by classical and neoclassical thought? Why?

2. Name the various pre-classical thinkers identified in this chapter. What ideas did each contribute to Enlightenment philosophy? What form did those ideas take in classical criminological thought?

3. Define *natural law*. Do you believe that natural law exists? If so, what types of behavior would be contravened by natural law? If not, why not?

4. What is meant by the idea of a social contract? How does the concept of social contract relate to natural law?

5. What were the central concepts that defined the Classical School of criminological thought? Which of those concepts are still alive? Where do you see evidence for the survival of those concepts?

6. Define *recidivism*. What is a recidivism rate? Why are recidivism rates so high today? What can be done to lower them?

# Student Exercises

## Activity #1

Your instructor will place you in groups and assign you to a public venue (a library, a grocery store, a video store, an office building, etc.). Your group is to inspect the location and answer the following questions:

1. What situational crime prevention techniques are in use in this location? What types of crime do they attempt to prevent? (For example, metal detectors help prevent the theft of library books.)

2. What additional techniques might be employed to reduce crime in this location?

## Activity #2

Your instructor will place you into groups. Your group is to read the U.S. Constitution (including the Bill of Rights) and prepare a short report on how this document was influenced by the principles of the classical school of criminology, including specific examples.

## Activity #3

Your instructor will provide you with a list of the UCR Part II offenses and ask you to classify each offense as either a *mala in se* or *mala prohibita* crime. You will then be placed into groups. Within each group, compare and contrast their classifications and determine where there is disagreement. Focus on the wide range of opinions present among a somewhat homogenous group (criminal justice majors at a university) and discuss possible reasons for these differing opinions.

# Criminology Today on the Web

### http://www.crimetheory.com/Archive/Beccaria/index.html

This site contains the text of Cesare Beccaria's essay *On Crimes and Punishment.*

### http://www.deathpenaltyinfo.org

This is the web site for the Death Penalty Information Center, a nonprofit organization which provides the public with information on a variety of topics related to the issue of capital punishment.

### http://www.yale.edu/lawweb/avalon/avalon.htm

This is the web site for Yale University's Avalon Project. It includes the text of many legal and historical documents, including the Code of Hammurabi and the Magna Carta.

### http://is.gseis.ucla.edu/impact/f96/Projects/dengberg

This site contains a virtual Panopticon.

# Student Study Guide Questions and Answers

## True/False

1. The new federal laws against sex-tourism are based on the belief that people make rational decisions to commit sex crimes involving children. **(True, p. 107)**

2. The Classical School sees humans as fundamentally rational. **(True, p. 107)**

3. Rape is a *mala in se* crime. **(True, p. 107)**

4. *Mala prohibita* acts are considered to be fundamentally wrong, regardless of the time or place in which they occur. **(False, p. 110)**

5. The Code of Hammurabi was developed in the city of Rome. **(False, p. 111)**

6. Common law is based on shared traditions and standards. **(True, p. 111)**

7. The Magna Carta was signed by King Edward the Confessor. **(False, p. 111)**

8. The Magna Carta has been expanded into the concept of due process of law. **(True, p. 112)**

9. Thomas Hobbes had a very positive view of human nature and social life. **(False, p. 112)**

10. John Locke focused primarily on the responsibilities of individuals to the societies of which they are a part. **(False, p. 112)**

11. The concept of a separation of powers between divisions of government was developed by Montisquieu. **(True, p. 112)**

12. Natural rights are inherent in the social contract between citizens and their government. **(True, p. 113)**

13. The Enlightenment contributed to the U.S. Constitution. **(True, p. 114)**

14. Under the development of the Classical School, crime came to be explained as a spiritual shortcoming. **(False, p. 114)**

15. Beccaria emphasized punishing offenders based on an assessment of their criminal intent. **(False, p. 114)**

16. Beccaria saw punishment as an end in itself. **(False, p. 114)**

17. Beccaria stated that punishment should be only severe enough to outweigh the personal benefits to be derived from the commission of the crime. **(True, p. 115)**

18. Beccaria was opposed to the death penalty under any circumstances. **(False, p. 115)**

19. According to Beccaria, an imperfect proof exists when there is still some possibility that the accused may be innocent. **(True, p. 115)**

20. Beccaria considered a jury of ones' peers to be useless. **(False, p. 115)**

21. Bentham advocated extreme and cruel punishments. **(False, p. 115)**

22. Probation and victim restitution fall into Bentham's concept of compulsive punishment. **(True, p. 116)**

23. Quasi-pecuniary punishment involves the use of fines. **(False, p. 116)**

24. Soft determinism suggests that crime results from forces beyond the control of the individual. **(False, p. 117)**

25. The original positivists completely rejected the notion of free will. **(True, p. 117)**

26. Robert Martinson's research resulted in the development of the justice model. **(False, p. 118)**

27. Routine activities theory is an extension of the rational choice perspective. **(False, p. 118)**

28. According to Jack Katz, crime may be sensually compelling to the offender. **(True, p. 120)**

29. Situational crime prevention focuses on the context in which crime occurs. **(True, p. 121)**

30. Rational choice theory assumes that not everyone is capable of making rational decisions. **(False, p. 124)**

31. Discouragement occurs when a crime is simply moved from one location to another, rather than being deterred altogether. **(False, p. 124)**

32. According to modern neoclassical thinkers, if a person chooses to commit a crime, s/he deserves to be punished. **(True, p. 124)**

33. Specific deterrence focuses on preventing recidivism among particular offenders. **(True, p. 126)**

34. A certain punishment is one that cannot be easily avoided. **(True, p. 126)**

35. The deterrence rate is used to measure the success of a given approach to the problem of crime. **(False, p. 126)**

36. High recidivism rates suggest that criminal punishments do not effectively deter crime. **(True, p. 126)**

37. Researchers generally find that murder rates are lower in states that have capital punishment than in states that have eliminated the death penalty. **(False, p. 127)**

38. According to the Death Penalty Information Center, minorities are disproportionately represented on death row in the United States. **(True, p. 127)**

39. White defendants are rarely executed for the murder of a black victim. **(True, p. 127)**

40. According to the Texas Defender Service, capital juries frequently include black or Hispanic members. **(False, p. 128)**

41. The expressive economics paradigm assumes that both the offender and the justice system are emotional. **(False, p. 132)**

42. Advocates of determinate sentencing believe that the fixed amount of punishment necessary for deterrence can be calculated and specified. **(True, p. 133)**

43. Selective incapacitation removes groups of dangerous individuals from society by changing legislation or sentencing patterns. **(False, p. 133)**

## Fill in the Blank

44. Of the terms used by Sumner, only __________ have been codified into formal strictures. **(laws, p. 107)**

45. Criminal homicide is a *mala* ________ crime. **(*in se*, p. 107)**

46. The _________ is one of the first known bodies of law to survive to the present day. **(Code of Hammurabi, p. 110)**

47. Common law was declared the law of the land in England by King_______. **(Edward the Confessor, p. 111)**

48. According to __________, governments are required to guarantee certain inalienable rights to their citizens. **(John Locke, p. 112)**

49. The concept of _________ suggests that certain immutable laws are fundamental to human nature and can be ascertained through reason. **(natural law, p. 113)**

50. According to Beccaria, oaths were ______ in a court of law. **(useless, p. 115)**

51. According to Bentham, ______ punishment included imprisonment and exile. **(chronic, p. 116)**

52. The __________ principle of the Classical School emphasizes deterrence as the best justification for punishment. **(punishment, p. 117)**

53. __________ determinism is a belief that crime results from forces beyond an individual's control. **(Hard, p. 117)**

54. The statement that offenders deserve punishment because of the choices they make is typical of the __________ model. **(justice, p. 118)**

55. _________ theory uses cost-benefit analysis. **(Rational choice, p. 118)**

56. Routine activities theory is also known as __________ theory. **(lifestyle, p. 118)**

57. Situation choice theory suggests that crime is a matter of both motivation and _________. **(opportunity, p. 119)**

58. A(n) __________ decision relates to particular instances of criminal opportunity. **(event, p. 119)**

59. Property identification falls into the _______ category of situational crime control. **(reducing anticipated reward, p. 120)**

60. The _______ model of criminal sentencing involves the belief that criminal offenders deserve their punishment. **(just deserts, p. 125)**

61. __________ is the repetition of criminal behavior by individuals who are already involved in crime. **(Recidivism, p. 126)**

62. The governor of __________ recently vetoed legislation passed by the legislature abolishing the death penalty. **(New Hampshire, p. 129)**

63. _______ requires judges to assess and make public the actual time an offender is likely to serve once sentenced to prison. **(Truth in sentencing, p. 133)**

64. The strategy of __________ uses imprisonment to reduce the likelihood that an offender will be capable of committing future offenses. **(incapacitation, p. 133)**

65. __________ uses changes in legislation or sentencing patterns to remove from society entire groups of individuals judged to be dangerous. **(Collective incapacitation, p. 133)**

66. Lawrence Sherman feels that the __________ paradigm offers the most hope for the future. **(emotional intelligence, p. 134)**

## Multiple Choice

67. Which of the following statements would probably *not* be made by an adherent of the Classical School?
    a. I believe that punishment is necessary to deter criminals from committing more crimes.
    b. I believe that people have certain basic rights and that if the government infringes upon these rights, it should be dissolved.
    c. I believe that people's behavior is determined by pain and pleasure.
    d. **I believe that forces beyond a person's control can affect his or her choice of criminal or non-criminal behavior. (p. 107)**

68. _________ are time-honored customs which are preferred but which do not threaten the survival of the social group if they are violated.
    a. Mores
    b. **Folkways (p. 107)**
    c. Laws
    d. Crimes

69. Which of the following is *not* a *mala prohibita* crime?
    a. Gambling
    b. Premarital sexual behavior
    c. Drug use
    d. **Theft (p. 110)**

70. Which of the following was *not* an early demonic era explanation of personal deviance?
    a. Free will **(p. 110)**
    b. Demonic possession
    c. Spiritual influences
    d. Temptation by fallen angels

71. Which of the following goals of punishment was emphasized by the Code of Hammurabi?
    a. Deterrence
    b. Rehabilitation
    c. **Retribution (p. 111)**
    d. Incapacitation

72. __________ was written around 450 B.C.
    a. The Code of Hammurabi
    b. The Common Law
    c. The Magna Carta
    d. **The Twelve Tables (p. 111)**

73. Which of the following was not one of the legal documents contained in the Justinian Code?
    a. **The Summary (p. 111)**
    b. The Institutes
    c. The Digest
    d. The Code

74. The Justinian Code was based on
    a. the Code of Hammurabi.
    b. common law.
    c. **early Roman law. (p. 111)**
    d. the Mosaic Code.

75. Which of the following was *not* a significant Enlightenment thinker?
    a. Thomas Hobbes
    b. John Locke
    c. Francis Bacon
    d. **William Sumner (p. 112)**

76. Which of the following works was written by Thomas Hobbes?
    a. *Essay Concerning Human Understanding*
    b. *The Spirit of Laws*
    c. *The Rights of Man*
    d. ***Leviathan* (p. 112)**

77. Which of the following works was written by Thomas Paine?
    a. *Essay Concerning Human Understanding*
    b. *The Spirit of Laws*
    c. ***The Rights of Man* (p. 112)**
    d. *Leviathan*

78. ________ is a concept which suggests that certain immutable laws are fundamental to human nature and can be ascertained through reason.
    a. **Natural law (p. 113)**
    b. Natural rights
    c. Positive law
    d. Hedonistic calculus

79. Which of the following was *not* one of the three types of crimes outlined by Beccaria?
    a. Crimes that ran contrary to the social order
    b. Crimes that threatened the security of the state
    c. Crimes that injured citizens or their property
    d. **Crimes that involved no victims other than society (p. 115)**

80. According to Bentham, ________ punishment included starvation and whipping.
    a. capital
    b. restrictive
    c. chronic
    d. **afflictive (p. 116)**

81. __________ punishment includes ordering an offender to make restitution.
    a. Pecuniary
    b. **Compulsive (p. 116)**
    c. Indelible
    d. Afflictive

82. The Panopticon was designed by
    a. Beccaria.
    b. Sumner.
    c. Locke.
    d. **Bentham. (p. 116)**

83. The principle of ________ is *not* one of the five fundamental principles of the Classical School.
    a. **subjectivity (p. 117)**
    b. rationality
    c. hedonism
    d. due process

84. The nothing works doctrine was based on the work of
    a. James Q. Wilson.
    b. David Fogel.
    c. **Robert Martinson. (p. 118)**
    d. Lawrence Cohen.

85. The justice model was developed by
    a. Robert Martinson.
    b. **David Fogel. (p. 118)**
    c. Marcus Felson.
    d. Ronald V. Clarke.

86. According to routine activities theory, which of the following is *not* necessary for a crime to occur?
    a. The presence of a motivated offender
    b. The absence of a capable guardian
    c. **The presence of a defensible victim (p. 118)**
    d. The presence of a suitable target

87. The situational choice perspective was developed by
    a. Lawrence Cohen and Marcus Felson.
    b. Hal Pepinsky and Richard Quinney.
    c. **Ronald Clarke and Derek Cornish. (p. 119)**
    d. Walter DeKeseredy and Jock Young.

88. Rational choice theory emphasizes primarily
    a. pleasure and pain.
    b. emotionality.
    c. **rationality and cognition. (p. 119)**
    d. none of the above

89. Which of the following techniques falls into the situational crime control category of reducing anticipated rewards?
    a. Formal surveillance
    b. Deflecting offenders
    c. **Target removal (p. 120)**
    d. Facilitating compliance

90. *The Seductions of Crime* was written by
    a. Marcus Felson.
    b. **Jack Katz. (p. 119)**
    c. David Weisburd.
    d. James Q. Wilson.

91. Those who advocate __________ see the primary utility of punishment as revenge.
    a. deterrence
    b. **retribution (p. 124)**
    c. rehabilitation
    d. uncapacitation

92. The Biblical injunction of "an eye for an eye" represents the concept of
    a. free will.
    b. **just deserts. (p. 125)**
    c. deterrence.
    d. rehabilitation.

93. According to modern-day advocates of general deterrence, which of the following is *not* required for punishment to be an effective impediment to crime?
    a. **The punishment must be harsh. (p. 126)**
    b. The punishment must be swift.
    c. The punishment must be severe.
    d. The punishment must be certain.

94. Recidivism rates in the United States reach levels of
    a. 10 to 20 percent.
    b. 40 to 50 percent.
    c. 60 to 70 percent.
    d. **80 to 90 percent. (p. 126)**

95. In 2000, the governor of ________ suspended all executions in the state.
    a. Texas
    b. **Illinois (p. 129)**
    c. Georgia
    d. Maryland

96. Which of Lawrence Sherman's paradigms of justice most closely mirrors the principles of classical and neoclassical thought?
    a. Expressive economics
    b. **Rational economics (p. 132)**
    c. Expression
    d. Emotional intelligence

97. The use of imprisonment or other means to reduce the likelihood that an offender will be capable of committing future crimes is known as
    a. deterrence.
    b. retribution.
    c. rehabilitation.
    d. **incapacitation. (p. 133)**

# Word Search Puzzle

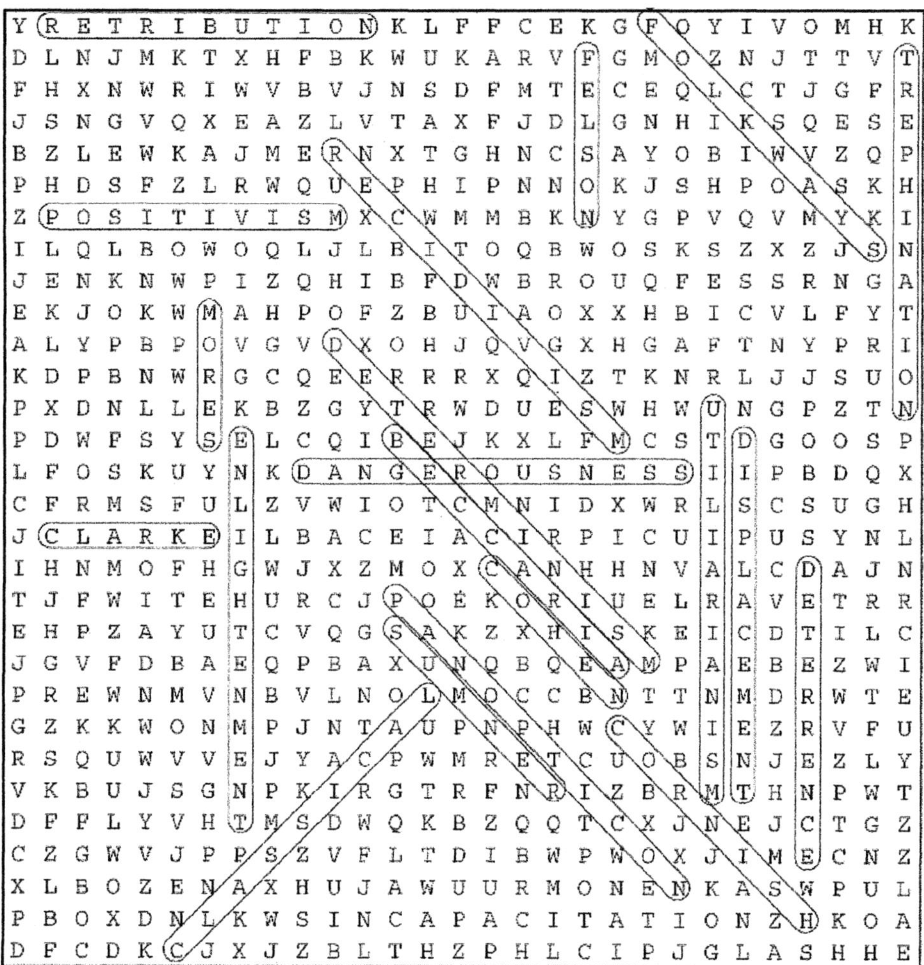

Beccaria
Clarke
Classical
Cohen
Cornish
Dangerousness
Determinism
Deterrence
Displacement
Enlightenment
Felson
Folkways
Mores
Panopticon
Positivism
Recidivism
Retribution
Sumner
Trephination
Utiliarianism

# Crossword Puzzle

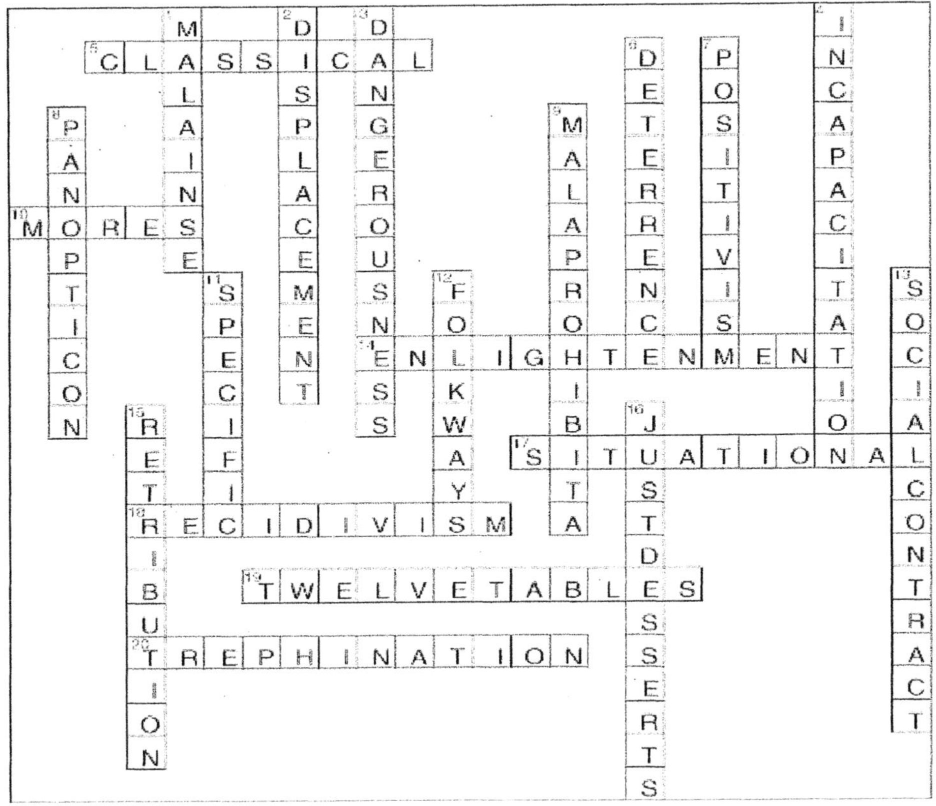


## Across

5. The ________ school suggests that humans are rational.
10. Behavioral proscriptions covering potentially serious violations of a group's values.
14. An 18th century social movement that built upon ideas such as empiricism, rationality, free will, and natural law.
17. A type of crime prevention focusing on the environment that makes crime possible.
18. The repetition of criminal behavior.
19. Early Roman laws which regulated family, religious, and economic life. (2 words)
20. A form of surgery typically involving bone, especially the skull.

## Down

1. Acts that are thought to be wrong in and of themselves. (3 words)
2. A shift of criminal activity from one location to another.
3. The likelihood that a given individual will later harm society or others.
4. The use of imprisonment to reduce an offender's ability to commit future crimes.
6. The prevention of crime.
7. The application of scientific techniques to the study of crime and criminals.
8. Jeremy Bentham's circular prison design.
9. Acts that are wrong only because they are forbidden. (2 words)
11. The type of deterrence that prevents a particular offender from recidivating.
12. Time-honored customs that carry the force of tradition.
13. The Enlightenment-era concept that human beings abandon their natural state of individual freedom to join together and form a society. (2 words)
16. The notion that criminal offenders deserve the punishment they receive at the hands of the law. (2 words)

# 5 Biological Roots of Criminal Behavior

## Learning Objectives

After reading this chapter, students should be able to:

1. Recognize the importance of biological explanations of criminal behavior
2. Identify the fundamental assumptions made by biological theorists of crime causation
3. Explain the relationship between human aggression and biological determinants
4. Describe the research linking genetics and crime
5. Explain the contributions of sociobiology to the study of criminality
6. Identify modern-day social policies that reflect the biological approach to crime causation
7. Assess the shortcomings of biological theories of criminal behavior

## Chapter Outline

Introduction
Major Principles of Biological Theories
Biological Roots of Human Aggression
- *Early Biological Theories*
- *Body Types*
- *Chemical and Environmental Precursors of Crime*
- *Hormones and Criminality*
- *Weather and Crime*

Genetics and Crime
- *Criminal Families*
- *The XYY "Supermale"*
- *Chromosomes and Modern-Day Criminal Families*
- *Behavioral Genetics*
- *The Human Genome Project*
- *Male-Female Differences in Criminality*

Sociobiology
Crime and Human Nature: A Contemporary Synthesis
Policy Implications of Biological Theories
Critiques of Biological Theories

# Chapter Summary

This chapter introduces biological theories of human behavior, an area that generates a considerable amount of skepticism and controversy among criminologists. Many early biological theories fall into the category of criminal anthropology: the scientific study of the relationship between human physical characteristics and criminality. These include physiognomy, a theory with roots in ancient Greece, and phrenology, developed by Franz Joseph Gall. One of the best-known early positivists was Cesare Lombroso, who developed the theory of atavism, suggesting that most offenders are born criminals. He also identified other categories of offenders, including criminaloids, or occasional criminals, insane criminals, and criminals incited by passion. A number of later researchers evaluated atavism; Charles Goring found no support for the theory, and Earnest Hooton concluded that criminals were physiologically inferior.

Constitutional theories examine body types. One of the best known constitutional theories is somatotyping, a theory associated with Ernest Kretschmer and William H. Sheldon. Sheldon identified four main body types, linked them to personality, and concluded that the mesomorph was most likely to be associated with criminality and delinquency.

Researchers have also linked criminal behavior to factors such as sugar or coffee consumption, food allergies, food additives, and vitamins, although the role of food and diet in producing criminal behavior has not been well established. Environmental pollution of lead, manganese, and other toxic metals also has been linked to violent crime. Prenatal exposure to substances such as tobacco smoke, alcohol, and marijuana have been found to be related to various behavioral factors, including delinquency. Various hormones, such as testosterone, serotonin, and cortisol, have been shown to be associated with aggression. Temperature has also been shown to have an influence on both violent and property crime, although it is moderated by temporal factors such as the time of day and day of the week.

Research into criminal families, such as the Jukes and the Kallikaks, led to the development of eugenic criminology and the eugenics movement of the late 1920s and early 1930s; this has been largely discredited. Research into the XYY or "supermale" has also concluded that XYY males are not predictably aggressive. More recently, Dutch criminologists may have identified a specific gene with links to criminal behavior. The use of twins to study genetic influences have found support for a substantial influence of heredity on delinquent and criminal behavior. The Human Genome Project may eventually help to uncover more information about the role of genetics in criminality. Gender differences in criminal behavior have remained extremely regular over time, refuting claims of criminologists such as Freda Adler, who suggest that cultural changes producing increased opportunity for female criminality would lead to an increase in crimes by women. Edward O. Wilson's paradigm of sociobiology involves systematic study of the biological basis of social behavior and emphasizes altruism and territoriality as determinants of behavior. Sociobiology has garnered considerable criticism as well as increased recognition.

A recent synthesis of biological and environmental factors was presented by James Q. Wilson and Richard Herrnstein in their book *Crime and Human Nature*. They identify a number of constitutional factors, such as age, gender, body type, intelligence, and personality, as contributing to crime.

The impact of biological theories on public policy has led to considerable controversy. Some fear issues such as racial prejudice or the resurgence of a new eugenics movement. In addition, contemporary criminologists have provided focused critiques of biological perspectives on crime, including methodological and other concerns. It does appear that various biological factors are correlated with various measures of criminal behavior, although the influence of social factors has overshadowed the relationship.

# Lecture Outline

I. Introduction
   A. Discuss the case presented by Russell Swerdlow and Jeffrey Burns regarding the child molester whose abnormal behavior may have been caused by a brain tumor
   B. The field of criminology has been slow to seriously consider biological theories of human behavior
      1. Criminology's academic roots are in the social sciences
      2. There are concerns that a biological focus on criminality might become racist

II. Major Principles of Biological Theories
   A. Outline the basic assumptions made by biological theories:
      1. The brain is the organ of the mind and the locus of personality
      2. The basic determinants of human behavior, including criminal tendencies, are to a considerable degree, constitutionally or genetically based
      3. Observed gender and racial differences in rates and types of criminality may be at least partially the result of biological differences between the sexes and/or between racially distinct groups
      4. The basic determinants of human behavior, including criminality, may be passed on from generation to generation
      5. Much of human conduct is fundamentally rooted in instinctive behavioral responses characteristic of biological organisms everywhere
      6. The biological roots of human conduct have become increasingly disguised, as modern symbolic forms of indirect expressive behavior have replaced more primitive and direct ones
      7. At least some human behavior is the result of biological propensities inherited from more primitive developmental stages in the evolutionary process
      8. The interplay between heredity, biology, and the social environment provides the nexus for any realistic consideration of crime causation
   B. Note that this is an overview and guide, and that these principles are discussed in greater detail later in the chapter

III. Biological Roots of Human Aggression
   A. Discuss Konrad Lorenz's 1966 work *On Aggression*
      1. Lorenz agreed with Darwin that intraspecies aggression favored the strongest and best animals in the reproductive process
         a. He suggested that aggression served other purposes as well, including ensuring an even distribution of a species over an inhabitable area and providing for defense against predators
         b. Human aggression serves similar purposes, although in more covert forms
      2. Lorenz claims that all human behavior is, to some degree, adapted instinctive behavior

3. He suggests that much crime is the result of overcrowding (which increases the likelihood of aggression) combined with contemporary socialization (which reduces legitimate opportunities for the effective expression of aggression)

B. Early biological theories
   1. Criminal anthropology is the scientific study of the relationship between human physical characteristics and criminality
      a. Physiognomy: the ancient Greek "science" of reading personality characteristics from facial features
      b. Franz Joseph Gall in his theory of phrenology, hypothesized that the shape of the human skill indicated personality and could be used to predict criminality
   2. The positivist school
      a. Cesare Lombroso's theory of atavism suggests that criminality is the result of primitive urges which survived the evolutionary process in modern-day human throwbacks
         (1) Lombroso stated that atavistic individuals are throwbacks to a more primitive biological state
         (2) He was the first criminologist of note to use the scientific method in his work and was one of the first notable positivists
      b. Positivism is built on two principles:
         (1) Acceptance of social determinism
         (2) Application of scientific techniques to the study of crime and criminology
      c. Lombroso studied and measured the bodies of executed and deceased offenders as well as examining living inmates to locate physical differences or abnormalities
         (1) He claimed to have found a variety of bodily features predictive of criminal behavior (e.g., exceptionally long arms, large teeth, ears lacking lobes, crooked nose, large amount of body hair, large lips)
         (2) He also identified characteristics of particular types of offenders
      d. Atavism implies that offenders are born criminals; Lombroso also identified other categories of offenders
         (1) Insane: mental and moral degenerates, alcoholics, etc.
         (2) Criminaloids/occasional criminals: persons pulled into crime by environmental influences
         (3) Criminals motivated by passion who surrendered to intense emotions
      e. Lombroso also studied female offenders and developed the masculinity hypothesis, suggesting that criminal women exhibited masculine features and mannerisms
   3. Evaluations of atavism
      a. Charles Buckman Goring studied Lombroso's atavism theory in the early 20th century
         (1) He compared prison inmates with university students, soldiers, and noncriminal hospital patients
         (2) Goring concluded that Lombrosian doctrine was fundamentally unsound
      b. Earnest A. Hooton conducted a similar study between 1927 and 1939, comparing prison inmates with nonincarcerated individuals

(1) Hooton claimed not only to have found physical differences between offenders and nonoffenders but also to have distinguished between regions of the country
(2) He concluded that criminals are physiologically inferior and that crime was the result of the impact of the environment upon low-grade human organisms

c. Discuss Schafer's criticisms of Hooton's work, especially the fact that his noncriminal control group may have included criminals who did not get caught and processed by the criminal justice system
d. Research into atavism continues today: a recent Canadian study concluded that subtle physical abnormalities were associated with an increased risk of behavioral and psychiatric problems

C. Body types

1. Constitutional theories or somatotyping emphasized body types as indicative of criminal tendencies
2. Ernst Kretschmer proposed a relationship between body build and personality type and outlined three main mental categories:
   a. Cycloid personality: heavyset, soft body; vacillate between normality and abnormality; primarily commit nonviolent property crimes
   b. Schizoids: usually have athletic, muscular bodies (could be thin and lean); more likely to be schizophrenic; usually commit violent crimes
   c. Displastics: a mixed group, highly emotional, unable to control themselves; commit mostly sexual offenses and crimes of passion
3. William H. Sheldon used measurement techniques to connect body type with personality and outlined four basic body types and associated temperaments and personalities:
   a. Endomorph: soft and round, overweight; relaxed and sociable
   b. Ectomorph: thin and fragile; restrained, shy, and inhibited
   c. Mesomorph: athletic and muscular, larger bones; most likely to be associated with delinquency
   d. Balanced type: average build
4. Later research on juvenile delinquency conducted by Sheldon and Eleanor Glueck also concluded that mesomorphy was associated with delinquency and supported Sheldon's work
5. The work of early biological theorists such as Gall, Lombroso, and Sheldon is generally discredited today

D. Chemical and environmental precursors of crime

1. Recent research has linked violent or disruptive behavior to eating habits, vitamin deficiencies, genetic inheritance, and other conditions affecting the body
2. Hypoglycemia (low blood sugar) has been linked to hyperactivity, aggressiveness, and crime
   a. Discuss the Dan White case
   b. More recent research did not find a link between sugar and hyperactivity; currently, the evidence on sugar's impact on behavior is unclear
3. Discuss recent research using PET scans, which found that murderers had lower levels of glucose uptake in the prefrontal cortex than controls
4. Food allergies and food additives (dyes, artificial flavorings, etc.) have also been associated with criminal violence, although the role of food and diet in producing criminal behavior has not been well established

5. Discuss the recent research into the relationship between other nutrients (e.g., omega-3 and omega-6 fatty acids) and behavior
6. A 1997 research study suggested that high levels of various environmental and industrial pollutants may cause people to commit violent crime
7. Enhancing brain levels of serotonin may lead to a decrease in aggression and impulsivity
8. Other environmental features linked to the likelihood of aggressive behavior include color and prenatal exposure to various substances (marijuana, tobacco smoke, and alcohol)

E. Hormones and criminality
1. Testosterone, a male sex hormone, has been linked to aggression
   a. Most research consistently has shown a relationship between high blood testosterone levels and increased male aggressiveness
   b. Aggressive behavior in men may also be influenced by high testosterone levels combined with low brain levels of serotonin
   c. Subtle changes in testosterone levels in women have also been linked to changes in personality and sexual behavior, but the research is limited and inconclusive
2. Fluctuation in female hormone levels (PMS) may also be linked to criminal behavior
   a. Discuss the cases of Christine English and Dr. Geraldine Richter
   . Research suggests that a drop in serotonin levels in the brain just prior to menstruation may explain the agitation and irritability sometimes associated with PMS
3. Other hormones (e.g., cortisol, thyroid hormone T3) have also been found to be related to delinquency and poor impulse control

F. Weather and crime
1. Research into the relationship between weather and criminal behavior suggests that temperature is the only weather variable consistently and reliably related to crime
2. Field research has found a definite positive correlation between temperature and violent crime, which appears to be moderated by temporal factors such as time of day, day of week, and season
   a. Cohn and Rotton have found temperature to be related to crimes such as assault, property offenses, domestic violence, and disorderly conduct
   b. Discuss how research by Cohn and Rotton is consistent with predictions that might be derived from routine activities theory
3. Other research suggests a link between barometric pressure and criminal offending

IV. Genetics and Crime

A. Criminal families
1. The field of criminal anthropology focused on criminal families, or families that appeared to show criminal tendencies through several generations
2. Richard L. Dugdale studied the Juke family
   a. Research into the family tree of the Juke family found a large percentage of murderers, thieves, and other criminals, as well as prostitutes and paupers
   b. Dugdale compared the Jukes with the descendants of Jonathan Edwards, a Puritan preacher and president of Princeton University; his

descendants included U.S. presidents, vice presidents, and successful businesspeople but no criminals

3. Henry H. Goddard performed a similar study of the Kallikak family
   a. He looked at two branches of the same family: same father, different mothers
      (1) The illegitimate branch resulted from a sexual liaison between the father and a barmaid and produced a large number of feebleminded (mentally retarded), epileptic, alcoholic, and criminal descendants
      (2) The legitimate branch resulted from the father's marriage to a righteous Quaker girl and produced only a few minor deviants
   b. Goddard concluded that a tendency toward feeblemindedness was inherited but criminality was not
4. This type of research led to the eugenics movement (1920s–1930s) and the development of eugenic criminology
   a. Eugenic criminology held that the root causes of criminality were passed down in the form of "bad genes"
   b. Social policies developed during the eugenics movement called for the sterilization of mentally handicapped women to prevent them from having children
   c. These policies were endorsed by the U.S. Supreme Court in the 1927 case of ***Buck* v. *Bell***
   d. Worldwide condemnation of Nazi genetic research, mass sterilization, and eugenics programs led to the end of the eugenics movement in the United States

B. The XYY "supermale"
1. Humans have 23 pairs of chromosomes; the last pair determines gender
   a. Males have an XY pair while females have an XX pair
   . It is possible to have unusual combinations resulting from a third X or Y chromosome (XXX, XYY, XXY)
2. A 1965 study of male Scottish prisoners found that a small number had an XYY chromosome; these were identified as potentially violent and labeled "supermale"
3. Discuss the use of chromosome-based defenses in court, including Richard Speck's unsuccessful attempt
4. Research of XYY males tend to show that they are taller than average, suffer from skin disorders, are of below-average intelligence, are overrepresented in prisons and mental hospitals, and come from families with less history of crime or mental illness
5. There is little evidence to suggest that XYY men commit crimes of greater violence than others, although they may commit somewhat more crimes overall

C. Chromosomes and modern-day criminal families
1. Discuss the recent Dutch research into criminal families: male descendants had near-normal IQs but showed a high proportion of arrests for violations of the criminal law
2. Roper and Brunner suggest that because males have only one X chromosome, they are more vulnerable to any defective gene, while women (with two X chromosomes) have a sort of backup system
3. They claim to have isolated the specific gene responsible for the family's criminality: the one responsible for production of the enzyme MAOA

a. MAOA breaks down serotonin and noradrenaline: excess amounts of these chemicals have been linked to aggressive behavior
b. If the body does not produce this enzyme, the brain is overwhelmed with stimulation, resulting in uncontrollable urges and criminal behavior

D. Behavioral genetics
1. Behavioral genetics is the study of genetic and environmental contributions to individual variations in human behavior
2. One way to separate out the role of heredity in crime causation is to study the criminal tendencies of fraternal (dizygotic or DZ) and identical (monozygotic or MZ) twins
a. If human behavior has a substantial heritable component, twins should tend to show similar behavioral characteristics despite variations in their social environment
b. Any observed relationship might be expected to be stronger among MZ than among DZ twins
3. Most twin studies have found support for a relationship between heredity and the risk of criminality
a. This may mean only that genes influence how people respond to their surroundings
b. Instead of inevitable producing antisocial behavior, "criminal genes" may be a genetic predisposition to respond in certain ways to a criminogenic environment

E. The Human Genome Project (HGP)
1. HGP is an international research project designed to construct detailed maps of the human genome by determining the complete nucleotide sequence of human DNA, localize all genes within the human genome, and determine the sequences of all the chemical base pairs that make up human DNA
2. Early results from HGP include the discovery of a pleasure-seeking gene that may play a role in deviant behavior, addictions, and violence
3. Discuss the new views of genes as enabling rather than causing human action

F. Male–female differences in criminality
1. Discuss the differences in male and female participation in crime
a. With the exception of crimes such as prostitution and shoplifting, the number of crimes committed by men far exceeds the number of crimes committed by women
b. Male-female criminality has been surprisingly stable over time
2. Suggestions that culture plays the major role in determining criminality are contradicted by the fact that the proportion of women participating in crime has remained fairly constant over a long period of time, despite cultural changes which have created new opportunities for women in crime
3. Although female criminality is probably culturally determined to a great extent, the issue of biology must also be examined
a. Some research supports the hypothesis that the relative lack of testosterone in women may lead them to commit future crimes
b. However, genetically based behavioral differences are greatly overshadowed by aspects of the social environment (socialization, expectations, culturally prescribed roles, etc.)

V. Sociobiology
  A. Sociobiology is a theoretical synthesis of biology, behavior, and evolutionary ecology introduced by Edward O. Wilson in 1975
    1. Wilson showed that particular forms of behavior, such as altruism, could contribute to the long-term survival of the social group
    2. His major focus was to show that the main determinant of human behavior was the need to ensure the survival and continuity of genetic material from one generation to the next
    3. Wilson emphasized the concept of territoriality
      a. Territoriality explains much human conflict (e.g., homicide, war) and results in tribalism, expressed through the increase in street gangs, racial tension, etc.
      b. The violence and aggression associated with territoriality are often reserved for strangers
  B. By the early 1980s, many criminologists saw sociobiology as a threat to the basic tenants of their field and advanced a significant amount of criticism, including:
    1. Sociobiology fails to convey the overwhelming significance of culture, social learning, and individual experiences in shaping behavior
    2. It is fundamentally wrong in its depiction of basic human nature because there is no credible evidence of genetically based or determined tendencies to act in certain ways
    3. It is an empirically unsupported rationale for the authoritative labeling and stigmatization of minorities who are despised, threatening, and powerless
    4. Humans are so different from other animal species that there is no rational basis for applying findings from animal studies to humans

VI. Crime and Human Nature: A Contemporary Synthesis
  A. In 1985, James Q. Wilson and Richard Herrnstein wrote *Crime and Human Nature*, a revival of biological criminology
    1. The purpose of the book was to revive discussions of biological cases of crime and move away from a totally sociological explanation
    2. They cited a variety of constitutional factors which contribute to crime, including gender, age, body type, intelligence, and personality
  B. Wilson and Herrnstein do recognize social factors in the development of personality
    1. They suggest that constitutional factors predispose one to specific types of behavior and that societal reactions to such predispositions may determine the form of continued behavior
    2. Thus, they emphasize the interplay between heredity, biology, and the social environment as crucial in any theory of crime causation

VII. Policy Implications of Biological Theories
  A. Discuss Steven Pinker's claim that social scientists unjustly ignore the biological basis of human behavior
  B. According to C. Ray Jeffrey, a number of elements should be included in any comprehensive biologically based crime prevention program
    1. Pre- and postnatal care for pregnant women and their infants
    2. Monitoring of children through early development to identify early symptoms of behavioral disorder

3. Monitoring of children through early development to reduce the risk of exposure to violence-inducing experiences
4. Neurological examinations
5. Biological research conducted in prisons and treatment facilities to help identify the root causes of aggression and violence

C. Discuss concerns that the possibility of links between race and crime could lead to a re-emergence of the eugenics movement

VIII. Critiques of Biological Theories

A. Discuss Nicole Hahn Rafter's critique of biological theories and her concern about the possible development of a contemporary eugenics movement based upon the findings of modern-day genetics

B. Discuss the critique of biological theories of crime causation by Glenn D. Walters and Thomas W. White and their conclusion that there is a need for caution in drawing causal inferences

1. Conceptualization of criminality is inadequate
2. Twin studies may incorrectly classify twins as MZ or DZ
3. There is difficulty in estimating the degree of criminality among sample populations
4. There are methodological problems, such as the lack of control or comparison groups, small sample sizes, high mortality rates, biased samples, and the use of inappropriate forms of statistical analysis
5. Research conducted outside the United States may not be applicable within this country (e.g., twin studies conducted in Sweden and Denmark)

# Key Concepts

**Atavism**: A concept used by Cesare Lombroso to suggest that criminals are physiological throwbacks to earlier stages of human evolution. The term is derived from the Latin term *atavus*, which means "ancestor."

**Behavioral genetics**: The study of genetic and environmental contributions to individual variations in human behavior.

**Biological theory:** A theory that maintains that the basic determinants of human behavior, including criminality, are constitutionally or physiologically based and often inherited.

**Born criminal**: An individual who is born with a genetic predilection toward criminality.

**Constitutional theory**: A theory that explains criminality by reference to offenders' body types, inheritance, genetics, or external observable physical characteristics.

**Criminal anthropology**: The scientific study of the relationship between human physical characteristics and criminality.

**Criminaloids**: A term used by Cesare Lombroso to describe occasional criminals who were pulled into criminality primarily by environmental influences.

**Cycloid**: A term developed by Ernst Kretschmer to describe a particular relationship between body build and personality type. The cycloid personality, which was associated with a heavyset, soft type of body, was said to vacillate between normality and abnormality.

**Displastic:** A mixed group of offenders described by constitutional theorist Ernst Kretschmer as highly emotional and often unable to control themselves. They were thought to commit mostly sexual offenses and other crimes of passion. The term is largely of historical interest.

**Ectomorph**: A body type originally described as thin and fragile, with long, slender, poorly muscled extremities and delicate bones.

**Endomorph**: A body type originally described as soft and round or overweight.

**Eugenic criminology**: A perspective that holds that the root causes of criminality are passed from generation to generation in the form of "bad genes."

**Eugenics**: The study of hereditary improvement by genetic control.

**Genetic determinism**: The belief that genes are the major determining factor in human behavior.

**Heritability**: A statistical construct that estimates the amount of variation in a population that is attributable to genetic factors.

**Hypoglycemia**: A condition characterized by low blood sugar.

**Juke family**: A well-known "criminal family" studied by Richard L. Dugdale.

**Kallikak family**: A well-known "criminal family" studied by Henry H. Goddard.

**Masculinity hypothesis:** (1) A belief (from the late 1800s) that criminal women typically exhibited masculine features and mannerisms. (2) In the late 1900s, the belief that, over time, men and women will commit crimes that are increasingly similar in nature, seriousness, and frequency. Increasing similarity in crime commission is predicted to result from changes in the social status of women (for example, better economic position, gender role convergence, socialization practices that are increasingly similar for both males and females, and so on).

**Mesomorph**: A body type described as athletic and muscular.

**Monozyotic (MZ) twins**: Twins that develop from the same egg and carry virtually the same genetic material.

**Paradigm**: An example, model, or theory.

**Phrenology**: The study of the shape of the head to determine anatomical correlates of human behavior.

**Schizoid:** A person characterized by schizoid personality disorder. Such disordered personalities appear to be aloof, withdrawn, unresponsive, humorless, dull, and solitary to an abnormal degree.

**Sociobiology**: "The systematic study of the biological basis of all social behavior."

**Somatotyping**: The classification of human beings into types according to body build and other physical characteristics.

**Supermale**: A male individual displaying the XYY chromosome structure.

**Testosterone**: The primary male sex hormone. Produced in the testes, its function is to control secondary sex characteristics and sexual drive.

# Additional Lecture Topics

Consider expanding on the discussion of positivism in the text. Outline the main propositions of early positivism:

- A rejection of the fundamental principles of classical criminology: positivists saw themselves as scientists rather than philosophers, emphasized a naturalistic rather than a legalistic definition of crime, and saw human behavior as determined by biological or genetic forces rather than individual free will

- An emphasis on the scientific study of crime: positivists demanded empirical investigation before drawing conclusions about the nature of crime

- A belief that criminals are fundamentally different from noncriminals either anatomically or physiologically (or both)

- An emphasis on the use of typologies to classify and identify offenders (e.g., the classification systems developed by Lombroso, Ferri, Sheldon, etc.)

In addition to the topic of twin studies, discuss the results of adoption research, which also lends support for the influence of genetics as well as social environment on criminality. For example, an early study by Hutchings and Mednick in Denmark matched criminal adoptees with a control group of noncriminal adoptees and found that the criminality of the biological father significantly predicted the criminality of the child.

# Discussion Questions

These discussion questions are found in the textbook at the end of the chapter. The instructor may want to focus on these questions during the coverage of Chapter 5.

1. This book emphasizes a social problems versus social responsibility theme. Which perspective is best supported by biological theories of crime causation? Why?

2. What are the central features of biological theories of crime? How do such theories differ from other perspectives that attempt to explain the same phenomena?

3. Why have biological approaches to crime causation encountered stiff criticism? Do you agree or disagree with those who are critical of such perspectives? Why?

4. What does the author of this book mean when he writes, "Open inquiry . . . requires objective consideration of all points of view and an unbiased examination of each for their ability to shed light on the subject under study"? Do you agree or disagree with this assertion? Why?

5. What are the social policy implications of biological theories of crime? What U.S. Supreme Court case, discussed in this chapter, might presage a type of policy based on such theories?

# Student Exercises

## Activity #1

Watch several episodes of a reality-based television show such as *Cops*. Observe the suspects in each crime/event and record as much information as possible about their physical characteristics. Do you notice any common physical characteristics among the suspects? Does there appear to be a "criminal type"?

In addition, watch several episodes of a non reality-based show and record information about the physical characteristics of the actors playing the criminals. Do fictional television shows cast actors of a certain physical type to play offenders? What characteristics (if any) are common to fictional criminals?

## Activity #2

Review the elements that C. Ray Jeffrey states should be included in a comprehensive biologically based program of crime prevention and control. Discuss the ethical implications of these components.

## Activity #3

In your university library, obtain information on the Youth Violence Initiative, a program proposed during the Bush administration in the early 1990s. Do you think that this program should have been canceled by President Clinton? Why or why not?

# Criminology Today on the Web

**http://www3.niu.edu/acad/psych/Millis/History/2004/phrenology.htm**

This Web site makes available an article about phrenology and the ideas behind it.

**http://www.crimetheory.com/Archive/BvB/index.html**

This Web site includes the U.S. Supreme Court's 1927 ruling in the case of *Buck v. Bell.*

**http://www.ornl.gov/sci/techresources/Human_Genome/home.shtml**

This is the home page of the Human Genome Project.

**http://www.crime-times.org**

This is the Web site of *Crime Times*, a national newsletter reporting on research conducted in the area of biological causes of crime.

# Student Study Guide Questions and Answers

## True/False

1. Criminology has embraced biological theories of deviant behavior. **(False, p. 143)**

2. Biological theories consider the brain to be the locus of personality. **(True, p. 144)**

3. A fundamental assumption of biological theories is that some humans may be further along the evolutionary ladder than others. **(True, p. 144)**

4. Charles Darwin wrote the book, *On Aggression*. **(False, p. 144)**

5. According to Lorenz, the drive to acquire wealth and power, which may contribute to criminal behavior, is part of a human mating ritual. **(True, p. 144)**

6. Konrad Lorenz's explanations apply only to violent crime. **(False, p. 145)**

7. Criminal anthropology is the scientific study of the relationship between human physical characteristics and criminality. **(True, p. 145)**

8. The theory of phrenology was developed by Konrad Lorenz. **(False, p. 145)**

9. According to Gall, poorly developed areas of the brain lead to a lack of associated personality characteristics. **(True, p. 145)**

10. Cesare Lombroso was a positivist. **(True, p. 147)**

11. Positivism emphasizes observation and measurement. **(True, p. 147)**

12. Cesare Lombroso's work was based on that of Charles Darwin. **(True, p. 147)**

13. Lombroso claimed that most offenders were biologically predisposed toward criminality. **(True, p. 147)**

14. Criminoloids do not exhibit atavism. **(False, p. 147)**

15. According to Lombroso, criminoloids differ from born criminals only in degree. **(True, p. 147)**

16. According to Lombroso, the quintessential female offender was the prostitute. **(True, p. 148)**

17. Earnest Hooton favored the development of rehabilitation programs. **(False, p. 149)**

18. According to Stephen Schafer, Earnest Hooton's research was flawed because the criminals he studied did not make up a representative sample of all criminals. **(True, p. 150)**

19. Hooton took into consideration the fact that some members of his noncriminal control group may have been criminals who had not been caught and processed by the criminal justice system. **(False, p. 150)**

20. Ernst Kretschmer's cycloid personality was associated with an athletic and muscular body. **(False, p. 151)**

21. An ectomorph is usually overweight. **(False, p. 151)**

22. The criminal courts do not agree that excess sugar consumption may be linked to crime. **(False, p. 152)**

23. Recent research published in the *New England Journal of Medicine* confirms the belief that diets high in sugar may lead to hyperactivity. **(False, p. 152)**

24. Food additives have been found to produce criminal violence. **(True, p. 152)**

25. Research has found that nutritional supplements can reduce antisocial behavior among incarcerated offenders. **(True, p. 153)**

26. Research has found a significant correlation between juvenile crime and high levels of lead. **(True, p. 153)**

27. Prenatal marijuana use is related to increased delinquency. **(True, p. 154)**

28. Increased levels of testosterone may be linked to increased aggressiveness in men. **(True, p. 155)**

29. PMS as a defense has been accepted by the courts. **(True, pp. 156-157)**

30. Elevated levels of serotonin in the blood correspond to elevated levels in the brain. **(False, p. 157)**

31. High cortisol levels appear to be linked to aggression. **(False, p. 157)**

32. Weather has no significant influence on human behavior. **(False, p. 158)**

33. The relationship between temperature and crime is not influenced by the day of the week. **(False, p. 158)**

34. Research does not support the notion of a link between barometric pressure and crime. **(False, p. 158)**

35. Goddard concluded that criminality was inherited. **(False, p. 159)**

36. The eugenics movement was prominent after World War II. **(False, p. 160)**

37. Both men and women can have Klinefelter's syndrome. **(False, p. 160)**

38. Lawrence E. Hannell was acquitted of murder because he was found to be a supermale. **(True, p. 160)**

39. The XYY defense has *never* been used successfully in court. **(False, p. 160)**

40. Recent research suggests that there is no relationship between XYY males and aggressive behavior. **(True, p. 160)**

41. Galton believed that heredity was related to criminality. **(True, p. 161)**

42. If human behavior has a substantial heritable component, any observed relationship might be expected to be stronger between monozygotic than between dizygotic twins. **(True, p. 161)**

43. Recent research at Florida State University using male twins found antisocial traits resulted to a significant degree from environmental factors. **(False, p. 163)**

44. Results associated with the Human Genome Project suggest that diminished dopamine function may be linked to deviant and addictive behavior. **(True, p. 164)**

45. Genes cause human action. **(False, p. 165)**

46. The proportion of homicides committed by men versus women has remained fairly constant for the last forty years. **(True, p. 165)**

47. Current research finds clear support for Freda Adler's theory that a new female criminal is emerging. **(False, p. 166)**

48. The fact that men commit more murders than women shows a genetic predisposition toward interpersonal violence that is present in men but not in women. **(False, p. 166)**

49. According to Arnold Lieber, nights around a full moon show an increase in crime. **(True, p. 169)**

50. *Crime and Human Nature* was written by Edward O. Wilson. **(False, p. 169)**

51. Wilson and Herrnstein said that individuals commit more crimes as they get older. **(False, p. 169)**

52. According to the blank slate myth, the human personality is malleable by society. **(True, p. 169)**

53. According to Ellis and Walsh, there are probably no genes for criminal behavior. **(True, p. 172)**

54. According to Nicole Han Rafter, genetic solutions to crime may be an oversimplification of a complex social issue. **(True, p. 172)**

55. It is possible for researchers conducing twin studies to make errors when classifying a pair of twins as monozygotic or dizygotic. **(True, p. 172)**

## Fill in the Blank

56. The 1992 National Institutes of Health-sponsored conference on biology and crime was cancelled for fear the meeting would be __________. **(racist, p. 143)**

57. Biological theories of crime causation assume that the basic determinants of behavior are __________ based. **(constitutionally/genetically, p. 144)**

58. Biological theories would suggest that __________ differences in criminality may be due in part to biological differences between the sexes. **(gender, p. 144)**

59. Phrenology is also known as __________. **(craniology, p. 145)**

60. According to Gall, the shape of the __________ is indicative of the personality. **(skull, p. 145)**

61. Positivism is based upon an acceptance of __________. **(social determinism, p. 147)**

62. Positivism emphasizes the application of __________ to the study of crime. **(scientific techniques, p. 147)**

63. The term "positivism" comes from the work of __________. **(Auguste Comte, p. 147)**

64. __________ conducted a study of Lombroso's theory and concluded that criminals show an overall physiological inferiority to the general population. **(Earnest Hooton, p. 149)**

65. __________ theories focus on an offender's body type. **(Constitutional/somatotype, p. 151)**

66. According to Ernst Kretschmer, __________ committed primarily nonviolent property crimes. **(cycloids, p. 151)**

67. Sheldon and Eleanor Glueck associated mesomorphy with __________. **(delinquency, p. 152)**

68. Early studies of chemical imbalances linked __________ to murder. **(hypoglycemia, p. 152)**

69. Dan White successfully used the "Twinkie Defense" to get a reduced sentence for the crime of __________. **(murder, p. 152)**

70. Research suggests that __________ brain levels of serotonin might reduce aggression. **(enhancing, pp. 153-154)**

71. According to research, specific shades of the color __________ could have a calming effect on people experiencing feelings of anger and agitation. **(pink, p. 154)**

72. Men whose brains lack sufficient amounts of __________ may feel frustration more acutely and respond to frustrating circumstances more aggressively. **(serotonin, p. 156)**

73. More __________ crime is reported to the police on warm than on cold days. **(violent, p. 158)**

74. Research has found a __________ correlation between temperature and violent crime. **(positive, p. 158)**

75. Richard Dugdale studied the __________ family. **(Juke, p. 158)**

76. __________ criminology focuses on the idea that the root causes of criminality are passed from one generation to the next in the form of "bad genes." **(Eugenic, p. 160)**

77. The eugenics movement policies were endorsed by the U.S. Supreme Court in the case of __________. **(*Buck* v. *Bell*, p. 160)**

78. A "normal" male individual has an __________ chromosome structure. **(XY, p. 160)**

79. Ropers and Brunner consider __________ to be more vulnerable to any defective gene because they have only one X chromosome. **(men, p. 161)**

80. __________ was the first western scientist to systematically study heredity and its possible influence on human behavior. **(Sir Francis Galton, p. 161)**

81. Identical twins are known as __________ twins. **(monozygotic, p. 161)**

82. The book *Sisters in Crime* was written by __________. **(Freda Adler, p. 166)**

83. The concept of __________ in sociobiology is used to explain conflict between humans. **(territoriality, p. 167)**

84. According to Wilson and Herrnstein, criminality is consistently associated with __________ intelligence. **(low, p. 169)**

85. According to __________, social scientists unjustly ignore the biological basis of human behavior. **(Steven Pinker, p. 169)**

86. According to __________, a comprehensive biologically based crime prevention program would include prenatal and postnatal care for pregnant women and their infants. **(C. Ray Jeffery, p. 169)**

## Multiple Choice

87. Which of the following is *not* one of the fundamental assumptions of biological theories of crime causation?
    1. The brain is the organ of behavior.
    2. **The basic determinants of criminal behavior are, to a considerable degree, the product of individual choice. (p. 144)**
    3. A tendency to commit crime may be inherited.
    4. They are all fundamental assumptions of biological theories.

88. The early biological theory which predicted personality characteristics from human facial features was known as
    1. atavism.
    2. **physiognomy. (p. 145)**
    3. somatotyping.
    4. phrenology.

89. The early biological theory which studied the shape of the head to predict criminality was known as
    1. atavism.
    2. physiognomy.
    3. somatotyping.
    4. **phrenology. (p. 145)**

90. __________ is a concept used by Cesare Lombroso to suggest that criminality is the result of primitive urges which survived the evolutionary process.
    1. Ectomorph
    2. **Atavism (p. 147)**
    3. Schizoid
    4. Criminaloid

91. An atavistic individual has an underdeveloped __________.
    1. **brain. (p. 147)**
    2. personality.
    3. emotional state.
    4. physique.

92. Which of the following traits is especially characteristic of a murderer, according to Lombroso?
    1. A diseased personality
    2. A nonstandard number of ribs
    3. A large amount of body hair
    4. **Cold glassy eyes (p. 147)**

93. According to Cesare Lombroso's categorization of offenders, occasional criminals were known as
    1. **criminaloids. (p. 147)**
    2. atavists.
    3. insane.
    4. criminals incited by passion.

94. *The Female Offender* was written by
    1. Charles Goring.
    2. **Cesare Lombroso. (p. 148)**
    3. Ernest Hooton.
    4. William Sheldon.

95. __________ reported finding physiological features characteristic of specific criminal types in individual states.
    1. Cesare Lombroso
    2. **Earnest Hooton (p. 149)**
    3. Charles Goring
    4. William Sheldon

96. Which of the following was *not* one of Ernst Kretschmer's mental categories?
    1. Schizoids
    2. **Criminaloids (p. 151)**
    3. Cycloids
    4. Displastics

97. Which of the following was *not* one of William Sheldon's basic body types?
    1. Ectomorphs
    2. Endomorphs
    3. Mesomorphs
    4. **Cyclothmorphs (p. 151)**

98. Which of Sheldon's body types is most likely to be relaxed and sociable?
    1. **An ectomorph (p. 151)**
    2. An endomorph
    3. A mesomorph
    4. A cyclothmorph

99. Which of the following foods has *not* been implicated in the production of criminal violence?
    1. Coffee
    2. MSG
    3. Processed foods
    4. **All of the above may possibly trigger antisocial behavior. (p. 152)**

100. The relationship between testosterone and aggressive behavior in young males appears to be moderated by
    1. age.
    2. **the social environment. (p. 156)**
    3. genetics.
    4. none of the above

101. The agitation and irritability sometimes associated with premenstrual syndrome may be explained by a decrease in __________ levels in the female brain just before menstruation.
    1. **serotonin (p. 157)**
    2. dopamine
    3. testosterone
    4. cortisol

102. According to Cohn and Rotton, the relationship between temperature and assaults is strongest during the __________ hours.
    1. **evening (p. 158)**
    2. morning
    3. afternoon
    4. midday

103. The studies of the Jukes and Kallikak families emphasized __________ as the primary source of criminality.
    1. environment
    2. ecology
    3. **genetics (p. 160)**
    4. psychology

104. The purpose of the Human Genome Project is to determine the complete sequence of
    1. **DNA. (p. 163)**
    2. RNA.
    3. XYY.
    4. MAOA.

105. Sociobiology was introducted by
    1. Freda Adler.
    2. Arnold L. Lieber.
    3. James Q. Wilson.
    4. **Edward O. Wilson. (p. 166)**

106. According to sociobiologists, the violence and aggressiveness associated with territoriality is often reserved for
    1. family members.
    2. relatives.
    3. acquaintances.
    4. **strangers. (p. 167)**

107. The __________ myth holds that everyone has an individual soul-like quality that can make choices independent of any biological predispositions.
    1. blank slate
    2. noble savage
    3. **ghost in the machine (p. 169)**
    4. scientific method

# Word Search Puzzle

Atavism
Criminaloids
Cycloid
Darwin
Displastic
Ectomorph
Endomorph
Eugenics
Galton
Heritability
Herrnstein
Hooton
Hypoglycemia
Kallikak
Lombroso
Mesomorph
Monozygotic
Paradigm
Phrenology
Sheldon
Sociobiology
Somatotyping
Supermale
Testosterone
Wilson

# Crossword Puzzle

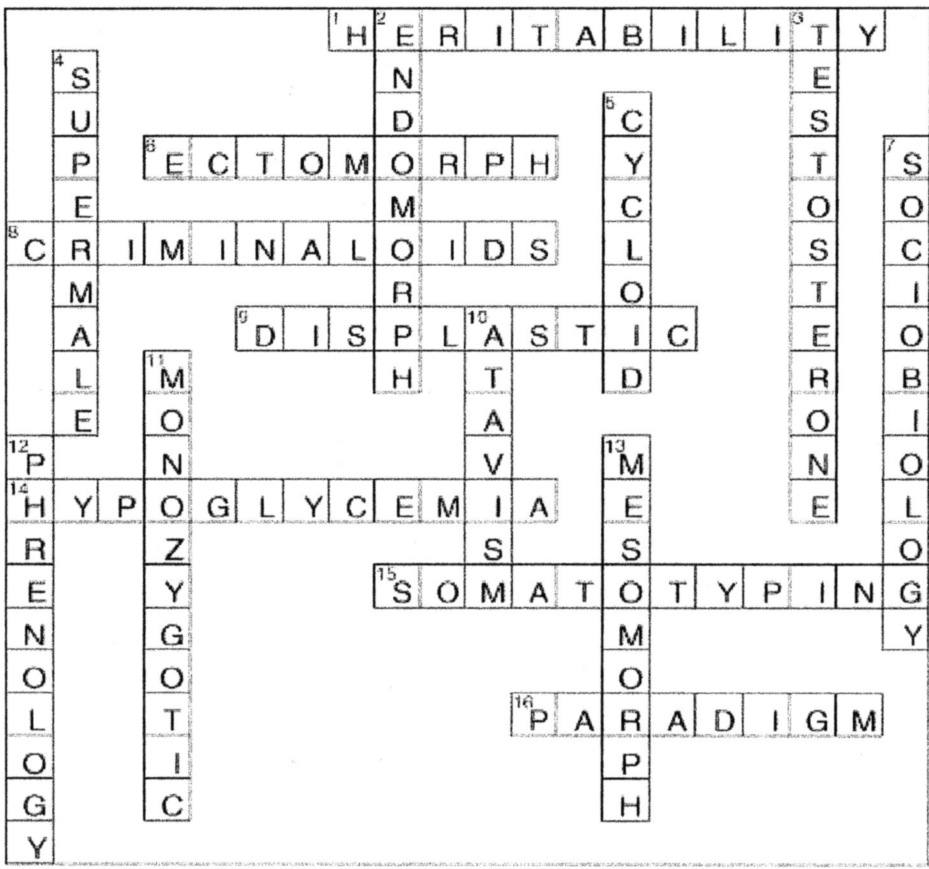

## Across

1. The amount of variation in a population attributable to genetic factors.
6. A body type that is thin and fragile.
8. Cesare Lombroso's term describing occasional criminals pulled into criminality by environmental influences.
9. Ernst Kretschmer's term describing a mixed group of offenders who are often unable to control themselves.
14. A condition characterized by low blood sugar.
15. Classifying humans according to body build.
16. An example, model, or theory.

## Down

2. A body type that is soft and round.
3. The primary male sex hormone.
4. An individual displaying the XYY chromosome structure.
5. Ernst Kretschmer's term describing a personality associated with a heavyset, soft type of body.
7. The systematic study of the biological basis of all social behavior.
10. Cesare Lombroso's concept that criminals are physiological throwbacks to earlier stages of human evolution.
11. Twins that develop from the same egg.
12. The study of the shape of the head to determine anatomical correlates of human behavior.
13. A body type that is athletic and muscular.

# 6

# Psychological and Psychiatric Foundations of Criminal Behavior

## Learning Objectives

After reading this chapter, students should be able to:

1. Identify the contributions of psychology and psychiatry to an understanding of criminal behavior
2. Explain the relationship between personality and criminal behavior
3. Recognize the importance of modeling theory to an understanding of criminality
4. Understand the unique characteristics of those found not guilty by reason of insanity
5. Identify current social policy that reflects the psychological approach to criminal behavior

## Chapter Outline

# Chapter Summary

This chapter introduces psychological and psychiatric theories of human behavior. Most early psychological theories emphasized either behavioral conditioning or personality disturbances and psychopathology. The concept of the psychopath or sociopath was developed by Hervey Cleckley. Currently, these terms have fallen out of favor and have been replaced by the concept of antisocial personality. Individuals with the characteristics of an antisocial personality are likely to become criminals at some point. Another theory emphasizing personality characteristics is biopsychology, which was developed by Hans Eysenck. Eysenck described three personality dimensions (psychoticism, extroversion, and neuroticism), each with links to criminality. He stated that personality traits were dependent on the autonomic nervous system; those whose nervous systems require stimulation are more likely to become offenders.

Sigmund Freud's psychoanalytic theory suggests that criminal behavior is maladaptive, the result of inadequacies inherent in the offender's personality. Psychoanalysis suggests that one possible cause of crime may be a poorly developed superego, which leaves the individual operating without a moral guide. Neurosis, a minor form of mental illness, may also lead to crime. In addition, more serious mental illness such as psychosis may result in criminal behavior, including violent crime. Freud's frustration–aggression link was more fully developed by researchers such as J. Dollard, who suggested that everyone suffers frustration and thus aggression is a natural part of life; it may be manifested in socially acceptable or unacceptable ways. Other theorists suggest that crime fulfills some purpose, such as the need to be punished or the need to reduce stress.

Modeling theory, as developed by Albert Bandura, is a form of social learning theory that suggests that people learn to act by observing others; observation of aggressive behavior teaches one how to behave aggressively. Behavior theory, developed by researchers such as B.F. Skinner, involves the use of rewards and punishments to control a person's responses, or operant behavior. Attachment theory suggests that the lack of a secure attachment between a child and his/her primary caregiver may lead to delinquent and criminal behavior later in life. Michael Gottfredson and Travis Hirschi developed a general theory of crime based on the concept that low self-control accounts for all types of crime.

Insanity is a legal rather than a clinical concept and is based on the claim of mental illness. Insanity is a defense to criminal prosecution and the burden of proof is on the defendant; a person is presumed sane at the start of a criminal trial. The 1984 federal Insanity Defense Reform Act (IDRA) created the verdict of not guilty by reason of insanity (NGRI), ensured that a federal defendant found NGRI will be hospitalized rather than released, and included a provision permitting mentally ill persons to be held for trial in the hopes that they will recover sufficiently to permit the trial to proceed. Several tests for insanity are used in the United States. The *M'Naughten* rule holds that people cannot be held criminally responsible for their actions if at the time of the crime they either did not know what they were doing or did not know that what they were doing is wrong. The irresistible-impulse test, which can be used alone or in conjunction with *M'Naughten*, holds that people are not guilty of criminal offenses if by virtue of their mental state or psychological condition, they were unable to resist committing the criminal act. Other tests include the *Durham* rule, the substantial-capacity test, and the *Brawner* rule. Some states permit verdicts of guilty but mentally ill (GBMI), which allows the defendant to be held responsible for a crime despite the presence of some degree of mental incompetence.

The use of psychological theories to predict or assess dangerousness has contributed to social policy. The concept of selective incapacitation is based on the notion of career criminals and relies on prediction of future criminality to determine sentencing policy. Correctional psychology is concerned with the diagnosis and classification of offenders, the treatment of correctional populations, and the rehabilitation of offenders. Psychological profiling is used to help police better understand people wanted for serious crimes.

# Lecture Outline

I. Introduction
   A. Discuss the cases of Persephone Muhammad, Jeffrey Dahmer, and Lorena Bobbitt and the possibility that their crimes may be the result of psychological factors
   B. Review the terminology used to describe the psychological study of crime and criminality:
      1. Forensic psychology/criminal psychology: the application of the science and profession of psychology to questions and issues relating to law and the legal system
      2. Forensic psychiatry: a medical subspeciality applying psychiatry to the needs of crime prevention and solution, criminal rehabilitation, and issues of the criminal law

II. Major Principles of Psychological Theories
   A. Discuss the central features of psychological theories of crime causation
      1. The individual is the primary unit of analysis
      2. Personality is the major motivational element within individuals, because it is the seat of drives and the source of motives
      3. Crimes result from abnormal, dysfunctional, or inappropriate mental processes within the personality
      4. Criminal behavior, although condemned by the social group, may be purposeful for the individual insofar as it addresses certain felt needs

5. Normality is generally defined by social consensus, which is what the majority of people in any social group agree is "real," appropriate, or typical
6. Defective, or abnormal, mental processes may have a variety of causes, including a diseased mind, inappropriate learning or improper conditioning, the emulation of inappropriate role models, and adjustment to inner conflicts

B. Note that this is an overview and guide, and that these points are discussed in more detail later in the chapter

III. Early Psychological Theories

A. Introduction
1. Early psychological theories emphasized either conditioning or personality disturbances and diseases of the mind
2. Discuss the work of Ivan Pavlov in popularizing the concept of conditioned behavior

B. The psychopath
1. Dinstinguish between psychopathy and psychopathology
   a. Psychopathology is any psychological disorder that causes distress to the individual or those in the individuals life (depressions, schizophrenia, alcoholism, bulimia, ADHD, etc.)
   b. Psychopathy is a specific personality disorder characterized by antisocial behavior and lack of affect.
2. A psychopath (also called a sociopath) is generally viewed as cruel and without thought or feeling for victims
3. The concept of a psychopathic personality was developed by Hervey Cleckley in his 1941 book *The Mask of Sanity*
   a. The key characteristic of a psychopath is poverty of affect, the inability to imagine accurately how others think and feel
   b. Discuss the characteristics of the psychopathic personality as outlined by Cleckley
4. Psychopaths frequently appear well-adjusted and happy and make a positive impression so that they can fool others into trusting them
5. Discuss early signs of psychopathology: bedwetting, cruelty to animals, fire-setting, lying, fighting, and stealing
6. A recent study of incarcerated psychopaths found they were not only emotionally impaired but were unable to process abstract words, understand metaphors, perform abstract categorization tasks, and process emotionally weighted words and speech

C. Antisocial personality disorder
1. Modern attempts to identify sociopathic individuals emphasize the type of behavior exhibited rather than identifiable personality traits
2. The American Psychiatric Association has replaced the terms psychopath and sociopath with the terms *antisocial* and *asocial personality*
   a. Individuals who are basically unsocialized and whose behavior pattern brings them into repeated conflicts with society
   b. Individuals who exhibit an antisocial personality are said to be suffering from antisocial personality disorder (ASPD, APD, ANPD)
   c. Discuss APA and WHO definitions of antisocial personality disorder and its characteristics

3. The causes of antisocial personality disorder are unclear
   a. Possible physiological causes may include a malfunctioning of the central nervous system (abnormally low levels of arousal) as well as brain abnormalities that may have been present from birth
   b. A lack of love or the sensed inability to depend unconditionally on a central loving figure (usually the mother) are often suggested as major psychogenic factors contributing to the development of antisocial personality disorder
4. Most research into antisocial personality disorder focus on males but the research into females with ASPD suggests they exhibit similar characteristics and behavior patterns

D. Personality types and crime
1. Hans Eysenck's 1964 book *Crime and Personality* explains crime as the result of fundamental personality characteristics
2. Eysenck identified three personality dimensions, each linked to criminality
   a. Psychoticism: characterized by a lack of empathy, creativeness, antisociability, hallucinations and delusions
   b. Extroversion: carefree, dominant, venturesome, high levels of energy
   c. Neuroticism: typical of people who are irrational, shy, moody, emotional
3. Psychotics are the most likely to be criminal because they combine high degrees of emotionalism and extroversion, are difficult to socialize and condition, and do not fully develop a conscience
4. This approach is known as biopsychology because it suggests that personality traits depend on physiology; people whose nervous system needs stimulation seek excitement and are more likely to turn to crime
5. Eysenck said that up to two-thirds of behavioral variance could be attributed to a strong genetic basis

E. Early psychiatric theories
1. Psychiatric criminology/forensic psychiatry suggests a complex set of drives and motives that operate from within the personality to determine behavior
2. Forensic psychiatry explains crime as caused by biological and psychological urges mediated through consciousness
3. Forensic psychiatry does not emphasize the role of the external environment

IV. Criminal Behavior as Maladaption

**Show the ABC News program *Eric Smith: Inside the Mind of a Child Killer* from the video library.**

A. The psychoanalytic perspective
1. Sigmund Freud coined the term *psychoanalysis* in 1896 and based his theory of human behavior on it
2. Psychoanalysis suggests that criminal behavior is maladaptive, the result of inadequacies inherent in the personality of the offender
3. Freud stated that the personality is made up of three components:

a. Id: the fundamental aspect of the personality from which drives, urges, and desires emanate
    (1) Operates on the pleasure principle, full and instant gratification of needs
    (2) Contains the motivation for crime, drives and urges that are kept in check only by other aspects of the personality
b. Ego: primarily charged with reality testing
    (1) Emphasizes how one's objectives can best be accomplished and develops strategies that maximize pleasure and minimize pain
    (2) Functions on the reality principle and recognizes the need to delay gratification to achieve a long-term goal
c. Superego: the moral guide to right and wrong; the conscience
    (1) Guides the ego to select strategies that are socially and ethically acceptable
    (2) Guilt may result when the superego's dictates are not followed
    (3) Also contains the "ego-ideal," a symbolic representation of what society values

4. The psychoanalytic perspective suggests that a poorly developed superego might result in criminal behavior
    a. The ego is left to operate without a moral guide and may select a strategy that is expedient but illegal
    b. Individuals with poor superego development frequently desire immediate gratification without concern for the long-term consequences of immediate choices
5. Another possible cause of crime is inadequate sublimation
    a. Sublimation is a process in which one item of consciousness is substituted symbolically for another
    b. It is frequently a healthy process; powerful sexual and aggressive drives may be sublimated into socially constructive activities
    c. Improper sublimation may lead to crime
6. Neurosis may also lead to crime
    a. A neurosis is a minor form of mental illness in which the person is in touch with reality but may be anxious or fearful of certain situations
    b. Examples include fear of heights, compulsive handwashing, and eating disorders
    c. Most neuroses do not lead to crime but some may, such as compulsive shoplifting

B. The psychotic offender
1. Psychotic disorders are characterized by a lack of contact with reality
2. Psychotics may suffer from hallucinations, delusions, breaks with reality
3. According to Nettler, there are three main characteristics of psychotic individuals
    a. Grossly distorted conception of reality
    b. Moods and mood swings
    c. Marked inefficiency in getting along with others and caring for oneself
4. There are two main types of psychotics:
    a. Schizophrenics: characterized by disordered or disjointed thinking
    b. Paranoid schizophrenics: suffer from delusions and hallucinations
5. Psychoses may lead to crime

C. The link between frustration and aggression
1. In his early writings, Freud said that aggression was a natural response to frustration
2. J. Dollard developed a frustration–aggression theory that held that although frustration can lead to various types of behavior, direct aggression toward others is its most likely consequence
a. Everyone suffers frustration throughout life; aggression is therefore a natural consequence of living
b. Aggression can be manifested in socially acceptable ways (e.g., sports, military, or law enforcement careers) or engaged in vicariously, through catharsis, by watching others act aggressively (e.g., on television or in the movies)
c. Some people respond violently and directly to the immediate source of frustration
3. Henry and Short suggest that how one responds to frustration may be determined by child-rearing practices
a. Children who are both punished and loved learn to suppress outward expressions of aggression
b. When children do not receive enough love, they may show immediate and direct anger and aggression because there is no fear of loss of love

V. Crime as Adaptive Behavior
A. Some psychiatric perspectives suggest that criminal behavior fulfills a certain aim or purpose, such as the need to be punished
1. Drives, motives, and wishes may be unconscious or repressed
2. Thus, the need for punishment may be unknown even to the offender
B. Crime can be adaptive in other ways as well
1. It may be an adaptation to life's stresses:
a. Alloplastic adaptation: crime reduces stress by producing changes in the environment
b. Autoplastic adaptation: crime reduces stress as a result of internal changes in beliefs and value systems
c. Other forms of behavior may also reduce stress: a person may select crime over other alternative behaviors if the crime has inherent advantages or when there are no reasonable alternatives
2. Stress may lead to aggression toward others or toward oneself, including self-destructive behaviors such as suicide, smoking, or substance abuse

VI. Modeling Theory
A. Discuss the work of Gabriel Tarde
1. Tarde made early attempts to explain crime as learned behavior rather than due to biology
2. Tarde suggested that the basis of society was imitation; he developed a theory of human behavior built upon three laws of imitation and suggestion:
a. People in close contact tend to imitate each other's behavior
b. Imitation moves from the top down
c. New acts and behaviors either reinforce or replace old ones

B. Albert Bandura developed a comprehensive modeling theory of aggression:
   1. He suggests that everyone is capable of aggression but must learn how to behave aggressively
   2. Social learning factors determine what forms aggressive behavior takes, its frequency, the situations in which it is displayed, and the targets selected for attack
   3. People learn to act (aggressively or otherwise) by observing others, either in person or in the media
   4. Aggression can be provoked in a variety of ways: physical assaults, verbal threats, thwarting one's hopes, obstructing one's goal-seeking behavior, etc.
   5. People may also become aggressive because they are rewarded for such behavior (discuss the concept of the "macho" male)
   6. People who devalue aggression may engage in it via a process of disengagement, where they construct rationalizations to overcome internal inhibitions
      a. Attributing blame to the victim
      b. Dehumanization through beuracratization, automation, urbanization, and high social mobility
      c. Vindication of aggression by legitimate authorities
      d. Desensitization from repeated exposure to aggression
   7. Modeling theory has been criticized for lacking comprehensive explanatory power (e.g., it cannot explain differences in sibling behavior)

VII. Behavior Theory
   A. Behavior theory is also known as the stimulus-response approach to behavior
      1. It emphasizes the concept of operant behavior: behavior choices operate on the environment to produce consequences for the individual
         a. When behavior results in rewards or desirable feedback, the behavior is reinforced and will probably become more frequent
         b. When behavior results in punishment, the frequency of that behavior decreases
         c. Behavior theory is often used by parents to control children through rewards and punishments
      2. Discuss the four conceptual categories of rewards and punishments:
         a. Positive rewards
         b. Negative rewards
         c. Positive punishments
         d. Negative punishments
   B. Behavior theory differs from other psychological theories in that the major determinants of behavior are in the surrounding environment rather than in the individual
      1. The best-known proponent of the theory is B.F. Skinner
      2. Behavior theory helps us understand the genesis of criminal behavior: crime results when people receive positive reinforcement for engaging in delinquent and criminal behavior
   C. Behavior theory has ben criticized for ignoring the role of cognition in human behavior

VIII. Attachment Theory
  A. First proposed by John Bowlby in the 1950s
    1. He suggested that healthy personality development requires that infants and young children have a warm, intimate, and continuous relationship with the mother or permanent mother substitute
    2. Bowlby identified three forms of attachment: secure attachment (a healthy form of attachment), anxious resistant attachment, and anxious avoidant attachment
    3. Delinquent behavior occurs when nonsecure attachments are created
  B. Tests of attachment theory seem to confirm that difficulties in early childhood produce adult criminality
    1. Children raised in insecure environments are likely to engage in violent behavior as adults
    2. Childhood insecurity leads to a relative lack of empathy, which may be the most important factor in whether or not a person conforms

IX. Self-Control Theory
  A. Self-control involves a person's ability to alter his/her states and responses
    1. It is most obvious when individuals act contrary to their preferences and impulses
    2. Psychologists have identified four types of self-control:
      a. Impulse control (resisting temptations)
      b. Control over the contents of the mind (e.g., suppression of unwanted thoughts)
      c. Control over emotional and mood states
      d. Control of performance
  B. Discuss the perspective on self-control outlined in Michael Gottfredson and Travis Hirschi's general theory of crime
    1. It suggests that low self-control accounts for all crime at all times and is the primary individual-level cause of crime
    2. Self-control is defined as the degree to which a person is vulnerable to momentary temptations
    3. Gottfredson and Hirschi reject the idea that some people have a propensity to commit crime; they suggest, rather, that some people have a tendency to ignore the long-term consequences of their behavior
  C. Harold Grasmick has built on the work of Gottfredson and Hirschi and has identified characteristics of individuals with low levels of self-control
    1. They are impulsive and seek immediate gratification
    2. They lack diligence, tenacity, and persistence
    3. They are risk-seekers
  D. Recent research has found considerable support for the idea that lack of self control is an important correlate of criminal behavior
  E. Thomas J. Bernard and Karen L. Hayslett-McCall have proposed a new theory combining elements of Gottfredson and Hirschi's theory with concepts from attachment theory
    1. They focus on disproportionate male offending, trying to explain the relationship between gender an criminality
    2. They suggest that gender-based differences in offending are caused by disruptions in attachments to primary caregivers early in childhood

3. These disruptions are more likely to occur to boys than girls because of cultural differences in how boys and girls are treated
4. Gender differences in attachment disruptions lead to low self-control among males

**Show the ABC News program *Losing It* from the video library.**

X. Insanity and the Law
   A. Psychological conceptions of mental illness (antisocial personality, psychopathy, etc.) are not applicable to the criminal justice system, which relies on the legal concept of insanity
      1. According to the criminal law, insanity is a legal determination that refers to a type of defense allowed by the criminal courts
         a. Using the defense of insanity, a criminal defendant may be found not guilty by reason of insanity and avoid punishment even when it is clear that he/she committed a criminal act
         b. The burden of proof is on the defendant as sanity is assumed at the start of a criminal trial
      2. The 1994 Insanity Defense Reform Act (IDRA) was passed by Congress after John Hinkley's attempted assassination of then-President Reagan
         a. The IDRA defines insanity as a severe mental disease or defect causing the defendant to be unable to appreciate the nature and quality or the wrongfulness of his/her acts
         b. The IDRA created a special verdict of "not guilty by reason of insanity" (NGRI)
            (1) If a defendant is found NGRI, he/she is held in custody pending a court hearing, which must occur within 40 days of the verdict
            (2) In the hearing, the court decides if the defendant should be hospitalized or released
         c. A provision of the IDRA permits mentally ill individuals to be held for trial in case they recover enough for their trial to proceed
   B. The *M'Naughten* rule
      1. In 1843, Daniel M'Naughten was accused of killing Edward Drummond, the secretary of British Prime Minister Sir Robert Peel; it appeared that he actually intended to kill Peel
      2. At the trial, the defense claimed that M'Naughten suffered from delusions which led to the crime
      3. The court accepted these claims, establishing the defense of insanity
      4. The judge's decision became known as the *M'Naughten* rule; it holds that individuals cannot be held criminally responsible for their actions at the time of the offense if either:
         a. They did not know what they were doing, or
         b. They did not know that what they were doing was wrong
      5. Many states still use the *M'Naughten* rule today
   C. The irresistible-impulse test
      1. Eighteen states use the irresistible-impulse test (sometimes in conjunction with the *M'Naughten* rule)

2. The irresistible-impulse test holds that a defendant is not guilty of a crime if he/she, by virtue of his/her mental state or psychological condition, was not able to resist committing the criminal act
3. Discuss the use of the irresistible-impulse test in the case of Lorena Bobbitt

D. The *Durham* rule
1. The *Durham* rule was developed in 1954 and states that a defendant is not criminally responsible if his or her unlawful act was the product of a mental disease or mental defect
2. The rule has led to considerable confusion because it encompasses a variety of mental diseases and defects, which may not be linked to criminality (cerebral palsy, Down's syndrome, dyslexia, etc.)

E. The substantial-capacity test
1. Nineteen states and the Model Penal Code use the substantial-capacity test, which combines elements of the *M'Naughten* rule and the irresistible-impulse test
2. The substantial-capacity test states that insanity is present when a person lacks the substantial capacity needed to appreciate the wrongfulness of his/her act or to conform his/her behavior to the requirements of the law
3. The problem with this test is defining what actually constitutes "substantial mental capacity"

F. The *Brawner* rule
1. This rule was created in 1972 in the case of *U.S.* v. *Brawner* and it not widely used today
2. It delegates to the jury the responsibility to determine what constitutes insanity - the jury basically must use its own sense of fairness

G. Guilty but mentally ill
1. Some states have enacted legislation allowing findings of "guilty but insane" or "guilty but mentally ill" (GBMI): a person can be held responsible for a criminal act even though there is a degree of mental incompetence
2. In most GBMI jurisdictions, a jury must return a finding of GBMI if:
   a. Every statutory element need for a conviction has been proven beyond a reasonable doubt
   b. The defendant is found to have been mentally ill at the time of the crime
   c. The defendant was not found to have been legally insane at the time of the crime
3. With a GBMI verdict, the judge may impose any sentence allowable under law for the crime; offenders are generally sent to a psychiatric hospital for treatment until cured and then transferred to a correctional facility to serve out their sentences

**Show the ABC News program *The Strange Tale of John Dupont* from the video library.**

H. Federal provisions for the hospitalization of individuals found NGRI
1. Federal law provides for defendants found NGRI to be confined in a suitable facility and requires the defendant to undergo a psychiatric or

psychological examination and a hearing within 40 days of the NGRI verdict

a. If the hearing court finds that the defendant's release would create a risk to persons or property due to a present mental disease or defect the court commits the defendant
b. To be later released, the person has the burden of proving that his/her release would not create any risk to persons or property
c. The person can be discharged when the director of the facility to which s/he is confined determines that s/he has recovered from the mental disease or defect

2. Many states use the federal statute as a model and some laws that differ from the federal model have been struck down as unconstitutional, especially if they permit the continued confinement of offenders who have be declared to be recovered even if they may still be dangerous

XI. Social Policy and Forensic Psychology

A. Discuss recent psychological theories and research

1. Recent research shows a stability of aggression over time: children who display early aggressive behavior are likely to continue such behavior as adults
2. This type of research is important for the assessment of dangerousness and the identification of personal characteristics that would allow for the prediction of dangerousness in individual cases
3. Selective incapacitation, a policy based on the idea of career criminality, involves predicting which individuals are habitual offenders
4. Career criminals were targeted in the 1984 Comprehensive Crime Control Act
   a. Sentencing guidelines include a criminal history factor: punishment may be increased significantly based on the offender's criminal history
   b. A career criminal is defined as:
      (1) Being at least 18 years of age at the time of the offense
      (2) Committing a crime of violence or trafficking in a controlled substance
      (3) Having at least two prior felony convictions of either a crime of violence or trafficking in a controlled substance
   c. One problem with this definition is that offenders with a history of minor drug trafficking are considered equal to violent offenders such as serial killers
5. Correctional psychology involves the diagnosis and classification of offenders, the treatment of correctional populations, and the rehabilitation of inmates and other law violators

B. Social policy and the psychology of criminal conduct (PCC)

1. D.A. Andrews and James Bonta wrote *The Psychology of Criminal Conduct* in 1994
2. They have not attempted to develop a new behavioral theory but ask for the objective application of what we now understand about the psychology of crime and criminal behavior
3. In other words, they say that we know something about what works; now we need to make use of that knowledge

XII. Criminal Psychological Profiling
  A. Discuss the early use of psychiatrists and psychologists in World War II to profile enemy leaders and predict their future moves
  B. Criminal psychological profiling (also known as criminal profiling or behavioral profiling) assists the police in better understanding persons wanted for serious offenses
    1. Profiling creates a behavioral composite of a subject by analyzing crime scene and autopsy data, using interviews and studies of past offenders
    2. It is based on the belief that almost any form of conscious behavior is symptomatic of a person's personality
    3. Thus, the specific activities of an offender help clarify the offender's motivations, personal characteristics, and likely future behavior
  C. Discuss the FBI's Behavioral Science Unit and their work on psychological profiling

# Key Concepts

**Alloplastic adaptation**: A form of adjustment that results from changes in the environment surrounding an individual.

**Antisocial (asocial) personality**: A term used to describe individuals who are basically unsocialized and whose behavior pattern brings them repeatedly into conflict with society.

**Antisocial personality disorder**: A psychological condition exhibited by individuals who are basically unsocialized and whose behavior pattern brings them repeatedly into conflict with society.

**Attachment theory**: A social-psychological perspective on delinquent and criminal behavior that holds that the successful development of secure attachment between a child and his or her primary caregiver provides the basic foundation for all future psychological development.

**Autoplastic adaptation**: A form of adjustment that results from changes within an individual.

**Behavior theory**: A psychological perspective that posits that individual behavior which is rewarded will increase in frequency, while that which is punished will decrease.

***Brawner* rule**: A somewhat vague rule for determining insanity that was created in the federal court case of *U.S. v. Brawner* (471 F.2d 969) and in which the jury is asked to decide whether the defendant could be *justly* held responsible for the criminal act with which he or she stands charged, in the face of any claims of insanity or mental incapacity.

**Conditioning**: A psychological principle that holds that the frequency of any behavior can be increased or decreased through reward, punishment, or association with other stimuli.

**Correctional psychology**: The branch of forensic psychology concerned with the diagnosis and classification of offenders, the treatment of correctional populations, and the rehabilitation of inmates and other law violators.

**Criminal psychology**: See **forensic psychology.**

***Durham* rule**: A standard for judging legal insanity that holds that an accused is not criminally responsible if his unlawful act was the product of mental disease or mental defect.

**Ego**: The reality-testing part of the personality. Also called the *reality principle*. More formally, the personality component that is conscious, most immediately controls behavior, and is most in touch with external reality.

**Electroencephalogram (EEG)**: The electrical measurement of brain wave activity.

**Forensic psychiatry**: A branch of psychiatry having to do with the study of crime and criminality.

**Forensic psychology**: The application of the science and profession of psychology to questions and issues relating to law and the legal system.

**Guilty but mentally ill (GBMI)**: A finding that offenders are guilty of the criminal offense with which they are charged, but because of their prevailing mental condition, they are generally sent to psychiatric hospitals for treatment rather than to prison. Once they have been declared cured, however, such offenders can be transferred to correctional facilities to serve out their sentences.

**Id**: The aspect of the personality from which drives, wishes, urges, and desires emanate. More formally, the division of the psyche associated with instinctual impulses and demands for immediate satisfaction of primitive needs.

**Insanity**

**Insanity (legal)**: A legally established inability to understand right from wrong or to conform one's behavior to the requirements of the law.

**Insanity (psychological)**: Persistent mental disorder or derangement.

**Irresistible-impulse test:** A standard for judging legal insanity that holds that a defendant is not guilty of a criminal offense if the person, by virtue of his or her mental state or psychological condition, was not able to resist committing the crime.

***M'Naughten* rule**: A standard for judging legal insanity which requires that offenders not know what they were doing, or if they did, that they not know it was wrong.

**Modeling theory**: A form of social learning theory that asserts that people learn how to act by observing others.

**Neurosis**: Functional disorders of the mind or of the emotions involving anxiety, phobia, or other abnormal behavior.

**Operant behavior**: Behavior that affects the environment in such a way as to produce responses or further behavioral cues.

**Paranoid schizophrenic**: A schizophrenic individual who suffers from delusions and hallucinations.

**Psychiatric criminology**: Theories derived from the medical sciences, including neurology, and which, like other psychological theories, focus on the individual as the unit of analysis. Psychiatric theories form the basis of psychiatric criminology. See also **forensic psychiatry**.

**Psychoanalysis**: The theory of human psychology founded by Sigmund Freud on the concepts of the unconscious, resistance, repression, sexuality, and the Oedipus complex.

**Psychological profiling**: The attempt to categorize, understand, and predict the behavior of certain types of offenders based on behavioral clues they provide.

**Psychological theory**: A theory derived from the behavioral sciences which focuses on the individual as the unit of analysis. Psychological theories place the locus of crime causation within the personality of the individual offender.

**Psychopath:** An individual with a personality disorder, especially one manifested in aggressively antisocial behavior, and who is lacking in empathy.

**Psychopathology**: Any psychological disorder that causes distress, either for the individual or for those in the individual's life. Also the study of pathological mental conditions — that is, mental illness.

**Psychosis**: A form of mental illness in which sufferers are said to be out of touch with reality.

**Psychotherapy**: A form of psychiatric treatment based on psychoanalytical principles and techniques.

**Punishment**: An undesirable behavioral consequence likely to decrease the frequency of occurrence of that behavior.

**Reward**: A desirable behavioral consequence likely to increase the frequency of occurrence of that behavior.

**Schizophrenic**: A mentally ill individual who is out of touch with reality and who suffers from disjointed thinking.

**Selective incapacitation**: A social policy that seeks to protect society by incarcerating the individuals deemed to be the most dangerous.

**Self-control**: A person's ability to alter his or her own states and responses.

**Sociopath**: See **psychopath**.

**Sublimation**: The psychological process whereby one aspect of consciousness comes to be symbolically substituted for another.

**Substantial-capacity test**: A standard for judging legal insanity that requires that a person lack the mental capacity needed to understand the wrongfulness of his or her act or to conform his or her behavior to the requirements of the law.

**Superego**: The moral aspect of the personality; much like the conscience. More formally, the division of the psyche that develops by the incorporation of the perceived moral standards of the community, is mainly unconscious, and includes the conscience.

**Thanatos**: A death wish.

# Additional Lecture Topics

One topic that is related to the issue of mental disorder is that of intelligence. Consider discussing the argument that low intelligence is related to, or even causes, crime. Research that could be referenced include:

- Travis Hirschi and Michael Hindelang's 1977 research linking IQ and crime, suggesting that criminals and noncriminals exhibit significant differences in IQ, even after controlling for socio-economic status and race.

- J.Q. Wilson and Richard Herrnstein's book *Crime and Human Nature*, which is also discussed in Chapter 5 and which suggested that there is an indirect link between IQ and crime: low intelligence contributes to poor performance in school which increases the likelihood of criminal involvement.

- Richard Herrnstein and Charles Murray's book *The Bell Curve* argued that intelligence is linked to a variety of factors, including crime. Individuals with a low IQ are more likely to commit crimes, more likely to be caught, and more likely to receive a sentence of incarceration. Herrnstein and Murray feel that intelligence is inherited, and therefore the link between intelligence and crime cannot be affected by the social environment.

While discussing this topic, it might be interesting to point out that researchers are operationalizing "intelligence" through the use of IQ. Consider the definition of "intelligence" and debate whether IQ really is a good measure of intelligence.

Another topic is that of moral development, a branch of cognitive theory. This approach was founded by Jean Piaget, who suggested that reasoning processes develop over time, from birth to about age 12. The concept of moral development was applied to crime by Lawrence Kohlberg, who postulated six stages through which people progress. Their decisions regarding right and wrong are made for different reasons, depending on their stage of moral development. He suggested that criminals generally reason at lower levels and have less developed moral judgment than that of noncriminals. Criminals generally are found to reason at the "preconventional" level (stages one and two), whereas most nonoffenders reach at least stages three and four. The stage of development may influence one's decision whether or not to commit crimes.

# Discussion Questions

These discussion questions are found in the textbook at the end of the chapter. The instructor may want to focus on these questions during the coverage of Chapter 6.

1. This book emphasizes a social problems versus social responsibility theme. Which perspective is best supported by psychological theories of crime causation? Why?

2. How do psychological theories of criminal behavior differ from the other types of theories presented in this book? How do the various psychological and psychiatric approaches presented in this chapter differ from one another?

3. How would the perspectives discussed in this chapter suggest that offenders might be prevented from committing additional offenses? How might they be rehabilitated?

4. How can crime be a form of adaptation to one's environment? Why would an individual choose such a form of adaptation over others that might be available?

5. Which of the various standards for judging legal insanity discussed in this chapter do you find the most useful? Why?

# Student Exercises

## Activity #1

Your instructor will assign you a state. Go to the web site of the Cornell University Law School's Legal Information Institute at **http://www.law.cornell.edu**, locate the statutes for this state, and find the definition of the insanity defense. Answer the following questions:

1. What test or tests are used to determine legal insanity?

2. Is the defendant presumed to be sane until proven otherwise?

3. Does the burden of proof for the defense of insanity lie with the defense or the prosecution?

4. If legal insanity is proved, what verdict is used, NGRI or GBI?

### Activity #2

Your instructor will place you in groups. Within your group, discuss different ways that you were taught right from wrong as a child. Using behavior theory, classify these techniques as positive rewards, negative rewards, positive punishments, or negative punishments. Which of the four types of rewards and punishments seemed to be most effective?

## Criminology Today on the Web

**http://www.psych.org/public_info/insanity.cfm**
This Web site provides information on the insanity defense from the American Psychiatric Association.

**http://www.forensic-psych.com/articles/artRebirth.html**
This Web site contains an article on forensic psychiatry and the insanity defense.

**http://www.mentalhealth.com/dis/p20-pe04.html**
**http://health.discovery.com/diseasesandcond/encyclopedia/2797.html**
These two sites provide information on antisocial personality disorder.

**http://faculty.ncwc.edu/toconnor/428/428lect01.htm**
This Web site makes available an article on the history of profiling.

**http://mentalhelp.net/**
This site provides information on mental health, disorders, and treatments.

## Student Study Guide Questions and Answers

### True/False

1. Persephane Elaine Muhammad was found not guilty by reason of insanity of the crime of murder. **(True, p. 180)**

2. Forensic psychologists generally hold Ph.D. degrees. **(True, p. 182)**

3. Psychological theories suggest that normality is defined by a small group of individuals wielding political power. **(False, p. 183)**

4. According to psychological theories, crimes result from normal and appropriate mental processes within the personality. **(False, p. 183)**

5. Psychopathology refers to a personality disorder characterized by antisocial behavior and lack of affect. **(False, p. 183)**

6. Poverty of affect means that the psychopath is unable to imagine accurately how others think and feel. **(True, p. 183)**

7. Poor intelligence is a characteristic of the psychopathic personality. **(False, p. 184)**

8. According to the PCL, traits associated with a chronic unstable and antisocial lifestyle include criminality. **(True, p. 184)**

9. Individuals suffering from antisocial personality disorder generally show a marked disregard for social norms and rules. **(True, p. 185)**

10. Individuals who manifest the characteristics of an antisocial personality are likely to violate the law. **(True, p. 185)**

11. Psychogenic causes of antisocial personality disorder are based on physiological features of the human organism. **(False, p. 185)**

12. Females with antisocial personality disorder exhibit different characteristics than their male counterparts. **(False, p. 185)**

13. Research suggests that most convicted felons have some type of mental impairment. **(True, p. 185)**

14. According to Eysenck, neurotics are the most likely to be criminal. **(False, p. 187)**

15. According to Eysenck, introverts rarely become criminal offenders. **(True, p. 187)**

16. The ego mainly focuses on how to best accomplish objectives. **(True, p. 188)**

17. The superego is a moral guide to right and wrong. **(True, p. 188)**

18. The Freudian concept of the ego-ideal is another term for the conscience. **(False, p. 188)**

19. According to Alfredo Niceforo, the superior ego developed as a consequence of socialization. **(True, p. 188)**

20. Sublimation is often a healthy process. **(True, p. 189)**

21. A neurosis is a serious form of mental illness. **(False, p. 189)**

22. Paranoid schizophrenics suffer from delusions and hallucinations. **(True, p. 190)**

23. According to Dollard, sublimation is the most likely consequence of frustration. **(False, p. 191)**

24. Frustration-aggression theory argues that aggression is a natural consequence of living. **(True, p. 191)**

25. When crime leads to stress reduction as a result of internal changes in beliefs and value systems, it is referred to as alloplastic adaptation. **(False, p. 193)**

26. Stress produces aggression only towards others. **(False, p. 193)**

27. According to Gabriel Tarde, individuals imitate the behavior of those they are in close contact with. **(True, p. 194)**

28. According to Bandura, aggressive behavior can be learned through watching television. **(True, p. 194)**

29. An increase of aversive treatment is one type of possible reward from aggression. **(False, p. 195)**

30. People who devalue aggression do not engage in it. **(False, p. 195)**

31. Operant behavior refers to the concept that an individual's behavior choices operate on the surrounding environment to produce consequences for the individual. **(True, p. 196)**

32. Allowing a good child to skip homework is an example of a negative reward. **(True, p. 197)**

33. A positive reward increases the frequency of approved behavior by giving adding something desirable to the situation. **(True, p. 197)**

34. Behavior theory focuses on the reformation of criminal offenders and not on the genesis of criminal behavior. **(False, p. 198)**

35. Attachment theory suggests that anxious avoidant attachment results in feelings of uncertainty. **(False, p. 198)**

36. Persisting in the face of adversity involves performance control. **(True, p. 199)**

37. Gottfredson and Hirschi suggest that self-control develops in adulthood. **(False, p. 199)**

38. Insanity is a clinical term used by psychiatrists and psychologists. **(False, p. 200)**

39. A defendant may be found not guilty by reason of insanity even when it is clear that the defendant committed a legally circumscribed act. **(True, p. 200)**

40. The U.S. Supreme Court case of *Sell v. United States* focused on the divergency between law and psychiatry in the understanding of mental impairment. **(False, p. 200)**

41. The end result of the *Durham* rule was to simplify the adjudication of mentally ill offenders. **(False, p. 202)**

42. The substantial capacity test is used in every state in the country. **(False, p. 202)**

43. The case of *Foucha v. Louisiana* dealt with the use of a guilty but mentally ill verdict. **(False, p. 203)**

44. Research suggests that aggressiveness appears to stabilize over time. **(True, p. 204)**

45. The best predictor of later antisocial behavior is early antisocial behavior. **(True, p. 204)**

46. Most crimes reported to the police are committed by only a small percentage of all offenders. **(True, p. 204)**

47. A major concern with the selective incapacitation strategy is the high rate of false positives. **(True, p. 204)**

48. Recent studies of criminal careers seem to show that involvement in crime decreases with age. **(True, p. 205)**

49. In their book *The Psychology of Criminal Conduct*, D. A. Andrews and James Bonta are attempting to develop a new behavioral theory. **(False, p. 205)**

50. According to Andrews and Bonta, treatment does not reduce recidivism. **(False, p. 205)**

51. Criminal profiling is useful in every case. **(False, p. 206)**

## Fill in the Blank

52. __________ psychology applies psychology to questions and issues relating to law and the legal system. **(Forensic, p. 182)**

53. __________ is a medical subspeciality applying psychiatry to the needs of crime prevention and solution, criminal rehabilitation, and issues of criminal law. **(Forensic psychiatry, p. 182)**

54. __________ popularized the concept of conditioned behavior. **(Ivan Pavlov, p. 183)**

55. A psychopath is also known as a(n) __________. **(sociopath, p. 183)**

56. __________ causes of antisocial personality disorder are based on physiological features. **(Somatogenic, p. 185)**

57. The inability to identify with one's parents during childhood and adolescence is a possible __________ cause of antisocial personality disorder. **(psychogenic, p. 185)**

58. Hans Eysenck wrote __________. **(*Crime and Personality*, p. 185)**

59. Hans Eysenck's approach has been termed __________. **(biopsychology, p. 187)**

60. Eysenck attributes up to __________ of all behavioral variance to a strong genetic basis. **(two-thirds, p. 187)**

61. __________ criminology envisions a complex set of drives and motives operating from hidden recesses deep within the personality to determine behavior. **(Psychiatric, p. 187)**

62. Psychiatric theories of crime focus on the __________ as the unit of analysis. **(individual, p. 188)**

63. Sigmund Freud developed the theory of __________. **(psychoanalysis, p. 188)**

64. Desires, wishes, and urges emanate from the __________, according to Freud. **(id, p. 188)**

65. According to Freud, the __________ contains the prerequisite motivation for criminal behavior. **(id, p. 188)**

66. According to Alfredo Niceforo, the __________ ego contains antisocial subconscious impulses representing a throwback to precivilized times. **(deep, p. 188)**

67. If the superego does not function properly, the mind falls back on the reality-testing ability of the __________. **(ego, p. 189)**

68. The psychological process by which one item of consciousness is symbolically substituted for another is known as __________. **(sublimation, p. 189)**

69. A __________ psychosis has no known physical cause. **(functional, p. 190)**

70. According to J. Dollard, contact sports would be an acceptable way of expressing __________. **(aggression, p. 191)**

71. Dollard stated that __________ involves satisfying aggressive urges through observation rather than direct action. **(catharsis, p. 191)**

72. The pressing need many offenders have to be punished comes out of a sense of __________. **(guilt, p. 191)**

73. According to Gabriel Tarde, the basis of any society is __________. **(imitation, p. 194)**

74. Gabriel Tarde's law of __________ says that new acts and behaviors tend to either reinforce or replace old ones. **(insertion, p. 194)**

75. __________ may result from attributing blame to one's victims. **(Disengagement, p. 195)**

76. More recent versions of modeling theory are known as __________ theory. **(cognitive social learning, p. 195)**

77. __________ theory is the "stimulus–response approach" to human patterns of being. **(Behavior, p. 196)**

78. According to behavior theory, giving a good child a treat is an example of a __________. **(positive reward, p. 197)**

79. The best known proponent of behavior theory is __________. **(B. F. Skinner, p. 197)**

80. John Bowlby developed the __________ theory of crime and delinquency. **(attachment, p. 198)**

81. __________ refers to a person's ability to alter his or her own states and responses. **(Self-control, p. 199)**

82. Because Gottfredson and Hirschi's theory claims that the operation of a single mechanism accounts for all crime at all times, it is known as a __________ theory. **(general, p. 199)**

83. Pratt and Cullen suggest that __________ is one of the strongest known correlates of crime. **(self-control, p. 200)**

84. After attempting to assassinate then-President Ronald Reagan, __________ was acquitted of the charges against him on the grounds of insanity. **(John Hinkley, pp. 200-201)**

85. According to the Insanity Defense Reform Act, the burden of proving insanity is placed on the __________. **(defendant, p. 201)**

86. The __________ for determining legal insanity was developed as a result of the murder of Edward Drummond, secretary of Sir Robert Peel. **(*M'Naughten* rule, p. 201)**

87. According to the *Durham* rule, __________ is a condition which is considered capable of improving or deteriorating. **(disease, p. 202)**

88. The __________ combines elements of the *M'Naughten* rule and the irresistible-impulse test. **(substantial capacity test, p. 202)**

89. Career criminals are also known as __________ offenders. **(habitual, p. 204)**

90. __________ psychology focuses on the diagnosis and classification of offenders and on offender rehabilitation. **(Correctional, p. 205)**

## Multiple Choice

91. Which of the following is *not* a fundamental assumption of most psychological theories of crime causation?
    1. The major motivational element within a person is personality.
    2. Defective mental processes may have a variety of causes.
    3. **Crimes result from individual choice. (p. 183)**
    4. Normality is generally defined by social consensus.

92. The concept of a psychopathic personality was developed by
    1. Hans Eysenck.
    2. Ivan Pavlov.
    3. **Hervey Cleckley. (p. 183)**
    4. Albert Bandura.

93. Which of the following is *not* one of the characteristics of the psychopathic personality described by Cleckley?
    1. Superficial charm
    2. Chronic lying
    3. Unreliability
    4. **Low intelligence (p. 184)**

94. Which of the following is *not* one of the early signs or indicators of psychopathy?
    1. Bed-wetting
    2. **Teenage pregnancy (p. 184)**
    3. Cruelty to animals
    4. Firesetting

95. A possible psychogentic cause of antisocial personality disorder is
    1. a low state of arousal.
    2. **a separation from the mother during the first six months of life. (p. 185)**
    3. a malfunction of some inhibitory mechanisms.
    4. none of the above

96. Which of the following was *not* one of the three personality dimensions described by Hans Eysneck in his study of personality characteristics and crime?
    1. Extroversion
    2. **Schizophrenism (p. 186)**
    3. Psychoticism
    4. Neuroticism

97. Eysenck suggests that __________ are the most likely to be criminal.
    1. extroverts
    2. neurotics
    3. **psychotics (p. 186)**
    4. introverts

98. According to Freud's psychoanalytic theory, the id conforms to the
    1. reality principle.
    2. **pleasure principle. (p. 188)**
    3. morality and conscience.
    4. unconscious mind.

99. The Freudian concept of a death instinct is called
    1. sublimination.
    2. ego-ideal.
    3. neurosis.
    4. **Thanatos. (p. 189)**

100. Which of the following is *not* an example of a neurosis?
    1. Fear of heights
    2. Compulsive hand washing
    3. An eating disorder
    4. **Schizophrenia (p. 189)**

101. A(n) __________ is a form of mental illness in which a person is said to be out of touch with reality in some fundamental way.
    1. **psychosis (p. 190)**
    2. operant behavior
    3. sociopath
    4. neurosis

102. Which of the following is *not* a characteristic of a psychotic individual?
    1. **Compulsive and obsessive behavior (p. 190)**
    2. A grossly distorted conception of reality
    3. Moods and mood swings
    4. A marked inefficiency in getting along with others and caring for oneself

103. Freud stated that aggression was a response to
    1. anger.
    2. **frustration. (p. 190)**
    3. psychosis.
    4. neurosis.

104. According to Dollard, violence directed against something or someone who is not the source of the original frustration is known as
    1. repression.
    2. catharsis.
    3. Thanatos.
    4. **displacement. (p. 191)**

105. When crime leads to stress reduction as a result of internal changes in beliefs and value systems, it is known as __________ adaptation.
    1. alternative
    2. alloplastic
    3. antiplastic
    4. **autoplastic (pp. 192-193)**

106. Which of the following behaviors is *not* aggression directed at one's self?
    1. Alcohol abuse
    2. Smoking
    3. Suicide
    4. **They are all forms of self-directed aggression. (p. 193)**

107. According to Gabriel Tarde's law of imitation, middle-class people would imitate
    1. lower class people.
    2. other members of the middle class.
    3. **upper-class individuals. (p. 194)**
    4. no one.

108. __________ is a psychological perspective that suggests people learn how to behave by modeling themselves after others.
    1. **Social learning theory (p. 194)**
    2. Operant behavior theory
    3. Psychoanalysis
    4. Forensic psychological theory

109. Spanking a bad child is an example of a
    1. positive reward.
    2. negative reward.
    3. **positive punishment. (p. 197)**
    4. negative punishment.

110. Which of the following is *not* one of the forms of attachment identified by Bowlby?
    1. Secure
    2. **Insecure (p. 198)**
    3. Anxious avoidant
    4. Anxious resistant

111. Attachment theory suggests that __________ attachment results in feelings of uncertainty which cause the child to feel anxious, to become fearful of its environment, and to cling to potential caregivers.
   1. anxious avoidant
   2. insecure
   3. **anxious resistant (p. 198)**
   4. secure

112. When people resist temptations, they engage in which type of self-control?
   1. Control over one's emotional and mood states
   2. Control over the contents of the mind
   3. **Impulse control (p. 199)**
   4. Performance control

113. Which of the following is the definition of insanity under the Insanity Defense Reform Act?
   1. Because of a mental state or psychological condition the defendant was unable to resist committing the act.
   2. **The defendant was suffering from a severe mental disease or defect and as a result was unable to appreciate the nature and quality or the wrongfulness of his acts. (p. 201)**
   3. The defendant's actions were the product of mental disease or defect.
   4. The defendant cannot justly be held responsible for the criminal act in the face of any claims of insanity.

114. The ___________ is a standard for judging legal insanity which considers whether a person was not able to resist committing the crime because of his or her mental state.
   1. *Durham* rule
   2. substantial capacity test
   3. **irresistible-impulse test (p. 202)**
   4. *Brawner* rule

115. The jury determines what constitutes insanity in states that use the
   1. *Durham* rule.
   2. substantial capacity test.
   3. irresistible-impulse test.
   4. ***Brawner* rule. (p. 202)**

# Word Search Puzzle

```
U X P K S M L B P H Y Y H G V Q H S O K I N H P H B D X L
A P Y Y H T S B V C A D O M S L X N J F G U W V Y I Y S Z
K S T B K S E C M K P K P G T E G C P E P B D V G Y V I P
I N U G T C T C G C P L X S Y H L Q M G X Q B F B B O P Q
L C M B L R I G O N L O K B Y U A F O E J X T R A S K I U
Z H W Z L V D L P K B B P I N C J N C N J M E E N U O L S
O O W O Z I H W Y R V F V Q E D H O A O L S M U D P N C L
H D R S H M M X P X R Y C C U C J O N T N W N D U E U W T
V X M C N Q W A I X W D D V R B E J P W O T N J R R J X X
B X S U E Q M G T C Z N W E O M N N O A B S R P A E B W J
N Z B H I Y G H S I P W Z D S T S W H F T J G O W G R R I
L K N B S E S E W J O W R E I Z A F L S B H R W L O M H T
V Q E Z S N B E M Z V N G O S H N L U C M Q W C H T U D P
Q W R M Q B D X N S G J B F V R W B P H S H T H D P X B W
Y C S K I N N E R C M O U L W F V U S R P Z Q F F U A V H
I J O G S S Y Q K O K I A J Z Q T G Y J S C L P R N L S R
J T D N D C V D B Y V M Y Q Y B D U C O Y V D D F I N J M
O G B T D H J D Y G T Y E E Q W V T H I C Y H K Q S F D A
V D V T P I H M W F P N L L Q S Z L O M H L B B Q H Y T E
G S L F I Z T S S Y M K L S L Y V I A C O W W X A M Z A H
Z A G P L O X I Q F R E W A R D T P N I T K M J C E Q S P
N D J Y J P H W O B A K J F N Z C U A N H D V H L N L E T
W Y R T Y H N T L N O S A G A O Q B L S E T G K E T U Y C
C I V L T R R W B J I G C V K Q J H Y A R W Q E C T H J B
Z W P B M E C P S U L N E T N M T Y S N A O J L K K B R T
Y D J M K N I A T A P J G G O U H Z I I P Y I L L H U H X
Y S W Z V I B R H N Y F R M O R O B S T Y L E Z E A Y Z C
V S S P G C E X J K B C H N O X A O L Y L T Y U Y H E P E
D U R P O P S Y C H O S I S S T U F L T P T K R Z Y H D R
G Y F Z Q U G H Z A J S I K F D M W O D O G C S Z O C Y F
```

**Bandura**
**Cleckley**
**Conditioning**
**Ego**
**Eysenck**
**Freud**
**Id**
**Insanity**
**Neurosis**
**Psychoanalysis**

**Psychopath**
**Psychosis**
**Psychotherapy**
**Punishment**
**Reward**
**Schizophrenic**
**Self control**
**Sublimation**
**Superego**
**Thanatos**

# Crossword Puzzle

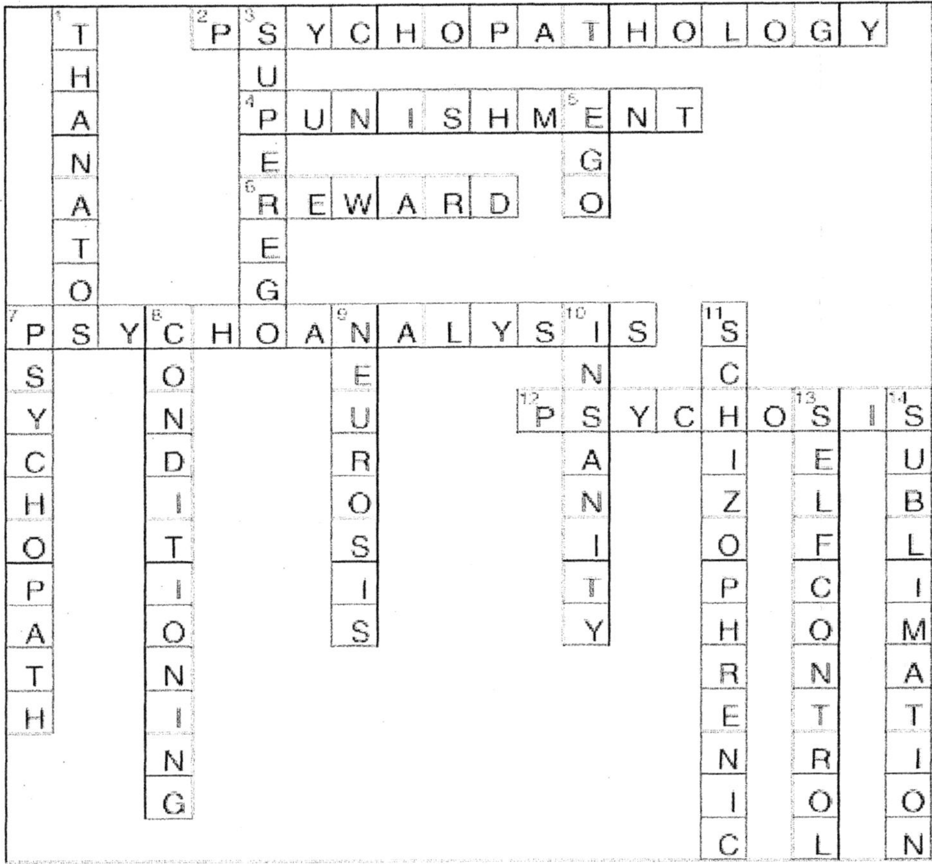

## Across

2. The study of mental illness.
4. Undesirable behavioral consequences likely to decrease the frequency of the behavior.
6. A desirable behavioral consequence likely to increase the frequency of the behavior.
7. Sigmund Freud's theory of human psychology.
12. A form of mental illness in which sufferers are said to be out of touch with reality.

## Down

1. A death wish.
3. The moral aspect of the personality.
5. The reality-testing part of the personality.
7. An individual with a personality disorder manifested in aggressively antisocial behavior.
8. A psychological principle which holds that the frequency of a behavior can be affected by reward or punishment.
9. A functional disorder of the mind or emotions.
10. Persistent mental disorder or derangement.
11. A mentally ill individual who is out of touch with reality and who suffers from disjointed thinking.
13. A person's ability to alter his or her own states and responses. (2 words)
14. Symbolically substituting one aspect of consciousness for another.

# Sociological Theories I: Social Structure

## Learning Objectives

After reading this chapter, students should be able to:

1. Explain how the organization and structure of society may contribute to criminality
2. Identify the role that cultural differences play in crime causation
3. Distinguish among a number of social structure theories of criminal behavior
4. Identify modern-day social policy that reflects the social structure approach
5. Assess the shortcomings of the social structure approach

## Chapter Outline

Introduction
Major Principles of Sociological Theories
Social Structure Theories Defined
Types of Social Structure Theories
*Social Disorganization Theories*
*Strain Theory*
*Culture Conflict*
Policy Implications of Social Structure Theories
Critique of Social Structure Theories

## Chapter Summary

This chapter begins with an introduction to the general assumptions of sociological theories before focusing specifically on social structure theories, theories that explain crime as the result of the institutional structure of society. The three main types of social structure theories are social disorganization theories, strain theories, and culture conflict perspectives.

Social disorganization or ecological theories are associated with the Chicago School of criminology. Robert Park and Ernest Burgess viewed cities in terms of concentric zones, with Zone II, surrounding the city center, seen as the zone of transition. Clifford Shaw and Henry McKay applied concentric zone theory to crime and found that rates of offending remained fairly constant within the zone of transition despite the arrival of various new immigrant groups. The most important contribution of the ecological school to criminology is its claim that the community has a major influence on human behavior. Recently, the emergence of environmental criminology or the criminology of place has revived ecological approaches. The broken windows thesis holds that physical deterioration in an area leads to increased concerns for personal safety among area residents and to higher crime rates in that area. The concept of defensible space is used by the criminology of place as a mechanism for reducing the risk of crime.

Strain theories see delinquency as adaptive behavior committed in response to problems involving frustrating and undesirable social environments. Classic strain theory was developed by Robert K. Merton, who developed the concept of anomie as a disjunction between socially approved means to success and legitimate goals. He outlined five modes of adaptation, or combinations of goals and means, and suggested that innovation was the mode most likely to be associated with crime. Stephen Messner and Richard Rosenfeld developed a contemporary version of Merton's theory, based on the concept of relative deprivation, the economic and social gap between rich and poor living in close proximity to one another. General strain theory, developed by Robert Agnew, reformulated strain theory and suggested that delinquency is a coping mechanism that helps adolescents deal with socio-emotional problems generated by negative social reactions.

Culture conflict or cultural deviance theory suggests that crime results from a clash of values between differently socialized groups over what is acceptable or proper behavior. Thorsten Sellin suggests that conduct norms are acquired early in life through childhood socialization. Primary conflict occurs when there is a fundamental clash of cultures, while secondary conflict occurs when smaller cultures within the primary one clash. Subcultural theory emphasizes the contribution to crime made by variously socialized cultural groups within a primary culture. Walter Miller identified focal concerns or key values of delinquent subcultures which encourage delinquent behavior. On the other hand, Gresham Sykes and David Matza suggest that offenders use techniques of neutralization to negate the norms and values of the larger society and overcome feelings of guilt at committing criminal acts. Franco Ferracuti and Marvin Wolfgang postulated the existence of violent subcultures, which are built around values that support and encourage violence. Differential opportunity theory, developed by Richard Cloward and Lloyd Ohlin, combines elements of subcultural and strain theories to suggest that delinquency may result from the availability of illegitimate opportunities for success combined with the effective replacement of the norms of the primary culture with expedient subcultural rules. Albert Cohen also combined elements of strain theory and the subcultural perspective in his theory of reaction formation, which states that juveniles who are held accountable to middle-class norms and who cannot achieve these norms may reject middle-class goals and turn to delinquency instead.

The gangs studied by early researchers were involved primarily in petty theft, vandalism, and turf battles; modern gangs are involved in more serious and violent crimes and drug dealing. However, recent researchers draw a distinction between juvenile delinquency and gang-related violence, suggesting that they are ecologically distinct community problems.

Social structure theories have influenced social policy, through programs such as the Chicago Area Project, Mobilization for Youth, and the War on Poverty. The social structural perspective is closely associated with the social problems approach and negates the claims of the social responsibility perspective. The chapter discusses a number of critiques of each type of social structure theory

# Lecture Outline

I. Introduction
   A. Review the case of the murder of James Jordan, father of Michael Jordan
   B. Discuss the concept of social and economic deprivation as a motivation for criminal behavior, in contrast to motivations derived from individual traits

II. Major Principles of Sociological Theories
   A. Discuss the central assumptions on which most of sociological theories of crime causation build:
      1. Social groups, social institutions, the arrangements of society, and social rules all provide the proper focus for criminological study
      2. Group dynamics, group organization, and subgroup relationships form the causal nexus out of which crime develops
      3. The structure of society and its relative degree of organization or disorganization are important factors contributing to the prevalence of criminal behavior
      4. Although it may be impossible to predict the specific behavior of a given person, statistical estimates of group characteristics are possible to achieve. Hence, the probability that a member of a given group will engage in a specific type of crime can be estimated
   B. Discuss the scope of sociological theories:
      1. They examine institutional arrangements within society (social structure) and the interaction between and among social institutions, individuals, and groups (social processes) as they affect socialization and have an impact on social behavior (social life)
      2. Emphasize that sociological theories have a macro perspective as compared to the micro approach of individualized psychological theories
   C. Review the three key sociological explanations for crime:
      1. Crime is the result of a person's location within the structure of society (social structure theories)
      2. Crime is the end product of various social processes (social process theories)
      3. Crime is the product of class struggle (conflict theories)

III. Social Structure Theories Defined
   A. Social structure theories explain crime by reference to the institutional structure of society
      1. The various formal and informal arrangements between social groups are seen as the root causes of crime and deviance
      2. These theories all have one thing in common: they emphasize aspects of society contributing to low socioeconomic status as significant causes of crime

3. Members of socially and economically disadvantaged groups are considered more likely to commit crime
4. Factors conducive to crime (poverty, lack of education, subcultural values, etc.) are all seen as predicated on social conditions surrounding early life experiences

B. The social structural perspective sees crime as primarily a lower-class phenomenon, while the criminality of the middle and upper classes is frequently considered to be less serious, less frequent, and less dangerous

IV. Types of Social Structure Theories
A. Social disorganization theory
1. This theory is closely associated with the ecological school of criminology
2. Discuss the early research of W.I. Thomas and Florian Znaniecki, who suggested that the cause of high crime rates among displaced immigrants may be due to social disorganization resulting from the immigrants' inability to transplant norms and values from the old to the new culture
3. The Chicago School
a. Robert Park and Ernest Burgess developed the field of social ecology or the ecological school of criminology in the 1920s and 1930s
(1) Their work linked the structure and organization of a community to interactions within its environment
(2) Park and Burgess viewed cities in terms of concentric zones, each of which had unique characteristics
(a) Zone I (The Loop): the city center, housing retail businesses and light manufacturing
(b) Zone II: the area surrounding the city center that housed recent immigrant groups, contained deteriorating housing, abandoned buildings, and factories, and was seen as being in transition from residential to business purposes
(c) Zone III: contained mostly working-class tenements
(d) Zone IV: occupied by middle-class citizens living in single-family homes
(e) Zone V: the commuter zone, consisting mainly of suburbs
(3) Park and Burgess found that residents of inner-city zones tend to migrate outward as their economic positions improve
b. Clifford Shaw and Henry McKay applied the concentric zone model to the study of juvenile delinquency
(1) They found that rates of offending remained constant over time within zones of transition despite high rates of immigration and movement from the inner cities to the suburbs
(2) They concluded that delinquency was caused by the nature of the environment in which the immigrants lived rather than by some characteristic of the immigrant groups themselves
(3) Shaw and McKay developed the concept of cultural transmission: traditions of delinquency are transmitted through successive generations of the same zone
c. The Chicago School showed the tendency for crime to be associated with urban transition zones characterized by lower property values, marginal individuals, and a general lack of privacy
d. Discuss the key contributions of the ecological school to criminology:
(1) Its claim that society significantly influences human behavior

(2) Its formalization of the use of official crime and population statistics as well as ethnographic information

4. The criminology of place/environmental criminology
   a. This is an emerging perspective building on routine activities theory, situational crime prevention, and ecological approaches and emphasizing the importance of location and architectural features in the prevalence of victimization
      (1) Discuss Lawrence Sherman's "hot spots" of crime research, which found that 3% of places in Minneapolis produced 50% of all calls to the police
      (2) Review Rodney Stark's theory of deviant neighborhoods, which discusses how neighborhoods can remain high in crime and deviance despite complete population turnovers
   b. The broken windows thesis holds that physical deterioration in a neighborhood leads to increased concerns for personal safety among residents, which leads to further deterioration and increased delinquency, vandalism, and crime
      (1) The broken windows perspective was first developed by James Q. Wilson and George L. Kelling
      (2) It has led to an increase in the use of order maintenance policing and a crackdown on quality-of-life offenses (panhandling, graffiti, littering, prostitution, etc.)
   c. Defensible space involves the use of architecture to reduce the risk of crime
   d. Places can be criminogenic because of the routine activities associated with them or because they provide the characteristics that facilitate the commission of crime

B. Strain theory
1. Strain theory sees delinquency as a form of adaptive, problem-solving behavior, usually committed in response to problems involving frustrating and undesirable social environments
2. Discuss Robert K. Merton's classic strain theory
   a. Merton suggested that anomie involved a disjunction between legitimate goals, which everyone desires, and socially approved means to success, which are not equally available to all members of society
   b. Crime and deviance are alternative means to success when individuals feel the strain of being pressed to succeed in socially approved ways when they lack the tools necessary for such success
   c. Review Merton's five modes of adaptation:
      (1) Conformity: most middle- and upper-class people accept legitimate goals and have access to approved means
      (2) Innovation (the mode most associated with crime): results when acceptance of legitimate goals is combined with a lack of access to approved means
      (3) Ritualism: results when people participate in socially desirable means but lack interest in achieving goals
      (4) Retreatism: people reject both the goals and means (e.g., dropouts, drug abusers, the homeless, and people involved in alternative lifestyles)

(5) Rebellion - people who wish to replace socially approved goals and means with an alternative system (e.g., political radicals and revolutionaries)

3. Discuss relative deprivation
   a. This is a contemporary version of Merton's theory proposed by Steven Messner and Richard Rosenfeld
   b. It suggests that the economic and social gap that exists between rich and poor who live in close proximity to one another contributes to criminal activity
   c. It is related to the concept of distributive justice: an individual's perception of his/her rightful place in the reward structure of society
4. General strain theory (GST) was developed by Robert Agnew
   a. GST suggests that delinquent behavior is a coping measure that helps adolescents deal with problems generated by negative social relations
   b. GST expands on traditional strain theory in several ways
      (1) It significantly widens the focus to include all types of negative relations between an individual and others
      (2) It maintains that strain may have a cumulative effect on delinquency after reaching a certain threshold
      (3) It provides a more comprehensive account of the various adaptations to strain
   c. Strain occurs when others do one of three things:
      (1) Prevent an individual from achieving positively valued goals
      (2) Remove positively valued stimuli
      (3) Present negatively valued stimuli
   d. Discuss recent research testing GST

C. Culture conflict/cultural deviance theory: suggests that the root cause of crime lies in a clash of values between differently socialized groups over what is acceptable behavior
1. Thorsten Sellin suggests that the root causes of crime are found in different values about what is acceptable or proper behavior
   a. Conduct norms provide the valuative basis for human behavior and are acquired early in life via socialization as a child
   b. The clash of norms between differently socialized groups results in crime
   c. Sellin described two types of culture conflict
      (1) Primary conflict occurs when a fundamental clash of cultures occurs
      (2) Secondary conflict occurs when smaller cultures within the primary one clash (e.g., middle-class values clash with lower-class norms)
2. Subcultural theory emphasizes the contribution made by variously socialized cultural groups to crime
   a. A subcutlure is a collection of values and preferences communicated to participants through a process of socialization
   b. Smaller groups within the larger culture may have values that do not conform to the national culture and may even encourage deviant activity
   c. Key subcultural theorists include Frederic M. Thrasher and William F. Whyte
3. Focal concerns (Walter B. Miller)
   a. Miller suggests the existence of a lower-class culture with its own values, behaviors, and attitudes

b. He also identified a number of focal concerns or key values of delinquent subcultures (trouble, toughness, smartness, excitement, fate, and autonomy)
c. He concluded that subculture crime and deviance result from specific values characteristic of such subcultures
d. Miller's work was based on a study of black, inner-city delinquents in Boston and may not generalize well to other places or times

4. Delinquency and drift (Gresham Sykes and David Matza)
   a. Members of delinquent subcultures also participate in the larger culture and thus may conform to two different sets of values simultaneously, those of the larger culture and those of a subculture
   b. Sykes and Matza suggest that offenders can do this through the use of five types of justifications:
      (1) Denial of responsibility: blame one's background of poverty, abuse, lack of opportunity, and so on
      (2) Denial of injury: claim that the crime did not hurt anyone or that the victim can afford the loss
      (3) Denial of victim: justify the harm done by claiming that the victim deserved it
      (4) Condemning the condemners: claim the victims are corrupt or responsible for their own victimization
      (5) Appeal to higher loyalties: claim that the crime was done to defend the honor of one's gang, family, neighborhood, and so on
   c. Matza later suggested that delinquents drift between criminal and conventional behavior, using these techniques of neutralization to overcome feelings of guilt
      (1) Techniques of neutralization allow the delinquent to commit crimes without being fully alienated from the larger society
      (2) Matza used the term "soft determinism" to describe drift
   d. Discuss recent research by Lois Presser supporting neutralization theory
5. Violent subcultures
   a. Franco Ferracuti and Marvin Wolfgang proposed the existence of a subculture emphasizing values that support violence and violent behavior
   b. They suggest that for members of these violent subcultures, violence can be a way of life and thus the users do not feel guilt about their aggressive behavior
   c. Discuss Frerracuti and Wolfgang's seven corollary propositions which extend their theory of subcultural violence
   d. Discuss the concepts of the "southern subculture of violence" and the "black subculture of violence"
6. Differential opportunity theory (Richard Cloward and Lloyd Ohlin)
   a. This theory blends concepts of subcultural and strain theory
   b. It suggests that there are two types of socially structured opportunities for success: legitimate and illegitimate
      (1) Individuals born into middle-class culture generally have access to legitimate but members of lower-class subcultures are often denied access to them
      (2) The illegitimate opportunity structure consists of preexisting subcultural paths to success not approved of by the wider culture

(3) Delinquent behavior may result from the availability of illegitimate opportunities combined with the replacement of the dominant culture's norms with the more expedient rules of the subculture

c. Cloward and Ohlin defined a delinquent act by two essential elements
   (1) Behavior that violates the basic norms of society
   (2) When it is officially known, it evokes a judgment by agents of criminal justice

d. They described three types of delinquent subcultures:
   (1) Criminal subcultures: provide criminal role models for those being socialized into the subculture
   (2) Conflict subcultures: participants seek status through violence
   (3) Retreatist subcultures: emphasize drug use and withdrawal from the wider society

e. Delinquent subcultures have at least three identifiable features
   (1) Acts of delinquency reflecting subcultural support are likely to recur with great frequency
   (2) Access to a successful adult criminal career sometimes results from participation in a delinquent subculture
   (3) The delinquent subculture imparts to the conduct of its members a high degree of stability and resistence to control or change

f. Cloward and Ohlin described four types of lower-class juveniles, based on their degree of commitment to middle-class values and material achievement:
   (1) Type I: desire entry to the middle class by improving their economic position
   (2) Type II: desire entry to the middle class but not improvement in their economic position
   (3) Type III: desire wealth without entry to the middle class (the most crime prone)
   (4) Type IV: dropouts who retreat from the cultural mainstream through drugs and alcohol

g. Differential opportunity theory significantly affected American social policy through the development of the Mobilization for Youth program in 1962, a delinquency prevention program creating employment and educational opportunities for deprived youth

7. Reaction formation (Albert Cohen)
   a. Cohen studied the gang behavior of delinquent youth
   b. He found that all juveniles, regardless of background, are generally held accountable to the norms of the wider society (the "middle-class measuring rod"), although not all juveniles are able to meet these expectations
   c. Juveniles from deprived backgrounds may turn to delinquency out of status frustration at being judged according to middle-class standards and goals they are unable to achieve
   d. Reaction formation is the process by which individuals reject something they want or aspire to but cannot obtain or achieve

8. The code of the street
   a. Elijah Anderson has done a study of social mores in modern American inner cities, focusing on African-American neighborhoods along Philadelphia's Germantown Avenue

b. He found that contemporary street code stresses an overinflated notion of manhood emphasizing respect or being treated right
c. The street subculture's violent nature means that a man cannot back down from threats, regardless of their seriousness
d. Anderson distinguished between two types of families
(1) Decent families try to uphold positive social values
(2) Street families are oriented toward the street, emphasizing the "thug life"

9. Gangs today
a. Modern gangs are significantly different from those studied by researchers such as Cohen, Thrasher, and Cloward and Ohlin
b. Discuss the 2002 National Youth Gang Survey, how it was conducted, and the results of the survey
c. Review the findings of Project Gangfact
d. Modern gangs generally have a name, a clothing style, tattoos, jewelry, and other symbols to identify them
(1) Along with traditional violent crime, many inner-city gangs are also involved in drug dealing
(2) Gang killings (e.g., drive-by shootings) have become common, and guns have become a way of life for many young gang members
e. Researchers suggest that gang activity and juvenile delinquency are separate problems
f. Many gang members are delinquent prior to their association with a gang

V. Policy Implications of Social Structure Theories
A. Theories that blame social structure for crime emphasize social action as a panacea
B. The Chicago Area Project was developed in the 1930s by Clifford Shaw as a way of reducing delinquency in transitional neighborhoods
1. The project attempted to reduce social disorganization in slum neighborhoods by creating community committees staffed with local residents
2. The project had three objectives:
a. Improve the physical appearance of poor neighborhoods
b. Provide recreational opportunities for youth
c. Involve project members directly in the lives of troubled youth through school and courtroom mediation
3. A 50-year review of the program declared that it was effective in reducing rates of juvenile delinquency
C. The Mobilization for Youth program was based on differential opportunity theory
1. It tried to provide new opportunities and to change social arrangements so as to address the root causes of crime and delinquency
2. The program emphasized community action that attacked entrenched political interests
D. The War on Poverty in the 1960s and later federal and state welfare programs providing supplement income assistance are examples of programs that may hold the potential to reduce crime rates through the redistribution of wealth

E. Recently, these programs have been criticized and the 1996 federal Welfare Reform Reconciliation Act reduced or eliminated long-term benefits and established stricter work requirements for welfare recipients

VI. Critique of Social Structure Theories
   A. The social structural perspective is associated with the social problems approach and seems to negate the claims of the social responsibility perspective
   B. Critiques of ecological theories
      1. They may give too much credence to the notion that spatial location determines crime and delinquency
         a. Changes in land-use patterns may affect the nature of a neighborhood and the quality of social organization found there
         b. Rates of neighborhood crime and delinquency may be an artifact of police decision-making practices and police bias
      2. It sometimes uses the incidence of delinquency as both an example of social disorganization and something caused by disorganization
      3. It does not explain crimes that occur outside socially disorganized areas
   C. Critiques of strain theory
      1. Merton's strain theory is not as applicable to modern society because of efforts toward improving success opportunities for everyone, regardless of ethnicity, race, or gender
      2. Recent studies have found that delinquents do not report being more distressed than other juveniles
   D. Critiques of subcultural theories
      1. They may lack explanatory power and can be tautological (circular)
      2. They may be racist because many so-called violent subcultures are said to be populated primarily by minorities; an observed correlation between race and violence does not necessarily explain the relationship
   E. General critiques of social structure theories
      1. Empirical studies of theories linking low levels of SES to high levels of delinquency have consistently found weak or nonexistent correlations between SES and self-reported delinquency
      2. They frequently fail to consider the role of nonsociological factors in crime causation
      3. They are unable to predict which individuals or what proportion of a given population will turn to crime

# Key Concepts

**Anomie**: A social condition in which norms are uncertain or lacking.

**Broken windows thesis**: A perspective on crime causation that holds that physical deterioration in an area leads to increased concerns for personal safety among area residents, and to higher crime rates in that area.

**Chicago Area Project**: A program focusing on urban ecology and originating at the University of Chicago during the 1930s, which attempted to reduce delinquency, crime, and social disorganization in transitional neighborhoods.

**Chicago School of criminology**: See **ecological theory**.

**Conduct norms**: Shared expectations of a social group relative to personal conduct.

**Criminology of place**: See **environmental criminology.**

**Cultural transmission**: The transmission of delinquency through successive generations of people living in the same area through a process of social communication.

**Culture conflict theory**: A sociological perspective on crime which suggests that the root cause of criminality can be found in a clash of values between variously socialized groups over what is acceptable or proper behavior.

**Defensible space**: The range of mechanisms that combine to bring an environment under the control of its residents.

**Distributive justice**: The rightful, equitable, and just distribution of rewards within a society.

**Ecological theory**: A type of sociological approach that emphasizes demographics (the characteristics of population groups) and geographics (the mapped location of such groups relative to one another) and sees the social disorganization that characterizes delinquency areas as a major cause of criminality and victimization. Also called *Chicago School of Criminology.*

**Environmental criminology**: An emerging perspective that emphasizes the importance of geographic location and architectural features as they are associated with the prevalence of criminal victimization. (Note: as the term has been understood to date, environmental criminology is not the study of environmental crime but, rather, a perspective that stresses how crime varies from place to place.) See also **criminology of place**.

**Focal concern**: A key value of any culture, especially a key value of a delinquent subculture.

**General strain theory (GST)**: A perspective that suggests that lawbreaking behavior is a coping mechanism that enables those who engage in it to deal with the socioemotional problems generated by negative social relations.

**Illegitimate opportunity structure**: Subcultural pathways to success that the wider society disapproves of.

**Negative affective states**: Adverse emotions that derive from the experience of strain, such as anger, fear, depression, and disappointment.

**Reaction formation**: The process by which a person openly rejects that which he or she wants or aspires to but cannot obtain or achieve.

**Relative deprivation:** A sense of social or economic inequality experienced by those who are unable, for whatever reason, to achieve legitimate success within the surrounding society.

**Social disorganization**: A condition said to exist when a group is faced with social change, uneven development of culture, maladaptiveness, disharmony, conflict, and lack of consensus.

**Social disorganization theory**: A perspective on crime and deviance that sees society as a kind of organism and crime and deviance as a kind of disease or social pathology. Theories of social disorganization are often associated with the perspective of social ecology and with the Chicago School of criminology which developed during the 1920s and 1930s.

**Social ecology**: An approach to criminological theorizing that attempts to link the structure and organization of human community to interactions with its localized environment.

**Social life**: The ongoing and (typically) structured interaction that occurs between persons in a society, including socialization and social behavior in general.

**Social pathology**: A concept that compares society to a physical organism and sees criminality as an illness.

**Social process:** The interaction between and among social institutions, individuals, and groups.

**Social structure**: The pattern of social organization and the interrelationships between institutions characteristic of a society.

**Social structure theory**: A theory that explains crime by reference to some aspect of the social fabric. These theories emphasize relationships between social institutions and describe the types of behavior which tend to characterize groups of people as opposed to individuals.

**Sociological theory:** A perspective that focuses on the nature of the power relationships that exist between social groups and on the influences that various social phenomena bring to bear on the types of behaviors that tend to characterize groups of people.

**Strain theory:** A sociological approach which posits a disjuncture between socially and subculturally sanctioned means and goals as the cause of criminal behavior. Also called *anomie theory*.

**Subcultural theory**: A sociological perspective that emphasizes the contribution made by variously socialized cultural groups to the phenomenon of crime.

**Subculture**: A collection of values and preferences which is communicated to subcultural participants through a process of socialization.

**Technique of neutralization**: A culturally available justification which can provide criminal offenders with the means to disavow responsibility for their behavior.

# Additional Lecture Topics

One topic for discussion would be to expand upon the text's discussion of Albert Cohen's theory of delinquent subcultures. For example, consider reviewing the three existing subcultures that he suggests most lower-class boys who fail to meet middle-class standards usually join: the corner boy, the college boy, and the delinquent boy

While covering the topic of strain theory, consider reviewing the work of Emile Durkheim, his version of the concept of anomie, and how it contributed to the development of strain theory.

Another topic is that of the recent application of opportunity theory to female criminality. Topics for discussion include the work of Freda Adler and Rita James Simon as well as more recent research by Darrell Steffensmeier and Meda Chesney-Lind.

Consider discussing in some detail the various crime-prevention strategies that have been based on strain theory, such as Operation Head Start, Job Corps, and the Perry Preschool Project.

# Discussion Questions

These discussion questions are found in the textbook at the end of the chapter. The instructor may want to focus on these questions during the coverage of Chapter 7.

1. What is the nature of sociological theorizing? What are the assumptions upon which sociological perspectives on crime causation rest?

2. What are the three key sociological explanations for crime that are discussed at the beginning of this chapter? How do they differ from one another?

3. What are the three types of social structure theories that this chapter describes? What are the major differences among them?

4. Do you believe ecological approaches have a valid place in contemporary criminological thinking? Why?

5. How, if at all, does the notion of a criminology of place differ from more traditional ecological theories? Do you see the criminology of place approach as capable of offering anything new over traditional approaches? If so, what?

6. What is a violent subculture? Why do some subcultures stress violence? How might participants in a subculture of violence be turned toward less aggressive ways?

# Student Exercises

## Activity #1

Obtain official crime data from the UCR on crime in various neighborhoods in a large city near you. Plot the crime data on a county map. Do you see a pattern? Discuss whether concentric zone theory fits the crime distribution in your city.

## Activity #2

Your instructor will place you into groups. Discuss the subcultures to which various members of the group belong. What norms and values of each subculture might conflict with the norms and values of the larger culture? Might any of these clashes lead to crime, delinquency, or deviance? How?

# Criminology Today on the Web

### http://www.gothicsubculture.com/

This Web site provides a detailed description of the gothic subculture, a modern subculture present in American society.

### http://faculty.washington.edu/bridges/soc271/lectures/presentation3/sld001.htm

This Web site provides a slide presentation of how social structure is linked to deviant behavior. It mentions many of the theories discussed in this chapter of the text.

### http://social-sciences.uchicago.edu/ssdnews/fixing.html

This Web site provides a briefarticle on a recent study examining the broken windows thesis.

### http://www.journals.uchicago.edu/AJS/home.html

This Web site provides online access to the *American Journal of Sociology*, which includes research on theories discussed in this and other chapters in the text.

### http://www.ncjrs.org/html/ojjdp/97_ygs/contents.html

This Web site provides the results of the 1997 National Youth Gang Survey.

### http://www.iir.com/nygc

This is the home page of the National Youth Gang Center.

**http://www.albany.edu/scj/jcjpc**

This is the home page of the *Journal of Criminal Justice and Popular Culture*. Volume 3 contains an article on culture, crime, and cultural criminology.

# Student Study Guide Questions and Answers

## True/False

1. Sociological theories argue that individual personality features create the motivation for crime. **(False, p. 215)**

2. Sociological theories attempt to predict the specific behavior of a given individual. **(False, p. 215)**

3. Sociological approaches generally use a micro perspective. **(False, p. 216)**

4. Strain theory is also known as the ecological approach. **(False, p. 216)**

5. According to Park and Burgess, the Loop, or central business district, is found in Zone II. **(False, p. 218)**

6. According to Shaw and McKay, rates of offending within zones of transition changed over time. **(False, p. 218)**

7. Early ecological theories used a methodology known as area studies. **(True, p. 219)**

8. Data that describes the lives of city inhabitants is known as demographic data. **(False, p. 219)**

9. Environmental criminology emphasizes the relationship between location and the prevalence of victimization. **(True, p. 219)**

10. According to Sherman's "hot spots" research, crime is geographically concentrated. **(True, p. 219)**

11. Places cannot be criminogenic in and of themselves. **(False, p. 221-222)**

12. Classic strain theory was developed by Robert Merton. **(True, p. 222)**

13. One's perception of the rightful distribution of rewards depends on cultural expectations. **(True, p. 226)**

14. Group relative deprivation involves a sense of injustice shared by members of the same group. **(True, p. 226)**

15. An individual experiencing personal deprivation is likely to feel socially isolated. **(True, p. 226)**

16. One of the factors that determines whether a person will respond to strain in a criminal or conforming manner is intelligence. **(True, p. 227)**

17. Research suggests that feelings of general strain are negatively related to later delinquency. **(False, p. 227)**

18. Culture conflict theory is incompatible with ecological criminology. **(False, p. 228)**

19. According to Thorsten Sellin, conduct norms are acquired early in life. **(True, p. 228)**

20. Secondary conflict occurs when smaller cultures within a primary culture clash with each other. **(True, p. 228)**

21. Most subcultures do not conform to the parameters of national culture. **(False, p. 228)**

22. According to Miller, subcultural crime and deviance are direct consequences of poverty and lack of opportunity. **(False, p. 229)**

23. The statement "I can take care of myself" best represents the focal concern of autonomy. **(True, p. 229)**

24. Miller primarily studied white male juvenile delinquents. **(False, p. 229)**

25. Claiming that the authorities are corrupt is an example of the technique of neutralization known as condemning the condemners. **(True, p. 230)**

26. Techniques of neutralization allow delinquents to participate in crime without being fully alienated from the larger society. **(True, p. 230)**

27. For participants in violent subcultures, violence can be a way of life. **(True, p. 230)**

28. Members of a violent subculture see violence as illicit behavior. **(False, p. 231)**

29. Participants in a violent subculture use techniques of neutralization to deal with feelings of guilt about their aggression. **(False, p. 231)**

30. James Clarke suggests that the high rate of black underclass homicide in the U.S. may result from a black subculture of violence. **(True, p. 231)**

31. According to differential opportunity theory, a lower-class youth who becomes addicted to drugs is probably involved in a conflict subculture. **(False, p. 232)**

32. According to Cloward and Ohlin, a Type II youth wants wealth but does not want to be a member of the middle class. **(False, p. 232)**

33. Gang crime during the 1920s involved primarily vandalism and petty theft. **(True, p. 234)**

34. According to the National Youth Gang Survey, gang-related activity increased between 1996 and 2002. **(False, p. 234)**

35. Most people who join gangs do not try to quit. **(False, p. 234)**

36. Most gangs are racially exclusive. **(False, p. 235)**

37. Inner-city gangs are often heavily involved with drug dealing. **(True, p. 235)**

38. Gang homicides and delinquency appear to be ecologically distinct community problems. **(True, p. 235)**

39. The Rand Corporation's review of the Chicago Area Project found it was effective in reducing rates of juvenile delinquency. **(True, p. 236)**

40. Social structural theories are consistent with the social problems approach. **(True, p. 236)**

## Fill in the Blank

41. Social __________ theories stress the contribution of interpersonal relationships and a lack of self control to crime. **(process, p. 216)**

42. Seeing crime as the product of class struggle is characteristic of __________theories. **(conflict, p. 216)**

43. Social structure theories explain crime by reference to the __________ structure of society. **(institutional, p. 216)**

44. All social structure theories highlight those aspects of society that contribute to the __________ of identifiable segments of society as significant causes of crime. **(low socioeconomic status, p. 216)**

45. Robert Park and Ernest Burgess developed the __________ movement. **(social ecology, p. 218)**

46. Social __________ occurs when a group is faced with social change, uneven cultural development, maladaptiveness, disharmony, conflict, and lack of consensus. **(disorganization/pathology, p. 218)**

47. According to Park and Burgess, Zone __________ was the commuter zone. **(V, p. 218)**

48. __________ data are gathered in the form of life stories. **(Ethnographic, p. 219)**

49. Criminology of place is also called __________ criminology. **(environmental, p. 219)**

50. The concept of deviant neighborhoods was proposed by __________. **(Rodney Stark, p. 219)**

51. __________ is a surrogate term for the range of mechanisms that combine to bring an environment under the control of its residents. **(Defensible space, p. 221)**

52. The term anomie was first popularized by __________ in the book *Suicide*. **(Emile Durkheim, p. 222)**

53. According to Robert K. Merton, __________ is a disjunction between socially approved means to success and legitimate goals. **(anomie, p. 222)**

54. The mode of adaptation that involves accepting the legitimate goals and the socially approved means of acquiring those goals is __________. **(conformity, p. 224)**

55. An individual who participates in socially desirable means but have little interest in achieving goals falls into the __________ mode of adaptation. **(ritualism, p. 224)**

56. According to Merton, __________ is the most common mode of adaptation. **(conformity, p. 226)**

57. The social gap between rich and poor living in close proximity to one another is known as __________. **(relative deprivation, p. 226)**

58. Culture conflict theory is also known as __________ theory. **(cultural deviance, p. 228)**

59. The book *Culture Conflict and Crime*, which described the culture conflict perspective, was written by __________. **(Thorsten Sellin, p. 228)**

60. According to Thorsten Sellin, __________ conflict arises from a fundamental clash of cultures. **(primary, p. 228)**

61. A subculture is communicated to participants through a process of __________. **(socialization, p. 228)**

62. The concept of focal concerns was developed by __________. **(Walter Miller, p. 229)**

63. Miller's term for the key values of delinquent subcultures was __________. **(focal concerns, p. 229)**

64. The technique of neutralization best described by the belief that the insurance company will pay for the stolen car is __________. **(denying injury, p. 230)**

65. According to Ferracuti and Wolfgang, the __________ involves legitimizing the use of violence as an appropriate way to resolve social conflicts. **(subculture of violence, p. 230)**

66. The subcultural ethos of violence is most prominent in the __________ age group **(adolescent through middle age, p. 230)**

67. The concept of a black subculture of violence was developed by __________. **(James Clark, p. 231)**

68. According to Cloward and Ohlin, participants in lower-class subcultures may be denied access to __________ opportunities. **(legitimate, p. 232)**

69. According to Cloward and Ohlin, __________ is an effort to conform to subcultural norms and expectations. **(deviance, p. 232)**

70. Individuals who openly reject what they want but cannot obtain are engaging in __________. **(reaction formation, p. 233)**

71. According to Anderson, contemporary street code emphasizes the issue of __________. **(respect, p. 233)**

72. Social structural theories negate the claims of the social __________ perspective. **(responsibility, p. 236)**

## Multiple Choice

73. Social __________ refers to institutional arrangements within society.
    a. **structure (p. 216)**
    b. life
    c. process
    d. pathology

74. Conflict theories see __________ as a fundamental cause of crime.
    a. social disenfranchisement
    b. a lack of self control
    c. the strength of the social bond
    d. **the nature of existing power relationships between social groups (p. 216)**

75. Social disorganization theory is closely associated with the __________ school of criminology.
    a. classical
    b. positivist
    c. **ecological (p. 216)**
    d. conflict

76. According to Thomas and Znaniecki, increased crime rates among recent immigrants to America was due to social
    a. **disorganization. (p. 217-218)**
    b. conflict.
    c. pathology.
    d. ecology.

77. The idea of viewing cities in terms of concentric zones was developed by
    a. Clifford Shaw and Henry McKay.
    b. **Robert Park and Ernest Burgess. (p. 218)**
    c. W.I. Thomas and Florian Znaniecki.
    d. Steven Messner and Richard Rosenfeld.

78. According to Park and Burgess, Zone __________ contained mostly working-class tenements.
    a. II
    b. **III (p. 218)**
    c. IV
    d. V

79. The concentric zone model was applied to the study of juvenile delinquency by
    a. **Clifford Shaw and Henry McKay. (p. 218)**
    b. Robert Park and Ernest Burgess.
    c. W.I. Thomas and Florian Znaniecki.
    d. Steven Messner and Richard Rosenfeld.

80. Based on the research conducted by Shaw and McKay, we would expect Zone __________ to have the highest rates of crime and delinquency.
    a. **II (p. 218)**
    b. III
    c. IV
    d. V

81. Early ecological theories of crime were collectively referred to as the __________ School of Criminology.
    a. Classical
    b. Positivist
    c. **Chicago (p. 219)**
    d. New York

82. Which of the following is *not* a characteristic of an urban transitional zone?
    a. Lower property values
    b. Impoverished lifestyles
    c. A general lack of privacy
    d. **The presence of a significant amount of retail businesses (p. 219)**

83. The idea that physical deterioration of a neighborhood leads to crime comes from __________ theory.
    a. routine activities
    b. strain
    c. deviant subculture
    d. **broken windows (p. 219)**

84. Merton's strain theory stresses
    a. the idea that although criminal behavior is not inherited, tendencies toward criminal behavior are inherited.
    b. the importance of a person's early family environment in determining attitudes towards crime.
    c. the sexual maladjustments of people as a main source of crime.
    d. **the idea that American society emphasizes common success goals without providing equal access to the means of obtaining them. (p. 222)**

85. According to Merton, an innovator
    a. accepts both the legitimate goals and the socially approved means of acquiring those goals.
    b. rejects legitimate goals and but accepts socially approved means.
    c. rejects both the legitimate goals and the socially approved means of acquiring those goals.
    d. **accepts the legitimate goals but rejects the socially approved means of acquiring those goals. (p. 224)**

86. __________ is an individual's perception of his or her rightful place in the reward structure of society.
    a. Relative deprivation
    b. **Distributive justice (p. 226)**
    c. Focal concerns
    d. Cultural transmission

87. According to general strain theory, strain occurs when which of the following events occurs?
    a. **Someone tries to prevent you from achieving positively valued goals. (p. 227)**
    b. Someone removes negatively valued stimuli.
    c. Someone presents you with positively valued stimuli.
    d. Someone helps you to achieve positively valued goals.

88. __________ theory is a sociological perspective that emphasizes the contribution made by variously socialized cultural groups to the phenomenon of crime.
    a. Conflict
    b. Strain
    c. **Subcultural (p. 228)**
    d. Anomie

89. The book *Street Corner Society*, which studied the Italian slum known as "Cornerville," was written by
    a. **William F. Whyte. (p. 228)**
    b. Walter B. Miller.
    c. Frederic M. Thrasher.
    d. Gresham Sykes.

90. Which of the following is *not* one of Miller's focal concerns?
    a. Trouble
    b. Toughness
    c. Autonomy
    d. **Control (p. 229)**

91. According to Miller, male involvement in fighting and sexual adventures while drinking represent which focal concern?
    a. **Trouble (p. 229)**
    b. Fate
    c. Autonomy
    d. Smartness

92. Which focal concern involves the ability to con or outsmart others?
    a. Excitement
    b. Toughness
    c. Autonomy
    d. **Smartness (p. 229)**

93. The technique of neutralization which involves a young offender claiming that the unlawful acts were "not my fault"is known as
    a. denying injury.
    b. **denying responsibility. (p. 229)**
    c. appealing to higher loyalties.
    d. condemning the condemners.

94. The development of favorable attitudes towards the use of violence involves
    a. **learned behavior. (p. 231)**
    b. biological factors.
    c. psychological traits.
    d. frustration or strain.

95. It appears that certain forms of violence are more acceptable in the __________ portion of the United States.
    a. Northeastern
    b. **Southern (p. 231)**
    c. Western
    d. Midwestern

96. The concept of "wholesale" and "retail" costs for homicide was developed by
    a. James Clark.
    b. Marvin Wolfgang.
    c. David Matza.
    d. **Franklin Zimring. (p. 232)**

97. According to Cloward and Ohlin, a Type __________ youth wants to desire wealth but not entry into the middle class.
    a. I
    b. II
    c. **III (p. 232)**
    d. IV

98. A juvenile who becomes addicted to drugs or alcohol is an example of Cloward and Ohlin's Type __________ youth.
    a. I
    b. II
    c. III
    d. **IV (p. 232)**

99. Reaction formation was developed by
    a. **Albert Cohen. (p. 233)**
    b. Thorsten Sellin.
    c. David Matza.
    d. Elijah Anderson.

100. __________ was based on the work of Cloward and Ohlin.
    a. **Mobilization for Youth (p. 236)**
    b. The Chicago Area Project
    c. The Welfare Reform Reconciliation Act
    d. Welfare-to-Work

101. Some researchers suggest that __________ theories fail to distinguish between the condition of social disorganization and the crimes that this condition is said to cause.
    a. **ecological (p. 237)**
    b. strain
    c. culture conflict
    d. subcultural

102. Which of the following is *not* a criticism of the subcultural approach?
    a. It is racist.
    b. It lacks explanatory power.
    c. It is tautological.
    d. **It overemphasizes the influence of spatial location. (p. 237)**

# Word Search Puzzle

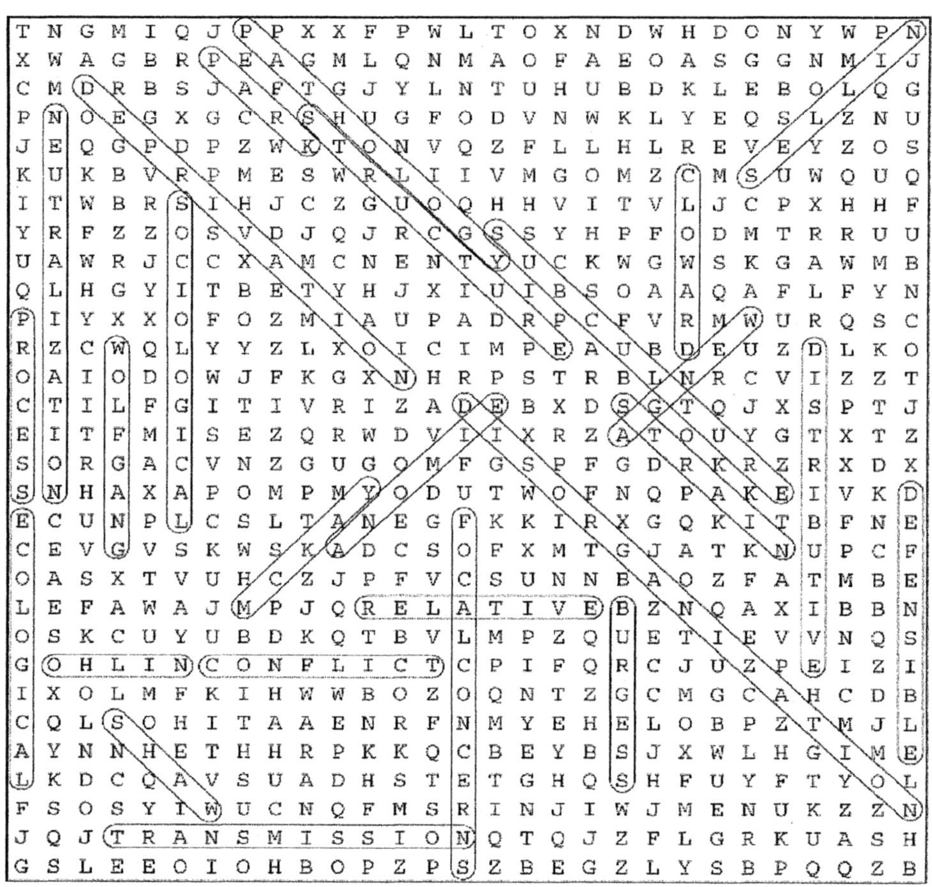

Agnew
Anomie
Burgess
Cloward
Conflict
Defensible
Deprivation
Disorganization
Distributive
Ecological
Focal concerns
McKay
Neutralization
Ohlin
Park
Pathology
Process
Relative
Sellin
Shaw
Sociological
Strain
Structure
Subculture
Transmission
Wolfgang

# Crossword Puzzle

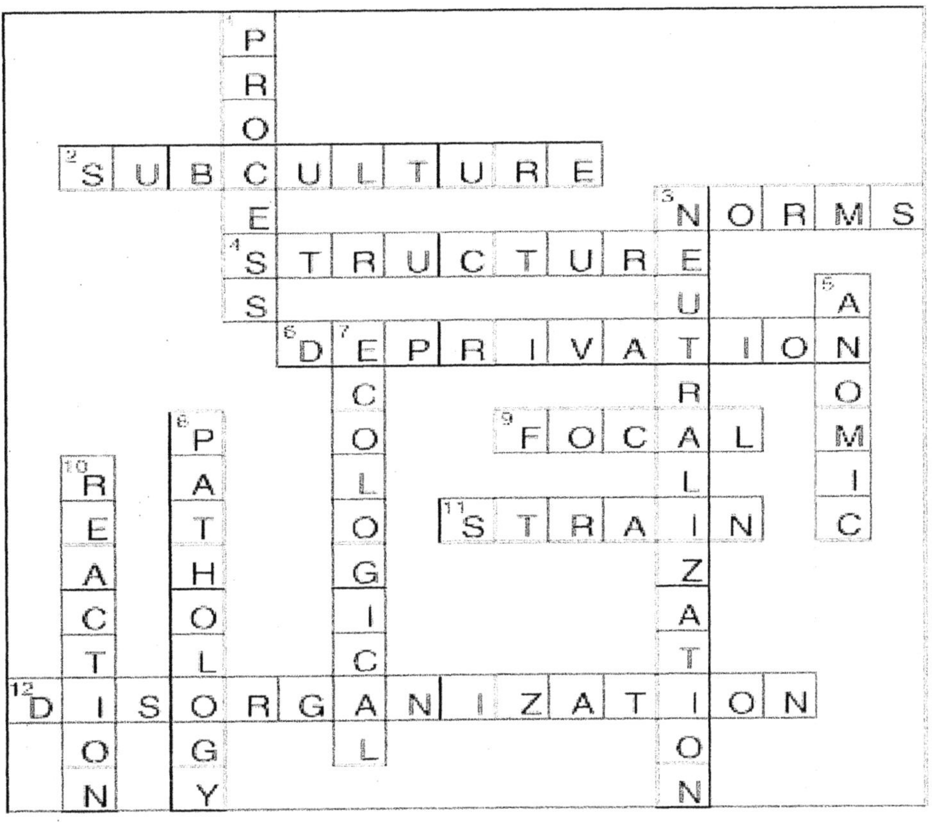


## Across

2 A collection of values communicated to participants through a process of socialization.

3. Conduct _______ are shared expectations of a social group relative to personal conduct.

4. Social _____ is the interrelationships between institutions characteristic of a society.

6. Relative ________ refers to the gap between the rich and the poor living in close proximity.

9. Miller's theory of _______ concerns focused on key values of delinquent subcultures.

11. A theory suggesting a disjuncture between socially sanctioned means and goals as the cause of crime.

12. Social _______ exists when a group is faced with social change, uneven culture development, and lack of consensus.

## Down

1. Social _______ is the interaction between and among social institutions, individuals, and groups.

3. Sykes and Matza proposed five techniques of ________.

5. A social condition in which norms are uncertain or lacking.

7. Social disorganization is associated with the ______ school of criminology.

8. Social ________ sees crime as an illness.

10. _______ formation involves rejecting what one wants or aspires to but cannot have.

# Sociological Theories II: Social Process and Social Development

## Learning Objectives

After reading this chapter, students should be able to:

1. Recognize how the process of social interaction between people contributes to criminal behavior
2. Identify and distinguish between a number of social process and social development perspectives
3. Identify current social policy initiatives that reflect the social development approach
4. Assess the shortcomings of the social process and social development perspectives

## Chapter Outline

Introduction
The Social Process Perspective
Types of Social Process Approaches
*Learning Theory*
*Social Control Theory*
*Labeling Theory*
*Reintegrative Shaming*
*Dramaturgy*
Policy Implications of Social Process Theories
Critique of Social Process Theories
The Social Development Perspective
Concepts in Social Development Theories
*The Life Course Perspective*
*Laub and Sampson's Age-Graded Theory*
*Moffitt's Dual Taxonomic Theory*

# Chapter Summary

This chapter begins with an introduction to social process theories or interactionist perspectives, which assume that everyone has the potential to violate the law, so that criminality is not an innate characteristic of certain individuals. The main types of social process theories are social learning theory, social control theory, labeling theory, the reintegrative shaming approach, and dramaturgy.

Learning theories suggest that crime, like all other types of behavior, is learned. One of the most influential learning theories is differential association, which was developed by Edwin Sutherland and which suggests that criminality is learned through a process of differential association with others who communicate criminal values and advocate the commission of crimes. Differential association-reinforcement theory adds the idea of reinforcement to Sutherland's theory; Robert Burgess and Ronald L. Akers integrated the concept of operant conditioning. Another theory building on Sutherland's work is Daniel Glaser's differential identification theory, which suggests that the process of differential association leads to an intimate personal identification with offenders, resulting in criminal acts.

Social control theories ask why people obey the laws instead of committing crimes. Containment theory, developed by Walter Reckless, suggests that individuals have control mechanisms, or containments, which protect them from crime; if these containments fail, people become vulnerable to criminal behavior. Howard Kaplan proposed the self-derogation theory of delinquency, which suggests that low self-esteem may promote delinquency, and that delinquent behavior may enhance self-esteem. Social bond theory, as proposed by Travis Hirschi, suggests that when the bond between an individual and a social group is weakened or broken, deviance and crime may result. Hirschi and Michael Gottfredson later proposed a general theory of crime which emphasized the lack of self-control as the key factor in explaining all types of crime. Charles Tittle's control-balance theory blends social bond and containment theory and includes the concept of a control ratio, which purports to predict not only the probability that one will engage in deviance but also the form that deviance will take.

Labeling theory focuses on society's reaction to deviance. Frank Tannenbaum developed the term *tagging* to explain how offenders become identified as bad and unredeemable after undergoing processing through the criminal justice system. The concepts of primary deviance (the offender's initial acts of deviance) and secondary deviance (continued acts of deviance) as developed by Edwin M. Lemert describe the development of a criminal career as a result of being tagged with the status of criminal. Howard Becker expanded on the labeling perspective, emphasizing that no act is intrinsically deviant, but must be so defined by society.

The concept of reintegrative shaming, developed by John Braithwaite, describes processes by which a deviant is labeled and sanctioned by society, but is then brought back into a community of conformity. According to Braithwaite, whereas stigmatic shaming destroys the moral bond between the offender and the community, reintegrative shaming strengthens the bond.

Finally, the dramaturgical perspective, developed by Erving Goffman, suggests that individuals play a variety of nearly simultaneous social roles which must be sustained in interaction with others. If discrediting information, or information that a person wants to hide, is revealed, the flow of interaction is disrupted and the nature of the performance may be changed substantially.

Social policy theories have influenced social policy through programs such as the Juvenile Mentoring Program, Preparing for the Drug Free Years, and the Montreal Preventive Treatment Program. The chapter discusses a number of critiques of each type of social policy theory.

Because the social development perspective focuses on human development on many levels, social development theories tend to be integrated theories. Major concepts in social development theories are discussed.

The life course perspective, developed by Robert J. Sampson and John Laub, focuses on the development of criminal careers over the life course and how these careers both start and finish. Laub and Sampson's age-graded theory involved reanalysis of data collected by Sheldon and Eleanor Glueck and emphasizes two key events in the life course (marriage and job stability) that seem to be particularly important in reducing the frequency of offending in later life.

Terrie Moffitt's dual taxonomic theory attempts to explain why, although adult criminality is almost always preceded by antisocial behavior during adolescence, most antisocial children do not become adult offenders. The theory discusses how positive developmental pathways may be fostered in adolescence. David P. Farrington and Donald J. West studied the issue of when offenders desist from crime. Other researchers using cohort analysis to study criminal careers include Marvin Wolfgang, who found that a small number of violent offenders were responsible for most of the crimes committed by the cohort. Lawrence E. Cohen and Richard Machalek developed the evolutionary ecology perspective, which attempts to explain how people acquire criminality, when and why they express it as crime, how individuals and groups respond to those crimes, and how this all interacts as a system evolving over time. Terence Thornberry's interactional theory integrates social control and social learning explanations of delinquency, suggesting that the fundamental cause of delinquency is a weakening of a person's bond to conventional society combined with the presence of an environment in which delinquency can be learned and in which rule-violating behavior can be positively rewarded. Thornberry says that delinquent peers are particularly important in providing the environment necessary for criminal behavior to develop. Because delinquents will seek out association with ever more delinquent groups if their delinquency continues to be rewarded, interactional theory sees delinquency as a process that unfolds over the life course.

A number of researchers are focusing on developmental pathways leading to criminality. The Program of Research on the Causes and Correlates of Delinquency is conducting a number of longitudinal studies of youth throughout their developmental years to understand the causes of delinquency and how it may be prevented. The Project on Human Development in Chicago Neighborhoods is a longitudinal study of how individuals, families, institutions, and communities evolve together and is tracing how criminal behavior evolves from birth to age 32.

Social development theories have influenced social policy. It is the foundation for the OJJDP's Comprehensive Strategy Program and for the Boys and Girls Clubs of America's Targeted Outreach program. The chapter discusses a number of critiques of social development theories.

# Lecture Outline

I. The Social Process Perspective
  A. This chapter focuses on social process theories or interactionist perspectives
    1. These theories depend on the process of interaction between individuals and society for their explanatory power
    2. These theories assume that everyone has the potential to violate the law; criminality is not an innate characteristic
    3. Criminal behavior is learned through interaction with others via socialization
    4. Groups important to the process of socialization include family, peers, work groups, and reference groups with which one identifies
  B. Social process theories hold that the process through which criminality is acquired, deviant self-concepts are established, and criminal behavior results is active, open-ended, and ongoing
    1. Individuals with weak stakes in conformity are more likely to be influenced by such social processes
    2. Criminal choices tend to persist because societal reaction to those identified as deviant reinforces them

**Show the ABC News program *Life and Death in First Grade* from the video library.**

II. Types of Social Process Approaches
  A. Learning theory
    1. Social learning theory suggests that all behaviors, including crime, are learned in much the same way
      a. Learning to commit crime from others includes the acquisition of norms, values, and patterns of behavior conducive to crime
      b. Criminal behavior is a part of the social environment, not an innate characteristic of some people
    2. Differential association
      a. One of the most influential forms of learning theory — developed in 1939 by Edwin H. Sutherland
      b. It suggests that criminality is learned through a process of differential association with others who communicate criminal values and advocate the commission of crimes
      c. Sutherland suggested that all significant human behavior is learned and that crime is not substantively different from any other form of behavior
      d. The theory has nine basic principles:
        (1) Criminal behavior is learned

(2) Criminal behavior is learned in interaction with other persons in a process of communication
(3) The principal part of the learning of criminal behavior occurs within intimate personal groups
(4) When criminal behavior is learned, the learning includes:
 (a) The techniques of committing the crime, which are sometimes very complicated, sometimes very simple
 (b) The specific direction of motives, drives, rationalizations, and attitudes
(5) The specific direction of motives and drives is learned from definitions of the legal codes as favorable or unfavorable
(6) A person becomes delinquent because of an excess of definitions favorable to violation of law over definitions unfavorable to violation of law
(7) Differential associations may vary in frequency, duration, priority, and intensity
(8) The process of learning criminal behavior by association with criminal and anticriminal patterns involves all of the mechanisms that are involved in any other learning
(9) While criminal behavior is an expression of general needs and values, it is not explained by those general needs and values, since noncriminal behavior is an expression of the same needs and values

3. Differential association-reinforcement theory
 a. In 1966, Robert Burgess and Ronald L. Akers added the concept of reinforcement to Sutherland's theory of differential association
  (1) They integrated in the concept of operant conditioning and reorganized Sutherland's nine principles into seven
  (2) They emphasized the belief that humans learn to define rewarded behaviors as positive and that an individual's criminal behavior is rewarded at least sometimes by those who value it
 b. Akers later identified two primary learning mechanisms:
  (1) Differential reinforcement/instrumental conditioning: behavior is a function of the frequency, amount, and probability of experienced and perceived contingent rewards and punishments
  (2) Imitation: the behavior of others and its consequence are observed and modeled
 c. Akers has redeveloped the theory into the social structure-social learning (SSL) theory of crime - discuss the seven key principles of the theory
  (1) Deviant behavior is learned according to the principle of operant conditioning
  (2) Deviant behavior is learned both in nonsocial situations that are reinforcing or discriminating and through that social interaction in which the behavior of other persons is reinforcing or discriminating for such behavior
  (3) The principal part of the learning of deviant behavior occurs in those groups that comprise or control the individual's major source of reinforcements
  (4) The learning of deviant behavior, including specific techniques, attitudes, and avoidance procedures, is a function of the effective and available reinforcers and the existing reinforcement contingencies

(5) The specific class of behavior learned and its frequency of occurrence are a function of the effective and available reinforcers, and the deviant or nondeviant direction of the norms, rules, and definitions that in the past have accompanied the reinforcement
(6) The probability that a person will commit deviant behavior is increased in the presence of normative statements, definitions, and verbalizations which, in the process of differential reinforcement of such behavior over conforming behavior, have acquired discriminative value
(7) The strength of deviant behavior is a direct function of the amount, frequency, and probability of its reinforcement. The modalities of association with deviant patterns are important insofar as they affect the source, amount, and scheduling of reinforcement

d. SSL integrates social structure and social learning by specifying the links between the larger social context and the individuals relationships that lead to crime

4. Differential identification theory (Daniel Glaser)
   a. This theory builds upon Sutherland's differential association theory, suggesting that the process of differential association leads to an intimate personal identification with offenders, resulting in criminal acts
   b. Essentially, a person pursues crime to the extent that s/he identifies with real or imaginary persons from whose perspective the criminal behavior seems acceptable
   c. The symbolic process of identification determines behavior and role models can be abstract ideas as well as actual persons
   d. Identification with noncriminals may assist in rehabilitation

B. Social control theory
1. Social control theories attempt to determine what personality and environmental factors keep people from committing crimes
   a. They go beyond personality and physical features of the environment to focus on the process through which social integration develops
   b. Social control theories ask why people actually obey the law instead of committing crimes
2. Containment theory (Walter C. Reckless)
   a. Containment theory compares committing crime to succumbing to an illness: only some people exposed to a disease actually come down with it and only some people exposed to social pressures to commit crime actually violate the law
   b. Crime results when control mechanisms or "containments" fail to protect the individual
      (1) External containments are provided by society: social groups such as families and communities help keep the individual within the bounds of conventional norms
      (2) Inner containment is the individual's ability to direct himself/herself to follow expected norms; it is enhanced by a positive self-image, a focus on socially approved goals, a good tolerance for frustration, and so on
   c. Pushes toward crime are factors within a person's background that might propel him/her toward criminal behavior (e.g., a criminogenic background, biological propensities toward deviant behavior, deprivation, psychological maladjustment)

d. Pulls toward crime are positive inducements or perceived rewards offered by crime (e.g., financial gain, sexual satisfaction, higher status)
e. A containment is a stabilizing force that, if effective, blocks pushes and pulls from leading a person into crime
f. According to Reckless, inner containment is more important than external containment in preventing crime

3. Delinquency and self-esteem
   a. Howard B. Kaplan developed the self-derogation theory of delinquency in the 1970s
      (1) He proposed that people who are ridiculed by their peers suffer a loss of self-esteem, assess themselves poorly, and lose the motivation to conform
      (2) Although research suggests that low self-esteem fosters delinquent behavior, it also appears that delinquency can enhance self-esteem for some delinquents
      (3) Research by Leung and Drasgow in 1986 testing Kaplan's self-derogation theory found that while white, African-American, and Hispanic youth groups all reported low self-esteem, low levels of self-esteem were only related to delinquent behavior among white youngsters
      (4) Other research found no differences in self-esteem and delinquency between African-American and white delinquents and nondelinquents
   b. The self-esteem approach of Oyserman and Markus suggests that the degree of disjunction between what one wants to be and what one fears one might become is a good potential predictor of delinquency
4. Social bond theory
   a. A form of control theory developed by Travis Hirschi in his 1969 book, *Causes of Delinquency*
   b. Hirschi suggests that successful socialization creates bonds between an individual and the social group and a weakened or broken bond may result in deviance and crime
   c. There are four components of the social bond
      (1) Attachment
         (a) A person's shared interests with others
         (b) Hirschi considers a psychopath to be someone whose attachment to society is nearly nonexistent
      (2) Commitment
         (a) The amount of energy and effort a person puts into activities with others
         (b) People who have invested time and energy in conventional activities must consider the costs of deviant behavior and the risk of losing the investment already made in conventional behavior
      (3) Involvement
         (a) The amount of time spent with others in shared activities
         (b) If a person spends a lot of time in legitimate activities, he/she will have little time or opportunity for criminal or deviant activities
      (4) Belief
         (a) Belief involves a shared value and moral system

(b) Unlike subcultural theory, control theory assumes a common value system and also assumes that the offender believes in this value system even though s/he is violating it

d. In 1990, Hirschi and Michael Gottfredson extended control theory further, developing a general theory of crime
   (1) Their theory is built on the classical or rational choice perspective: the belief that crime is a natural consequence of unrestrained human tendencies to seek pleasure and avoid pain
   (2) Offenders are people who have little self-control over their own desires: when personal desires conflict with long-term interests, they are more likely to choose immediate gratification, even if it results in criminal behavior
   (3) A well-developed social bond will result in the creation of effective mechanisms of self-control
   (4) Gottfredson and Hirschi consider self-control to be the key concept in explaining all forms of behavior, including all types of crime
   (5) Differences in crime rates between groups may be explained by differences in self-control management

5. Control-balance theory (Charles Tittle)
   a. Control-balance theory blends social bond and containment perspectives and suggests that too much self-control can be as dangerous as too little
   b. The control ratio is the amount of control to which a person is subject versus the amount of control the person exerts over others
      (1) The control ratio predicts not only the probability that a person will engage in deviance but also the form that deviance will take
      (2) People with high levels of control (control surplus) can exercise a lot of control over others and will work to increase this control, leading to deviance involving exploitation, plunder, and decadence
      (3) People with low levels of control (control deficit) are unable to exercise much control over others and attempt to escape repressive control through deviant behavior, such as predation, defiance, and submission
   c. A control imbalance only sets the stage for deviance, which occurs when a person realizes that acts of deviance can reset the control ration in a favorable way
   d. Opportunity also affects the actual likelihood of the occurrence of deviance

C. Labeling theory
   1. Discuss the controversy surrounding the case of James Hann, convicted offender who entered law school after being paroled, and how it provides an example of how society's reaction to crime can change the course of an offender's life
   2. This perspective is based on the study of society's reactions to deviance and to offenders
   3. Frank Tannenbaum's 1938 research used the term "tagging" to describe what happens to offenders after arrest, conviction, and sentencing
      a. Tannenbaum said crime is the result of two opposing definitions of the situation - those of the delinquent and of the community at large
      b. As the community's attitude hardens into a demand for suppression, there is a shift from the definition of specific acts as evil to a definition

of the offender as evil, so that all of the offender's future acts are also suspect

c. Dramatization of evil is the process by which an offender becomes seen as irrevocably "bad"
    (1) Once a person has been tagged (defined as "bad"), access to legitimate opportunities is limited, and only others who have been similarly defined by society are available to associate with him or her
    (2) Continued association with negatively defined others leads to continued crime

4. Edwin M. Lemert developed the concepts of primary and secondary deviance
    a. Primary deviance is the initial act, which may occur as a way of solving an immediate problem or meeting the expectations of a subcultural group
    b. If the offender is tagged with a criminal status, secondary deviance may occur as a way to adjust to the negative status
5. Howard Becker is most closely associated with labeling theory through his 1963 book *Outsiders: Studies in the Sociology of Deviance*
    a. Becker suggested that deviance and the deviant person are created by society through society's response to circumscribed behaviors
    b. Deviance is not a quality of the action but a consequence of the application of rules and sanctions, and a deviant is one to whom the label has been applied successfully
    c. According to Becker, no act is intrinsically deviant or criminal but must be defined as such by others
    d. Becker emphasized the concept of "moral enterprise:" the efforts made by a particular interest group to have its sense of moral or ethical propriety enacted into law (such as the Women's Christian Temperance Union's impact on Prohibition)
    e. Becker focused on the description of the development of deviant or criminal careers
        (1) He suggested that initially most deviance is transitory and unlikely to occur again
        (2) However, a pattern of criminal behavior may be created through the labeling process: once a person is labeled deviant, opportunities for conforming behavior are limited significantly and the most accessible behavioral opportunities are primarily deviant ones
        (3) Throughout his or her career, the deviant increasingly participates in deviant behavior not out of personal choice but because his or her choices have been limited by society
        (4) Near the completion of a deviant career, the labeled person internalizes society's negative label, assumes a negative self-concept, and may join a deviant subgroup
6. Labeling theory contributed several unique ideas to criminology:
    a. Deviance is the result of social processes involving the imposition of definitions, rather than the consequence of any quality inherent in human activity itself
    b. Deviant individuals achieve their status by virtue of social definition, rather than because of inborn traits

   c. The reaction of society to deviant behavior and to actors who engage in such behavior is the major element in determining the criminality of the person and of the behavior in question
   d. Negative self-images follow from processing by the formal mechanisms of criminal justice, rather than precede delinquency
   e. Labeling by society and handling by the justice system tend to perpetuate crime and delinquency rather than reduce it
7. Becker developed a topology of delinquents
   a. Pure deviants commit norm-breaking behavior and are labeled as deviant by society
   b. Falsely accused deviants are innocent but are still labeled as deviant
   c. Secret deviants commit norm-breaking behavior, but society does not notice and does not label them as deviant
8. Labeling theory has recently been redefined as a developmental theory because of its emphasis on processes over time
   a. Labeling is seen as one factor contributing to cumulative disadvantages in life chances
   b. Discuss the recent research by Bernburg and Krohn that found that official intervention during adolescence led to increased criminality during early adulthood and that poor people were more negatively impacted by official processing

D. Reintegrative shaming
1. This is a contemporary offshoot of labeling theory developed in Australia by John Braithwaite and colleagues
   a. Traditional labeling theory emphasizes stigmatization and the resulting amplification of deviance
   b. Reintegrative shaming focuses on labeling and sanctioning deviants and then bringing them back into a community of conformity through words, gestures, or rituals
2. Reintegrative Shaming Experiments (RISE) conducted in Canberra, Australia, compared traditional court processing of criminal offenders with the restorative justice approach of diversionary conferencing, which involved emotionally intense meetings involving the police, admitted offenders and their supporters, and the victim and his/her supporters
3. Braithwaite suggests that two kinds of shame exist:
   a. Stigmatic shaming destroys the moral bond between the offender and the community and labels the individual as untrustworthy and as someone who is expected to commit more crimes
   b. Reintegrative shaming strengthens the moral bond between the offender and the community
      (1) It condemns the crime rather than the criminal and gives the offender an opportunity to rejoin the community as a law-abiding citizen
      (2) Offenders must express remorse for their past behavior, apologize to their victims, and repair the harm caused by the crime
4. Preliminary results from RISE support the claimed value of reintegrative shaming

**Show the ABC News program *Shame on You* from the video library.**

E. Dramaturgy (Erving Goffman)
  1. The dramaturgical perspective suggests that people play a variety of nearly simultaneous social roles that must be sustained in interaction with others
  2. Social actors define the situations in which they are involved through verbal and nonverbal communications, which establishes rules of interpersonal interaction
     a. Impression management involves constant exchanges of information to create an overall definition of a given situation
     b. If discrediting information, or information that an actor-individual wants to hide, is revealed, the flow of interaction is disrupted and the nature of the performance may be changed substantially.
  3. Society responds differently to discredited or stigmatized individuals than to "normal" individuals
     a. If the discredited person is known to others in advance, normal people approach the stigmatized person expecting to encounter further stigmatizing behavior
     b. If the discrediting information is not known in advance, the stigmatized person may attempt to conceal it through misrepresentation, the use of aliases, etc.
  4. Total institutions are facilities in which communal life is extremely circumscribed and from which people can rarely come and go (prisons, convents, seminaries, mental hospitals, etc.)
     a. Residents of total institutions may bring their former cultures into the facilities with them
     b. During their time in the institution, they undergo a period of disculturation, during which they drop aspects of the presenting culture and are socialized into the institutional culture instead

III. Policy Implications of Social Process Theories
  A. Social process theories emphasize crime prevention programs that work to enhance self control and build prosocial bonds
  B. The Juvenile Mentoring Program (JUMP) is run by the Office of Juvenile Justice and Delinquency Prevention (OJJDP)
     1. JUMP attempts to build strong social bonds while teaching positive values to juveniles
     2. JUMP places at-risk youth in a one-on-one relationship with favorable adult role models
     3. As of August 2004, 9,200 youths were enrolled in over 200 JUMP programs throughout the United States with an average age of enrollment at just under 12 years
     4. Both youth and mentors are very positive when rating the mentoring experience
  C. Preparing for the Drug Free Years (PDFY) is also run by OJJDP
     1. This social control program emphasizes strong bonding to positive influences as a way of reducing the probability of delinquency and other problem behaviors
     2. PDFY works with parents of children in grades 4–8 to teach effective parenting skills as an attempt to reduce drug abuse and other behavioral problems

D. The Montreal Preventive Treatment Program
   1. This program emphasizes the development of self-control, targeting boys from low socioeconomic backgrounds who have displayed disruptive behavior in kindergarten and engaging them and their parents in training sessions
   2. An evaluation of the program suggests that it is effective at keeping boys from joining gangs

IV. Critique of Social Process Theories
   A. Criticisms of differential association theory
      1. One key criticism is the claim that Sutherland's initial formation of differential association is not applicable at the individual level: not everyone who experiences an excess of definitions favorable to crime will become a criminal, and some individuals who rarely associate with deviants may turn to crime
      2. Most people experience a wide variety of definitions and must interpret what these experiences mean, possibly making the theory untestable
      3. Some critics suggest that differential association is not a sufficient explanation for crime and does not provide for free choice in individual circumstances or explain why some people can maintain non-criminal values even when surrounded by criminal associates
      4. The theory does not account for the emergence of criminal values, only their communication
   B. Criticisms of labeling theory
      1. The theory does not explain the origin of crime and deviance
      2. There is little empirical support for the concept of secondary deviance or for the claim that criminals have a criminal self-image
      3. There is also little empirical support for the claim that contact with the criminal justice system affects offenders' personal lives negatively
      4. The theory does not discuss secret deviants
   C. Criticisms of dramaturgy
      1. Goffman's work has been seen as providing a set of linked concepts rather than a consistent theoretical frame
      2. The theory does not make suggestions for institutional change or for treatment modalities based on its assumptions

V. The Social Development Perspective
   A. This perspective suggests that human development begins at birth and occurs in a social context
   B. Human development occurs on many simultaneous levels: psychological, biological, familial, interpersonal, cultural, societal, and ecological
   C. Social development theories tend to be integrated theories, combining various points of view on the process of development

VI. Concepts in Social Development Theories
   A. Unlike sociological theories, which study groups, social development theories focus on individual rates of offending and changes in rates of offending over the life course
      1. They generally emphasize the use of longitudinal studies

2. One critical transition period occurs as a person moves from childhood to adulthood — discuss the seven developmental tasks American adolescents confront during this transition period

B. The life course perspective
  1. While traditional theories lack a developmental perspective, developmental theories focus on the patterns that criminal behavior follows across the life cycle
  2. Life course theory developed out of a 1986 National Academy of Sciences panel report that emphasized the study of criminal careers and of crime over the life course
     a. The panel defined a criminal career as the longitudinal sequence of crimes committed by an individual offender
     b. They outlined four dimensions of criminal careers:
        (1) Participation: the fraction of a population that is criminally active
        (2) Frequency: the number of crimes committed by an individual offender per unit of time; this is not constant but varies over the life course
        (3) Duration: the length of the criminal career
        (4) Seriousness: the seriousness of the crimes committed by the offender during a criminal career
  3. Life course criminology was so named by Robert J. Sampson and John Laub
     a. The life course has been defined as "pathways through the life span involving a sequence of culturally defined, age-graded roles and social transitions enacted over time"
     b. Life course theories recognize that criminal careers may develop as the result of criminogenic influences affecting individuals over the course of their lives
  4. Three key concepts are important to the life course perspective:
     a. Activation: the ways that delinquent behaviors, once initiated, are stimulated and the processes by which the continuity, frequency, and diversity of delinquency are shaped
        (1) Acceleration is an increased frequency of offending over time
        (2) Stabilization is increased continuity over time
        (3) Diversification is the propensity of individuals to become involved in more diverse delinquent activities
     b. Aggravation: the existence of a developmental sequence of activities that escalate or increase in seriousness over time
     c. Desistance: a reduction in offending
        (1) Deceleration is a slowing down in the frequency of offending
        (2) Specialization is a slowing down in the variety of offending
        (3) Deescalation is a slowing down in the seriousness of the offenses committed
  5. Another important principle in life course theories is the concept of linked lives, which refers to the fact that human lives are embedded in social relationships with family and friends across the life span and that these people have considerable influence on most people's life course
  6. Glen Elder identified four important principles which provide a summary of life course theory

   a. The principle of historical time and place: the life course is embedded in and shaped by the historical times and places individuals experience over their lifetime
   b. The principle of timing in lives: the developmental impact of various life transitions or vents depends on when they occur in a person's life
   c. The principle of linked lives: lives are lived interdependently and historical influences are expressed through this network of shared relationships
   d. The principle of human agency: individuals construct their own life course through their choices and actions within the opportunities and constraints of history and social circumstances
7. Sheldon Glueck and Eleanor Glueck
   a. In the 1930s, the Gluecks studied the life cycles of delinquent boys, following the careers of known delinquents to identify the causes of delinquency
   b. They concluded that family dynamics were extremely important in the development of criminality
   c. They also found that juvenile delinquent careers tended to lead to adult criminal careers
   d. Their early research supports modern life course theories

C. Laub and Sampson's age-graded theory
1. In the 1980s, John Laub and Robert Sampson reanalyzed the Gluecks' data and found that juveniles who became delinquent generally had trouble at school and at home and had friends who were already involved in delinquency
2. They also found that marriage and job stability were key life course events that helped reduce the frequency of offending later in life
3. They developed an age-graded theory of informal social control
   a. Delinquency is more likely to occur when social bonds are weak or broken
   b. Social ties embedded in adult transitions explain variations in crime that is not accounted for by childhood deviance
4. A key element in their approach is the concept of turning points in a criminal career
   a. The two especially significant turning points are employment and marriage
   b. Others may occur in association with leaving home, having children, getting divorced, graduating, and so on
5. The concept of life course interdependence suggests that the effect of prosocial ties as a deterrent to crime varies as a function of criminal predisposition
6. Laub and Sampson also developed the concept of social capital: the degree of positive relations with individuals and institutions that are built up over the life course and which reduce the likelihood of criminal activity

D. Moffitt's dual taxonomic theory (Terrie E. Moffitt)
1. This two-path (dual taxonomic) theory helps to explain why most antisocial children do not become adult criminals even though adult criminality is almost always preceded by adolescent antisocial behavior,
2. Moffit identified two types of offenders
   a. Life course persistent offenders/life course persisters

(1) People who display fairly constant patterns of misbehavior throughout life, possibly as a result of the combination of neurophysological deficits, poverty, and family dysfunction
(2) They tend to fail in school and become involved in delinquency at an early age, resulting in increasingly limited opportunities for legitimate success

b. Adolescence-limited offenders
(1) Teenagers who go through limited periods where they exhibit high probabilities of offending and who are led to offending primarily by structural disadvantages such as status anxiety and maturity gap
(2) These offenders may display inconsistencies in antisocial behavior but that much of their behavior will remain within socially acceptable bounds

3. Research into this theory suggests that positive developmental pathways are fostered when adolescents are able to develop all of the following:
   a. A sense of industry and competency
   b. A feeling of connectedness
   c. A belief in their ability to control their future
   d. A stable identity

E. Farrington's delinquent development theory
1. Persistence describes continuity in crime or the continual involvement in offending
2. Desistance refers to the ending of criminal activity or of a criminal career and can be of two forms:
   a. Unaided desistance occurs without the formal intervention or assistance of the criminal justice system
   b. Aided desistance involves the criminal justice system and is usually known as rehabilitation
3. Early criminologists identified the desistance phenomenon, which involves offenders who were heavily involved in crime during their teens and 20s but who stop their criminal activities by about age 35
   a. Marvin Wolfgang described the process as one of spontaneous remission
   b. It was also discussed by criminologists such as Adolphe Quetelet and the Gluecks
4. David P. Farrington and Donald J. West have conducted longitudinal studies of crime in the life course and found greater diversity in ages of desistance than ages of onset
   a. In 1982 they began the Cambridge Study in Delinquent Development, tracking a cohort of 411 boys born in London in 1953, in an effort to explain the heterogeneity of developmental pathways
   b. They found that persistent offenders suffered from a variety of risk factors for delinquency, including hyperactivity, broken homes, low family income, and harsh discipline
   c. They found offending tends to peak around age 17 or 18 and then decline, and that by age 35, many subjects in the study had assumed conforming lifestyles
5. Rolf Loeber and Marc LeBlanc have identified four components of desistance
   a. Deceleration: a slowing down in the frequency of offending
   b. Specialization: a reduction in the variety of offenses

c. Deescalation: a reduction in the seriousness of offending
d. Reaching a ceiling: remaining at a certain level of offending and not committing more serious offenses

**Show the ABC News program *What If...?* from the video library.**

F. Evolutionary ecology
1. Life course researchers generally use cohort analysis designs tracing the development from birth to some predetermined age of a population whose members share common characteristics
2. Marvin Wolfgang's analysis of a birth cohort in the 1960s found that a small number of chronic juvenile offenders (6% of the cohort) accounted for a disproportionately large number of juvenile arrests (52%)
3. Lawrence Cohen and Richard Machalek developed the evolutionary ecology approach, which attempts to explain how people acquire criminality, when and why they express it as crime, how those crimes are responded to, and how all these factors interact

G. Thornberry's interactional theory
1. Terence Thornberry's interactional theory of crime integrates social control and social learning explanations of delinquency
2. The theory says the fundamental cause of delinquency is a weakening of a person's bond to conventional society combined with the presence of an environment in which delinquency can be learned and in which rule-violating behavior can be positively rewarded
3. Thornberry says that delinquent peers (including gang membership) are particularly important in providing the environment necessary for criminal behavior to develop
4. Because delinquents will seek out association with ever more delinquent groups if their delinquency continues to be rewarded, delinquency is seen as a process that unfolds over the life course

H. Developmental pathways
1. Manifestations of disruptive behaviors by children and adolescents are often age dependent
   a. As children grow older, they develop verbal coping skills that help them deal with conflict
   b. Children who are unable to develop adequate verbal coping skills are more likely to commit acts of intense aggression and to be characterized by their parents as having a difficult temperament
2. OJJDP's Program of Research on the Causes and Correlates of Delinquency involves longitudinal studies attempting to understand life pathways leading to criminality
   a. Each project involves repeated contacts with inner-city youth who are at high risk for involvement in drug abuse and delinquency
   b. Discuss the results of the program to date
   c. The most significant result may be the finding that there are three separate developmental paths to delinquency, which are not necessarily mutually exclusive and which can converge:
      (1) The authority conflict pathway

(2) The covert pathway
(3) The overt pathway
d. Simultaneous progression along two or more pathways leads to higher rates of delinquency

I. The Chicago Human Development Project
1. The Project on Human Development in Chicago Neighborhoods (PHDCN) is a longitudinal analysis of how individuals, families, institutions, and communities evolve together: it is tracing how criminal behavior develops from birth to age 32
2. The project involves two studies combined into a single comprehensive design
a. One is an intensive study of Chicago's neighborhoods, evaluating the social, economic, organizational, political, and cultural components of each neighborhood as a way of identifying changes occurring over the eight year period of the study
b. The other is a series of coordinated longitudinal evaluations of 7,000 subjects, looking at the changing circumstances of their lives to identify personal characteristics that may lead toward or away from antisocial behavior
3. Early results of the project have led to targeted interventions intended to lower rates of offending

VII. Policy Implications of Social Development Theories
A. OJJDP has adopted the social development model as the foundation for its Comprehensive Strategy Program, which helps communities develop programs for preventing and responding to delinquency and crime and for early intervention
B. The Boys and Girls Clubs of America's Targeted Outreach program diverts at-risk juveniles into activities intended to develop a sense of belonging, competence, usefulness, and self-control

VIII. Critique of Social Development Theories
A. One key critique centers around definitional issues: precise definitions of key terms are necessary for the testing of hypotheses derived from life course theories
B. Social development theories are associated with the social problems approach, which leads to the question of what role, if any, individual choice plays in human development

# Key Concepts

**Cambridge Study in Delinquent Development:** A longitudinal (life-course) study of crime and delinquency tracking a cohort of 411 boys born in London in 1953.

**Cohort analysis:** A social scientific technique that studies over time a population that shares common characteristics. Cohort analysis usually begins at birth and traces the development of cohort members until they reach a certain age.

**Containment**: Aspects of the social bond that act to prevent individuals from committing crimes and which keep them from engaging in deviance.

**Containment theory**: A form of control theory that suggests that a series of both internal and external factors contributes to law-abiding behavior.

**Control ratio**: The amount of control to which a person is subject versus the amount of control that person exerts over others.

**Criminal career**: The longitudinal sequence of crimes committed by an individual offender.

**Desistance**: The cessation of criminal activity or the termination of a period of involvement in offending behavior.

**Differential association**: The sociological thesis that criminality, like any other form of behavior, is learned through a process of association with others who communicate criminal values.

**Differential identification theory**: An explanation for crime and deviance that holds that people pursue criminal or deviant behavior to the extent that they identify themselves with real or imaginary people from whose perspective their criminal or deviant behavior seems acceptable.

**Discrediting information**: Information that is inconsistent with the managed impressions being communicated in a given situation.

**Dramaturgical perspective**: A theoretical point of view that depicts human behavior as centered around the purposeful management of interpersonal impressions. Also called *dramaturgy*.

**Evolutionary ecology**: An approach to understanding crime that draws attention to the ways people develop over the course of their lives.

**Human development**: The relationship between the maturing individual and his or her changing environment, as well as the social processes that the relationship entails.

**Impression management**: The intentional enactment of practiced behavior which is intended to convey to others one's desirable personal characteristics and social qualities.

**Interactional theory**: A theoretical approach to explaining crime and delinquency that blends social control and social learning perspectives.

**Interactionist perspective:** See **social process theory**.

**Labeling**: An interactionist perspective that sees continued crime as a consequence of limited opportunities for acceptable behavior which follow from the negative responses of society to those defined as offenders. Also, the process by which a negative or deviant label is imposed.

**Learning theory (sociology)**: A perspective that places primary emphasis upon the role of communication and socialization in the acquisition of learned patterns of criminal behavior and the values that support that behavior.

**Life course**: Pathways through the age-differentiated life span. Also, the course of a person's life over time.

**Moral enterprise**: The efforts made by an interest group to have its sense of moral or ethical propriety enacted into law.

**Persistence**: Continuity in crime. Also, continual involvement in offending.

**Primary deviance**: Initial deviance often undertaken to deal with transient problems in living.

**Project on Human Development in Chicago Neighborhoods (PHDCN)**: An intensive study of Chicago neighborhoods employing longitudinal evaluations to examine the changing circumstances of people's lives in an effort to identify personal characteristics that may lead toward or away from antisocial behavior.

**Reintegrative shaming**: A form of shaming, imposed as a sanction by the criminal justice system, that is thought to strengthen the moral bond between the offender and the community.

**Secondary deviance**: Deviant behavior that results from official labeling and from association with others who have been so labeled.

**Social bond**: The link, created through socialization, between individuals and the society of which they are a part.

**Social capital**: The degree of positive relationships with others and with social institutions that individuals build up over the course of their lives.

**Social control theory**: A perspective that predicts that when social constraints on antisocial behavior are weakened or absent, delinquent behavior emerges. Rather than stressing causative factors in criminal behavior, control theory asks why people actually obey rules instead of breaking them.

**Social development perspective**: An integrated view of human development that examines multiple levels of maturation simultaneously, including the psychological, biological, familial, interpersonal, cultural, societal, and ecological levels.

**Social process theory:** A theory that asserts that criminal behavior is learned in interaction with others and that socialization processes that occur as the result of group membership are the primary route through which learning occurs. Also called the *interactionist perspective*.

**Stigmatic shaming**: A form of shaming, imposed as a sanction by the criminal justice system, that is thought to destroy the moral bond between the offender and the community.

**Tagging**: The process whereby an individual is negatively defined by agencies of justice. Also called *labeling*.

**Total institution**: A facility from which individuals can rarely come and go and in which communal life is intense and circumscribed. Individuals in total institutions tend to eat, sleep, play, learn, and worship (if at all) together.

## Additional Lecture Topics

Consider expanding on the discussion of labeling theory with the example of William Chambliss's study of the Saints and the Roughnecks. The Saints were a group of eight upper-middle-class white boys, who while earning good grades and participating in school activities were also involved in delinquent activities, such as vandalism, petty theft, and underage drinking. The Roughnecks were a group of six lower-class white boys who did not do well in school and engaged in similar delinquent activities. However, while the Saints were seen as "good boys" and did not have any serious encounters with teachers and the police, the Roughnecks were labeled "bad boys" and were frequently in trouble with the police and with school officials.

Discuss some of the sources from which individuals may learn the motives and the techniques for committing crimes. These include:

- The individual's peer group
- The community in which the person lives, particularly if local adult offenders are present to serve as role models and instructors
- The values of the culture in which the person is brought up
- The influence of sports and professional athletes who are involved in criminal activities
- The visual media, including violent television programs and movies
- The print media, including publishers who print "how to" books such as *The Anarchist Cookbook*, *The Ultimate Sniper*, and *Hit Man*

When reviewing the life course perspective, consider discussing how one exits or disengages successfully from a criminal career. Neil Shover's model of the exiting process suggests that increased ties to another person (e.g., a positive relationship with a member of the opposite sex or with a family member) and increased ties to a line of activity (e.g., finding a good job that reinforces a non-criminal identity) lead an offender to a "modified calculus" which results in a reduction in both the frequency and visibility of criminal activity or in a complete cessation of involvement in criminal behavior.

# Discussion Questions

These discussion questions are found in the textbook at the end of the chapter. The instructor may want to focus on these questions during the coverage of Chapter 8.

1. This chapter describes both social process and social development perspectives. What are the significant differences between these two perspectives? What kinds of theories characterize each?

2. This textbook emphasizes a social problems versus social responsibility theme. Which of the perspectives discussed in this chapter (if any) best support the social problems approach? Which (if any) support the social responsibility approach? Why?

3. This chapter contains a discussion of the labeling process. Give a few examples of the everyday imposition of positive, rather than negative, labels. Why is it so difficult to successfully impose positive labels on individuals who were previously labeled negatively?

4. Do you believe that Erving Goffman's dramaturgical approach, which sees the world as a stage and individuals as actors upon that stage, provides any valuable insights into crime and criminality? If so, what are they?

5. What kinds of social policy initiatives might be suggested by social process theories? By social development theories? Which do you think might be most effective? Why?

6. What are the shortcomings of the social process perspective? Of the social development perspective?

# Student Exercises

## Activity #1

Your instructor will place you into groups and assign you one of the theories discussed in this chapter. Develop a crime reduction and/or prevention policy that is based on this theory. Explain how the theory justifies the policy and why you expect the policy to reduce or prevent crime.

## Activity #2

According to Hirschi's social bond theory, four elements of a social bond work together to promote law-abiding behavior and prevent involvement in crime and delinquency: attachment, commitment, involvement, and belief. Explain how youth organizations such as the Boy Scouts, Girl Scouts, and 4-H Clubs (or similar groups) work to strengthen these four elements of the social bond and encourage members to engage in normative behaviors.

## Activity #3

Currently, there is considerable debate over the belief that violent video games may lead to criminal behavior among juveniles. Explain how this belief could be supported by the theories discussed in this chapter.

# Criminology Today on the Web

### http://www.sonoma.edu/cja/info/Edintro.html

This Web site was created in memory of Edwin Lemert, who died in 1996. It includes links to some of his articles and to an interview with him.

### http://www.aber.ac.uk/media/Functions/mcs.html

This Web site, which is part of the University of Wales, Aberystwyth Media and Communications Program, includes links to articles and other information on the relationship between television and violence.

### http://www.ncjrs.org/works/

This site makes available a comprehensive report on the effectiveness of crime prevention that was mandated by Congress in 1996. It includes information on the relationship between various theories of crime causation and public policy, including many of the theories discussed in this chapter.

### http://www.cfmc.com/adamb/writings/goffman.htm

This article discusses Erving Goffman's dramaturgy perspective.

### http://www.crimetheory.com/Archive/Response/index.html

This site includes a discussion of various "social response" theories, including labeling theory.

### http://www.aic.gov.au/rjustice/rise/

The Australian Institute of Criminology has a web site providing information on the Reintegrative Shaming Experiments project in Australia.

# Student Study Guide Questions and Answers

## True/False

1. Social process theories assume that criminality is an innate human characteristic. **(False, p. 245)**

2. According to Sutherland, the process of learning criminal behavior is substantively different from learning other forms of behavior. **(False, p. 247)**

3. Sutherland suggested that criminality occurs when there is a disjunction of socially approved goals and legitimate means. **(False, p. 247)**

4. According to differential association, the principal part of the learning of criminal behavior occurs within intimate personal groups. **(True, p. 247)**

5. Criminal behavior is explained by general needs and values. **(False, p. 247)**

6. According to Akers, differential reinforcement is also known as imitation. **(False, p. 247)**

7. According to Akers, criminal or deviant behavior is learned only in social situations. **(False, p. 248)**

8. According to Glaser, a role model must be an actual person. **(False, p. 248)**

9. Containment theory was developed by Howard Becker. **(False, p. 249)**

10. According to Reckless, society provides individuals with meaningful roles and activities, which are an important factor in inner containment. **(False, p. 249)**

11. A perceived reward that may be offered by crime is an external containment. **(False, p. 249)**

12. Delinquent behavior may enhance self-esteem. **(True, p. 252)**

13. Gottfredson and Hirschi's theory is based on a rational choice perspective. **(True, p. 253)**

14. A control surplus is frequently seen in cases of white collar crime. **(True, p. 254)**

15. Deviance engendered by a control deficit usually takes the form of decadence and exploitation. **(False, p. 254)**

16. Secondary deviance is usually undertaken to solve an immediate problem or to meet the expectations of one's subcultural group. **(False, p. 255)**

17. Essentially, labeling theory denies the concept of *male in se*. **(True, p. 255)**

18. According to labeling theory, no act is intrinsically deviant. **(True, p. 255)**

19. Throughout an individual's criminal career, s/he increasingly exhibits deviant behavior out of choice. **(False, p. 256)**

20. According to labeling theory, deviance is the result of social processes involving the imposition of definitions. **(True, p. 256)**

21. According to labeling theory, negative self images precede delinquency. **(False, p. 256)**

22. A secret deviant is not guilty but has still been labeled deviant. **(False, p. 256)**

23. Only about half of the states in the United States have laws that hamper the ability of former offenders to reenter society. **(False, p. 256)**

24. The concept of reintegrative shaming emphasizes stigmatization and amplification of deviance. **(False, p. 257)**

25. According to Goffman, dramatic realization occurs when impression management has been successful. **(True, p. 258)**

26. Preliminary results from JUMP suggest that while adult mentors were very positive, youth participants were negative when rating the mentoring experience. **(False, p. 259)**

27. Labeling theory does not focus on secret deviants. **(True, p. 260)**

28. According to theories of social development, a critical transitional period occurs as a person moves from childhood to adulthood. **(True, p. 261)**

29. Criminality is relatively common during childhood. **(False, p. 262)**

30. Offenders with long criminal careers usually commit serious crimes. **(False, p. 262)**

31. Deceleration involves a reduction in the variety of offending. **(False, p. 263)**

32. Early research conducted by Sheldon and Eleanor Glueck concluded that delinquent careers rarely carried over into adulthood. **(False, p. 264)**

33. Turning points can occur at any time in the life course. **(True, p. 264)**

34. Individuals with a history of conventional behavior will not begin offending in response to turning points. **(False, p. 265)**

35. Unaided desistance is also known as rehabilitation. **(False, p. 266)**

36. Specialization involves a reduction in the variety of offenses. **(True, p. 267)**

37. Thornberry sees delinquency as a process that unfolds over the life course. **(True, p. 267)**

38. Children who do not develop adequate verbal coping skills are more likely to commit aggressive acts. **(True, p. 270)**

39. Independence is the final developmental task necessary for successful prosocial development during childhood and adolescence. **(True, p. 270)**

40. The first step on the covert pathway to delinquency is minor aggression such as bullying. **(False, p. 271)**

41. Simultaneous progression along multiple pathways to delinquency leads to higher rates of delinquency. **(True, p. 271)**

42. Social development theories have been criticized for definitional issues. **(True, p. 276)**

## Fill in the Blank

43. Sutherland's theory of differential association has a total of _________ principles. **(nine, p. 247)**

44. Burgess and Akers added the concept of _________ to Sutherland's original idea of differential association. **(reinforcement, p. 247)**

45. Glaser suggests that identification with _________ offers the possibility of rehabilitation. **(noncriminals, p. 249)**

46. According to Reckless, _________ containments are more important in preventing law violations. **(inner, p. 249)**

47. The _________ element of the social bond refers to the person's shared interests with others. **(attachment, p. 252)**

48. According to Hirschi, a _________ has little or no attachment to society. **(psychopath, p. 253)**

49. The idea that keeping a person busy with legitimate pursuits reduces opportunity for crime and deviance refers to the _________ aspect of the social bond. **(involvement, p. 253)**

50. Charles Tittle proposed _________ theory. **(control-balance, p. 253)**

51. The _________ is the amount of control to which a person is subject versus the amount of control that person exerts over others. **(control ratio, p. 254)**

52. According to Tittle, people with a control _________ can exercise a lot of control over others. **(surplus, p. 254)**

53. Frank Tannenbaum popularized the term _________ to describe what happens to offenders following processing through the criminal justice system. **(tagging, p. 254)**

54. Tannenbaum used the term _________ to explain the process by which an offender comes to be seen as ultimately and irrevocably "bad." **(dramatization of evil, p. 255)**

55. _________ deviance may be undertaken to solve an immediate problem. **(Primary, p. 255)**

56. The name most often associated with labeling theory is __________. **(Howard Becker, p. 255)**

57. A criminal who is caught in the act of committing a crime and who is then convicted and punished for the offense is an example of a(n) __________ deviant. **(pure, p. 256)**

58. A(n) __________ deviant violates social norms but does not encounter any negative societal reactions. **(secret, p. 256)**

59. The __________ approach involves an emotionally intense meeting between offenders and victims, and supporters for both. **(diversionary conferencing, p. 257)**

60. __________ shaming destroys the moral bond between the offender and the community. **(Stigmatic, p. 257)**

61. __________ shaming condemns the crime but not the criminal. **(Reintegrative, p. 257)**

62. A(n) __________ is a facility from which people can come and go and in which communal life is circumscribed. **(total institution, p. 259)**

63. The __________ perspective suggests that development occurs primarily with a social context. **(social development, p. 261)**

64. The __________ dimension of a criminal career refers to the fraction of the population that is criminally active. **(participation, p. 262)**

65. __________ refers to the length of the criminal career. **(Duration, p. 262)**

66. A __________ is a pathway or line of development through life which is marked by a sequence of transitions. **(trajectory, p. 263)**

67. Age grading is also known as __________. **(age differentiation, p. 263)**

68. The __________ type of activation involves an increased frequency of offending over time. **(acceleration, p. 263)**

69. __________ involves a reduction in the seriousness of offending. **(Deescalation, p. 263)**

70. The concept of __________ refers to the fact that human lives are typically embedded in social relationships with family and friends. **(linked lives, p. 263)**

71. Elder's principle of __________ suggests that individuals construct their own life course through the choices they make. **(human agency, p. 264)**

72. Sampson and Laub consider the two most significant turning points to center on employment and __________. **(marriage, p. 265)**

73. Laub and Sampson's concept of __________ refers to the degree of positive relationships with other persons and with social institutions that people build up over the course of their lives. **(social capital, p. 265)**

74. According to Moffitt, __________ display constant patterns of misbehavior throughout life. **(life course persisters, p. 265)**

75. Moffit suggests that __________ offenders are led to offending primarily by structural disadvantages such as status anxiety. **(adolescence-limited p. 265)**

76. According to Moffit, a(n) __________ occurs because biological maturity occurs before society permits the assumption of autonomous adult roles. **(maturity gap, p. 266)**

77. Marvin Wolfgang described the desistance phenonenon as __________. **(spontaneous remission, p. 266)**

78. The __________ component of desistance involves a slowing down in the frequency of offending. **(deceleration, p. 267)**

79. Life course researchers usually use longitudinal research designs involving __________ analysis. **(cohort, p. 267)**

80. The __________ perspective on crime control was pioneered by Lawrence Cohen and Richard Machalek. **(ecological, p. 267)**

81. The first step on the overt pathway to delinquency occurs around age __________. **(11 or 12, p. 270)**

## Multiple Choice

82. Social __________ theories assume that everyone has the potential to violate the law.
    a. development
    b. **process (p. 245)**
    c. structure
    d. disorganization

83. Which of the following is *not* considered to be one of the most important groups contributing to the process of socialization, according to social process theories?
    a. Family
    b. **Acquaintances (p. 245)**
    c. Work groups
    d. Peers

84. According to learning theory, criminal behavior is
    a. **a product of the social environment. (p. 247)**
    b. an innate characteristic of particular people.
    c. present as a genetic predisposition.
    d. none of the above

85. Edwin Sutherland developed
    a. dramaturgy.
    b. societal reaction theory.
    c. **differential association theory. (p. 247)**
    d. differential identification theory.

86. According to differential association theory, criminal behavior is
    a. inherited.
    b. **learned. (p. 247)**
    c. a function of culture conflict.
    d. none of the above

87. Burgess and Akers developed
    a. differential association theory.
    b. **differential association-reinforcement theory. (p. 247)**
    c. differential identification theory.
    d. none of the above

88. The idea that the behaviors of others are observed and modeled is the basis of which of Akers' primary learning mechanisms?
    a. **Imitation (p. 248)**
    b. Differential reinforcement
    c. Instrumental conditioning
    d. Differential identification

89. Differential identification theory was developed by
    a. Ronald Akers.
    b. Edwin Sutherland.
    c. **Daniel Glaser. (p. 248)**
    d. Howard B. Kaplan.

90. Rather than focusing on factors which cause criminal behavior, __________ theories examine factors that keep people from committing crimes.
    a. subcultural
    b. **social control (p. 249)**
    c. strain
    d. differential opportunity

91. According to containment theory, a positive self-image is an important __________ containment.
    a. outer
    b. **inner (p. 249)**
    c. external
    d. personal

92. Self-derogation theory was developed by
    a. Daniel Glaser.
    b. **Howard Kaplan (p. 252)**
    c. Walter Reckless.
    d. Robert Sampson.

93. Social bond theory postulates that
    a. crime occurs when there is a disparity between societal goals and the legitimate means available to reach those goals.
    b. criminal behavior is learned in the same way any other type of behavior is learned.
    c. **crime occurs when a person's links to society are weakened or broken, thus reducing the likelihood of conformity. (p. 252)**
    d. crime occurs because the criminal justice system stigmatizes individuals, forcing them into a deviant lifestyle.

94. The __________ element of a social bond refers to the amount of energy and effort put into activities with other people.
    a. attachment
    b. belief
    c. **commitment (p. 252)**
    d. involvement

95. The __________ element of a social bond refers to a shared value and moral system.
    a. attachment
    b. **belief (p. 252)**
    c. commitment
    d. involvement

96. According to Gottfredson and Hirschi's general theory of crime, the key concept in explaining all forms of criminal behavior is
    a. social bonds.
    b. **self-control. (p. 253)**
    c. sensitivity.
    d. intelligence.

97. Which of the following crimes would probably *not* be committed by an individual with a control deficit?
    a. **Exploitation (p. 254)**
    b. Sexual assault
    c. Submission
    d. Vandalism

98. According to Becker, deviance is
    a. **created by society. (p. 255)**
    b. an innate characteristic of certain individuals.
    c. an intrinsic characteristic of some behaviors.
    d. none of the above

99. The Women's Christian Temperance Union is an early example of
    a. tagging.
    b. labeling.
    c. **moral enterprise. (p. 255)**
    d. reintegrative shaming.

100. Once an individual is labeled "deviant," opportunities for conforming behavior are
    a. seriously increased.
    b. slightly increased.
    c. **seriously reduced. (p. 256)**
    d. slightly reduced.

101. According to Becker's typology, a person who is punished for a crime he or she did not commit is a(n) __________ deviant.
    a. pure
    b. secret
    c. **falsely accused (p. 256)**
    d. innocent

102. The dramaturgical perspective was developed by
    a. Howard Becker.
    b. Edwin Lemert.
    c. **Erving Goffman. (p. 258)**
    d. Ronald Akers.

103. Which of the following programs is based on concepts basic to social process theories?
    a. OJJDP's Comprehensive Strategy Program
    b. Targeted Outreach
    c. Mobilization for Youth
    d. **OJJDP's Juvenile Mentoring Program (p. 259)**

104. Which of the following is *not* a criticism of differential association theory?
    a. The theory may not be applicable at the individual level
    b. The theory does not account for the emergence of criminal values, only their communication
    c. **The theory does not explain the origin of crime and deviance (p. 260)**
    d. The theory is not a sufficient explanation for crime

105. Life course criminology was given its name in a seminal book written by
    a. Michael Gottfredson and Travis Hirschi.
    b. Sheldon and Eleanor Glueck.
    c. **Robert Sampson and John Laub. (p. 262)**
    d. Terrie E. Moffitt.

106. Which of the following is *not* one of the three types of activation that are possible?
    a. Acceleration
    b. Diversification
    c. Stabilization
    d. **Desistance (p. 263)**

107. The dynamic process of __________ refers to the existence of a developmental sequence of activities that increase in seriousness over time.
    a. **activation (p. 263)**
    b. duration
    c. activation
    d. desistance

108. Elder's principle of __________ refers to the fact that the developmental impact of a succession of life transitions is contingent on when in a person's life they occur.
    a. linked lives
    b. human agency
    c. **timing in lives (p. 264)**
    d. historical time and place

109. The __________ theory was developed by Laub and Sampson.
    a. **age-graded (p. 264)**
    b. dual taxonomic
    c. delinquent development
    d. evolutionary ecology

110. The concept of turning points in a criminal career was first identified by
    a. Sheldon and Eleanor Glueck.
    b. **G.B. Trasler. (p. 264)**
    c. Terrie E. Moffitt.
    d. Richard Machalek.

111. Which of the following factors would *not* enhance a person's social capital?
    a. Education
    b. Getting married
    c. **Losing a job (p. 265)**
    d. Having a "clean" record

112. The __________ theory was developed by Terrie E. Moffitt.
    a. age-graded
    b. **dual taxonomic (p. 265)**
    c. delinquent development
    d. evolutionary ecology

113. The dual taxonomic theory of criminality identifies ________ paths to criminality.
   a. **two (p. 265)**
   b. three
   c. four
   d. five

114. According to Moffit's theory, which of the following is *not* a positive outcome of the developmental process?
   a. Competency
   b. Connectedness
   c. Control
   d. **Cohort (p. 266)**

115. Farrington and West found that offending tends to peak around age
   a. 13.
   b. **17. (p. 267)**
   c. 25.
   d. 35.

116. The __________ component of desistance involves a reduction in the seriousness of offending
   a. deceleration
   b. **deescalation (p. 267)**
   c. reaching a ceiling
   d. specialization

117. Terence Thornberry developed __________ theory.
   a. age-graded
   b. delinquent development
   c. **interactional (p. 267)**
   d. dual taxonomic

118. Which of the following is *not* one of the preliminary results of the Causes and Correlates of Delinquency Program?
   a. Delinquency is related to individual risk factors such as impulsivity.
   b. **Being on welfare is associated with a fairly low risk of delinquency. (p. 270)**
   c. A lack of commitment to school is associated with higher involvement in delinquency.
   d. Serious involvement in drugs is related to serious involvement in delinquency.

119. According to the Causes and Correlates of Delinquency Program research, the __________ pathway to delinquency begins with behaviors such as frequent lying or shoplifting around age 10.
   a. overt
   b. authority conflict
   c. multiple disruption
   d. **covert (p. 270)**

120. PHDCN is using a(n) __________ research design to study the development of criminal behavior.
   a. experimental
   b. quasi-experimental
   c. **longitudinal (p. 271)**
   d. participant observation

121. The primary goal of the __________ program is to provide a positive alternative to gangs for at-risk youth.
   a. Comprehensive Strategy
   b. PDHDCN
   c. JUMP
   d. **Targeted Outreach (p. 276)**

# Word Search Puzzle

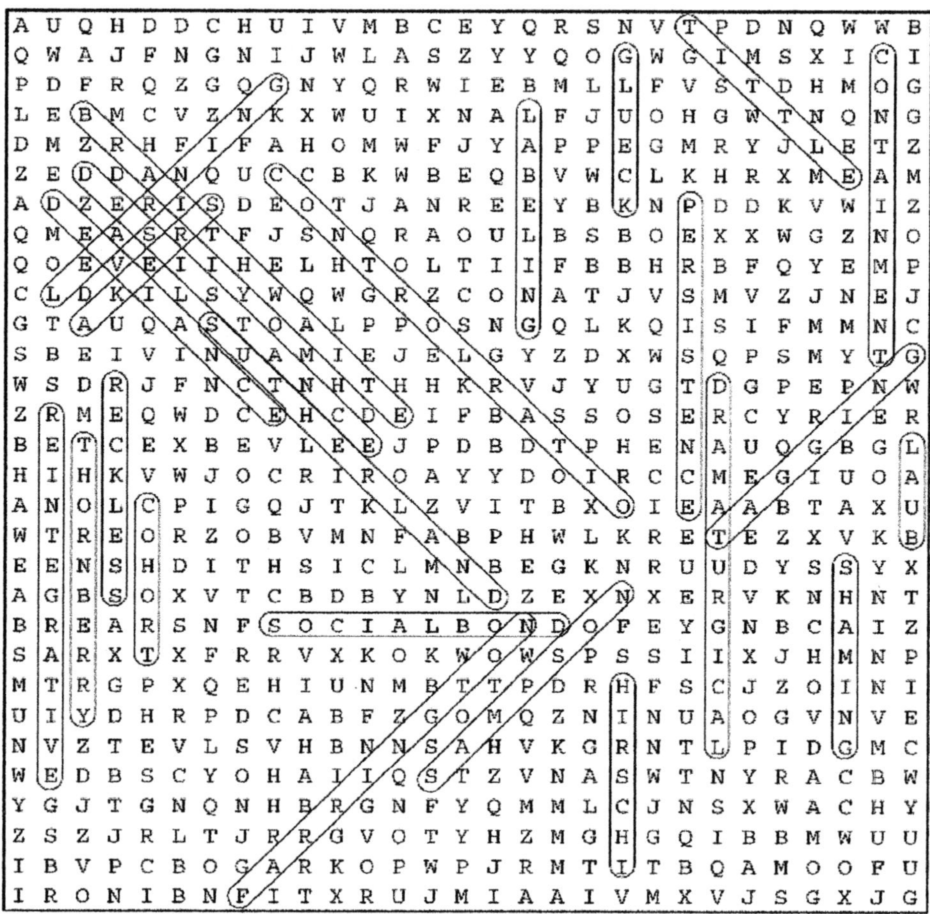

Akers

Braithwaite
Cohort
Containment
Control ratio
Desistance
Deviance
Dramaturgical
Farrington
Glueck
Hirschi
Labeling

Laub
Learning
Persistence
Reckless
Reintegrative
Sampson
Shaming
Social bond
Sutherland
Tagging
Thornberry
Tittle

# Crossword Puzzle

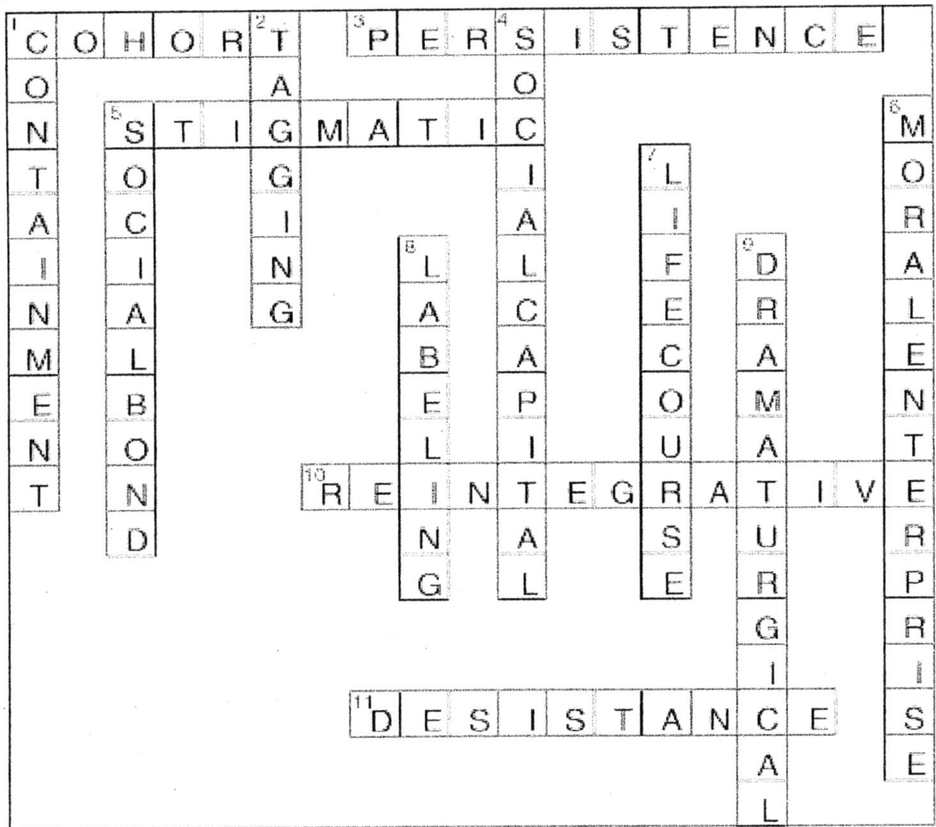

## Across

1. A group of individuals sharing common social characteristics.
3. Continual involvement in offending.
5. A form of shaming that destroys the moral bond between the offender and the community.
10. A form of shaming that strengthens the moral bond between the offender and the community.
11. The cessation of criminal activity.

## Down

1. A theory suggesting that internal and external factors contribute to law-abiding behavior.
2. The process whereby an individual is negatively defined by agencies of justice.
4. The degree of positive relationships with others that individuals build up over the course of their lives. (2 words)
5. The link between individuals and the society of which they are a part. (2 words)
6. Efforts made by an interest group to have its sense of ethical propriety enacted into law. (2 words)
7. Pathways through the age-differentiated life span. (2 words)
8. The process by which one is negatively defined by agencies of justice.
9. A perspective that sees behavior as centered around the purposeful management of interpersonal impressions.

# Sociological Theories III: Social Conflict

## Learning Objectives

After reading this chapter, students should be able to:

1. Recognize the ways in which power conflict between social groups contributes to crime and criminal activity
2. Understand the distinctions between a number of social conflict theories
3. Identify those social policy initiatives that reflect the social conflict approach
4. Assess the shortcomings of the social conflict perspective

## Chapter Outline

Introduction
Law and Social Order Perspectives
- *The Consensus Perspective*
- *The Pluralist Perspective*
- *The Conflict Perspective*

Radical Criminology
- *Critical Criminology*
- *Radical–Critical Criminology and Policy Issues*
- *Critique of Radical–Critical Criminology*

Emerging Conflict Theories
- *Left-Realist Criminology*
- *Feminist Criminology*
- *Postmodern Criminology*
- *Peacemaking Criminology*

Policy Implications of Social Conflict Theories

# Chapter Summary

This chapter begins with a discussion of three analytical perspectives: consensus, pluralist, and conflict. The consensus perspective is based on the premise that most members of society agree on what is right and wrong and share a set of core values. This perspective assumes that the criminal law reflects the collective will of the people and serves everyone equally, and believes that criminals are unique. The pluralistic perspective assumes that there is a variety of different viewpoints, values, and beliefs, but that most individuals agree on the usefulness of law as a formal means of dispute resolution, so that the law is a peace-keeping tool used to resolve conflict. The conflict perspective holds that there is no consensus on what is right and wrong, that conflict is a fundamental aspect of social life, and that the law is a tool of the powerful that is used to maintain their power.

The conflict perspective is based on the writings of Karl Marx, who believed that conflict was inevitable in any capitalist society. The six key elements of the conflict perspective are outlined and the concept of social class, a topic central to the conflict perspective, is discussed. Other early conflict theorists include George Vold, who described crime as the result of political conflict between groups, Ralf Dahrendorf, who considered conflict to be a normal part of any society, and Austin Turk, who considered crime a natural consequence of intergroup conflict.

Modern radical criminology suggests that crime causes are rooted in social conditions empowering the wealthy and politically well-organized and disenfranchising those less fortunate. William Chambliss, a modern radical thinker, emphasizes the power gap between the powerful and powerless as helping to create crime. Richard Quinney outlined six Marxist principles for an understanding of crime. He stated that crime is inevitable under capitalist conditions and that the problem of crime can only be solved by the development of a socialized society.

A distinction is made between critical criminology, which is a way of critiquing social relationships that lead to crime, and radical criminology, which is a proactive call for radical change in the social conditions leading to crime. Most modern radical-critical criminologists focus on promoting a gradual transition to socialized forms of government activity. Critiques of radical-critical criminology include its overemphasis on methods at the expense of well-developed theory, its failure to recognize the existence of a fair degree of public consensus about the nature of crime, and its inability to explain low crime rates in some capitalist countries or the problems existing in communist countries.

There are a variety of new innovative conflict theories. Left-realist criminology portrays crime in terms understandable to those most affected by it, shifting the focus to a pragmatic assessment of crime and the needs of victims. Key scholars include Walter DeKeseredy and Jock Young. A key principle of left realism is that radical ideas must be translated into realistic social policies. Critiques of left-realist criminology include the claim that it represents more of an ideological emphasis than a theory and the belief that realist criminologists build upon existing theoretical frameworks but rarely offer new testable propositions or hypotheses. Feminist criminology attempts to include gender awareness in the thinking of mainstream criminologists, pointing out inequities inherent in patriarchal forms of thought. Early researchers include Freda Adler and Rita J. Simon, who suggested that gender differences in crime rates were due to socialization, not biology. However, despite increased gender equality, the criminal behavior of men and women has not become more similar. Key contemporary theorists include Kathleen Daly and Meda Chesney-

Lind, who are concerned about androcentricity in criminology. There are several schools of feminist thought, including radical feminism, liberal feminism, and social feminism, as well as a perspective developed by women of color emphasizing feminism's sensitivity to the interplay of gender, class, and race oppression. John Hagan developed power-control theory, which suggests that the social distribution of criminality is passed on by the family. Modern feminist thinkers suggest social policies such as increasing controls over male violence towards women, creating alternatives for women facing abuse, and the protection of children. Critiques of feminist theory suggest that it may be a theory in formation, rather than a completely developed theory of crime. Some critics argue that a feminist criminology is impossible, although feminist thought may inform criminology.

Postmodern criminology applies understandings of social change inherent in postmodern philosophy to criminological theorizing and to issues of crime control. Much is deconstructionist, challenging existing criminological perspectives and working toward replacing them with perspectives more relevant to the postmodern era. Two key postmodern criminologists are Stuart Henry and Dragan Milovanovic, who focus on constitutive criminology, claiming that crime and crime control are constructions produced through a social process involving the offender, victim, and society and stating that crime should be understood as an integral part of society. Critics of postmodern theory claim that the terminology is vaguely defined and the approaches are often incoherent and confusing, and that postmodernism challenges traditional theories but fails to offer viable alternatives for crime prevention and control. Peacemaking criminology is a new form of postmodernism that suggests citizens and social control agencies need to work together to alleviate social problems and reduce crime. Key theorists include Harold Pepinsky and Richard Quinney, who suggest the problem of crime control is not "how to stop crime" but rather "how to make peace." Peacemaking emphasizes a peace model of crime control, focusing on ways of developing a shared consensus on critical issues such as crime. Programs such as dispute resolution are based on the participatory justice principle. Restorative justice is a social movement stressing healing over retribution. Peacemaking criminology has been criticized as being naive and utopian and for failing to recognize the realities of crime control and law enforcement.

Social conflict theory suggests that reducing conflict will lead to a reduction in crime rates. The various schools of thought have different views of how to reduce conflict, ranging from the use of conflict resolution to the replacement of the existing capitalist system with a socialist economic structure.

# Lecture Outline

I. Introduction: discuss the case of Theodore Kaczynski, the "Unabomber," and the possible motivations for his actions

II. Law and Social Order Perspectives
   A. Explain how Kaczynski's idealism resembled European thought during the mid- to late-1800s
      1. Karl Marx and Friedrich Engels wrote *The Communist Manifesto* in 1848 suggesting that communism was going to replace capitalism
      2. Communism came to represent a totalitarian system in which one political party controls the government, which in turn owns the means of production

and distributes wealth with the professed aim of establishing a classless society

3. Three key analytical perspectives in criminology emphasize an understanding of the relationship between law and social order and how social conflict affects criminality:
   a. The consensus perspective
   b. The pluralist perspective
   c. The conflict perspective

B. The consensus perspective (refer back to the discussion in Chapter 1)
1. The consensus model is based on the assumption that most members of society agree on right and wrong and that the various elements of society work together toward a shared view of the greater good
2. Raymond J. Michalowski identified the four main principles characterizing the consensus perspective:
   a. A belief in the existence of core values
   b. The notion that the law reflects the collective will of the people
   c. The assumption that the law serves everyone equally
   d. The idea that criminals represent a unique subgroup with some distinguishing features
3. The consensus perspective characterized social scientific thought in the United States throughout much of the early 1900s
   a. Roscoe Pound, legal scholar, suggested that the law is a tool for engineering society and can be used to fashion society's characteristics and major features
   b. Discuss Pound's five jural postulates

C. The pluralist perspective
1. Despite the assumptions of consensus thinkers, it appears that not everyone agrees on what the law should say
   a. Modern society involves conflicting values and ideals (abortion, euthanasia, death penalty, social justice, etc.)
   b. There are many social groups, each with a separate agenda and a different point of view regarding right and wrong
2. The pluralist perspective suggests that there are many different values and beliefs in any complex society and that each social group will have its own set of beliefs, values, and interests
   a. A key assumption is that although different viewpoints exist, most people agree on the usefulness of law as a formal means of dispute resolution
   b. The law is a peacekeeping tool used to settle disputes
3. The basic principles of the pluralistic perspective
   a. Society consists of many and diverse social groups
   b. Each group has its own set of values, beliefs, and interests
   c. A general agreement exists as to the usefulness of formalized laws as a mechanism for dispute resolution
   d. The legal system is value neutral
   e. The legal system is concerned with the best interests of society
4. The pluralistic perspective suggests that conflict is resolved through the peacekeeping activities of unbiased government officials exercising objective legal authority

D. The conflict perspective

**Show the ABC News program *The Clinic — Living under Siege* from the video library.**

1. This perspective suggests that conflict is a fundamental aspect of social life that cannot be fully resolved
   a. Formal social control agencies coerce the unempowered to comply with rules established by those in power
   b. The law is a tool of the powerful used to keep control of social institutions
   c. Social order rests on the exercise of power through law - those in power work to remain there
2. One of the best known writers on social conflict was Karl Marx
   a. According to Marx, there are two main social classes within any capitalist society
      (1) The proletariat is the working class, who are without power and must earn a living by selling their labor (the "have-nots")
      (2) The bourgeoisie are the capitalists or wealthy owners of the means of production (the "haves")
   b. These groups are engaged in ongoing conflict or class struggle: according to Marx, the natural outcome of this struggle would be the overthrow of the capitalist social order and the birth of a communistic (classless) society
3. Willem Bonger described the ongoing struggle between the haves and the have-nots as a natural consequence of a capitalist society and said that in capitalist societies only those without power are routinely subject to the criminal law
4. The six key elements of the conflict perspective are that:
   a. Society is made up of diverse social groups
   b. Each group holds to differing definitions of right and wrong
   c. Conflict between groups is unavoidable
   d. The fundamental nature of group conflict centers on the exercise of political power
   e. Law is a tool of power and furthers the interests of those powerful enough to make it
   f. Those in power are inevitably interested in maintaining their power against those who would usurp it
5. A key element of radical criminology is the concept of social class, which usually involves distinctions made between individuals on the basis of significant defining characteristics (race, religion, profession, income, wealth, housing, etc.)
   a. Most social scientists consider there to be at least three classes: upper, middle, and lower
   b. Some have distinguished between five classes, which are further subdivided according to ascribed characteristics like race and religion
6. George Vold saw crime as the result of political conflict between groups and as a natural expression of the struggle for power and control

a. He considered conflict to be a universal form of interaction that intensifies the loyalty of group members to their respective groups
b. Vold stated that the process of law making, law breaking, and law enforcement reflects conflicts between interest groups
(1) Powerful groups make laws that express and protect their interests
(2) Law is a political statement, and crime is a political definition imposed on those whose interests do not lie with what the powerful define as acceptable
c. Crime is seen as a manifestation of needs and values denied by society
7. Ralf Dahrendorf saw conflict as a fundamental part of society, so that an absence of conflict would be abnormal
a. Power and authority lead to conflict between groups, and conflict leads to either destructive or constructive change
b. Destructive change lessens social order whereas constructive change increases social cohesiveness
8. Austin Turk saw the law as a tool serving social groups seeking control over others and saw crime as the natural consequence of intergroup struggles because it resulted from the definitions imposed by the laws of the powerful upon the disapproved strivings of the unempowered

III. Radical Criminology
A. Introduction
1. The conflict perspective is based in radical criminology, also known as new, critical, or Marxist criminology
2. It developed out of thee historical circumstances
a. The 19th century social utopian thinkers (Marx, Engels, Hegel, Bonger, Weber, etc.)
b. The rise of conflict theory in the social sciences
c. The radicalization of American academia in the 1960s and 1970s
3. Contemporary radical criminology suggests that the causes of crime are rooted in social conditions empowering the wealthy and politically well organized while disenfranchising the less fortunate
4. William Chambliss states that what makes a behavior criminal is the coercive power of the state to enforce the will of the ruling class
a. In 1971, Chambliss and Robert T. Seidman published *Law, Order, and Power*, which helped to bridge conflict and radical theories
(1) They stated that the more economically stratified a society becomes, the more necessary it is for dominant groups to enforce through coercion the conduct norms that guarantee their dominance
(2) Their position is outlined in four main propositions:
(a) The conditions of one's life affect one's values and norms
(b) Complex societies are therefore composed of highly disparate and conflicting sets of norms
(c) The probability of a given group having its particular normative system embodied in law is not equally distributed but is related to the group's political and economic position
(d) The higher the group's political or economic position, the greater the probability that its views will be reflected in laws
(3) Chambliss also stated that middle- and upper-class criminals are less likely to be apprehended and punished by the criminal justice system

  b. By 1975, Chambliss's work had become more Marxist and suggested that socialist societies would have less crime than capitalist societies because of less intense class struggles
5. Richard Quinney is one of the most influential radical criminologists
  a. He set forth six key Marxist propositions:
    (1) American society is based on an advanced capitalist economy
    (2) The state is organized to serve the interests of a capitalist ruling class
    (3) Criminal law is a tool of the state and ruling class to maintain and perpetuate the existing social and economic order
    (4) Crime control in a capitalist society is accomplished through institutions and agencies administered by a governmental elite, representing the interests of the ruling class
    (5) The contradictions of advanced capitalism require the oppression of the subordinate classes by any necessary means, including the coercion and violence of the legal system
    (6) The crime problem will be solved only if capitalist society is eliminated and a socialist society established instead
  b. Quinney suggests that lower-class crimes are necessary for the survival of the members of those classes and that crime is inevitable in a capitalist society
  c. His solution to the problem of crime is the development of a socialist society
6. Modern radical criminology is divided into two schools:
  a. Structural Marxism sees capitalism as a self-maintaining system in which the law and justice systems work to perpetuate the existing system of power relationships
  b. Instrumental Marxism sees the criminal law and justice system as tools used by the powerful to control the poor

B. Critical criminology
1. Critical criminology is sometimes distinguished from radical criminology
  a. Critical criminology is a way of critiquing social relationships that lead to crime
  b. Radical criminology is a proactive call for radical change in the social conditions leading to crime
2. Elliott Currie's work is an example of the critical perspective in contemporary criminology
  a. Currie claims that market societies are especially likely to have high levels of violent crime because the striving after personal economic gain becomes paramount
  b. Discuss the seven mechanisms that Currie says operate in a market society to produce crime:
    (1) The progressive destruction of livelihood
    (2) The growth of extremes of economic inequality and material deprivation
    (3) The withdrawal of public services and supports
    (4) The erosion of informal and communal networks of mutual support, supervision, and care
    (5) The spread of a materialistic, neglectful, and "hard" culture
    (6) The unregulated marketing of the technology of violence
    (7) The weakening of social and political alternatives

c. Currie predicts that as more countries copy America's market society culture, crime rates will rise and there will be more emphasis on punishment and the growth of large prison systems worldwide

C. Radical–critical criminology and policy issues

1. Most radical-critical criminologists are focusing on promoting a gradual transition to socialism and socialized forms of government activity
2. Middle-range policy alternatives include equal justice in the bail system, abolishing mandatory sentences, prosecuting corporate crimes, reducing prison overcrowding, increasing equality within criminal justice system employment, etc.
3. The emphasis is on creating economic equality or employment opportunities as a way of combating crime

D. Critique of radical–critical criminology

1. The field emphasizes methods of social change at the expense of well-developed theory
2. It fails to recognize that there seems to be a fair degree of consensus about the nature of crime: crime is undesirable and criminal activity should be controlled
3. Marxist thinkers seem to confuse issues of personal politics with social reality, thus sacrificing their objectivity
4. Marxist criminology does not seem to appreciate the many problems contributing to the problem of crime
5. Discuss Carl Klockars' classic critique of radical criminology
   a. Marxist criminology does not explain the low crime rates in some capitalist countries (e.g., Japan) or address the problems of communist countries with poor records of human rights
   b. He stated that Marxist criminology resembled a religion more than a science, since criminologists were unwilling to examine their beliefs objectively
6. The collapse of the former Soviet Union contributed to a loss of prestige and impact of Marxist criminology

IV. Emerging Conflict Theories

A. Left-realist criminology

1. Realist criminology portrays crime in terms understandable to those most affected by it
   a. It criticizes radical–critical criminology for romanticizing street crime and criminals and for falsely seeing street criminals as political resistors in an oppressive capitalist society
   b. It shifts the focus onto a pragmatic assessment of crime and the needs of victims
2. Realist criminology is generally considered synonymous with left realism, also known as "radical realism" or "critical realism"
3. Key scholars include Walter DeKeseredy in North America and Jock Young in England
   a. They refocused leftist theories onto the serious consequences of street crime and on lower-class crime
   b. They argue that victims are often the poor and disenfranchised
   c. The criminal justice system is seen as consisting of institutions that could offer useful services if modifications were made to reduce the use of force and increase sensitivity

4. A key principle of left realism is that radical ideas must be translated into realistic social policies
5. Critique of left-realist criminology
   a. It represents more of an ideological emphasis than a theory
   b. Realist criminologists build upon existing theoretical frameworks but rarely offer new testable propositions or hypotheses
6. Realist criminologists tend to suggest crime control policies that focus on the needs of the victimized (e.g., community policing, neighborhood justice centers, dispute resolution) rather than on punitive measures

B. Feminist criminology
1. This is a model intended to redirect the thinking of mainstream criminologists to include gender awareness
   a. It points out inequities inherent in patriarchal (male dominated) forms of thought
   b. Traditional criminology has been male-centered, with women largely ignored by criminologists
2. Early researchers include Freda Adler and Rita J. Simon, who both published books on feminist criminology in 1975
   a. They suggested that gender differences in crime rates were due to socialization rather than biology
   b. As gender equality increased, they said the criminal behavior of men and women would become more similar
   c. However, despite increased gender equality in the past 30 years, this has not happened
3. Two key contemporary theorists are Kathleen Daly and Meda Chesney-Lind, who state that gender differences bring into question traditional assumptions about crime, especially that it is a normal part of social life
4. Feminist thinking combines a female mental perspective with a sensitivity for social issues that primarily influence women
   a. A key principle is that feminism views gender in terms of power relationships
   b. According to feminist approaches, men traditionally have held more power in society, creating a patriarchal social structure that excluded women from much decision making and perpetuated gender inequality
5. There are several schools of feminist thought:
   a. Radical feminism sees men as aggressive and violent individuals who control women through sexuality; this view suggests that eliminating male domination should reduce crime rates for women
   b. Liberal feminists blame gender inequities on the development of separate areas of influence and traditional attitudes about the roles of men and women; they suggest that eliminating traditional divisions of labor and power would eliminate inequity
   c. Socialist feminists see gender oppression as a result of the economic structure of society and suggest that a socialist society would eliminate gender and class divisions
   d. A fourth alternative framework developed by women of color emphasizes feminism's sensitivity to the interplay of gender, class, and race oppression
6. John Hagan developed an approach known as power control theory, which suggests that the family passes on gender relations and the social distribution of criminality

a. In a paternalistic model of family dynamics, common in most middle- and upper-middle-class families, the father works and the mother cares for the children
b. Boys are less closely controlled than girls and are relatively free to deviate from social norms, resulting in higher levels of male delinquency
c. In lower-middle- and lower-class families, the paternalistic model is less common, resulting in less gender socialization and more female delinquency

7. Much current feminist thought emphasizes the need for gender awareness in criminological theory design, so that theories of crime causation can apply to both men and women
   a. Some researchers have asked whether theories of male crime apply to women
   b. Others study the process by which laws are made, suggesting that the criminal law represents traditionally male ways of organizing the social world
8. Feminist thinkers suggest social policies such as increasing controls over male violence toward women, creating alternatives for women facing abuse, and for the protection of children
9. Critique of feminist theory
   a. It may be a theory in formation rather than a completely developed theory of crime
   b. Although the gender gap in crime still exists, despite increasingly balanced opportunities, gender disparities in arrests are rarely found, nor do sentencing practices seem to favor women
   c. Some critics argue that a feminist criminology is impossible, although feminist thought may inform criminology

C. Postmodern criminology
1. Postmodern criminology applies understandings of social change inherent in postmodern philosophy to criminological theorizing and to issues of crime control
   a. It is a group of criminological perspectives bound together by the tone of postmodernism, including paradigms such as chaos theory, discourse analysis, topology theory, and anarchic criminology
   b. All postmodern criminologies build upon the idea that past approaches have failed to realistically assess the true causes of crime and to offer workable crime control solutions, or that if they have, the theories and solutions are no longer applicable to the postmodern era
   c. As a result, much postmodern criminology is deconstructionist
2. Deconstructionist theories challenge existing criminological perspectives and work toward replacing them with perspectives more relevant to the postmodern era
3. Two key postmodern criminologists are Stuart Henry and Dragan Milovanovic, who focus on constitutive criminology
   a. Their work claims that crime and crime control are constructions produced through a social process involving the offender, victim, and society
   b. They assert that people both shape and are shaped by their society, so the behaviors of offenders and victims cannot be understood outside their society

c. Milovanovic suggests the application of semiotics to the study of law, suggesting that everything we do, say, know, think, and feel is mediated through signs (e.g., the multiple meanings and interpretations of the term "mental illness")
d. Henry and Milovanovic suggest that crime should be understood as an integral part of society rather than something separate and apart from society

4. Critique of postmodern theory:
   a. The terminology is vaguely defined and the approaches are often incoherent and confusing
   b. Postmodernism challenges traditional theories but fails to offer feasible alternatives for crime prevention and control

D. Peacemaking criminology
   1. This is a relatively new form of postmodern criminology, suggesting that citizens and social control agencies need to work together to alleviate social problems and reduce crime
      a. Key theorists include Harold Pepinsky and Richard Quinney, who suggest that the problem of crime control is not "how to stop crime" but "how to make peace"
      b. Peacemaking criminology emphasizes rising above personal dichotomies to end the political and ideological divisiveness in society
   2. Restorative justice
      a. Peacemaking criminology emphasizes crime control through the adoption of a peace model based on cooperation rather than retribution
      b. The peace model of crime control focuses on effective ways for developing a shared consensus on critical issues such as crime
      c. Alternative dispute resolution programs such as mediation are characterized by cooperative efforts to resolve disputes rather than by adversarial proceedings
      d. Dispute resolution is based on the participatory justice principle in which all parties accept a form of binding arbitration by neutral parties
      e. The restorative justice movement, which stresses healing over retribution, is based on three principles:
         (1) Crime causes injury to victims, the community, and the offender
         (2) The criminal justice process should help repair those injuries
         (3) A protest of the government's apparent monopoly over social responses to crime
   3. Critique of peacemaking criminology
      a. It has been criticized as being naive and utopian and for failing to recognize the realities of crime control and law enforcement
      b. However, peacemaking criminology envisions positive change on the social and institutional level rather than suggesting that victims should try to effect personal changes in offenders

V. Policy Implications
   A. Social conflict theory suggests that reducing conflict will lead to a reduction in crime rates
   B. Various schools of thought have different views of how to reduce conflict
      1. Radical–Marxist criminologists argue that the only effective way is to replace the existing capitalist system with a socialist economic structure
      2. Peacemaking criminology calls for the use of conflict resolution

3. Left-realism and feminist criminology offer a variety of solutions ranging from reducing paternalism to recognizing the consequences of crime to victims

# Key Concepts

**Androcentricity**: A single-sex perspective, as in the case of criminologists who study only the criminality of males.

**Bourgeoisie**: In Marxian theory, the class of people who own the means of production.

**Conflict perspective:** An analytical perspective on social organization that holds that conflict is a fundamental aspect of social life itself and can never be fully resolved.

**Consensus model**: An analytical perspective on social organization that holds that most members of society agree about what is right and what is wrong and that the various elements of society work together in unison toward a common vision of the greater good.

**Critical criminology**: See **radical criminology**.

**Deconstructionist theory**: A postmodernist perspective that challenges existing criminological theories in order to debunk them and that works toward replacing traditional ideas with concepts seen as more appropriate to the postmodern era.

**Feminist criminology**: A self-conscious corrective model intended to redirect the thinking of mainstream criminologists to include gender awareness.

**Gender gap**: The observed differences between male and female rates of criminal offending in a given society, such as the United States.

**Instrumental Marxism**: A perspective that holds that those in power intentionally create laws and social institutions that serve their own interests and that keep others from becoming powerful.

**Left-realism**: A conflict perspective that insists on a pragmatic assessment of crime and its associated problems. Also called *realist criminology*.

**Left-realist criminology**: See **left realism**.

**Liberal feminism:** A perspective that holds that the concerns of women can be incorporated within existing social institutions through conventional means and without the need to drastically restructure society. Criminal laws, such as the Violence Against Women Act, for example, have been enacted in order to change the legal structure in such a way that it becomes responsive to women's issues.

**Marxist criminology**: See **radical criminology.**

**Participatory justice**: A relatively informal type of criminal justice case processing which makes use of local community resources rather than requiring traditional forms of official intervention.

**Patriarchy**: The tradition of male dominance

**Peacemaking criminology**: A perspective that holds that crime control agencies and the citizens they serve should work together to alleviate social problems and human suffering and thus reduce crime.

**Peace model**: An approach to crime control that focuses on effective ways for developing a shared consensus on critical issues which could seriously affect the quality of life.

**Pluralist perspective**: An analytical approach to social organization that holds that a multiplicity of values and beliefs exists in any complex society but that most social actors agree on the usefulness of law as a formal means of dispute resolution.

**Postmodern criminology**: A brand of criminology that developed following World War II and that builds on the tenets inherent in postmodern social thought.

**Power-control theory**: A perspective that holds that the distribution of crime and delinquency within society is to some degree founded upon the consequences which power relationships within the wider society hold for domestic settings and for the everyday relationships between men, women, and children within the context of family life.

**Proletariat**: In Marxist theory, the working class.

**Radical criminology**: A perspective that holds that the causes of crime are rooted in social conditions which empower the wealthy and the politically well organized but disenfranchise those less fortunate. Also called *critical criminology*; *Marxist criminology*.

**Radical feminism**: A perspective that holds that any significant change in the social status of women can be accomplished only through substantial changes in social institutions such as the family, law, and medicine. Radical feminism argues, for example, that the structure of current legal thinking involves what is fundamentally a male perspective, which should be changed to incorporate women's social experiences and points of view.

**Restorative justice**: A postmodern perspective that stresses "remedies and restoration rather than prison, punishment and victim neglect."

**Social class**: Distinctions made between individuals on the basis of important defining social characteristics.

**Socialist feminism**: A perspective that examines social roles and the gender-based division of labor within the family, seeing both as a significant source of women's subordination within society. This perspective calls for a redefinition of gender-related job status, compensation for women who work within the home, and equal pay for equal work regardless of gender.

**Structural Marxism**: A perspective that holds that the structural institutions of society influence the behavior of individuals and groups by virtue of the type of relationships created. The criminal law, for example, reflects class relationship and serves to reinforce those relationships.

# Additional Lecture Topics

One topic for discussion is to review Mark Colvin and John Pauly's integrated structural-Marxist theory, which is primarily a macro-level theory focusing on juvenile delinquency. Colvin and Pauly state that capitalism and the workplace structure create competition and produce differential attitudes toward authority. The key variables in their theory appear to be the social class of the parents and the level of coerciveness found in workplace social control. Parents experiencing coercive social control in the workplace bring those negative experiences home and employ them in the family structure, creating strain and alienation in their children. The conflict created in juveniles may be exacerbated by factors such as a coercive school environment and may lead them to choose to associate with peers who are similarly alienated, reinforcing the feelings of strain and alienation. If these peer groups emphasize deviant or violent behavior, the juvenile will be more likely to be drawn into delinquency. This theory includes not only a Marxist component, but also elements of social learning and opportunity theories. Note that Chambliss, in his critique of this theory, claims that Colvin and Pauly are assuming that juvenile delinquency is primarily a lower-class phenomenon.

Consider briefly discussing how current enforcement of laws against corporate and white-collar crimes (illegal restraint of trade, price fixing, false advertising, environmental pollution, insider trading, etc.) reflect the views of Marxist criminologists. Offenders frequently receive much more lenient punishments than those who commit street-level property crimes (e.g., theft, burglary).

# Discussion Questions

These discussion questions are found in the textbook at the end of the chapter. The instructor may want to focus on these questions during the coverage of Chapter 9.

1. This book emphasizes a social problems versus social responsibility theme. Which of the theoretical perspectives discussed in this chapter (if any) best support the social problems approach? Which (if any) support the social responsibility approach? Why?

2. Explain the differences among the consensus, pluralistic, and conflict perspectives. Which comes closest to your way of understanding society? Why?

3. What is Marxist criminology? How, if at all, does it differ from radical criminology? From critical criminology?

4. Does the Marxist perspective hold any significance for contemporary American society? Why?

5. What are the fundamental propositions of feminist criminology? How would feminists change the study of crime?

6. What does it mean to say that traditional theories of crime need to be "deconstructed"? What role does deconstructionist thinking play in postmodern criminology?

# Student Exercises

## Activity #1

Your instructor will place you into groups and assign you one of the radical–critical theories discussed in this chapter. Develop a crime reduction and/or prevention policy that is based on this theory. Explain how the theory justifies the policy and why you expect the policy to reduce or prevent crime.

## Activity #2

Locate a program in your community that emphasizes restorative justice (e.g., an alternative dispute resolution program). Describe the program and how it works to reintegrate offenders back into the community after they have been punished by the criminal justice system. Discuss the success/failure rate of the program.

# Criminology Today on the Web

### http://www.critcrim.org

This is the Web site for the American Society of Criminology's Critical Criminology Division.

### http://online.anu.edu.au/polsci/marx/marx.html

This site, the Marxism Page, is devoted to Karl Marx and includes a considerable amount of information on Marxism.

### http://www.westga.edu/~jfuller/peace.html

This site contains information on the peacemaking model of criminal justice.

### http://www.restorativejustice.org

This site is devoted to the topic of restorative justice.

**http://www.umsl.edu/~rkeel/200/powcontr.html**
This Web site provides a discussion of power-control and feminist theories.

# Student Study Guide Questions and Answers

## True/False

1. The idea that communism would inevitably replace capitalism as the result of a natural historical process or dialetic was advanced by Karl Marx and Friedrich Engels. **(True, p. 286)**

2. The consensus perspective holds that the laws reflect the will of the interest group holding political and economic power. **(False, p. 286)**

3. According to the pluralist perspective, law violators suffer from some lapse that makes them unable to participate in the widespread agreement on values and behavior. **(False, p. 286)**

4. According to Roscoe Pound, the law is designed to meet the needs of everyone living together in society. **(True, p. 286)**

5. The pluralistic perspective holds that conflict is a fundamental aspect of social life. **(False, p. 289)**

6. According to the pluralistic perspective, the legal system is value neutral. **(True, p. 289)**

7. According to the pluralistic perspective, the legal system focuses primarily on the needs of the rich and politically powerful. **(False, p. 289)**

8. The conflict perspective sees laws as a tool of the disenfranchised. **(False, p. 289)**

9. Karl Marx defined the proletariat as the "haves." **(False, p. 289)**

10. Karl Marx believed that the natural outcome of the struggle between the proletariat and the bourgeoisie would be the overthrow of a communistic social order. **(False, p. 289)**

11. According to Willem Bonger, in capitalist societies, individuals who have power are routinely subject to the criminal law. **(False, p. 289, 292)**

12. According to the conflict perspective, conflict between groups can be avoided through the use of the legal system. **(False, p. 292)**

13. Race is an example of an achieved characteristic. **(False, p. 292)**

14. George Vold compared a criminal with a soldier, using crime to fight for the survival of his or her group. **(True, p. 293)**

15. According to Ralf Dahrendorf, conflict is ubiquitous. **(True, p. 293)**

16. Chambliss suggested that upper-class criminals are more likely to escape punishment by the criminal justice system because they are smarter and thus more capable of hiding their crimes. **(False, p. 295)**

17. Richard Quinney sees criminal law as an instrument of the state. **(True, p. 295)**

18. Instrumental Marxism sees the criminal law and the criminal justice system as tools used to keep the poor disenfranchised. **(True, p. 296)**

19. Currie suggests that in the 21st century, there will be a greater worldwide emphasis on prison building. **(True, p. 297)**

20. Most radical-critical criminologists today are focusing on a sudden and total reversal of existing political arrangements within the United States. **(False, p. 297)**

21. One criticism of radical-critical criminology is its failure to recognize that there is a fair degree of public consensus about the nature of crime. **(True, p. 297)**

22. Modern radical criminologists are calling for the abolition of capital punishment. **(True, p. 298)**

23. Left realism is more conservative than traditional Marxist criminology. **(True, p. 298)**

24. Left realism sees the criminal justice system and its agents as pawns of the powerful. **(False, p. 299)**

25. Traditional criminological theory assumes men and women are the same. **(True, p. 299)**

26. According to Freda Adler and Rita Simon, existing differences in crime rates between men and women are due primarily to biology. **(False, p. 299)**

27. *Women in Crime* was written by Freda Adler. **(False, p. 299)**

28. According to early feminist criminology, as gender equality increased, male and female criminality would take on similar characteristics. **(True, p. 299)**

29. According to feminist thought, gender is a natural fact. **(False, p. 300)**

30. Radical feminists would suggest that the elimination of male domination would reduce rates of female crime and male violence against women. **(True, p. 300)**

31. Liberal feminists blame the present inequalities on the development within culture of separate spheres of influence and traditional attitudes about gender roles. **(True, p. 300)**

32. Power-control theory would suggest that a paternalistic model of family structure would result in higher levels of female delinquency. **(False, p. 301)**

33. According to feminist criminologists, criminal laws reflect traditionally male ways of organizing the social world. **(True, p. 302)**

34. The gender gap in crime refers to the differential treatment of men and women by the criminal justice system. **(False, p. 302)**

35. Gender differences in crime appear to exist in every society that has been systematically studied. **(True, p. 302)**

36. Postmodern criminology is a theory. **(False, p. 303)**

37. Semiotic criminology attempts to identify how language systems communicate values. **(True, p. 303)**

38. Adversarial court proceedings are based on the principle of participatory justice. **(False, p. 305)**

39. Restorative justice stresses retribution. **(False, p. 306)**

40. Peacemaking criminology has been criticized for being naive and utopian. **(True, p. 306)**

41. Peacemaking criminologists primarily envision positive change on an individual level. **(False, p. 306)**

## Fill in the Blank

42. Theodore Kaczynki was also known as the __________. **(Unabomber, p. 284)**

43. According to the __________ perspective, the law serves all people equally. **(consensus, p. 286)**

44. The champion of the consensus perspective was __________. **(Roscoe Pound, p. 286)**

45. According to the __________ perspective, the law is a peacekeeping tool that allows agencies within the government to settle disputes effectively. **(pluralistic, p. 289)**

46. According to the conflict perspective, formal agencies of __________ coerce the unempowered to comply with the rules established by those in power. **(social control, p. 289)**

47. The __________ are the capitalists, according to Marx. **(bourgeoisie, p. 289)**

48. In 1905, __________ described the struggle between the haves and the have-nots as a natural consequence of a capitalist society. **(Willem Bonger, p. 289)**

49. According to most sociologists, the concept of __________ entails distinctions made between individuals on the basis of significant defining characteristics. **(social class, p. 292)**

50. Level of education is an example of a(n) __________ characteristic. **(achieved, p. 292)**

51. __________ was the author of *Theoretical Criminology*. **(George Vold, p. 292)**

52. George Vold described crime as the product of __________ conflict between groups. **(political, p. 292)**

53. According to Ralf Dahrendorf, the __________ of conflict would be surprising and abnormal. **(absence, p. 293)**

54. According to Chambliss, __________ societies should reflect lower crime rates than capitalist societies. **(socialist, p. 295)**

55. According to Richard Quinney, the solution to the crime problem involves the collapse of the __________ society. **(capitalist, p. 295)**

56. According to __________ Marxists, the legal system keeps control in the hands of those who are already powerful. **(Instrumental, p. 296)**

57. According to Jeffrey Reiman, the criminal justice system is biased against the __________. **(poor, p. 296)**

58. __________ criminology is a proactive call for change in the social conditions leading to crime. **(Radical, p. 296)**

59. According to Elliott Currie, __________ societies tend to have high levels of violent crime. **(market, p. 296)**

60. __________ has been credited with popularizing left realism in North America. **(Walter DeKeseredy, p. 298)**

61. According to __________, radical ideas must be translated into realistic social policies. **(left realism, p. 299)**

62. __________ is a term referring to male dominance. **(Patriarchy, p. 299)**

63. Feminist criminology points out the inequities inherent in __________ forms of thought. **(patriarchal, p. 299)**

64. The book *Women and Crime* was written by __________. **(Rita Simon, p. 299)**

65. According to __________ theory, family class structure affects the social distribution of delinquency. **(power-control, p. 301)**

66. Postmodern criminological theories are sometimes called __________ theories. **(deconstructionist, p. 303)**

67. Anarchic criminology is a form of __________ criminology. **(postmodern, p. 303)**

68. A central feature of __________ criminology is the assertion that individuals both shape and are shaped by their world. **(constitutive, p. 303)**

69. The __________ model of crime control focuses on effective ways for developing a shared consensus on critical issues that have the potential to seriously affect the quality of life. **(peace, p. 305)**

70. Alternative dispute resolution programs play an important role in __________ perspectives. **(peacemaking, p. 305)**

71. Miami-Dade County's drug court program expands on the concept of __________ by also providing offenders with treatment. **(diversion, p. 305)**

72. __________ criminology emphasizes practical applications of the principles of conflict resolution. **(Peacemaking, p. 306)**

## Multiple Choice

73. The work *The Communist Manifesto* was written by
    a. **Karl Marx and Friedrich Engels. (p. 286)**
    b. Dragan Milovanovic.
    c. Raymond J. Michalowski.
    d. Richard Quinney.

74. Which of the following is *not* one of the three main analytical perspectives discussed in the text?
    a. Consensus
    b. **Radical (p. 286)**
    c. Conflict
    d. Pluralist

75. The idea that those who violate the law represent a unique subgroup with some distinguishing feature is a key principle of the __________ perspective.
    a. pluralist
    b. conflict
    c. **consensus (p. 286)**
    d. radical

76. The __________ perspective holds that conflict is a fundamental aspect of social life that can never be fully resolved.
    a. pluralistic
    b. **conflict (p. 289)**
    c. consensus
    d. radical

77. According to Karl Marx, the __________ are the exploited working class who are without power.
    a. **proletariat (p. 289)**
    b. bourgeoisie
    c. petit bourgeoisie
    d. materialists

78. According to the conflict perspective, the fundamental nature of group conflict centers on
    a. **the exercise of political power. (p. 292)**
    b. the accumulation of wealth.
    c. socially significant differences.
    d. None of the above

79. Which of the following is *not* an ascribed characteristic?
    a. Race
    b. Gender
    c. **Income (p. 292)**
    d. Family background

80. Most social scientists today identify __________ social classes.
    a. two
    b. **three (p. 292)**
    c. four
    d. five

81. According to George Vold, as intergroup conflict intensifies, the loyalty of individual members to their groups
    a. **increases. (p. 292)**
    b. decreases.
    c. stays about the same.
    d. Vold did not discuss this topic.

82. The conflict view of crime as a manifestation of denied needs and values was espoused by
    a. Ralf Dahrendorf.
    b. Willem Bonger.
    c. **George Vold. (p. 293)**
    d. Karl Marx.

83. Ralf Dahrendorf suggested that class conflicts arose over
    a. wealth.
    b. **authority. (p. 293)**
    c. race.
    d. crime.

84. According to Ralf Dahrendorf, constructive change increases __________within society.
    a. **cohesiveness (p. 294)**
    b. tension
    c. conflict
    d. stasis

85. The book *Criminality and Legal Order* was written by
    a. Ralf Dahrendorf.
    b. Willem Bonger.
    c. George Vold.
    d. **Austin Turk. (p. 294)**

86. According to __________, a spokesperson for modern radical thinkers, criminal behavior results from the coercive power of the state to enforce the will of the ruling class.
    a. Ralf Dahrendorf
    b. **William Chambliss (p. 294)**
    c. Harold Pepinsky
    d. Richard Quinney

87. According to Richard Quinney, the state is organized to serve the interests of the
    a. proletariat.
    b. working class.
    c. **dominant economic class. (p. 295)**
    d. petty bourgeoisie.

88. Richard Quinney suggests that the problem of crime will be solved only by the creation of
    a. a class structure.
    b. **a socialist society. (p. 295)**
    c. hedonistic values.
    d. a capitalist society.

89. Which of the following books was written by Jeffrey Reiman?
    a. *Class, State, and Crime*
    b. *Law, Order and Power*
    c. ***The Rich Get Richer and the Poor Get Prison* (p. 296)**
    d. *Class and Class Conflict in Industrial Society*

90. __________ criminology consists of a proactive call for change in the social conditions leading to crime, whereas __________ criminology is a way of critiquing social relationships leading to crime.
    a. Critical; radical
    b. **Radical; critical (p. 296)**
    c. Radical; pluralistic
    d. Critical; pluralistic

91. Modern radical criminologists have escalated their demands for
    a. **an end to police misconduct. (p. 298)**
    b. increased use of capital punishment.
    c. mandatory sentencing guidelines.
    d. increased funding for new prison construction.

92. Which of the following probably would *not* be expected of a modern radical criminologist?
    a. A call for the abolition of capital punishment
    b. A demand for the elimination of gender and racial inequity in the criminal justice system
    c. **An emphasis on increasing funding for the construction of new prisons (p. 298)**
    d. A call for the elimination of police misconduct

93. __________ was an early feminist criminologist.
    a. Meda Chesney-Lind
    b. **Rita Simon (p. 299)**
    c. Kathleen Daly
    d. John Hagan

94. A demand for the elimination of the traditional divisions of power and labor between the sexes would probably come from a(n) __________ feminist.
    a. socialist
    b. radical
    c. **liberal (p. 300)**
    d. alternative (women of color)

95. The alternative feminist framework developed by women of color was identified by
    a. Rita J. Simon.
    b. Kathleen Daly.
    c. Meda Chesney-Lind.
    d. **Sally S. Simpson. (p. 300)**

96. Stuart Henry and Dragan Milovanovic are known for their development of __________ criminology.
    a. **constitutive (p. 303)**
    b. anarchic
    c. peacemaking
    d. semiotic

97. Which of the following is a criticism of postmodern criminology?
    a. It is a theory in formation rather than a completely developed theory of crime.
    b. Postmodernists build upon existing theoretical frameworks but rarely offer new testable propositions or hypotheses.
    c. **Postmodernists use terminology that is only vaguely defined. (p. 304)**
    d. It is naive and utopian.

98. A peace model is based on
    a. **cooperation. (p. 305)**
    b. retribution.
    c. just deserts.
    d. All of the above

# Word Search Puzzle

```
N C T A O R M E T K U E E X N M L S E B T P H D Y O K U J
S W L B C L I D R J T X T L P Z A R T E M B A Z Q M N N Q
Z D A O I D L L Y U F P P W Y Z S Q O S B U B X E D S H J
O H M U I C H K A J Q K G Z W J H C C S B O C L R Y N M M
B A L R M D N B X O T K P R P J Q U B A J K N O T S I N V
Q G I G A S U H I Q W T M T K I T K S N N J B G B T U H D
Y A K E R Q O L H Q P T G V Z E K P F F F J N Y E Y Y R E
R N Q O X Y H N C S S P G E H S C L L S T V F I D R J U Z
V B M I I X J P O I P R P C Y J D U I L I B C E Q H Z Y Z
A V B S S A T Y N U M M R B C Y A R D E X D O J I N B O U
J K J E M R I I V C T N M D X D H A Y Q B E N P K U H I F
K Q F I I B M K G K L M R N O G R L O C O C S R Z Q W P H
U X V O D E K W D L K Y A Q Y Y E I U A C O E J Q U H U X
E T Q J F F O O T U H D D U Z Y N S N N M N N A X E O C D
E X R J T R Q C B C B A I I P D D T G D Q S S E T T O O V
U H I T B U O H R Q A S C N D N O S B R F T U L L C G N O
Y T M D O F E A Y D V V A N O P R Z P O F R S X U I O F L
G M H C D Y I M G K N R L E I T E V E C N U J A R I D L D
H A M A T R N B T M K M Q Y T G R Q A E G C M D K X Y I C
K D E J T Z V L Z P Y V Y F T M Y I C N T T V U K T Y C R
W L G A B N M I I O O L T R D J E L E T L I B F R E E T I
S E P X O W R S K S J R P K S L R J M R Z O B A I F Q L T
X R P B V W Z S X T S P P O G J H P A I W N T M M A T U I
K N N H K P L N S M Q W P I W Z Z M K C T I I L E R H B C
G L J G B G E R E O C K L O L H K G I I J S S X A V O Y A
S C S F L L B H Y D V R M C X D K K N T T T Q X F P M Y L
H N F W F K P F W E J V I N L B S F G Y K L I J K V Z G K
A K I M R Z C U P R E M M Y E J E X W G C L A V Z K H B V
Y N X J H H Q G H N K N I C B B W P E Z Y S K S D C S W F
Q J J B A O B H P R O L E T A R I A T X X A T B V N X P F
```

Adler
Androcentricity
Bonger
Bourgeoise
Chambliss
Conflict
Consensus
Critical
Dahrendorf
Deconstructionist
Feminist
Hagan
Marxism
Patriarchy
Peacemaking
Pluralist
Postmodern
Proletariat
Quinney
Radical
Vold
Young

# Crossword Puzzle

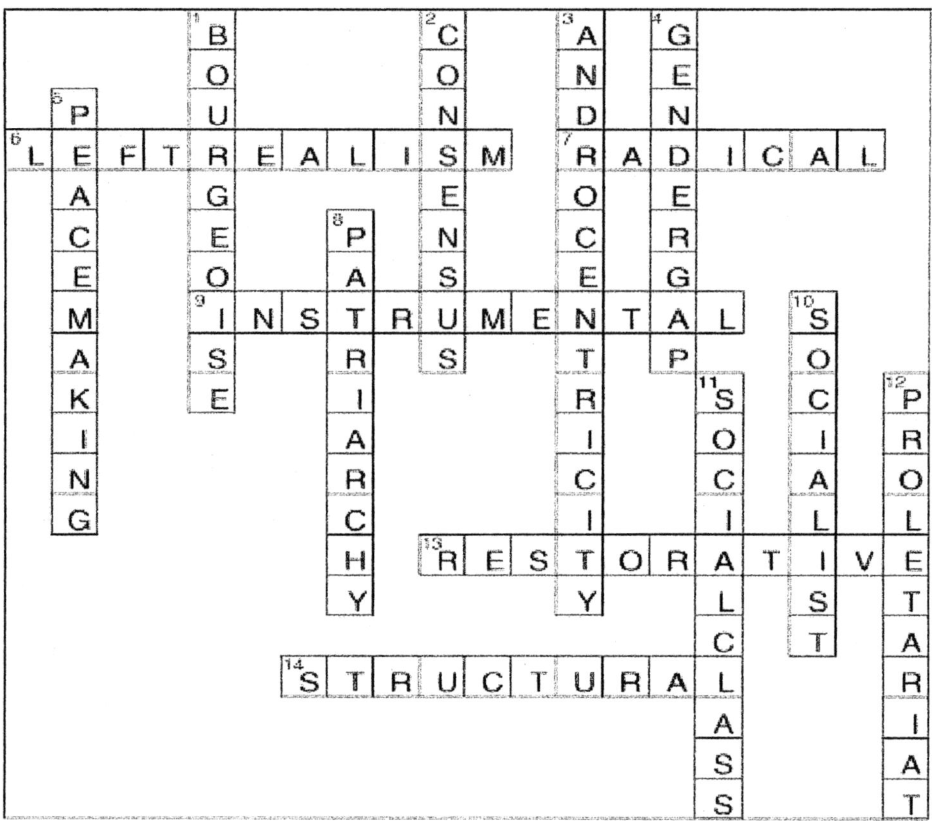

## Across

6. A conflict perspective that insists on a pragmatic assessment of crime and its associated problems. (2 words)
7. The feminist perspective suggesting that eliminating male dominance should reduce crime rates for women.
9. ______ Marxism sees the criminal law as a tool used by the powerful to control the poor.
13. _________ justice is a postmodern perspective stressing remedies over prison and punishment.
14. _________ Marxism holds that social institutions influence individual and group behavior because of the type of relationships created.

## Down

1. In Marxian theory, the class of people who own the means of production.
2. A model suggesting that society generally agrees on what is right and wrong.
3. A single-sex perspective, such as criminologists who only study the criminality of males.
4. The observed differences between male and female rates of criminal offending in a society. (2 words)
5. The perspective which holds that citizens and crime control agencies should work together to alleviate social problems and human suffering and thus reduce crime.
8. The tradition of male dominance.
10. The feminist perspective which examines social roles and the gender-based division of labor within the family.
11. Distinctions made between individuals based on important defining social characteristics. (2 words)
12. In Marxian theory, the working class.

# 10 Crimes Against Persons

## Learning Objectives

After reading this chapter, students should be able to:

1. Describe typologies of violent crime
2. Understand the key issues in explaining patterns of homicide
3. Understand the key issues in explaining patterns of violent crime
4. Identify the different types of terrorism and possible methods for the control of terrorism
5. Explain the major patterns of stalking

## Chapter Outline

Introduction
Violent Crime Typologies
Homicide
- *The Subculture of Violence Thesis and Structural Explanations*
- *The Victim–Offender Relationship*
- *Instrumental and Expressive Homicide*
- *Victim Precipitation*
- *Weapon Use*
- *Alcohol and Drug Use*
- *Gangs*
- *Serial Murder*
- *Mass Murder*

Rape
- *Rape Myths*
- *The Common Law Definition of Rape*
- *Rape Law Reform*
- *The Social Context of Rape*
- *Theoretical Perspectives on Rape*
- *Typologies of Rapists*

Robbery
- *The Lethal Potential of Robbery*
- *Criminal Careers of Robbers*
- *Robbery and Public Transportation*

# Chapter Summary

This chapter discusses various types of violent crime in America, including homicide, rape, robbery, assault, workplace violence, stalking, and terrorism. Homicide research focuses on two main theoretical frameworks, using subcultural and structural explanations to understand variations in homicide offending. Examinations of the relationship between the victim and the offender have found that homicides frequently involve family members, friends, or acquaintances. Victim precipitation studies characteristics of victims which may have precipitated their victimization, although the focus is not on "blaming the victim" for the crime. Factors such as weapons availability and the use of alcohol and drugs may also be associated with homicide. Gang membership may influence homicides; research shows several differences between homicides involving gang and nongang members. Serial and mass murder are also discussed, and several typologies are presented

It is difficult to measure the extent of rape in this country because the figures vary depending on the source used. Because many rapes are not reported to the police, official statistics frequently underestimate the extent of rape in the U.S. today. Rape myths, which are false assumptions about rape, inhibit reporting of this crime. The common law definition of rape, which was recognized in the U.S. until the 1970s, did not recognize male victims or rape within marriage; common law rules of evidence required victims to demonstrate physical resistance and to have some form of corroboration that the rape occurred. Rape law reform is designed to make the legal understanding of rape similar to that of other violent crime. All states have made significant changes in the common law crime of rape, although the impact of these reforms varies widely. The majority of rapes involve victims and offenders who are acquainted. College and university campuses typically have a high incidence of rape. Law reform has eliminated the marital exemption for rape and the text presents a typology of men who rape their wives. Same-sex rape is common in both male and female correctional institutions, although the patterns vary: rape within female prisons primary involves the attack of inmates by male staff while in male prisons the assault involves only inmates. Theoretical perspectives surrounding rape include feminist perspectives, the psychopathological perspective, Baron and Strauss' integrated theory of rape, and evolutionary and biological perspectives. Various typologies of rapists have been developed, often based on offender motivation.

Robbery is considered a violent crime because the use or threat of force is involved in the crime. There is a high potential for injury and even death for robbery victims. Most robbers are generalists; few specialize in robbery alone. Many robbers are motivated by direct financial need. Offenders specializing in street robbery frequently target other criminals, especially lower-level drug dealers, both because of the opportunity to obtain not only money but also drugs, and because these victims would be less likely to report their victimization to the police. With the exception of rape, robbery may be the most gender differentiated serious crime in the U.S., as the vast majority of offenders are male. Male and female offenders differ significantly in how they carry out street robberies, although the primary motivation for both is economic.

Assault is the most frequent violent crime and is similar psychologically, although not legally, to homicide. The offender profiles for homicide and assault are extremely similar. The majority of assaults involve victims and offenders who are known to each other, frequently in a familial or intimate relationship. Research into familial violence has been hindered by the belief that the family is a private institution. NIBRS data on family assaults shows some differences from aggravated assaults generally. Intimate partner assault involves assaultive behavior between individuals involved in an intimate relationship. The majority of victims are female, although men may also be victims.

Workplace violence, which includes a variety of violent crimes committed against persons who are at work or on duty, is a significant problem in America today. Approximately 18 percent of all violent crime involves workplace violence. There is a variety of job-related factors which increase the risk of workplace violence and a number of prevention strategies which may be employed.

Stalking involves ongoing patterns of behavior that cause victims to fear for their personal safety. All states, and the federal government, currently have anti-stalking laws. Stalking behaviors can include making telephone calls, following the victim, sending letters, making threats, vandalizing property, or watching the victim. Data on the extent of stalking is available from the National Violence Against Women Survey. The majority of victims are women and the majority of stalkers are men. Women are more likely to be stalked by an intimate partner while men are more likely to be stalked by strangers or acquaintances. Cyberstalking involves using electronic communication such as e-mail or the Internet to harass individuals.

Terrorism has been defined by the U.S. State Department as "premeditated, politically motivated violence perpetrated against noncombatant targets by subnational groups or clandestine agents, usually intended to influence an audience." Terrorist acts are distinguished from other violent crimes by the political motivation or ideology of the offender. Various typologies of terrorist activities have been developed. The U.S. has to deal with both international and domestic terrorism. A recent development is that of cyberterrorism, which uses technology to plan and carry out terrorist attacks against the economic, business, and military infrastructure of a country. A number of commissions have been formed to study terrorism and the country's prepardness to deal with terrorist threats. The Department of Homeland Security was created in 2002 to protect the United States' critical infrastructure from terrorism.

# Lecture Outline

I. Introduction
   A. Discuss the 2002 sniper shootings in the Washington, D.C. area by John Muhammad and Lee Malvo
      1. Sniper killings are not typical homicides — most are individual events motivated by personal animosity
      2. Muhammad and Malvo are not typical serial killers — most are white and most target people who fall into specific categories
   B. This chapter focuses on violent crimes: homicide, rape, robbery, assault, workplace violence, stalking, and terrorism

II. Violent Crime Typologies
   A. A crime topology categorizes offenses against persons using a particular dimension
      1. These may include legal categories, offender motivation, victim behavior, situation aspects of the event, or offender characteristics
      2. Typologies simplify social reality by creating homogeneous groups of crime behaviors that differ from other groups of crime behavior
   B. Typologies may use a single variable to explain variation in criminal offending or may suggest several variables that may interact to produce patterns in offending
      1. Gottfredson and Hirschi's general theory of crime is an example of a single-variable typology
      2. Developmental and life course theories use several variables

III. Homicide
   A. Basic homicide statistics
      1. Statutes distinguish between types of homicide based on factors such as intent, circumstances, and age
      2. Homicides are fairly rare: in 2003, less than 0.1% of all crimes reported to the police were homicides
      3. Most homicides involve acquaintances or family: only about 13% involve strangers
      4. Approximately 17% of homicides occur during the commission of another felony

**Show the ABC News program *The Peterson Story* from the video library.**

   B. The subculture of violence thesis and structural explanations
      1. The subculture of violence thesis proposed by Marvin Wolfgang and Franco Ferracuti (refer back to Chapter 7) has been the primary theoretical perspective used to explain the similarity between homicide victims and offenders in two ways:
         a. Homicide statistics show that victims and offenders have similar sociodemographic characteristics; for example, African-Americans are represented disproportionately in homicide statistics as both victims and offenders

b. Victims and offenders who are intimately known to each other are disproportionately represented in homicide statistics: approximately 60% of victims and offenders have some prior relationship

2. Research has shown that the racial composition of an area did not have a significant effect on the homicide rates for whites or African-Americans
3. There are regional variations in subcultural patterns
   a. Subcultural theorists have suggested that the history of high rates of homicide in the South is due to an adherence to a set of violence-related norms that have become outdated in other regions of the country
   b. However, some researchers claim that the influence of structural variables such as poverty may provide alternative explanations for regional variations in homicide rates
   c. Currently, we are not certain whether the high rates of violence in the South are due to a subculture of violence or to structural factors, but there is evidence that the South differs from other regions in frequency of homicides

C. The victim–offender relationship

1. Discuss the results of Marvin Wolfgang's study of homicides in Philadelphia
   a. Approximately 25% of homicides were between family members, with women more likely than men to be both offenders and victims in this category than in any other
   b. Males were more likely to be killed by friends or strangers than by family members, except that if a male was killed by a female, it was more likely to be his spouse
2. Discuss Smith and Parker's research differentiating homicide according to victim-offender relationships
   a. They distinguished between two classifications of homicide:
      (1) Primary homicides: most frequent; involve family members, friends, and acquaintances; usually characterized as expressive crimes resulting from acts of interpersonal hostility
      (2) Nonprimary homicides: victims and offenders have no prior relationship; usually occur in the course of another crime; usually characterized as instrumental crimes because they involve some premeditation and are less likely to be victim precipitated
   b. They found that structural variables are important predictors of differences in primary homicide but not for non primary homicide rates
3. Williams and Flewelling found that factors such as poverty and population size have different effects on different types of homicide, so that both the victim–offender relationship and the context of the event must be considered in explaining homicide patterns
4. The recent decline in the rate of intimate partner homicides has led to the development of the exposure-reduction theory of intimate homicide, proposed by Dugan, Nagin, and Rosenfeld
   a. They suggest that factors such as declining domesticity, the improved economic status of women, and the increase in domestic violence resources help to reduce exposure to the violent dynamics that usually precede intimate-partner homicide
   b. As resources supporting dissolution or a nonviolent exit from a violent relationship increase, rates of intimate homicide decrease

D. Instrumental and expressive homicide
   1. In both instrumental and expressive homicide, the homicide may not be intended (a robbery motivated by instrumental ends or an argument that precedes an unplanned homicide)
   2. A sibling offense is an incident that begins a homicide; considering these offenses and trying to understanding the patterns of nonlethal violence may assist in the prevention of lethal violence

E. Victim precipitation
   1. Victim precipitation focuses on victim characteristics that may have precipitated their victimization
   2. The concept is not to blame the victim but to examine individual and situational factors that may have contributed to and initiated the crime
   3. Researchers have found gender patterns of victim precipitation in intimate-partner homicide: a large number of homicides committed by women are victim precipitated, whereas only a small number of homicides committed by men are victim precipitated
   4. There is also a positive significant association between alcohol use and victim-precipitated homicides

F. Weapon use: instrumentality versus availability in the relationship between guns and homicide
   1. Instrumentality refers to the fact that the type of weapon used in an encounter can affect whether the encounter becomes lethal
   2. The presence of a gun as the weapon in a criminal event increases the likelihood of a fatality
   3. Availability refers to issues surrounding how access to guns may increase their presence in all types of interactions, including criminal interactions

G. Alcohol and drug use
   1. Robert Nash Parker developed a theory of selective disinhibition to explain the role that alcohol plays in homicide
   2. He suggests that the disinhibiting effect of alcohol is social rather than biochemical, so that the presence of alcohol in some situations may suspect factors that could restrain violence and may also put into play factors that could increase the occurrence or lethal nature of violence
   3. Research has found that alcohol significantly predicts most types of primary homicide

H. Gangs
   1. Research suggests that gang homicides are more likely to involve minority males, to involve gun use, to occur in public places, and to involve victims and offenders with no prior relationship
   2. There are two types of gang homicides:
      a. Gang-motivated violence: violent crime as the direct result of gang activity
      b. Gang-affiliated violence: individual gang members are involved in crime but not as a purposeful result of gang activity
   3. During the early 1990s gang-motivated homicides declined but gang-affiliated homicides increased — researchers suggest this is due to the continued involvement of gang members (but not gangs) in the drug trade

**Show the ABC News program *Crime and Justice* from the video library.**

I. Serial murder

1. Serial murder involves the killing of several victims in three or more events
   a. Estimates suggest that approximately 100 murders per year are the result of serial killings
   b. The typical offender is a white male in his late 20s or 30s who targets strangers at or near home or work
   c. Most serial killers are not insane or psychotic, although many are diagnosed as sociopaths
2. Typologies of serial killers
   a. Ronald Holmes and J. DeBurger developed a typology of four types of serial killers:
      (1) Visionary serial killers hear voices and have visions that are the basis for the compulsion to murder
      (2) Comfort serial killers kill for financial or material gain
      (3) Hedonistic serial killers murder for the pleasure of the killing
      (4) Power seekers operate from some position of power over others
   b. James Alan Fox and Jack Levin developed a three-part typology of serial killers
      (1) Thrill-motivated killers (most common) involve sexual sadism or dominance
      (2) Mission-oriented killers generally have a reformist or visionary orientation
      (3) Expedience-directed killers are motivated by profit or protection
         (a) Profit-driven killers kill for financial or material gain
         (b) Protection-oriented killers commit murders to mask other crimes (e.g., robbery)
3. Female serial killers
   a. The vast majority of serial killers are male but the patterns of activities of female serial killers differ from those of male serialists
      (1) Holmes and DeBurger's typology applies to women but female serialists are rarely hedonistic serial killers
      (2) Female serialists generally target victims who they know (unlike male serialists, w ho generally target strangers) and generally are geographically stable (male serialists may be stable or transient)
      (3) A disciple killer, who kills under the influence of a charismatic personality, is usually a woman
   b. Female serial killers have longer careers than those of males, possibly because they tend to be more systematic
4. Apprehending serial killers is difficult because of their caution and skill
   a. The FBI's Violent Criminal Apprehension Program (VICAP) was established in 1985 to increase the efficiency and effectiveness of serial murder apprehension
      (1) Problems with VICAP include the complexity of the data and the associated record keeping, and the difficulty in recognizing patterns
      (2) VICAP is more a detection than an apprehension tool
   b. Other methods include profiling and geomapping techniques

**Show the ABC News program *The Zodiac Killer* from the video library.**

J. Mass murder
   1. Mass murder involves killing more than three people at the same time in the same event (e.g., the Oklahoma City bombing)
   2. Levin and Fox have developed a four-part typology based on motivation
      a. The categories include revenge (the most common motive), love, profit (e.g., eliminating witnesses to a crime), and terror (e.g., the Charles Manson murders)
      b. Levin and Fox suggest that mass murders motivated by anger or love are expressive while those motivated by profit or terror are more instrumental
   3. Levin and Fox have also identified factors or elements that may lead to mass murder:
      a. Predisposers: long-term stable preconditions incorporated into the offender's personality
      b. Precipitants: short-term acute triggers or catalysis
      c. Facilitators: situational conditions that increase the likelihood of violence but are not necessary to produce it
   4. Mass murders are easier to apprehend than serial killers either because they stay on the scene long enough to be caught or because they commit suicide after the killings

IV. Rape
   A. Introduction
      1. Social awareness of the nature and extent of violence against women has increased significantly in recent years, as evidenced by the passage of the Violence Against Women Act (VAWA) in 1994 and its reauthorization in 2000.
      2. Figures representing the extent of rape in the United States vary depending on the data source used
         a. According to the UCR, over 90,000 completed or attempted rapes were reported to the police in 2001, with approximately 64 out of every 100,000 females in the United States reported victims of forcible rape
         b. According to the NCVS, there were over 198,000 rape incidents in 2003
         c. Estimates from the National Violence Against Women Survey show that 17.6% of women reported either a completed or an attempted rate at some point during their lifetime
   B. Rape myths (false assumptions about rape)
      1. Rape myths include the idea that women bring false charges to get even with men, that women ask for it by wearing provocative clothing or going to bars alone, and that women say "no" when they mean "yes"
      2. Rape myths are culturally based and inhibit reporting of rape by victims
   C. The common law definition of rape
      1. Rape was a common law crime in the United States until the 1970s and in Canada until the 1980s
      2. The common law definition of rape was "the carnal knowledge of a woman not one's wife by force or against her will"
         a. This definition did not recognize male victims or rape within marriage
         b. It also did not allow for acts of sexual penetration other than vaginal penetration by a penis or for various means by which force could occur

3. Rules of evidence required that the victim demonstrate physical resistence, have some form of corroboration that the rape occurred, and allowed the victim's previous sexual history to be admitted as relevant information

D. Rape law reform
1. Rape law reform emphasizes making the legal understanding of rape compatible with those of other violent crimes, to keep victims from undergoing further trauma during the investigation and trial
2. Cassia Spohn and Julie Horney identified four common themes in rape law reforms:
   a. Redefining rape and replacing the single crime of rape with a series of graded offenses
   b. Changing the consent standard by eliminating the requirement that the victim resist the attacker physically
   c. Eliminating the need for corroboration of the victim's testimony
   d. Placing restrictions on the introduction of evidence of the victim's prior sexual conduct
3. Rape shield laws were first introduced in the 1970s and were intended to protect rape victims by ensuring that irrelevant facts about the victim's sexual past were not introduced into evidence by the defendant
4. Spohn and Horney identified four general changes anticipated as a result of rape law reform:
   a. An increase in the reporting of rapes
   b. Symbolic change emphasizing the violent nature of rape
   c. A change in the decision-making structure of the criminal justice system because consideration of extralegal factors was eliminated
   d. Removal of barriers preventing more effective prosecution and higher conviction rates for rape
5. The effects of rape law reform
   a. Legal impact studies commonly find that new legislation has limited impact on courtroom work group behavior unless they embrace the changes or instrumental changes are forced upon them
   b. Legal reforms take time to produce large scale change and must be evaluated continually for more evidence of how change is occurring

E. The social context of rape
1. Acquaintance rape
   a. This occurs primarily when the victim and offender have some prior relationship, although not necessarily an intimate or family relationship (including rape within the context of a dating relationship)
   b. The vast majority of rapes are acquaintance rapes and many are unreported
   c. Rape on college campuses
      (1) Although research has found high levels of rape on college campuses, societal awareness and concern about rape on college campuses did not emerge until the 1980s
      (2) The 1992 Campus Sexual Assault Victims' Bill of Rights Act requires campus authorities to conduct appropriate disciplinary hearings, treat sexual assault victims and defendants with respect, make their rights and legal options clear, and cooperate with them in fully exercising those rights
      (3) Much of the research on rape in college settings focuses on identifying factors in college life that may be conducive to rape

(4) Although social organizations (e.g., fraternities) may reinforce rape myth ideology, other social organizations on campus challenge this ideology
(5) Because of the increased awareness of rape as a problem on college campuses, more services and programs are available for victims and to present information challenging rape myths
(6) Recent programs focus on rape as an issue for men as well as women, such as the creation of groups of men organized for the purpose of developing programs involving men in the effort to stop rape

2. Marital rape
 a. Under common law, there was no crime of spousal rape
 b. Rape law reform emphasized elimination of the marital exemption for rape — the first state to remove the marital exemption from its rape statutes was Oregon in 1978
 c. Discuss the case of John Rideout, the first American husband indicted for raping his wife
 d. Diane E.H. Russell developed a typology of men who rape their wives
  (1) Husbands who prefer raping their wives to having consensual sex with them
  (2) Husbands who enjoy both rape and consensual sex with their wives or who are indifferent to which type it is
  (3) Husbands who prefer consensual sex with their wives but are willing to rape them if their sexual advances are refused
  (4) Husbands who might like to rape their wives but do not act out these desires

3. Rape in prison
 a. Although same-sex rape can be common in correctional institutions, the victimization of prisoners does not seem to produce the same level of social outrage that occurs when the victim is "law abiding" leading male victims of prison rape to be known as the "forgotten victims"
 b. Patterns of rape differ in male and female prisons: rape within female prisons involves primarily male staff attacking female inmates, whereas rape within male prisons involves only inmates

F. Theoretical perspectives on rape

1. Feminist perspectives include several common elements:
 a. They see gender as a social construct rather than a biological given
 b. They do not separate the patriarchal structures within society that contribute to the privileged status of males from rape itself because rape serves as a social control mechanism
 c. Rape is seen as an act of power or domination, with sex as the tool used to subordinate
 d. A rape culture exists that sees male aggression as normal and blames women for their own rape

2. The psychopathological perspective
 a. This perspective is based on two assumptions:
  (1) Rape is the result of idiosyncratic mental disease
  (2) Rape often includes uncontrollable sexual impulses
 b. Nicholas Groth identified three types of rapists:
  (1) Power rapists, who rape to exert control over the women, are the most common

(2) Anger rapists attack their victims in anger, generally impulsively, and with no prior planning
(3) Sadistic rapes, which are fairly rare, involve a combination of power and anger motives and frequently involve torture

c. Although Groth's model does not appear to characterize the majority of men who rape, it has often been applied as if it did

3. An integrated theory of rape (Larry Baron and Murray A. Straus)
   a. This model argues that higher levels of gender inequality, social disorganization, and support for legitimate violence combine to produce higher rape rates at large macro levels (e.g., states)
      (1) Support for legitimate violence refers to norms justifying the expression of violence in certain contexts, so that high rates of rape would be associated with high rates of other violent crime
      (2) Gender inequality is related to rape rates because as women's status in society increases, rape as a mechanism of social control over women is challenged
      (3) Social disorganization refers to community inability to sustain social institutions that serve as a buffer to social ills such as crime
   b. Baron and Straus have found support for the direct effect of gender inequality on rape rates and for social disorganization as well.
   c. They have not found direct support for the relationship between legitimate violence and rape but argue for the presence of an indirect effect where states with higher rates of gender equality have higher rates of legitimate violence
4. Evolutionary/biological perspectives
   a. This suggests that motives and ends conducive to rape may be traits that are adaptations over generations
   b. Different traits that have developed in males and females are believed to have evolved through sexual selection: the idea that some traits survive because they further the attainment of mates or defense against competition over mates
   c. Evolutionary perspectives argue that the feminist position of rape, equating rape with expressions of violence, ignores the existence of a biologically based sexual motivation

G. Typologies of rapists
1. Robert Hazelwood and Ann Burgess developed a four-part typology of rapists based on offender motivation
   a. Power-assertive rapists plan their crimes and use force to subdue the victim
   b. Power-reassurance rapists (the most common type among stranger rapists) act out of a sense of social and sexual inadequacy
   c. Anger-retaliatory rapists are motivated by anger and express the anger through rape
   d. Anger-excitation rapists are sexually stimulated by the victim's response to the rape; these rapes usually involve the most planning
2. Dennis J. Stevens' typology is also based on offender motivation and is based on interviews with 61 serial rapists
   a. Lust rapists use minimal force and select victims based on availability
   b. Righteous rapists see the victim as responsible for the attack
   c. Peer rapists hold friendship responsible for the rape

d. Control and anger rapes include excessive violence, with the rape secondary to the violence
e. Supremacy rapists also involve excessive violence and emphasize the punishment given to the victim
f. Fantasy rapists focus on attaining some imaginary ideal or goal
g. A small percentage of rapists lack any clearly identifiable motive

3. Diana Scully interviewed 114 convicted rapists and organized them based on the rationalizations used
   a. Admitters (the largest category) included those men who acknowledged their offense as a rape but who purposefully downplayed the amount of force used or other key facts about the rape
   b. Deniers argue that the sex was consensual and they did not commit rape

**Show the ABC News program *Rape Survivor* from the video library.**

V. Robbery
   A. Robbery combines elements of violence (the threat or use of force) as well as property crime (the purpose of the crime is to take the property of another)
      1. Personal robbery includes robberies in residences and "muggings" (robberies on the highway or street)
         a. These may be deterred by the presence of security precautions, especially in neighborhoods characterized by a well-developed social control structure
         b. Security precautions appear to be much less effective in socially disorganized neighborhoods
      2. Institutional robbery occurs in commercial settings (gas stations, convenience stores, banks, etc.) and may often be prevented through environmental and policy changes (e.g., situational crime prevention techniques)
   B. The lethal potential of robbery
      1. Robberies are very likely to produce injury, including lethal injury, to the victim
      2. According to data from NIBRS, one in every three robbery victims receives at least a minor injury
      3. Overall, 8% of homicides occur in the context of a robbery
      4. In 2003, approximately 17% of all homicides occurred during the commission of another felony; of these, 46% occurred during the commission of a robbery
      5. The most commonly used weapon in robbery homicides is a firearm, particularly a handgun
   C. Criminal careers of robbers
      1. Most robbers are generalists who do not specialize in robbery
      2. Research with prison inmates have found that very few convicted robbers specialized exclusively in robbery
   D. Robbery and public transportation
      1. Crime prevention strategies for robbery may be effective in public transportation settings, as robbery on mass transit is fairly rare

2. Taxicab drivers run the greatest risk of robbery of any transit worker; robbery prevention strategies for taxicab drivers include carrying a weapon, passenger screening, and protection partitions

E. The motivation of robbers
  1. Most robberies involve very little planning on the part of the offender
  2. Bruce Jacobs and Richard Wright have conducted research into the motivational context of street robbery
    a. They found that the decision to offend occurs as part of ongoing social action mediated by prevailing situations and subcultural conditions
    b. Immediate financial need combined with street culture provides the motivation to offend
    c. Alternatives that robbers could have employed for money include legal work, borrowing, and committing other crimes

F. Drug robberies
  1. Richard Wright and Scott Decker found that 60% of offenders specializing in street robberies targeted individuals also involved in lawbreaking; most of these are not reported to the police and do not appear in the official statistics
  2. Many targeted minor drug dealers
    a. The robbers were able to acquire both money and drugs
    b. Drug dealers were unlikely to report victimization to the police

G. The gendered nature of robbery
  1. Robbery is the most gender-differentiated serious crime in the United States, with the exception of forcible rape
  2. Only approximately 10% of all robberies involve women offenders
  3. The primary motivation for both men and women is economic, but the methods of carrying out street robberies differ by gender
    a. Men generally use physical violence and/or a gun, rob other males more frequently, and target victims involved in street life
    b. Women robbers do not have one clear style, although they rarely use guns unless robbing a man
      (1) The most common approach is to rob females in a physically confrontational manner
      (2) Others include using their sexuality to attract male victims and acting as accomplices to males in robberies of other men

VI. Assault

A. Assault is the most frequent violent crime and the starting point for more serious interpersonal violence events
  1. There is a legal but not necessarily a psychological difference between assault and homicide
  2. The typical aggravated assault offender is the same as that of homicide: disproportionate involvement of males, African-Americans, those 15–34 years old, those of lower socioeconomic status, those with prior arrest records, and those showing little evidence of offense specialization
  3. Most aggravated assaults are spontaneous
  4. The majority of assaults are simple rather than aggravated

B. Stranger assault
  1. Although most people fear stranger violence, the probability of being seriously injured by a stranger is low

2. Likelihood of stranger victimization varies by demographic characteristics (age, gender, marital status, lifestyle, etc.)
3. There are two primary types of stranger violence:
   a. Crimes that involve exploiting a setting (e.g., a robbery where the store is cased prior to the crime)
   b. Spontaneous encounters between strangers in routine settings (the typical assault setting)
4. Stranger assaults are more likely than family assaults to involve victims and offenders of similar ages

C. Assault within families
1. The majority of assaults involve victims and offenders known to each other, often in familial or intimate relationships
2. Invading the castle
   a. Family violence is difficult to research because the family is a private social institution, and discussing violence among family members involves violating this privacy
   b. Hindelang found in the 1970s that two of the most frequent reasons for not reporting crimes to the police were that it was a private matter and fear of reprisal; current research continues to support these findings
3. Early studies of family violence
   a. Initial research involved official records and small clinical studies
   b. The first National Survey on Family Violence (NSVF) was conducted in 1976 and the second, in 1985; they found that the rate of violence between spouses was higher than estimates produced from studies such as the NCVS
4. Current survey information on family violence
   a. NIBRS includes information on family violence: 1998 NIBRS data showed that 27% of violent crimes involved victims and offenders who were family
   b. Compared to aggravated assaults generally, in those within a family, firearms are less likely and personal weapons and knives more likely to be present
   c. Women are more likely to be assault victims within the family than in the general population
5. Intimate-partner assault
   a. Intimate-partner assault involves assaultive behavior between individuals involved in an intimate relationship
   b. The vast majority of victims of marital violence within heterosexual relationships are women, although men can also be victims of violence
   c. Separation assault is a particularly violent response by the male partner that occurs after a woman leaves a violent relationship
   d. Violent relationships between intimate partners are characterized by a cycle of violence using numerous forms of social control, including physical and emotional attacks and threats or attacks against children
   e. James Ptacek has developed a typology of the types of strategies men use to control women in violent relationships
      (1) Separation assault involves the use of violence to prevent women from leaving or to get back at them for leaving
      (2) Punishment, coercion, and retaliation against women's actions concerning children involves attacking a woman during pregnancy, if

she challenges his parental authority with children, or if she requests child support through the courts

(3) Retaliation or coercion against women's pursuit of court or police remedies involves violence in response to legal action that women take other than requests for child support

(4) Retaliation for other perceived challenges to authority involves any violence in response to any comment or behavior that women might have made concerning their male partner's behavior

f. The National Violence Against Women Survey has attempted to estimate the nature and extent of physical abuse among intimate partners

(1) At some point during their lifetime 22% of women and slightly more than 7% of men report having been physically assaulted by an intimate partner

(2) Most physical assaults involve grabbing and shoving rather than the use of a gun or knife

(3) Most intimate-partner violence is perpetrated by men

(4) There is an increased risk of assault for men and women who are separated from intimate partners

**Show the ABC News program *Upscale Abuse* from the video library.**

VII. Workplace Violence

A. Workplace violence is a significant problem in America today

1. It includes murder, rape, robbery, and assault committed against persons who are at work or on duty
2. Approximately 18% of all violent crime in the United States involves workplace violence
3. Police officers are at the highest risk of victimization from workplace violence; college and university professors are among those at lowest risk
4. Discuss the results of the 2001 Bureau of Justice Statistics study on workplace violence

B. There are a variety of job-associated factors that increase the risk of workplace violence, including having contact with the public; being involved in the exchange of money; delivering passengers, goods, or services; having a mobile workplace (e.g., a taxicab); working with unstable or volatile persons; working late night or early morning hours; guarding valuables; and working in community-based settings

C. Prevention strategies include environmental design factors, enhanced administrative controls, and training and educating employees in conflict resolution strategies

VIII. Stalking

A. This behavior has recently become of significant social concern, enough to be criminalized

1. Discuss some of the recent high-profile stalkers, such as John Hinkley and Mark David Champan
2. California passed the first antistalking statute in 1990; today, all states and the federal government have antistalking laws

3. The Model Antistalking Code for States defines stalking as "a course of conduct directed at a specific person that involves repeated visual or physical proximity, nonconsensual communication, or verbal, written or implied threats, or a combination thereof, that would cause a reasonable person fear"
4. Stalking-related behaviors include making phone calls, following the victim, sending letters, making threats, vandalizing property, or watching the victim

B. The extent of stalking: the National Violence Against Women (NVAW) Survey is the only source of national-level data on the nature and extent of stalking
   1. Survey results based on the strictest definition of stalking, requiring repeated behaviors falling within the scope of stalking and a high level of fear reported by the stalking victim
      a. About 8% of women and 2% of men reported being stalked at some point during their life
      b. The annual prevalence rate was 1% of all women surveyed and 0.4% of all men
      c. Ninety percent reported being stalked by only one person during their lifetime
   2. When a lower fear threshold was used, the estimates increased significantly

C. Victim–offender relationships in stalking: results from the NVAW
   1. Four out of every five stalking victims are women and the majority of stalkers are men
   2. The majority of victims are between 18 and 39 years of age
   3. The majority of victims know the stalker: most female victims are likely to be stalked by an intimate partner, while male victims are more likely to be stalked by a male stranger or acquaintance

D. Stalking in intimate partner relationships: results from the NVAW
   1. Stalking can occur prior to the end of a relationship or after it has ended, or both before and after the end of an intimate-partner relationship
   2. Physical and sexual assault of women stalked by intimate partners are common

E. Consequences of stalking
   1. Consequences that affected the lives of victims negatively included more concern about personal safety, the need for counseling, and time lost from work
   2. Reasons why victims failed to report the stalking to the police are similar to those often given for not reporting other crimes

F. Cyberstalking
   1. There is no standard definition of cyberstalking, but the term refers to the use of electronic communications to harass people
   2. Discuss the 1999 U.S. Attorney General's report and the recommendations made to control cyberstalking

IX. Terrorism

A. The U.S. Department of State defines terrorism as "premeditated, politically motivated violence perpetrated against noncombatant targets by subnational groups or clandestine agents, usually intended to influence an audience"
   1. Terrorist acts are inherently criminal because they violate the criminal law, involve criminal activity, and produce criminal results

2. The primary distinction between violent criminal acts and terrorist acts is the political motivation or ideology of the offender: criminal acts committed for individual or pecuniary gain and which do not involve political or social objectives are not terrorism
3. The Council on Foreign Relations has developed a typology of terrorism (although some groups such as Hezbollah or the Japanese Red Army may fit into multiple categories)
   a. Nationalist terrorists want to form a separate state of their own and depict their acts as a fight for liberation from a hostile political entity (e.g., Irish Republican Army)
   b. Religious terrorists use violence to bring about social and cultural changes that support their vision of divine will (e.g., Al-Qaeda, HAMAS)
   c. State-sponsored terrorists are groups used by radical states as foreign policy tools (e.g., Hezbollah, the Japanese Red Army)
   d. Left-wing terrorists want to destroy free-market economies and replace them with socialist or communist economic systems (e.g., Red Brigades)
   e. Right-wing terrorists are motivated by fascist ideals and the dissolution of democratic governments (e.g., Neo-Nazis, white supremacists)
   f. Anarchist terrorists are revolutionaries who want to overthrow all established forms of government
4. The United States has to deal with two main types of terrorism
   a. Domestic terrorism is the unlawful use of force or violence by a group or individual who is based and operates entirely within the United States and its territories without any foreign direction and whose acts are directed at elements of the U.S. government or population
   b. International terrorism is the unlawful use of force or violence by a group or individual who has a connection to a foreign power or whose activities transcend national boundaries against persons or property to intimidate or coerce a government, the civilian population, or any segment thereof, in furtherance of political or social objectives
   c. International terrorism is sometimes incorrectly called foreign terrorism, which really refers only to acts of terrorism occurring outside the United States

B. International terrorism
1. In 2003, the U.S. State Department identified 208 acts of international terrorism, a slight increase over 2002 but a significant decrease from 2001
2. Most of the attacks during Operation Iraqi Freedom and Operation Enduring Freedom do not qualify as international terrorism because they were directed at combatants (members of U.S. and Coalition armed military forces); attacks against noncombatants were considered to be terrorist attacks

C. Domestic terrorism - discuss some of the recent acts of terrorism within the U.S. borders (e.g., the 1995 Oklahoma City bombing, the 2001/2002 anthrax mailings)

D. Cyberterrorism
1. Cyberterrorism uses high technology (especially computers, the Internet, and the World Wide Web) in planning and carrying out terrorist attacks
   a. Rather than targeting people and things, cyberterrorism targets the virtual world (software, information, communications, etc.)

b. Cyberterrorism involves cyberattacks on the economic, business, and military infrastructure of a country

2. Discuss the various commissions and acts relating to cyberterrorism
   a. The President's Commission on Critical Infrastructure Protection: formed by President Clinton to study critical components of the country's infrastructure, determine areas of vulnerability, and develop a strategy to protect them in the future
   b. The National Infrastructure Protection Center: an agency serving as a focal point within the U.S. government for threat assessment, warning, investigation, and response to threats or attacks against the country's critical infrastructure (these duties are now the responsibility of the Department of Homeland Security)
   c. The Critical Infrastructure Assurance Office: created to coordinate the federal government's initiatives on critical infrastructure protection (these duties are now the function of the Department of Homeland Security)
3. GovNet is a new Internet being built by the U.S. government that will have no connectivity with commercial or public networks; its purpose is to protect vital American interests from future acts of terrorism

E. Terrorism commissions and reports
   1. A number of governments and private groups have issues reports on terrorism and the country's preparedness to deal with threats of terrorism
   2. The Gilmore Commission presents annual reports to the President and Congress
   3. The U.S. Commission on National Security in the 21st Century (the Hart-Rudman Commission) has issued three reports on terrorism in the word today and on important antiterrorism priorities for the future
   4. The National Commission on Terrorism (the Bremmer Commission) issued a report including information on the changing face of international terrorism and suggestions for diplomatic, intelligence, and law enforcement options for addressing the threat of international terrorism
   5. The 9/11 Commission's 2004 report states that the United States is not prepared to adequately deal with terrorist threats and calls for the creation fo a new federal intelligence-gathering agency

F. Countering the terrorist threat
   1. Discuss the Bremmer Commission's findings and recommendations
   2. Foreign terrorist organizations
      a. The U.S. Department of State has the authority to designate any group external to the United States as a foreign terrorist organization (FTO) if it meets certain requirements
         (1) It must be foreign
         (2) It must engage in terrorist activity as defined by the Immigration and Nationality Act
         (3) It must threaten national security or the security of U.S. nationals
      b. There are several legal consequences if an organization is designated an FTO
         (1) It is illegal for a person in the United States or subject to United States jurisdiction to provide funds or material support to an FTO
         (2) Representatives and some members of a designated FTO may be denied visas or kept from entering the United States if they are aliens

(3) U.S. financial institutions are required to block funds of designated FTOs and their agents and report the blockage to the U.S. Department of the Treasury

c. The State Department also has the authority to designate selected foreign governments as state sponsors of international terrorism: the text lists seven countries that have been so designated

d. The Terrorist Exclusion List within the 2001 USA Patriot Act allows the government to deport aliens living in the United States who provide material assistance to organizations on the list and to refuse entry to the United States to anyone assisting these organizations

3. The Department of Homeland Security

a. The Department of Homeland Security (DHS) was created in 2002 by the Homeland Security Act and contains five directorates

(1) Border and Transportation Security
(2) Emergency Preparedness and Response
(3) Science and Technology
(4) Information Analysis and Infrastructure Protection
(5) Management

b. Other agencies within the DHS include the U.S. Coast Guard, the U.S. Secret Service, the Office of State and Local Government Coordination, the Office of Private Sector Liaison, and the Office of Inspector General

# Key Concepts

**Acquaintance rape:** Rape characterized by a prior social, though not necessarily intimate or familial, relationship between the victim and the perpetrator.

**Crime typology:** A classification of crimes along a particular dimension, such as legal categories, offender motivation, victim behavior, or the characteristics of individual offenders.

**Cyberstalking:** An array of activities in which an offender may engage to harass or "follow" individuals, including e-mail and the Internet.

**Cyberterrorism**: A form of terrorism that makes use of high technology, especially computers and the Internet, in the planning and carrying out of terrorist attacks.

**Domestic terrorism**: The unlawful use of force or violence by a group or an individual who is based and operates entirely within the United States and its territories without foreign direction and whose acts are directed at elements of the U.S. government or population.

**Exposure-reduction theory:** A theory of intimate homicide which claims that a decline in domesticity, accompanied by an improvement in the economic status of women and a growth in domestic violence resources, explains observed decreases in intimate-partner homicide.

**Expressive crime**: A criminal offense that results from acts of interpersonal hostility, such as jealousy, revenge, romantic triangles, and quarrels.

**Institutional robbery**: Robbery that occurs in commercial settings, such as convenience stores, gas stations, and banks.

**Instrumental crime**: A goal-directed offense that involves some degree of planning by the offender.

**International terrorism**: The unlawful use of force or violence by a group or an individual who has a connection to a foreign power or whose activities transcend national boundaries against people or property to intimidate or coerce a government, the civilian population, or any segment thereof in furtherance of political or social objectives.

**Intimate-partner assault:** A gender-neutral term used to characterize assaultive behavior that takes place between individuals involved in an intimate relationship.

**National Violence Against Women (NVAW) Survey**: A national survey of the extent and nature of violence against women conducted between November 1995 and May 1996 and funded through grants from the National Institute of Justice and the U.S. Department of Health and Human Services' National Center for Injury Prevention and Control.

**Nonprimary homicide:** Murder that involves victims and offenders who have no prior relationship and which usually occurs during the course of another crime, such as robbery.

**Personal robbery:** Robbery that occurs on the highway or street or in a public place (and that is often referred to as “"mugging”) and robbery that occurs in residences.

**Primary homicide:** Murder involving family members, friends, and acquaintances.

**Rape myth:** A false assumption about rape such as, “When a woman says no, she really means yes.” Rape myths characterize much of the discourse surrounding sexual violence.

**Rape shield law:** A statute providing for the protection of rape victims by ensuring that defendants do not introduce irrelevant facts about the victim's sexual history into evidence.

**Selective disinhibition**: A loss of self-control due to the characteristics of the social setting, drugs or alcohol, or a combination of both.

**Separation assault:** Violence inflicted by partners on significant others who attempt to leave an intimate relationship.

**Sibling offense:** An offense or incident that culminates in homicide. The offense or incident may be a crime, such as robbery, or an incident that meets a less stringent criminal definition, such as a lover’s quarrel involving assault or battery.

**Spousal rape:** The rape of one spouse by the other. The term usually refers to the rape of a woman by her husband.

**Stalking:** A course of conduct directed at a specific person that involves repeated visual or physical proximity; nonconsensual communication; verbal, written, or implied threats; or a combination thereof, which would cause a reasonable person fear.

**Terrorism:** Premeditated, politically motivated violence perpetrated against noncombatant targets by subnational groups or clandestine agents, usually intended to influence an audience.s

**Victim precipitation:** Contributions made by the victim to the criminal event, especially those that led to its initiation.

**Violence Against Women Act (VAWA):** A federal law enacted as a component of the 1994 Violent Crime Control and Law Enforcement Act and intended to address concerns about violence against women. The law focused on improving the interstate enforcement of protection orders, providing effective training for court personnel involved with women's issues, improving the training and collaboration of police and prosecutors with victim service providers, strengthening law enforcement efforts to reduce violence against women, and on increasing services to victims of violence. President Clinton signed the reauthorization of this legislation, known as the Violence Against Women Act 2000, into law on October 28, 2000.

**Violent Criminal Apprehension Program (VICAP):** The program of the Federal Bureau of Investigation focusing on serial murder investigation and the apprehension of serial killers.

**Workplace violence:** The crimes of murder, rape, robbery, and assault committed against persons who are at work or on duty.

# Additional Lecture Topics

When discussing the topic of rape, consider including a brief discussion of statutory rape, which involves consensual sexual relations between an adult and a minor. Review the laws relating to statutory rape, including the statutory age of consent. Some states limit the crime to underage minor females engaged in sex with an adult male. Most states consider it irrelevant whether the adult offender was aware of the victim's true age or if the adult offender was misled by the victim. One case that could be discussed is that of Mary Kay LeTourneau, a teacher who had an affair with one of her sixth-grade students, a 12-year-old.

When discussing assault, consider covering child abuse as well as intimate-partner abuse. Review the various types of child abuse: physical abuse, emotional abuse, sexual abuse, and neglect. Estimates suggest that there are as many as # million reported cases of child abuse annually. Child abuse can be committed by family members, strangers, or caregivers (e.g., day care center employees). The issue of elder abuse may also be discussed at this time.

Review the topic of hate or bias crimes: violent crimes directed toward an individual or group because of some racial, ethnic, religious, or gender characteristic. Consider this as a motive for some of the violent crimes discussed in this chapter.

When discussing workplace violence, consider introducing the typology created by the California Occupational Safety and Health Administration, which groups workplace violence into four main categories. Type I (criminal intent) involves an offender who has no legitimate relation to the business or its employees but who is a criminal targeting the business. Type II (customer/client) involves an offender who has a legitimate relationship with the business and who becomes violent while being served by business. Type III (worker on worker) involves an offender who is a current or former employee attacking or threatening another employee in the workplace. Type IV (personal relationship) involves an offender who has no relationship with the business but does have a personal relationship with the intended victim (frequently a domestic dispute that spills over into the workplace).

# Discussion Questions

These discussion questions are found in the textbook at the end of the chapter. The instructor may want to focus on these questions during the coverage of Chapter 10.

1. Why are crime typologies useful for understanding violent crime patterns?

2. What are the most common forms of violent crime? What characterizes these types of crimes?

3. What are the least common forms of violent crime? What characterizes these types of crimes?

4. Why was rape law reform necessary? What have been the beneficial aspects of this reform for rape victims?

5. Is robbery primarily a rational activity? Why?

6. What types of terrorism has this chapter identified?

7. What is cyberterrorism? How does it differ from other types of terrorism?

8. How might terrorism be controlled?

# Student Exercises

## Activity #1

Recent legislation requires that universities publish statistics on crime on campus. Obtain information about violent crime occurring at your university campus.

Compare the rates of serious violent crimes on campus to the rates in neighboring jurisdictions. How safe does your university appear to be?

### Activity #2

Locate programs and other resources that are available on your university campus for victims of domestic violence and/or stalking. Bring these materials into class for discussion.

### Activity #3

Obtain NCVS and UCR data on murder and aggravated assault and compare and contrast the two crimes. What are the similarities, and what are the differences between them? Consider factors such as the characteristics of the offenders and the victims, characteristics of the event (location, weapon used, when the crime occurred, etc.), and arrest and clearance rates.

### Activity #4

Select three theories that you have discussed in previous chapters and discuss how each of these might explain the crimes of assault and robbery.

## Criminology Today on the Web

**http://www.icpsr.umich.edu/HRWG/**

This is the home page of the Homicide Research Working Group, which was organized by the American Society of Criminology in 1991.

**http://www.pbs.org/kued/nosafeplace**

This Web site provides a link to a 1998 PBS program discussing violence against women. The site includes the program script, links and other resources, and other material.

**http://www.cavnet2.org**

This is the home page of CAVNET, the Communities Against Violence Network, which addresses domestic violence, sexual assault, rape, stalking, and other types of violent crime.

**http://www.ojp.usdoj.gov/nij/pubs-sum/181867.htm**

This web site provides a link to results from the National Violence Against Women Survey, which asked respondents about their experiences as victims of various types of intimate-partner violence, including rape, assault, and stalking.

**http://www.ojp.usdoj.gov/vawo**

This is the home page of the U.S. Department of Justice Violence Against Women Office.

**http://www.usdoj.gov/criminal/cybercrime/cyberstalking.htm**
This site makes available the 1999 Attorney General's report on cyberstalking.

**http://www.antistalking.com**
This is the home page of the antistalking Web site.

**http://www.fbi.gov/ucr/ucr.htm#hate**
This site makes available hate crime statistics published by the FBI.

**http://www.lib.umich.edu/govdocs/usterror.html**
This is a link to the University of Michigan Documents Center, which has a wealth of information on the 9/11 terrorist attacks and the aftermath.

**http://www.terrorism.com/index.php**
This is the home page of the Terrorism Research Center.

# Student Study Guide Questions and Answers

## True/False

1. Most homicides involve multiple victims. **(False, p. 314)**

2. African-Americans like John Muhammad and John Lee Malvo are typical of serial killers. **(False, pp. 314-315)**

3. Homicide is one of the most common types of violent crime. **(False, p. 316)**

4. The most frequent circumstance that precedes a homicide is an argument. **(True, p. 316)**

5. Homicide victims and offenders share similar demographic characteristics. **(True, p. 316)**

6. The racial composition of a neighborhood significantly affects the homicide rates for whites and blacks. **(False, p. 316)**

7. Evidence suggests that the South differs from other regions in terms of the frequency of homicide. **(True, p. 316)**

8. Wolfgang found that the majority of homicides involved family members. **(False, p. 316)**

9. Men are more likely than women to be offenders and victims of homicides involving family members. **(False, p. 316)**

10. An instrumental crime involves some degree of premeditation by the offender. **(True, p. 317)**

11. The rate of intimate-partner homicide has been increasing since the 1980s. **(False, p. 317)**

12. Homicide offenders always intend to kill their victims. **(False, p. 318)**

13. A homicide that occurs during an incident that began as a robbery is an example of an instrumental homicide. **(True, p. 318)**

14. Instrumental homicides are preceded by an argument between the victim and the offender. **(False, p. 318)**

15. Victim characteristics may affect whether a particular encounter ends up as an assault or a homicide. **(True, p. 318)**

16. According to Wolfgang, most victims of spousal homicide had been drinking at the time of the crime. **(True, p. 318)**

17. Instrumentality refers to the fact that the type of weapon used in a particular encounter has an effect on whether the encounter ends in death. **(True, p. 318)**

18. According to the availability factor, access to guns may increase their presence in all types of interactions, not just criminal interactions. **(True, p. 318)**

19. Gun availability is a stronger factor in explaining lethal violence than gun instrumentality. **(True, p. 318)**

20. The concept of economic compulsion suggests that crimes are committed to support a drug habit. **(True, p. 318)**

21. Alcohol is a variable that significantly predicts non-primary homicides. **(False, p. 321)**

22. Gang-affiliated violence involves violence as a direct result of gang activity. **(False, p. 321)**

23. African-American males are more likely to be participants in gang-motivated violence. **(True, p. 321)**

24. Serial killers generally use a standard pattern of offending and method of killing. **(False, p. 322)**

25. The typical serial killer is under 40 years of age. **(True, p. 322)**

26. Serial murder is a form of instrumental violence. **(False, p. 322)**

27. Most serial killers are psychotic. **(False, p. 322)**

28. Female serial killers follow a pattern similar to that of male serialists. **(False, p. 323)**

29. According to Kelleher and Kelleher, the black widow kills individuals in her care. **(False, p. 323)**

30. Serial killers are generally easy to identify. **(False, p. 323)**

31. VICAP is primarily a tool for detecting offenders. **(True, p. 324)**

32. According to Levin and Fox, a profit motivation for a mass murder would involve the elimination of witnesses to a crime. **(True, p. 324)**

33. A predisposer is a long-term stable precondition that is incorporated into the mass murder's personality. **(True, p. 324)**

34. Mass murderers are more difficult to apprehend than serial killers. **(False, p. 325)**

35. The NCVS suggests that there are significantly more rapes in the United States than are reported in the UCR. **(True, p. 325)**

36. A rape myth is a true assumption about rape. **(False, p. 325)**

37. Rape myths increase the likelihood that rape victims will report the crime to the police. **(False, p. 326)**

38. The common law definition of rape recognized rape within marriage. **(False, p. 326)**

39. Rape law reforms have eliminated the requirement that the victim physically resist the attacker. **(True, p. 326)**

40. Rape law reforms require that the victim's testimony be corroborated. **(False, p. 326)**

41. Rape law reforms have resulted in a greater percentage of convicted rape offenders being sentenced to incarceration. **(False, p. 327)**

42. College campuses typically have a high incidence of rape. **(True, p. 330)**

43. Rape law reform involved creation of the marital exemption for rape. **(False, p. 330)**

44. Prison rape only occurs in male institutions. **(False, p. 331)**

45. Feminist perspectives view gender as a biological given. **(False, p. 331)**

46. According to Groth, anger rapes generally involve no prior planning on the part of the offender. **(True, p. 332)**

47. Sadistic rapes frequently involve torture. **(True, p. 332)**

48. Baron and Straus suggest that high rates of rape are associated with high rates of other violent crime. **(True, p. 333)**

49. Supremacy rapists are more interested in the punishment given to the victim than to the sexual contact, according to Dennis Stevens. **(True, p. 334)**

50. According to Diana Scully, rape is a socially learned behavior. **(True, p. 334)**

51. Institutional robberies occur in commercial settings. **(True, p. 335)**

52. Institutional robberies may be prevented by environmental changes. **(True, p. 335)**

53. The weapon most often used in a robbery homicide is a handgun. **(True, p. 336)**

54. Most bank robbers visit the targeted bank to "case" it prior to committing the actual robbery. **(False, p. 337)**

55. Street robbers frequently target drug dealers. **(True, p. 337)**

56. Anonymity maintenance involves robbers who target drug dealers and who make a significant effort to ensure they will have no contact with the victim after the crime. **(False, p. 338)**

57. Most aggravated assaults are spontaneous. **(True, p. 339)**

58. Firearms are less likely to be used during family assaults than in other aggravated assaults. **(True, p. 341)**

59. Stalking is an offense that occurs once. **(False, p. 344)**

60. Men and women are equally likely to be victims of stalking. **(False, p. 344)**

61. Homosexual men are at greater risk of stalking than heterosexual men. **(True, p. 345)**

62. The primary distinction between acts of terrorism and violent crimes revolves around the political motivation of the offender. **(True, p. 346)**

63. A bombing or hostage-taking that is undertaken for individual or pecuniary gain is not terrorism. **(True, p. 346)**

64. Religious terrorists seek to destroy economies based on free enterprise. **(False, pp. 346-347)**

65. Right-wing terrorists want to destroy economies based on free enterprise and replace them with socialist or communist economic systems. **(False, p. 347)**

66. Domestic terrorism refers only to acts of terrorism occurring outside of the United States. **(False, pp. 347-348)**

67. According to the 9/11 Commission, America is not properly prepared to deal with terrorist threats. **(True, p. 352)**

## Fill in the Blank

68. A crime __________ categorizes offenses using a particular dimension such as legal categories or offender motivation. **(typology, p. 315)**

69. __________ homicides are generally motivated by interpersonal hostility. **(Primary, p. 317)**

70. Gottfredson and Hirschi's general theory of crime is an example of a(n) __________ typology. **(single-variable, p. 315)**

71. __________ homicides involve victims and offenders who have no prior relationship. **(Nonprimary, p. 317)**

72. Victim __________ focuses on characteristics of victims that may have led to their victimization. **(precipitation, p. 318)**

73. Victim precipitated homicides are more likely to be committed by __________. **(women, p. 318)**

74. Robert Nash Parker developed the theory of __________. **(selective disinhibition, p. 319)**

75. Serial murder involves killing several victims in at least __________ separate events. **(three, p. 322)**

76. According to the typology developed by Holmes and DeBurger, the __________ serial killer hears voices that are the basis for a compulsion to murder. **(visionary, p. 322)**

77. A comfort serial killer is motivated by __________. **(financial gain/material gain, p. 322)**

78. The most frequently occurring type of serial killer, according to the Fox and Levin typology, is the __________ killer. **(thrill-motivated, p. 323)**

79. According to Fox and Levin, __________ killers tend to be genuinely psychotic. **(visionary, p. 323)**

80. A __________ killer is a female serial killer who murders as the result of the influence of a charismatic personality. **(disciple, p. 323)**

81. According to FBI profiling theory, __________ killers have higher levels of intelligence and social skills. **(organized nonsocial, p. 324)**

82. __________ murder involves killing at least four victims at one location within one event. **(Mass, p. 324)**

83. According to Levin and Fox, a __________ is a situation condition which increases the likelihood of a violent outburst. **(facilitator, p. 324)**

84. Some states have changed their terminology, replacing the crime of "rape" with the offense of __________. **(sexual assault, p. 326)**

85. __________ laws protect rape victims by ensuring that defendants do not introduce irrelevant facts of the victim's sexual past into evidence. **(Rape shield, p. 326)**

86. The most common scenario for rape is __________ rape. **(acquaintance, p. 327)**

87. The typology of men who rape their wives was developed by __________. **(Diana E.H. Russell, p. 331)**

88. Rape of inmates by inmates is more common in __________ correctional institutions. **(male, p. 331)**

89. According to Groth, __________ rapists generally plan their crimes. **(power, p. 332)**

90. According to Baron and Straus, __________ refers to norms that justify the expression of violence in certain contexts. **(support for legitimate violence, p. 332)**

91. According to Baron and Straus, __________ refers to the inability of communities to sustain viable social institutions that serve as a buffer for social ills such as crime. **(social disorganization, p. 333)**

92. According to the evolutionary perspective on rape, __________ is the key to survival of a trait. **(propagation, p. 333)**

93. According to Hazelwood and Burgess, the most common type of stranger rapist is the __________ rapist. **(power-reassurance, p. 334)**

94. According to Dennis Stevens, __________ rapists select victims based on the most available target and use a minimal amount of force. **(lust, p. 334)**

95. Dennis Stevens' typology of rapists suggests that __________ rapists hold friendship responsible for the rape. **(peer, p. 334)**

96. According to Dennis Stevens, __________ rapists are trying to regain some imaginary goal that had been part of their past. **(fantasy, p. 334)**

97. Scully labeled rapists who claim that the sexual relations with the victims were consensual as __________. **(deniers, p. 335)**

98. A mugging is __________ robbery. **(personal, p. 335)**

99. Among homicides occurring during the commission of another felony, __________ is the most likely felony to result in a homicide. **(robbery, p. 336)**

100. Most robbers are motivated by __________ considerations. **(economic, p. 337)**

101. __________ refers to how robbers who target drug dealers consciously devote a significant amount of time and effort into ensuring they will not have contact with the victim after the robbery. **(Hypervigilance, p. 338)**

102. Approximately __________ percent of all robberies are committed by women. **(10, p. 339)**

103. __________ is the most frequently occurring violent crime. **(Assault, p. 339)**

104. __________ assaults are more likely to involve victims and offenders of similar ages. **(Stranger, p. 340)**

105. __________ violence involves violent crimes committed against persons who are on duty or at work. **(Workplace, p. 343)**

106. __________ involves the use of electronic communication to harass individuals. **(Cyberstalking, p. 346)**

107. __________ terrorists are revolutionaries who seek to overthrow all established forms of government. **(Anarchist, p. 347)**

108. __________ terrorism involves the unlawful use of force or violence by a group or individual who is based and operates entirely within the U.S. and whose acts are directed at elements of the U.S. government or population. **(Domestic, p. 347)**

109. __________ targets the virtual world. **(Cyberterrorism, p. 350)**

110. The private Internet being created by the U.S. government is known as __________. **(GovNet, p. 351)**

111. A group external to the U.S. that engages in terrorist activity may be considered for designation as a __________. **(foreign terrorist organization/FTO, p. 354)**

112. The Terrorist Exclusion List was created by the __________ Act. **(USA Patriot, p. 359)**

113. The federal Department of __________ is responsible for protecting the country's critical infrastructure against terrorism. **(Homeland Security, p. 359)**

## Multiple Choice

114. Approximately __________ percent of the crimes reported to the police in 2003 were homicides.
   a. **0.1 (p. 316)**
   b. 0.5
   c. 2
   d. 5

115. The subculture of violence thesis was originally proposed by
   a. Emile Durkheim.
   b. **Marvin Wolfgang and Franco Ferracuti. (p. 316)**
   c. K.R. Williams and R.L. Flewelling.
   d. Robert Nash Parker.

116. African-Americans are disproportionately represented in the homicide statistics as
   a. victims.
   b. offenders.
   c. **both victims and offenders. (p. 316)**
   d. neither victims nor offenders.

117. Homicides that involve victims and offenders who have no prior relationship are classified as
   a. primary homicides.
   b. expressive crimes.
   c. **nonprimary homicides. (p. 317)**
   d. none of the above

118. According to Williams and Flewelling, __________ is a stronger predictor of family homicide than of stranger homicide.
   a. **poverty (p. 317)**
   b. population size
   c. the context of the event
   d. the victim–offender relationship

119. The exposure-reduction theory focuses on explaining rates of __________ homicide.
   a. stranger
   b. **intimate-partner (p. 317)**
   c. acquaintance
   d. All of the above

120. The connection between drugs and drug trafficking is described by the concept of
   a. **systemic violence. (p. 319)**
   b. economic compulsion.
   c. psychopharmacology.
   d. selective disinhibition.

121. __________ focuses on explaining the role that alcohol plays in homicide.
   a. The general theory of crime
   b. The subculture of violence thesis
   c. **Selective disinhibition theory (p. 319)**
   d. The critical criminological perspective

122. Which of the following is *not* one of the ten myths of serial murder outlined by Fox and Levin?
   a. All serial killers are insane.
   b. Serial killers are primarily motivated by pornography.
   c. Serial killers are primarily sexual sadists.
   d. **Serial killers do not want to be apprehended. (p. 322)**

123. Reasonable estimates suggest that approximately __________ murders each year are the result of serial killings.
   a. 50
   b. **100 (p. 322)**
   c. 1,000
   d. 5,000

124. Serial killers generally target
   a. **strangers. (p. 322)**
   b. acquaintances.
   c. family members.
   d. co-workers.

125. The __________ serial killer frequently plays a "cat and mouse" game with the victim before committing the murder.
   a. visionary
   b. comfort
   c. hedonistic
   d. **power seeker (p. 323)**

126. Which of the following is a type of mission oriented serial killer?
   a. The dominance killer
   b. The profit driven killer
   c. **The reformist (p. 323)**
   d. The sexual sadist

127. Male serial killers are more likely to target __________ as victims.
   a. family members
   b. relatives
   c. acquaintances
   d. **strangers (p. 323)**

128. According to Levin and Fox's typology of mass murder, the most common motive for such a crime is
   a. **revenge. (p. 324)**
   b. love.
   c. profit.
   d. terror.

129. The UCR data set includes __________ rapes than the NCVS.
   a. significantly more
   b. **significantly less (p. 325)**
   c. about the same number of
   d. slightly more

130. Which of the following was *not* required by the rules of evidence under the common-law definition of rape?
   a. The victim had to demonstrate physical resistance to the act.
   b. The victim must have some form of corroboration that the rape occurred.
   c. The victim's previous sexual history could be admitted as relevant information.
   d. **The victim had to be the spouse of the offender. (p. 326)**

131. The first state to eliminate the marital exemption for rape was
   a. California.
   b. Michigan.
   c. Indiana.
   d. **Oregon. (p. 330)**

132. According to feminist researchers, male and female are defined as opposite poles of social existence, with "male" being defined by
   a. inferiority.
   b. subordinance.
   c. **dominance. (p. 332)**
   d. patriarchy.

133. Which of the following is *not* one of the types of rape identified in Groth's typology of rapists?
   a. Power rape
   b. Anger rape
   c. Sadistic rape
   d. **Erotic rape (p. 332)**

134. According to Groth, __________ rapes involve eroticized aggression.
   a. power
   b. anger
   c. **sadistic (p. 332)**
   d. erotic

135. __________ developed an integrated theory of rape.
   a. **Larry Baron and Murray A. Straus (p. 332)**
   b. Travis Hirschi and Michael Gottfredson
   c. Randy Thornhill and Craig T. Palmer
   d. Robert Hazelwood and Ann Burgess

136. According to the Hazelwood and Burgess typology of rapists, __________ rapists plan their crimes and use a lot of force to subdue the victim.
    a. anger-excitation
    b. power-reassurance
    c. anger-retaliatory
    d. **power-assertive (p. 333)**

137. According to Hazelwood and Burgess, __________ rapists generally stalk their victims in advance and generally act out of a sense of social and sexual inadequacy.
    a. anger-retaliatory
    b. anger-excitation
    c. **power-reassurance (p. 334)**
    d. power-assertive

138. According to the Hazelwood and Burgess typology of rapists, the blitz approach is used by the __________ category of rapist.
    a. anger-excitation
    b. power-reassurance
    c. **anger-retaliatory (p. 334)**
    d. power-assertive

139. According to Dennis Stevens, the __________ rape motive involves an offender who believes that the victim is responsible for the attack because she consented to the sex in some "silent deal."
    a. lust
    b. **righteous (p. 334)**
    c. peer
    d. supremacy

140. Which of the following types of robbery is most likely to be affected by crime prevention strategies?
    a. Muggings
    b. Robberies of commercial establishments
    c. **Robberies on mass transit (p. 336)**
    d. Personal robberies

141. Robbers who target drug dealers they do not know are employing the technique of
    a. **anonymity maintenance.(p. 338)**
    b. intimidation.
    c. hypervigilance.
    d. selective disinhibition.

142. Which of the following is a characteristic of female robbers?
    a. They almost always use guns.
    b. They target victims involved in street life.
    c. **They frequently rob females in a physically confrontational manner. (p. 339)**
    d. They have one clear style of robbery.

143. Which of the following is *not* typical of an aggravated assault offender?
    a. Lower socioeconomic status
    b. Prior arrest record
    c. African American male
    d. **Evidence of offense specialization (p. 339)**

144. The currently accepted term for assaultive behavior that takes place between individuals involved in an intimate relationship is
    a. spouse assault.
    b. women battering.
    c. wife assault.
    d. **intimate-partner assault. (p. 341)**

145. The most common workplace violent incident is a(n)
    a. robbery.
    b. homicide
    c. **assault. (p. 343)**
    d. rape.

146. Which of the following is *not* a risk factor for workplace violence?
    a. Having a mobile workplace
    b. Being involved in the exchange of money
    c. **Working during the daytime (p. 344)**
    d. Having contact with the public

147. The first antistalking statute was passed in
    a. New York.
    b. **California. (p. 344)**
    c. Washington, D.C.
    d. Texas.

148. Stalking behaviors include
    a. following the victim.
    b. making phone calls.
    c. vandalizing property.
    d. **All of the above (p. 344)**

149. __________ terrorists claim that they are fighting for liberation from an unfair and repressive political entity.
    a. Left-wing
    b. Right-wing
    c. **Nationalist (p. 346)**
    d. Anarchist

150. Al-Qaeda is an example of __________ terrorism.
    a. **religious (p. 347)**
    b. right-wing
    c. anarchist
    d. nationalist

151. The __________ was formed by President Clinton to study critical components of the country's infrastructure.
    a. **President's Commission on Critical Infrastructure Protection (p. 350)**
    b. Critical Infrastructure Assurance Office
    c. Department of Homeland Security
    d. National Infrastructure Protection Center

152. The __________ Commission issues annual reports to the President and Congress on domestic response capabilities for terrorism.
    a. Hart-Rudman
    b. Bremmer
    c. **Gilmore (p. 351)**
    d. 9/11

153. The Bremmer Commission considers the country's *first* priority to be
    a. **preventing terrorist attacks. (p. 352)**
    b. catching known terrorists.
    c. dealing with the aftermath of terrorist attacks in the U.S.
    d. prosecuting known terrorist groups.

154. Which of the following is *not* a consequence of designation as a foreign terrorist organization?
    a. It is illegal for a person in the U.S. or subject to U.S. jurisdiction to provide funds or material support to a foreign terrorist organization.
    b. Representatives and some members of designated foreign terrorist organizations may be denied visas or kept from entering the U.S. if they are aliens.
    c. U.S. financial institutions are required to block funds of designated foreign terrorist organizations and their agents and report the blockage to the U.S. Department of the Treasury.
    d. **Members of designated foreign terrorist organizations may be deported by the U.S. Department of State without review. (p. 356)**

# Word Search Puzzle

```
K C G D G G E I X U H D I N K W W T I V Q Q A P M R W A J
U W N D L K I N S T R U M E N T A L Y M W D Z W V B X M M
A R O J C V G O X N H G T U O G K X G S V S C S X E L O T
G T I W X Y K W E A Z R J V B S A H R N O T D G C X B G U
S T L Y H X B J I V C S C K W S F B N X B V E Q P P Z E D
E C X I N Q K E Y C T S M X M Z R K M Y V E C E O R L H F
K T A T E N K F R T V L A I Z R I C X K Z G O A D E O R V
K S W G R Y V L S S Q M K Z H M F P S T S F J A M S A G N
N C Q P R F S S Y B T X R T A K L C V S N N H W M S V U Y
P V W Y S U E T E O X A K J N H S S P F L T F X B I L V Y
C N K Y T G C Y A J M J L T I H T Y P O L O G Y I V K M H
B V Y E R D I V S L I I F K U R F P Y D X P V K H E R E L
O L T U A J I C P R K W G K I M E K V R N M L T S I D L S
R X B A U O M K O O T I Y T B N K G P I W O R K P L A C E
B G C Y S P O X H N T J N B U I G X N G C W P Z O R C C Q
P B M G F S F N N I Z R T G W N K I P C T A T U C N X C T
B C L P P I A W Q T L A P D R Y X P H Y N Q P X Y U M H O
H F X D V Q V L Y Q Q V V G X C O K K B F Z K Z B V O T M
V X D O A A C Q U A I N T A N C E A Z E W B A S I U M V M
F K W E W L R W R A D M X I U X Q O E R G M L S F P W S B
L P E Q A Z K V G Y N J W B L A M X F T V I R S W J I G S
D S V Y T J R A P E M Y T H S Y X A D E X O I O R R E I P
R P X Q C N N A W S Q N D P O F H I H R S Y K R O Z R X P
L D X H M M R S X M W N B M X X W S J R V N Q R G O Z Y G
A C Q N V W T P Z O L Z U G O N X I M O U E R D R R K J A
P O T L V C Q M W G A T A E X K L O F R J E I R S L O X V
X B I N F R A S T R U C T U R E F Y B I T V E N A J Q T M
N Q A Y T D M E P A T R T W T H D S D S B T G X R D L J H
M K K D P V F Z T Z Q U V V V U A B E M P J A Y F S S K M
V T A V Z N Q J F E R M X H O Z M W F Z E R L W X I X P K
```

Acquaintance
Burgess
Cyberstalking
Cyberterrorism
Expressive
Groth
Infrastructure
Instrumental

Rape myths
Spohn
Stalking
Terrorism
Typology
VAWA
VICAP
Workplace

# Crossword Puzzle

## Across

2. Mugging is an example of _________ robbery.
6. A goal-directed crime that involves some degree of planning by the offender.
7. A crime resulting from acts of interpersonal hostility.
8. An offense that culminates in a homicide.
9. A(n) _________ homicide involves family members, friends, and acquaintances.
12. Politically motivated violence against noncombatant targets by subnational groups or clandestine agents.
13. Activities using the Internet or email to harass a victim.
14. The victim's contributions to the criminal event.

## Down

1. Repeated behaviors directed at a specific person that would cause a reasonable person fear.
3. A(n) ______ homicide involves victims and offenders who have no prior relationship.
4. The robbery of a gas station is an example of ________ robbery.
5. A form of terrorism that makes use of high technology.
10. Classification of crimes along a particular dimension, such as legal categories.
11. __________ rape involves a prior social relationship between the victim and the offender.

# 11 Crimes Against Property

## Learning Objectives

After reading this chapter, students should be able to:

1. Understand the distinction between professional criminals and other kinds of property offenders
2. Identify the major forms of property crime
3. Explain the rationalizations and motivations characteristic of property offenders
4. Understand the application of various typologies to property offenses
5. Describe how stolen goods are distributed

## Chapter Outline

Introduction
Persistent and Professional Thieves
*Criminal Careers of Property Offenders*
*Property Offenders and Rational Choice*
Larceny-Theft
*Prevalence and Profile of Larceny-Theft*
*Theft on College Campuses*
*Motor Vehicle Theft*
*Shoplifting and Employee Theft*
Burglary
*The Social Ecology of Burglary*
*Types of Burglars*
*Burglary Locales*
*The Motivation of Burglars*
*Target Selection*
*Costs of Burglary*
*The Burglary-Drug Connection*
*The Sexualized Context of Burglary*
Stolen Property
*The Role of Criminal Receivers*
Arson
*Fire Setters*

# Chapter Summary

This chapter discusses various types of property crime in the United States, including larceny/theft, burglary, stolen property, and arson. The difference between persistent thieves and professional criminals is examined briefly. Professional offenders commit crime with some skill, make a living from crime, and spend relatively little time incarcerated. Persistent thieves are those who continue in common-law property crimes despite having at best an ordinary level of success. Most property offenders do not specialize in one type of crime. The issue of property crimes as rational choice is also discussed.

Larceny/theft, which does not involve the use of force or illegal entry, is the most frequently occurring property crime, with theft from a motor vehicle being the largest category. Theft on college campuses is influenced by the size and design of the campus. Motor vehicle theft can include a variety of means of transportation, but automobiles are the vehicle most commonly stolen. It is the crime where the largest percentage of victims miss time from work as a result of the crime. Most completed motor vehicle thefts are reported to the police. Theft of external car parts may be committed for a variety of reasons; theft from motor vehicles also includes taking items from within the vehicle (stereo equipment, cameras, briefcases, etc.). Joyriding involves opportunistic car theft committed by groups of teenagers for fun or thrills; the preferred vehicle is an American-made sports car. Jockeys are professional car thieves who are regularly involved in steal-to-order jobs; they are rarer but represent the most costly and serious form of auto theft.

Employee theft and shoplifting are both increasing. Employee theft costs retailers more than customer shoplifting and is often perceived as more serious. Historically, shoplifting was pervasive among middle-class women. Today, it is a crime that crosses class lines and is not committed primarily by women; juveniles are overrepresented in current statistics on offending. Research suggests that shoplifting is one of the largest categories of unofficial delinquency and may be a gateway offense leading to more serious and chronic types of offending. Various typologies of shoplifters are discussed.

Burglary is usually a victim-avoiding crime; offenders prefer to avoid direct confrontation with their victims. Burglary is more common in large metropolitan areas and in the Midwest. Changes in routine activities since World War II may help explain changes in burglary rates. A typology of burglars is discussed. The primary motivation for burglary is the need for fast cash, often to maintain the offender's street status or to support a party lifestyle. Commercial targets are selected based on their suitability, with retail establishments being the most common choice. Residential burglars rarely target homes of family or friends but may target homes of people otherwise known to them. Other key elements in target selection include a reluctance to burglarize occupied dwellings, residences with complex security devices, and residences with a dog that could make noise or injure the offender. The recent increase in robbery and decrease in burglary may be linked to the increased demand for crack cocaine. Some burglaries have sexual motivations, such as voyeuristic or fetish burglaries; there may also be a link between burglary and later sexual offending.

Receiving stolen property involves three key elements: buying and selling, stolen property, and knowing property to be stolen. The fence is a middleman who takes on the role of moving stolen goods from the professional thief to the customer; most thieves do not use a professional fence to dispose of stolen goods. Paul Cromwell's typology of criminal receivers is discussed.

The FBI records an incident as an arson only after it has been investigated and officially classified as arson by the proper investigative authorities; fires of suspicious or unknown origin are not included in the FBI's arson statistics. The recent wave of church arsons in the United States and the motivations behind these crimes are discussed. Arson for profit is fairly rare. The majority of those involved in arson are juveniles.

# Lecture Outline

I. Persistent and Professional Thieves
   A. Explain that offenses such as larceny and burglary may be legally different but they are all basically property crimes of theft, and in some way all such offenders are thieves
   B. There are several basic differences between persistent thieves and professional criminals
      1. Neil Shover defines professional criminals as those "who commit crime with some degree of skill, earn reasonably well from their crimes, and despite stealing over long periods of time, spend rather little time incarcerated"
      2. Persistent thieves continue in property crimes despite having, at best, an ordinary level of success: most do not specialize but alternate among a variety of crimes (e.g., burglary, robbery, car theft, con games)
      3. Offense specialization, a preference for a certain type of offense, is limited among property offenders
      4. Property offenders are often designated as occasional offenders because of the short-term and sporadic nature of offending
         a. Occasional refers not to the frequency of offending but to the nature and character of the offending
         b. Occasional property offenders commit crimes when there is an opportunity or situational inducement

**Show the ABC News program *Diamond Heist* from the video library.**

   C. Criminal careers of property offenders
      1. The concept of a criminal career implies a rational and planned progression through defined stages, with some type of planning or logic to the progression
      2. Alfred Blumstein suggests that a criminal career in property offending has three phases
         a. The break-in period characterizes the offender's early years and may last for the first 10 to 12 years of the offender's career
         b. The stable period is the time of highest commitment and the period when the offender most closely identifies with a criminal lifestyle
         c. The burnout phase is characterized by increasing dropout rates and a reduced commitment to a criminal lifestyle

3. Other researchers suggest that the criminal careers of violent offenders are much shorter
4. The assumption that career offending becomes more serious and frequent over time has recently been challenged by the belief that crime may be a more fragmented pursuit

D. Property offenders and rational choice
1. Research on property crimes is often conducted from the perspective of rational choice theories (refer back to Chapter 4)
2. Research suggests that the use of rationality is common, although partial and limited rather than total
3. Rationality is not a dichotomous variable but a continuum with offenders at one end using more rationality while those at the other end may sometimes show behavior that appears totally senseless
4. This chapter examines both the professional and the persistent occasional thief and examines a variety of research on typologies of property crime offending to consider whether property crimes are rational pursuits for either expressive or instrumental gains
5. The major property crimes examined in this chapter are larceny/theft, motor vehicle theft, burglary, and arson (refer back to Chapter 2 for offense definitions and prevalence information)

II. Larceny/Theft

A. Introduction
1. Larceny/theft is defined by the UCR and NIBRS as "the unlawful taking, carrying, leading, or riding away of property from the possession, or constructive possession, of another"
2. Unlike burglary, it does not involve the use of force or other means of illegal entry, making it more a crime of opportunity and thus seemingly less frightening

**Show the ABC News program *Master Thief* from the video library.**

B. Prevalence and profile of larceny-theft
1. According to the FBI and the NCVS, larceny is the most frequently occurring property crime
2. The largest categories include theft from motor vehicles followed by shoplifting and theft from building
3. The aggregate economic loss is high, but slightly over one-third of all individual losses are under $50.
4. Personal items (jewelry, camera equipment, etc.) are most frequently stolen, constituting almost one-fourth of all stolen items
5. According to the NCVS, theft from motor vehicles account for almost 13% of all items stolen

C. Theft on college campuses
1. College campuses provide many opportunities for crime and the most frequent crime on college campuses is larceny
2. The Crime Awareness and Campus Security Act of 1990 (refer to Chapter 2) mandates that institutions of higher learning compile and make public

data on some index crimes, but theft is not included in this requirement, which may present a misleading picture of crime on campus

3. Research into theft on college campuses found that campus size and design were more important determinates of theft rates on campus than the rates of theft in the surrounding area
4. Research testing routine activity theory found that measures of individual lifestyle such as how a person spends leisure time can be important predictors of victimization
   a. Students spending a large amount of time away from their residence (studying, involved in campus organizations, etc.) have an increased risk of major theft victimization
   b. Self-protective measures (increased locks on doors, owning a dog, etc.) were effective deterrents to victimization

D. Motor vehicle theft
1. The UCR defines motor vehicle theft as "the theft or attempted theft of a motor vehicle," which includes various means of transportation (refer to Chapter 2)
   a. The most commonly stolen vehicle is an automobile
   b. There are several reasons why motor vehicle theft is analyzed separately from other theft
      (1) The frequency of motor vehicle thefts
      (2) The cultural association of automobiles with status and the social definition of individuals
   c. Auto theft represents an invasion of the victim's possessions as well as a significant inconvenience
2. Prevalence and profile of motor vehicle theft
   a. In 2003, approximately 1.23 million vehicles were reported stolen, with an estimated total value of $8.2 billion
   b. Many crimes occur at or near the victim's residence
   c. Approximately 90% of all completed and 54% of all attempted motor vehicle thefts are reported to the police, with the rate of reporting increasing with household income level
   d. Approximately 62% of stolen cars are recovered, although they may not be found in pretheft condition
   e. Reasons for theft include joyriding, temporary transportation needs, use in a crime, and stripping
   f. Models preferred by thieves include Honda Accords and Toyota Camrys
3. Theft of car parts
   a. The Motor Vehicle Theft Law Enforcement Act, passed by Congress in 1984, called for marking major sheet metal parts of high-theft cars with VINs to deter theft of stolen parts to the auto body repair industry
   b. 1998 British Crime Survey data suggest that the items most frequently stolen from motor vehicles were external parts of the vehicle, followed by stereo equipment and other items (e.g., bags, briefcases, cameras, clothing)
   c. Reasons for stealing external car parts (body panels, windshield wipers, mirrors, antennas, tires, wheels, etc.) include the expense of replacing car parts, the lack of availability of car parts for older models, acquiring the license plate, and youth crazes; research primarily supports the first two of these explanations
4. Joyriders: car theft for fun

a. Joyriding involves car thefts that are usually opportunistic and usually committed by groups of teenagers for the purpose of fun or thrills
b. Most vehicles stolen by joyriders are recovered, although they are often found abandoned and often after they have been crashed
c. Patterns of joyriding theft differ from those of other types of auto theft
(1) The type of car stolen tends to be an American-made sports car
(2) Joyriders are more likely to select a car belonging to someone they know, whereas most auto thefts involve victims and offenders who are unknown to each other

5. Jockeys: car theft for profit
a. A jockey is a car thief who is regularly involved in stealing to order
b. Professional thefts are the most costly and most serious type of auto theft but are not as common as thefts for other uses
c. Professional auto thieves generally operate in groups and engage in planning and calculation in target selection
d. They generally target luxury cars that may be driven out of the country or shipped overseas
e. Professional auto thefts have the lowest recovery rate

E. Shoplifting and employee theft

1. Employee theft accounts for 47% of loss to US retailers while shoplifting accounts for 32% of loss, with employee theft increasing at a faster rate than shoplifting
a. Most employees stealing cash or merchandise are short-term and typically work in retail establishments with higher-than-average sales and a high degree of management turnover
b. Many retailers see internal theft to be a more serious problem than consumer shoplifting

2. Technology is used to address both types of crime (e.g., computerized inventory counts to track merchandise; electronic detection systems; antitheft tags attached to goods)

3. During the late 1800s and early 1900s, shoplifting was pervasive among middle-class females, leading to several possible explanations
a. Changes in the production, distribution, and marketing of goods that created a greater desire for merchandise
b. Kleptomania was used as an explanation for middle-class shoplifters and as a way to legitimize the actions of stores and courts that dismissed or acquitted such offenders

4. Who shoplifts?
a. Discuss the case of Winona Ryder and explain why she is not a typical shoplifter, although her case was highly publicized due to her fame as an actress
b. Juveniles are overrepresented in shoplifting statistics
c. Shoplifting by adolescents is typical among all social classes, although the most serious and chronic forms are found less among the more economically disadvantaged members of society
d. Early research suggested that females were more likely to be apprehended for shoplifting than males but more recent research challenges this finding, suggesting that males were more highly involved — one explanation for the different results may relate to different types of research subjects

5. An adolescent phase?

a. Shoplifting is one of the largest categories of delinquency not detected by formal authorities according to research in the United States and in other countries
b. Shoplifting appears to be one of several forms of deviant behavior engaged in during adolescence

6. Shoplifting as a gateway offense
a. Because shoplifting has been found to be part of the early offense history of a certain segment of property offenders, it may be a gateway offense or a starting point leading to more serious and chronic types of offending, although research results supporting this are mixed
b. Research does not support the idea that offenders move systematically from lesser to more serious forms of property offending: rather than moving in a linear fashion from one type of property offense to another, their progression is more sporadic and fragmented

7. Meaningful typologies for shoplifting
a. Mary Owen Cameron's topology distinguishes between professional shoplifters (boosters) and novice shoplifters (snitches)
(1) Boosters comprise a small percentage of those apprehended for shoplifting and most commonly sell the items they steal rather than shoplifting for their own personal consumption
(2) Snitches are more common and are characterized by a tendency to steal items of often small monetary value for their own personal gratification
b. Richard H. Moore's topology considers motivation, although because his sample consisted only of convicted shoplifters it is unclear how well the typology would apply to the majority of shoplifters, who are never apprehended
(1) Impulsive shoplifters were inexperienced, rarely planned the crime in advance, and were remorseful when apprehended
(2) Occasional shoplifters committed crimes more frequently and were motivated primarily by peer pressure
(3) Episodic shoplifters generally had psychological problems and were the smallest group
(4) Amateur shoplifters, the most common type, who committed crimes fairly regularly and in a way that was calculated to maximize profit and minimize risk
(5) Semiprofessional shoplifters had the most skill and expertise and preferred more expensive items, frequently for resale to others
c. Frank J. McShane and Barrie A. Noonan used cluster analysis to create a typology that considered relevant demographic characteristics, prior offending history, psychological factors, and measures of life purpose
(1) Rebels: younger females with a significant prior history of offending and who often had the economic ability to pay for the stolen items
(2) Reactionaries: older persons, more likely to be male, married, with higher levels of education, also had the economic ability to pay for the stolen items, reported occupational pressure as the only psychosocial stressor
(3) Enigmas: almost half the sample, older persons, slightly more likely to be male, low likelihood of prior offending, lacked apparent psychosocial stressors preceding apprehension

(4) Infirm: more likely to be female, category most likely to contain the elderly, tended to have experienced more previous episodes of chronic illness

8. The thrill of it all
   a. Because many shoplifters have the economic means to afford the items they steal, there must be a motivation other than economic gain
   b. Some research suggests that shoplifting may be a thrill-seeking activity, with the crime making the stolen object desirable

III. Burglary
A. Introduction
1. Burglary is a highly prevalent crime: victimization data suggests that 72% of U.S. households will be burglarized at least once over the average lifetime
2. Burglary involves unlawful entry into a structure for the purpose of committing a felony, usually a theft (refer to Chapter 2)
3. Force is not a required element of burglary, although burglaries are differentiated by whether force is used
4. 2003 UCR data provides some information on burglary
   a. The majority of burglaries do involve forcible entry, followed by unlawful entry and then by attempted forcible entry
   b. A slight majority of burglaries occurred during the day but residential burglaries are more likely to occur during the evening
5. Burglary, unlike robbery, is a crime where the offender avoids the victim when possible

B. The social ecology of burglary
1. Burglary rates are higher in large metropolitan areas and in the midwestern region of the United States
2. Lifestyle and routine activity theory have affected explanations of how the nature and level of property crime offending has changed in response to changes in the routine activities and structures of daily living
   a. The three minimal ingredients necessary for a crime to occur are a motivated offender, a suitable target, and the lack of a capable guardian
   b. Technological advances and changes affect individuals, families, and communities
   c. Changes in crime rate trends since World War II are not related to an increase in motivated offenders but to changes in patterns of routine activities that affect the risk of victimization
3. Research suggests that the type of area is the strongest predictor of burglary victimization, although the relationship between income and victimization risk is not linear, as households with the highest and lowest incomes had the greatest risk of victimization
4. Research using data from the British Crime Survey attempted to estimate the risk for crimes including burglary
   a. The study found that the highest victimization risk for burglary was found within single-adult households (compared to households with at least two adults)
   b. Victimization risks were highest for people living in areas characterized by a high percentage of unemployed, high building density, primary-individual households, and single-parent households with children

c. Victimization risk for personal theft was lower for individuals who are married, older, and male, and higher for women and individuals with more education

C. Types of burglars: Mike Maguire's typology

1. Low-level burglars are primarily juveniles, who often commit crimes impulsively, usually work with others, are easily dissuaded from a particular target by security devices, do not gain significant rewards, and frequently desist from burglary as they get older
2. Middle-range burglars are generally older, move back and forth between legitimate and criminal pursuits, more commonly use alcohol and other drugs, are easily dissuaded from a target by security devices, gain larger rewards from their crimes than do low-level burglars, but lack connections to permit constant and large-scale dealing in stolen goods
3. High-level burglars are professionals, work in organized groups, engage in careful planning and target selection, and earn a significant living from their crimes

D. Burglary locales

1. Nighttime residential and daytime commercial burglary are considered more serious by the police because of the increased risk of a confrontation between the offender and other persons
2. Burglary is considered a "cold" crime because there is generally little physical evidence and because the crime is often discovered long after it actually occurred (especially if it is a residential burglary)

E. The motivation of burglars

1. The most prevalent rationale behind the crime of residential burglary is economic (the need for fast cash to maintain street status, buy drugs, provide basic necessities, etc.)
2. The majority of residential burglars live a party lifestyle and use much of the money obtained from burglary to maintain this lifestyle, which includes illicit drugs, alcohol, and sexual pursuits
3. Commercial burglaries are even more associated with instrumental ends such as economic gain
4. Professional burglars are also motived by economic gain
5. Many offenders choose burglary because it is familiar, is less risky than other crimes (such as selling drugs or robbery), or because they do not have the equipment necessary for robbery (such as a gun)
6. A small number of burglars commit crimes for the excitement rather than for the money

F. Target selection

1. Commercial burglars select sites on the basis of the target's suitability, with retail establishments four times more likely to be burglarized than other times of commercial establishments
2. Most residential burglars have potential targets in mind prior to committing the crime, usually selected based on knowledge of the occupants, receipt of a tip, or through observation
   a. Some residential burglars do target residences of persons known to them, although generally not residences of close friends or relatives
   b. Selection based on information from tipsters is not common, as most burglars lack such connections
   c. Burglary targets are rarely chosen impulsively, although the amount of observation prior to selection is usually fragmented

3. Other elements also influence target selection
    a. Looking for occupancy is very important, as most burglars do not want to burglarize occupied dwellings
    b. Most residential burglars avoid residences with complex security devices because they do not have the skill to bypass these devices
    c. Dogs will also deter offenders from potential targets because of the possibility of injury and because of the potential for noise by the dog

G. Costs of burglary
1. Over 85% of household burglaries involve some type of economic loss, with approximately 20% involving losses of over $1,000
2. Items stolen from homes include personal times such as jewelry and clothing, household furnishings, tools, and cash
3. A small percentage of victims also lose time from work as a result of the victimization
4. Property crimes appear to have a larger effect than violent crimes on the victim's decision to move, especially if there has been repeated property victimization near the home

H. The burglary–drug connection
1. During the 1980s, burglary began to decrease and robbery increase
2. One possible explanation for this may be increased demand for crack cocaine
    a. Offenders using crime to fund drug habits need to rely on crimes such as robbery that produce quick cash
    b. Burglary is more likely to result in stolen goods rather than cash
3. The illicit market for crack has driven down the street value of stolen goods, reducing preference for burglary as a crime

I. The sexualized context of burglary
1. Although economic gain is the primary motive for most burglaries, there is a category of burglaries motivated by sexual forces
    a. Fetishes involve the offender stealing particular items because they provide an outlet for sexual gratification
    b. Voyeuristic burglaries may involve looking around but not actually taking anything
2. A study of sexual murderers found that the majority had a history of burglary, suggesting that burglary may constitute part of a pattern of sexual offending
3. Residential rape and burglary both involve the unlawful entry of a structure by stealth and may have similar opportunity structures

IV. Stolen Property

A. Introduction
1. The basic elements of the crime involves buying and receiving stolen property while knowing it to be stolen
2. Receiving stolen property involves various levels of profits for people with various levels of skill
    a. Some burglars commit crimes specifically to obtain something they know someone wants and sell the item directly to the customer
    b. Burglars may also sell stolen goods to people known to them or take the stolen goods to flea markets, auctions, and so on
    c. Some burglars sell stolen merchandise to merchants while representing it as legal goods

d. The use of a professional fence to dispose of stolen goods is the most common method for professional burglars but the least common method for the majority of thieves

3. Darrell Steffensmeier used the case study method to study Sam Goodman, a white male fence
   a. He links the rise of the fence to the availability of mass-produced products made possible by industrialization
   b. Steffensmeier defines a fence as someone who "purchases stolen goods both on a regular basis and for sale"
   c. According to Steffensmeier, a professional fence has direct contact with thieves, engages in the buying and selling of stolen goods regularly and persistently, and is a public dealer
   d. There are also occasional fences; their receipt of stolen goods is infrequent in both quality and quantity

B. The role of criminal receivers
1. Paul Cromwell and colleagues developed a three-part topology of criminal receivers
   a. Professional receivers meet Steffensmeier's definition
      (1) Most residential burglars do not use professional fences; connections to professional receivers often distinguish high level burglars from the more typical residential burglar
      (2) A professional fence provides a safe and quick way to dispose of goods and is often the best outlet for a large volume of stolen goods
      (3) Some are generalists who deal in a wide variety of stolen goods, while others specialize in only certain types of stolen goods
      (4) Most are involved in a legitimate business that serves as a cover for and facilitates their criminal activity (e.g., secondhand stores)
   b. Avocational receivers are involved in buying of stolen property on a part-time basis: it is secondary to but usually associated with their primary business activity
      (1) They may be involved in respectable occupations (e.g., the lawyer or bail bondsman who provides professional services in exchange for stolen property) or in illegitimate occupations (e.g., drug dealers who accept stolen goods in exchange for drugs)
      (2) They are distinguished from the professional by the frequency of purchase, volume of activity, and level of commitment to the criminal enterprise
   c. Amateur receivers are otherwise honest people who buy stolen property on a relatively small scale, primarily for personal use; they make up for lack of volume with sheer numbers

V. Arson

A. Introduction
1. The FBI defines arson as "any willful or malicious burning or attempt to burn, with or without intent to defraud, a dwelling, house, public building, motor vehicle or aircraft, personal property of another, etc." (refer to Chapter 2)
2. The FBI records a fire as arson only after it has been investigated and officially classified as arson by the proper authorities; fires of suspicious or unknown origins are not included in FBI arson statistics

3. Discuss the Earth Liberation Front (ELF) arsonists and the use of arson as a hate crime

B. Fire setters
1. Arson for profit is only a minor part of the loss due to arson and the businessperson committing arson to collect insurance money is atypical of arsonists in general
2. The majority of those involved in arson are juveniles
   a. Approximately 50 percent of all cleared arson cases involve juvenile offenders
   b. Juveniles are more likely to be involved in arsons in cities than in suburbs or rural areas and commit both residential and commercial arson
3. Arson is the third leading cause of residential fires and the second leading cuase of residential fire deaths
4. There are three main types of juvenile fire setters
   a. Children under the age of 7, who generally start fires accidentally or out of curiosity
   b. Children between the ages of 8 and 12, who may start fires out of curiosity or more likely because of underlying psychosocial conflicts
   c. Children between the ages of 13 and 18 who have a history of fire setting, usually undetected

# Key Concepts

**Booster:** A frequent shoplifter.

**Fence;** An individual or group involved in the buying, selling, and distribution of stolen goods. Also called *criminal receiver*.

**Gateway offense:** An offense, usually fairly minor in nature, that leads to more serious offenses. Shoplifting, for example, may be a gateway offense to more serious property crimes.

**Jockey:** A professional car thief involved regularly in calculated, steal-to-order car thefts.

**Joyriding:** An opportunistic car theft, often committed by a teenager seeking fun or thrills.

**Occasional offender:** A criminal offender whose offending patterns are guided primarily by opportunity.

**Offense specialization:** A preference for engaging in a certain type of offense to the exclusion of others.

**Persistent thief**: One who continues in common-law property crimes despite no better than an ordinary level of success.

**Professional criminal:** A criminal offender who makes a living from criminal pursuits, is recognized by other offenders as professional, and engages in offending that is planned and calculated.

**Snitch:** An amateur shoplifter.

# Additional Lecture Topics

When discussing the topic of auto theft, consider reviewing some of the new types of antitheft devices that have been developed recently. These include car alarms, steering column locks such as "The Club," fuel cutoff switches, ignition kill switches, chip-encoded ignition keys, and electronic tracking systems such as "Lo-Jack." Discuss the impact of these devices as a deterrent to various types of car thieves and as a way of preventing car theft.

Consider reviewing some specific additional types of fraud and theft, such as confidence games, check forgery, counterfeiting, embezzlement, insurance fraud, and credit card fraud.

Currently, less than 10% of all burglars apprehended are female. Consider discussing female burglars and whether there are gender-based differences in burglars today . One source of information for this topic is a recent research study on female residential burglars:

> Decker, S.H., R. Wright, A. Redfern, and D. L. Smith (1993). "A Woman's Place Is in the Home: Females and Residential Burglary." *Justice Quarterly*, v.10 #1, pp. 143-162.

# Discussion Questions

These discussion questions are found in the textbook at the end of the chapter. The instructor may want to focus on these questions during the coverage of Chapter 11.

1. Explain the differences between professional property offenders and persistent property offenders.

2. To what extent are property offenders rational actors? Use examples from larceny, burglary, and receipt of stolen property to illustrate your answer.

3. Why is so much attention given to shoplifting among adolescents? Should it be? Why?

4. How are drugs involved in the offending patterns of some burglars? Might effective drug-treatment programs reduce the number of burglaries committed? Why?

5. What does the "sexualized context" of burglary mean? How can burglary have a sexual component or motivation?

6. How are "honest" citizens and professional criminal receivers connected?

7. To what extent is "thrill seeking" a motivation behind certain types of property offenses? How might it contribute to the crime of shoplifting?

# Student Exercises

## Activity #1

Recent legislation requires that universities publish statistics on crime on campus. Obtain information about property crime occurring at your university campus. Compare the rates of property crime on campus to the rates in neighboring jurisdictions. How safe does your university appear to be?

## Activity #2

Your instructor will place you in groups and assign each group to a building on campus (e.g., the university library, the student union, a dormitory). Examine this building and its occupants for vulnerability to property crime (burglary, theft, etc.). Develop at least three workable techniques for reducing the likelihood of property crime victimization for the occupants of this building.

# Criminology Today on the Web

### http://www.ojp.usdoj.gov/bjs/cvict.htm

This site provides summary findings from the National Crime Victimization Survey. Click on the property crime chart for more information about property crime trends in the United States.

### http://www.fbi.gov/hq/cid/arttheft/arttheft.htm

The FBI has a division specializing in art theft.

### http://www.ojp.usdoj.gov/bjs/glance/mvt.htm

This link provides information from the Bureau of Justice Statistics on the rates of motor vehicle theft in the United States.

### http://www.bayou.com/~captjim/cheklist.html

The Rushton Police Department and the National Sheriff's Association have developed a home burglary prevention checklist to allow individuals to make security surveys of their own homes.

**http://www.atf.treas.gov**

This is the home page of the Bureau of Alcohol, Tobacco, Firearms and Explosives, which is the agency responsible for the investigation of arson of federal buildings.

**http://www.usfa.fema.gov/safety/campaigns/mediainfo/ffwf-9.shtm**

The U.S. Fire Administration's arson prevention page.

# Student Study Guide Questions and Answers

## True/False

1. Professional criminals are rare in the world of theft. **(True, p. 370)**

2. Occasional offenders are so named because of the infrequency of their offenses. **(False, p. 372)**

3. According to Alfred Blumstein, property offenders are most committed to a criminal career during the break-in phase. **(False, p. 372)**

4. Larceny involves the use of force. **(False, p. 374)**

5. The Crime Awareness and Campus Security Act of 1990 requires universities to make public data on thefts occurring on campus. **(False, p. 375)**

6. Faculty members are most likely to be victims of theft on college campuses. **(False, p. 375)**

7. According to research on theft, a college student who is involved in a large number of campus organizations and activities is at less risk of major theft victimization. **(False, p. 375)**

8. Theft of a motor vehicle is included in the "larceny-theft" category of the UCR. **(False, p. 376)**

9. Victims of motor vehicle theft are less likely to miss time from work as a result of the crime than victims of violent crime. **(False, p. 376)**

10. The largest percentage of stolen vehicles are taken from a parking lot or garage. **(True, p. 376)**

11. Victims are more likely to report a completed motor vehicle theft than an attempted one. **(True, p. 376)**

12. The majority of stolen cars are recovered. **(True, p. 376)**

13. Police are less able to identify stolen car parts than stolen vehicles. **(True, p. 376)**

14. The item most frequently stolen from a motor vehicle is the stereo. **(False, p. 377)**

15. The majority of auto thefts involve victims and offenders who are known to each other. **(False, p. 377)**

16. Cars stolen by jockeys are likely to be recovered by the police. **(False, p. 378)**

17. Employee theft is a more serious problem than shoplifting to retailers. **(True, p. 378)**

18. During the early 1900s, shoplifting was commonly committed by middle-class women. **(True, p. 378)**

19. Shoplifting today is restricted primarily to the lower class. **(False, p. 378)**

20. Today, shoplifting is committed primarily by women. **(False, p. 378-379)**

21. Winona Ryder is not a typical shoplifter. **(True, p. 379)**

22. Shoplifting may be a gateway offense leading to more serious and chronic offending. **(True, p. 381)**

23. Boosters primarily keep the items they shoplift. **(False, p. 381)**

24. The least common type of shoplifter is the occasional, according to Richard Moore. **(False, p. 381)**

25. Most shoplifters do not have the means to afford the items they steal. **(False, p. 382)**

26. The majority of burglars are professionals. **(False, p. 382)**

27. Residential burglaries are more likely to occur during the morning hours. **(False, p. 382)**

28. Burglary is generally a victim-avoiding crime. **(True, p. 382)**

29. Burglary rates are highest in the southern part of the United States. **(False, p. 382)**

30. Burglary rates are higher in rural areas. **(False, p. 382)**

31. According to Mike Maguire, middle-range burglars are more likely to be juveniles. **(False, p. 384)**

32. Residential burglary that occurs at night is considered to be more serious. **(True, p. 385)**

33. Commercial burglary that is committed during nighttime hours is considered by the police to be more serious. **(False, p. 385)**

34. Property crimes generally do not involve known victims. **(True, p. 387)**

35. The pattern of victim–offender relationship found in property crimes is different from that found in violent crimes. **(True, p. 387)**

36. Burglars generally do not have connections with tipsters. **(True, p. 387)**

37. Burglary targets are rarely chosen on the spur of the moment. **(True, p. 387)**

38. Most offenders are reluctant to burglarize occupied dwellings. **(True, p. 387)**

39. Most household burglaries involve economic loss. **(True, p. 388)**

40. The majority of burglary victims lose time from work as a result of their victimization. **(False, p. 388)**

41. Property crimes may have more of an effect than violent crimes on a victim's decision to move . **(True, p. 388)**

42. Prior to the 1980s, burglary and robbery rates paralleled. **(True, p. 388)**

43. Research on active burglars has found that in areas characterized by a strong trade in crack cocaine, there is an increased preference for burglary. **(False, p. 388)**

44. Research suggests that there may be a link between burglary and sexual offenses. **(True, p. 389)**

45. The use of a professional fence is the most common method of disposing of stolen goods for most thieves. **(False, p. 389)**

46. The majority of professional fences are involved in a legitimate business that act as a cover for criminal activities. **(True, p. 390)**

47. As a front for criminal activity, a pawnshop would be viewed as strictly clean. **(False, p. 390)**

48. Avocational receivers are usually professional fences. **(False, p. 390)**

49. Fires that are of suspicious or unknown origin are classified by the FBI as arson. **(False, p. 393)**

50. The majority of those involved in arson are juveniles. **(True, p. 393)**

51. Adults are more likely to be involved in commercial arson than juveniles. **(False, p. 394)**

52. For juveniles between the ages of 8 and 12, fire setting generally represents underlying psychosocial conflicts. **(True, p. 394)**

## Fill in the Blank

53. Larceny and burglary offenders are both __________. **(thieves, p. 371)**

54. A(n) __________ thief continues in common law property crimes despite having an ordinary level of success, at best. **(persistent, p. 371)**

55. Offense __________ is a preference for a certain type of offense. **(specialization, p. 371)**

56. According to Alfred Blumstein, the __________ period is the initial phase of a property offender's criminal career. **(break-in, p. 372)**

57. __________ is defined as activities identified by their impersonal, methodical, efficient, and logical components. **(Rationality, p. 372)**

58. __________ is the most frequently occurring property offense. **(Larceny, p. 375)**

59. __________ are the most commonly stolen vehicles. **(Automobiles/cars, p. 376)**

60. Removing air bags, radios, seats, and other parts from a stolen car is known as __________. **(stripping, p. 376)**

61. The Motor Vehicle Theft Law Enforcement Act requires the major sheet metal parts of high-theft automobiles to be marked with __________. **(Vehicle Identification Numbers/VINs, p. 376)**

62. Joyriding offenses are usually committed by __________. **(teenagers, p. 377)**

63. A car thief who is regularly involved in stealing cars to order is a(n) __________. **(jockey, p. 378)**

64. In Finland, shoplifting is most prevalent among __________. **(adolescents, p. 380)**

65. The most common reason why Finnish adolescents desist from shoplifting is __________. **(boredom, p. 380)**

66. According to Richard Moore's typology of shoplifters, __________ shoplifters are inexperienced, rarely plan the crime in advance, and are remorseful when apprehended. **(impulsive, p. 381)**

67. According to Richard Moore, the __________ shoplifter is most likely to steal merchandise for resale to others. **(semiprofessional, p. 381)**

68. According to McShane and Noonan's typology of shoplifters, members of the __________ group were characterized by a lack of apparent psychosocial stressors preceding apprehension. **(enigma, pp. 381-382)**

69. According to victimization data, approximately __________ percent of households in the United States will be burglarized at least once over an average lifetime. **(72, p. 382)**

70. According to Mike Maguire's typology of burglars, __________ burglars are professionals. **(high-level, p. 384)**

71. Commercial burglaries are generally associated with __________ ends. **(instrumental/economic, p. 386)**

72. Commercial burglary locations are usually selected based on the __________ of the target. **(suitability, p. 386)**

73. Retail establishments are __________ times as likely to be burglarized as other commercial establishments. **(four, p. 386)**

74. Crack users are more likely to commit __________ than burglary. **(robbery, p. 388)**

75. __________ burglaries occur when the offender steals particular items because they provide an outlet for sexual gratification. **(Fetish, p. 389)**

76. A professional fence who deals in only certain types of stolen goods is known as a(n) __________. **(specialist, p. 390)**

77. A(n) __________ fence is one whose illicit lines of goods are distinct from those of legitimate commerce. **(noncovered, p. 390)**

78. The Church Arson Prevention Act was signed into law by President Clinton in __________. **(1996, p. 393)**

## Multiple Choice

79. Malcolm Kline used the term __________ to refer to the heterogeneous and unplanned nature of offending found among gang members.
    a. professional criminal activity
    b. offense specialization
    c. **cafeteria-style offending (p. 371)**
    d. persistent offending

80. According to Alfred Blumstein, the break-in period of a property offender's criminal career lasts approximately __________ years.
    a. 5
    b. **10 (p. 372)**
    c. 20
    d. 25

81. The most frequent type of larceny, according to the UCR, is
    a. shoplifting.
    b. **theft from a motor vehicle. (p. 375)**
    c. theft from a building.
    d. purse snatching.

82. The most common index crime occurring on college campuses is
    a. **larceny. (p. 375)**
    b. burglary.
    c. assault.
    d. rape.

83. Which of the following cars is most likely to be preferred by car thieves?
    a. **Toyota Camry (p. 376)**
    b. Ford Taurus
    c. Dodge Intrepid
    d. Mitsubishi Gallant

84. The primary motivation for the crime of joyriding is
    a. profit.
    b. **fun. (p. 377)**
    c. to meet a long-term need for transportation.
    d. to meet an immediate need for transportation.

85. The most costly form of auto theft is
    a. joyriding.
    b. **professional theft. (p. 378)**
    c. theft for use in a crime.
    d. stripping.

86. Shoplifting is
    a. **increasing. (p. 378)**
    b. decreasing.
    c. remaining the same.
    d. Research has not addressed this.

87. One of the best ways to address both shoplifting and employee theft is
    a. security personnel.
    b. **technology. (p. 378)**
    c. severe penalties.
    d. warning notices.

88. Today, __________ are overrepresented in offense statistics on shoplifting.
    a. **juveniles (p. 378)**
    b. young adults
    c. senior citizens
    d. middle class women

89. Research by __________ suggests that males are more likely to shoplift than females.
    a. Mary Owen Cameron
    b. **Lloyd W. Klemke (p. 380)**
    c. Richard H. Moore
    d. Frank J. McShane and Barrie A. Noonan

90. According to Mary Owen Cameron's typology, professional shoplifters were known as
    a. **boosters. (p. 381)**
    b. impulsive shoplifters.
    c. snitches.
    d. enigmas.

91. According to Mary Owen Cameron's typology, shoplifters who primarily stole for their own personal gratification were known as
    a. boosters.
    b. impulsive shoplifters.
    c. **snitches. (p. 381)**
    d. enigmas.

92. According to Richard Moore's typology of shoplifters, __________ shoplifters generally had psychological problems.
    a. impulsive
    b. **episodic (p. 381)**
    c. amateur
    d. occasional

93. According to McShane and Noonan's typology of shoplifters, the __________ category includes persons who are older, with higher levels of education than other groups, and more likely to be married and male.
    a. rebel
    b. enigma
    c. **reactionary (p. 381)**
    d. infirm

94. According to UCR data, the most common type of burglary involves __________ entry.
    a. **forcible (p. 382)**
    b. attempted forcible
    c. unlawful
    d. lawful

95. According to routine activities theory, which of the following elements is *not* necessary for a criminal act to occur?
    a. **The presence of a capable guardian (p. 382)**
    b. The presence of a motivated offender
    c. The absence of a capable guardian
    d. The presence of a suitable target

96. Which of the following individuals has the greatest risk of being a victim of personal theft?
    a. A young unmarried woman
    b. An older married woman
    c. A young unmarried man
    d. **An older married man (p. 383)**

97. According to Mike Maguire's typology of burglars, juveniles committing crimes on the spur of the moment fall into the category of __________ burglars.
    a. high-level
    b. mid-range
    c. **low-level (p. 384)**
    d. multilevel

98. The most common commercial establishment to be targeted for burglary is a __________ establishment.
    a. wholesale
    b. **retail (p. 386)**
    c. service
    d. banking

99. Which of the following is *not* one of the ways residential burglars generally select targets?
    a. Through their knowledge of the occupants
    b. **Through spur of the moment selection (p. 387)**
    c. Through receiving a tip
    d. Through observing a potential target

100. Which of the following is *not* an element considered when selecting a target for a burglary?
    a. Whether the residence has a security device
    b. Whether a dog lives in the residence
    c. Whether the residence is unoccupied
    d. **They are all elements considered by the offender when selecting a target. (p. 387)**

101. A fence commits the crime of
    a. burglary.
    b. robbery.
    c. **receiving stolen property. (p. 389)**
    d. motor vehicle theft.

102. __________ conducted a case study of Sam Goodman, a professional fence.
    a. Carl Klockars
    b. **Darrell Steffensmeier (p. 389)**
    c. Vincent Swaggi
    d. Paul Cromwell

103. According to Cromwell's typology of criminal receivers, the __________ receiver is most likely to be used by high-level burglars.
    a. **professional (p. 390)**
    b. avocational
    c. amateur
    d. episodic

104. Among the businesses fences use as a front for their criminal activity, a(n) __________ is perceived as strictly clean.
    a. **restaurant (p. 390)**
    b. auto parts shop
    c. pawnshop
    d. antique shop

105. According to Cromwell's typology of criminal receivers, __________ receivers generally buy stolen property primarily for personal consumption.
    a. professional
    b. avocational
    c. **amateur (p. 390-392)**
    d. episodic

106. Young children under the age of seven generally start fires
    a. **accidently. (p. 394)**
    b. due to underlying psychosocial conflicts.
    c. for revenge.
    d. for personal motives.

# Word Search Puzzle

```
D T J P V R E W D N N J R O N G N S D W J I Z F O D P Y G
A K I Y V D S W J D V J K O L F T E F J P S T B Y W J V O
W S D I V O V T I O H S F V R H P A C F F W Y R E P W O B
N S Z T N B A P G N C P A K C G R M M X Z J H B U L G U G
T I N J Y L J I R P H K Q L F I U H X C J J C F E Z A D R
Z Z M R O W J K E K O X E L A K N G J B N Q W G K X U L W
X N G X K Y C W Y Y B G K Y J B Y G A T E W A Y X O H Q X
Q U R R L P R E B L E A Y Y Y P G T C K E Q M B H T Q X K
G E Z U X N L I C D A Z E T Q V F J I C C W S R E R X N Q
J A Q B O Z I J D A R S T E F F E N M E I E R O R H H D F
S K E N B O R F D I L P R O D O H W V O S L G F Y Q T T Z
P Z E O Y S J O W Q N Z A A J Q P T B U R H D G T B P Y A
E Z F S X R S M Y F I G B Z H L G I F J U V O Z E X E F Y
C J R E L B F Y U L C J P Q S X R L M G N R C V U C Y T O
I H Z K T O D P J S M T K J J S S X Q W Z H O X E B K C I
A F C Z B L B L E F U S C J X P W H B J N A W C M R V I T
L A H K Y X Q R R X A J M D F G M N Q L B Q T L V T E A E
I Z J D Q D L R Q B G W H L E G C U A C K G T Y N K X S H
Z E U C T K S S N P E R S I S T E N T V A P D A W M M I R
A X R I Q Y N D T C D P A V T U O T L S D M K K Y J W U D
T G O A D A I S A T L X B V X I Z W V X Z A E B N C B E S
I H Q W F I T Z L S B W O A S Z J R K Z L N R R R X C Q X
O O B E F O C S S G P G F S C Z X A L Z S K W L O N E Z V
N G F O S A H W U A B L E V V N R S O C J S K Y E N D P P
Q W J R O C W L X R S F C U R O J R C Q R L G F J T L O U
M Z M T V S V W A K O S V S E K D M K R H B G X Y L D A R
C U D B I X T G A R O E Z T V J J N E U X F F B U Q S L X
D M J I B T U E P S B V B P C H W Q R L E W H C Z C D P J
N R D Q W B V I R D E B T D P K X X S M L H P A Z K G P N
X B V O C C A S I O N A L Q Y Q H P M C X S B N S G N A R
```

**Booster**
**Cameron**
**Fence**
**Gateway**
**Jockey**
**Joyriding**
**Klockers**
**Occasional**
**Persistent**
**Professional**
**Shover**
**Snitch**
**Specialization**
**Steffensmeier**

## Crossword Puzzle

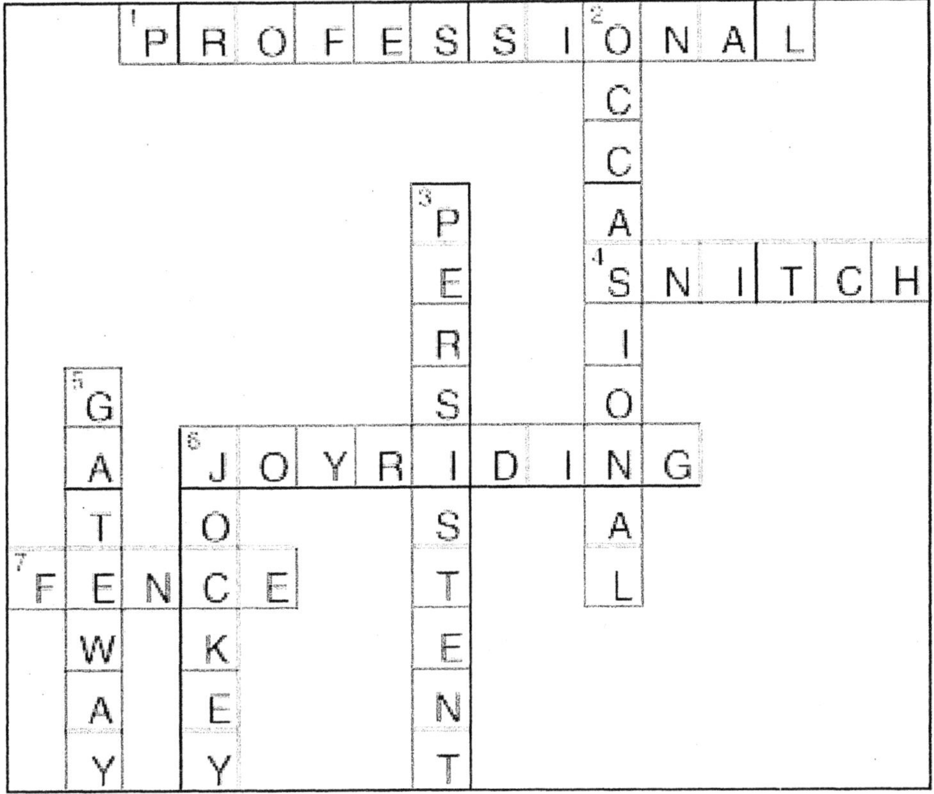


**Across**

1. A criminal who makes a living from crime.
4. An amateur shoplifter.
6. An opportunistic car theft, often committed by a teenager seeking fun or thrills.
7. An individual involved in the buying, selling, and distribution of stolen goods.

**Down**

2. An offender whose offending patterns are guided primarily by opportunity.
3. A(n) ________ thief continues committing property crimes despite no better than an ordinary level of success.
5. Shoplifting may be a(n) ________ offense to more serious crime.
6. A professional car thief involved in steal-to-order car thefts.

# 12

# White-Collar and Organized Crime

## Learning Objectives

After reading this chapter, students should be able to:

1. Discuss white-collar crime and its etiology
2. Describe the nature of corporate crime
3. Explain the history of organized crime in the United States, including La Cosa Nostra
4. Identify new and emerging organized criminal groups within the United States
5. Discuss the relationship between organized crime and the law

## Chapter Outline

Introduction
White-Collar Crime
*Definitional Evolution of White-Collar Crime*
*Corporate Crime*
*Causes of White-Collar Crime*
*Curtailing White-Collar and Corporate Crime*
Organized Crime
*History of Organized Crime in the United States*
*A Rose by Any Other Name—La Cosa Nostra*
*Prohibition and Official Corruption*
*The Centralization of Organized Crime*
*La Cosa Nostra Today*
*Activities of Organized Crime*
*Code of Conduct*
*Other Organized Criminal Groups*
*Transnational Organized Crime*
*Organized Crime and the Law*
Policy Issues: The Control of Organized Crime

# Chapter Summary

This chapter reviews two specific categories of crime: white-collar crime and organized crime. Edwin Sutherland's original 1939 definition of white-collar crime focused on the social standing of the offender; today, the focus has shifted to the type of offense committed. Currently, one commonly used term is *occupational crime*, which includes any criminal act committed through opportunities created in the course of a legal occupation. Gary S. Green developed a typology of occupational crime which includes four categories: organizational occupational crime, state authority occupational crime, professional occupational crime, and individual occupational crime. Corporate crime, another form of white-collar crime, is committed for the benefit of the corporation rather than the individual employee. One new area of corporate crime is environmental crime. There have been a number of attempts to explain white-collar crime. Sutherland applied elements of differential association theory to white-collar crime. Travis Hirschi and Michael Gottfredson stated that white-collar criminals are motivated by the same forces that drive other offenders and suggest that a general theory of crime can explain white-collar crime and other forms of crime as well. John Braithwaite states that white-collar criminals are motivated by a disparity between corporate goals and legitimate means and suggests that business subcultures encourage illegal behavior. Dealing with white-collar crime may require ethical, enforcement, structural, and political reforms.

Criminal societies such as La Cosa Nostra and the Mafia began in Italy several centuries ago and migrated to the United States during a period of Italian immigration during the late 1800s. Prohibition, which began after the passage of the Eighteenth Amendment to the U.S. Constitution in 1919, established the wealth and power of modern organized crime syndicates and effectively institutionalized official corruption. The Wickersham Commission specifically mentioned the corrupting influence that Prohibition was having on professional law enforcement in the United States. During this period, organized crime leaders also worked to consolidate power. The repeal of the Eighteenth Amendment, in 1933, ended Prohibition. Organized crime activities went underground for the next twenty years. National attention was again focused on organized crime in 1951, when the federal Kefauver Committee reported that a nationwide crime syndicate was operating in many large U.S. cities. Eventually, federal investigations established the existence of twenty-four crime families operating in the United States under the direction of a commission.

Organized crime activities include racketeering, vice, theft/fence rings, gangs, and terrorism. The primary motivation for all organized crime activities is money. Members of organized Sicilian-American criminal groups are governed by a strict code of conduct known as *omerta*, which functions to concentrate power in the hands of the crime bosses as well as ensuring their protection. The two key requirements imposed by the code are to obey one's superiors and to keep silent; the penalty for failing to adhere to these rules is death. Transnational organized crime involves unlawful activity undertaken and supported by organized criminal groups operating across national boundaries; it is becoming a key challenge to law enforcement agencies. The most important piece of federal legislation ever passed to target organized crime activities is RICO, which includes a provision for asset forfeiture, making it possible for federal officials to seize all proceeds of persons involved in racketeering. Organized crime is difficult to control; the text discusses various approaches to the control of organized criminal activity.

# Lecture Outline

I. Introduction
   A. Discuss the 2002 collapse of the Enron Corporation
   B. Discuss the crimes committed by top executives of WorldCom, Inc.
   C. Briefly review the early Teapot Dome scandal, which involved the Harding administration

**Show the ABC News program *Martha Stewart* from the video library.**

II. White-Collar Crime
   A. Introduction
      1. White-collar crime was first defined by Edwin Sutherland during his presidential address to the American Sociological Society
         a. Sutherland defined white-collar crime as "a crime committed by a person of respectability and high social status in the course of his occupation"
         b. He felt that criminologists fail to understand that violations of public and corporate trust by people in positions of authority are just as criminal as predatory acts committed by persons of lower social status
         c. He also pointed out that white-collar criminals are less likely to be investigated, arrested, or prosecuted than other types of offenders, and if they do happen to be convicted, they are much less likely to be incarcerated
         d. He claimed that this was due primarily to the social standing of white-collar criminals
      2. Discuss some contemporary examples of white-collar crime, such as Ivan Boesky's insider trading scam, Michael Milken's conviction for securities fraud, and the savings and loan disaster of the 1980s, as well as the various offenses that have been uncovered since the collapse of Enron and the bankruptcy of WorldCom, Inc.
      3. Review the terminology of white-collar crime as presented in Table 12-1
   B. Definitional evolution of white-collar crime
      1. The concept of white-collar crime has changed significantly since Sutherland's first definition — the emphasis today is on the type of crime committed rather than on the social class or occupation of the person committing the crime
      2. Discuss definitions developed by scholars such as Herbert Edelhertz and Gilbert Geis
      3. Occupational crime is any act punishable by law that is committed through opportunity created during the course of a legal occupation
      4. Gary Green developed a topology of occupational crime with four categories:
         a. Organizational occupational crime: crime committed for the benefit of an employing organization
         b. State authority occupational crime: crimes by officials through the exercise of their state-based authority
         c. Professional occupational crime: crimes committed by professionals in their capacity as professionals (e.g., physicians, lawyers)

   d. Individual occupational crime: crimes by individuals as individuals (e.g., personal income tax evasion, employee theft, falsifying expense reports)

**Show the ABC News program *Fools Gold* from the video library.**

C. Corporate crime
   1. Corporate crime involves violation of a criminal statute by a corporate entity or by its executives, employees, or agents acting on behalf of and for the benefit of the corporation
   2. Discuss some recent examples of corporate crime:
      a. The conviction of Arthur Andersen for obstruction of justice for the destruction of documents relating to the Enron Corporation audits
      b. The conviction of SabreTech for their part in the crash of a Valujet airplane in 1996
      c. The class action suit brought against makers and sellers of silicon gel breast implants
      d. Negligence by Union Carbide Corporation that resulted in a chemical leak at their storage facilities in Bhopal, India
      e. The tobacco industry liability settlement
   3. One relatively new area of corporate and white-collar crime is environmental crime, which involves violations of the criminal law (by businesses, business officials, or other individuals or organizations) which damage some protected or significant aspect of the natural environment
      a. Examples of environmental crime include whaling and intentional pollution
      b. The Exxon *Valdez* supertanker that spilled 11 million gallons of crude oil over 1700 miles of Alaskan coastline was an example of corporate negligence contributing to environmental criminality

D. Causes of white-collar crime
   1. Sutherland applied elements of his own differential association theory to white-collar crime, suggesting that white-collar crime, like other systematic criminality, is learned
   2. Travis Hirschi and Michael Gottfredson (refer to Chapters 6 and 8) have applied their general theory of crime to white-collar crime
      a. They suggest that white-collar offenders are motivated by the same forces that drive other criminals: self interest, the pursuit of pleasure, and the avoidance of pain
      b. They conclude that white-collar crime is fairly rare because the personal characteristics of most white-collar workers are those that are expected to produce conformity, not criminality (e.g., high levels of education, commitment to the status quo, personal motivation to succeed)
   3. John Braithwaite suggests that white-collar criminals are motivated by a disparity between corporate goals and the limited opportunities available through conventional business practices
      a. When corporate officers are pressured to achieve goals that may not be available within the framework of laws and regulations, they may turn to crime to meet the demands of the organization
      b. Braithwaite suggests that a general theory explaining both white-collar and other forms of crime can be developed by focusing on inequality as

the central explanatory variable in criminal activity: greed can motivate successful people to violate the law to acquire more power and wealth

c. The corporate culture socializes executives into modalities that make it easier for them to violate the law when pressured to perform, and the hostile relationship that often exists between businesses and government regulatory agencies further encourages executives to evade the law
d. He suggests that the potential for shame associated with discovery is a powerful deterrent to most corporate executives
e. Braithwaite recommends the use of an accountability model which would hold accountable everyone responsible for corporate crimes
f. Thus, Braithwaite's integrated theory combines elements of strain, subcultural, labeling, and control theories

E. Controlling white-collar and corporate crime
1. White-collar crimes are difficult to investigate, prosecute, and convict for a number of reasons
   a. It is often difficult for prosecutors to show that a crime has actually occurred
   b. White-collar criminals are generally better educated than other offenders and better able to conceal their crimes
   c. Cases against white-collar criminals frequently have to be built on evidence of a continuing series of offenses, rather than a single crime
   d. The evidence involved in white-collar crimes is only understood by financial or legal experts and is difficult to explain to jurors
   e. Business executives can hire excellent defense attorneys and tie up the courts with motions and appeals
2. Discuss the Sarbanes-Oxley Act, signed by President George W. Bush in 2002, and review some of the earlier federal legislation relating to the conduct of American business
3. Some types of occupational crime, such as individual occupational crimes, may be easier to deal with and reduce
4. However, as long as professional occupational criminals continue to enjoy relative immunity from prosecution, they are not likely to be deterred by sanctions or threats
5. James Coleman suggests four areas of reform through which white-collar crime might effectively be addressed:
   a. Ethical reforms: establishing stronger and more persuasive codes of business ethics
   b. Enforcement reforms: center on the belief that white-collar offenders must be more severely punished but also includes items such as more funding for enforcement agencies, larger research budgets for regulatory investigators, and insulating enforcement personnel from undue political influence
   c. Structural reforms: making basic changes in corporate structure to make white-collar crimes more difficult to commit
   d. Political reforms: center on eliminating campaign contributions from businesses and corporations but also include increasing the level of fairness in determining government grants, purchases, and contracts

III. Organized Crime
   A. Discuss the history of Jonathan Wild, who ran the largest criminal organization in England in the early 1700s
   B. History of organized crime in the United States
      1. Italian secret societies came to the United States in the late nineteenth and early twentieth centuries; organizations such as the Mafia and the Black Hand specialized in intimidating Italian immigrants
      2. The Mafia became a quasi-police organization in Italian ghetto areas in the early twentieth century
      3. During the 1930s and 1940s, the Mafia became very antifascist, which made them popular during World War II; after the war, they resumed traditional positions of power within Italian society and increased linkages between American and Italian criminal organizations
   C. A rose by any other name—La Cosa Nostra
      1. Prior to the influx of Italian immigrants in the late 1800s, other organized criminal groups flourished in New York City, including Jewish and Irish gangs
      2. Ethnic succession, the continuing process by which one immigrant or ethnic group succeeds another through assumption of a particular place in society, has been a reality in organized crime as in most other aspects of American life
      3. During the last 50 years, organized criminal activity in the United States has largely been the domain of Italian-American immigrants and their descendants, especially those of Sicilian descent
      4. The terms *Mafia* and *La Cosa Nostra* have been used interchangeably to refer to Sicilian-American organized criminal groups
   D. Prohibition and official corruption
      1. Prohibition, which began after the 1919 passage of the Eighteenth Amendment to the U.S. Constitution, gave organized crime a significant financial boost
         a. Prior to Prohibition, Mafia operations were relatively small in scale, focusing primarily on gambling, protection, and loan-sharking
         b. Prohibition allowed the Mafia to establish significant wealth and power
      2. The profits from bootlegging led to significant corruption of public officials, including the police
      3. The Wickersham Commission, appointed in 1929 by President Herbert Hoover, produced a series of reports that mentioned the corrupting influence that Prohibition was having on professional law enforcement
      4. Although Prohibition was repealed in 1933, with the passage of the Twenty-first Amendment to the U.S. Constitution, its heritage of corruption remains, and official corruption has become an institutionalized part of life in some parts of the country
      5. In 1967, President Johnson's Task Force on Organized Crime concluded that organized crime flourishes where local officials have been corrupted
   E. The centralization of organized crime
      1. During the Prohibition era, organized crime leaders worked to consolidate power, which resulted in gang warfare
      2. One famous gangland war occurred in Chicago in the 1920s when Al Capone created a crime syndicate and declared himself to be the leader of all Chicago's organized crime families
      3. Nationally, similar efforts at consolidation occurred

a. In September 1931, a large number of gang-ordered executions of Mafia leaders took place, leading to the transformation of the Mafia into an integrated, coordinated criminal organization able to settle most disputes internally and to shield its activities from investigators
b. After this, Mafia activity went underground so successfully that many thought it had died

4. Organized crime returned to public attention again in 1951, when the federal Special Committee to Investigate Organized Crime in Interstate Commerce (the Kefauver Committee) reported that a national crime syndicate known as the Mafia operated in many large cities and that its leaders control the most lucrative rackets in these cities
5. The 1967 President's Commission reported that organized criminal groups in the United States consisted of twenty-four crime families operating under the direction of a national body of overseers
   a. Family organization included a boss, an underboss, a counselor/advisor, lieutenants, and soldiers
   b. Organized crime members swear allegiance to a strict code of conduct which protects the bosses and gives them power over the organization

F. La Cosa Nostra today
1. Of the twenty-four organized crime families of Sicilian-American heritage that some believe continue to operate throughout the United States today, the largest number (five) operate out of New York
2. Other influential Cosa Nostra families operate out of Chicago, Philadelphia, New Orleans, New England, and Kansas City, Missouri

G. Activities of organized crime
1. According to the 1976 federal Task Force on Organized Crime, the five types of activities that may qualify as organized crime are racketeering, vice operations, theft/fence rings, gangs, and terrorism
2. The primary motivation for all organized criminal activity is money
3. Today, Sicilian-American cartels are involved in a variety of activities, including gambling, loansharking, drug trafficking, fencing, infiltration of legitimate businesses, and labor union racketeering
4. Organized crime appears increasingly to be involved in illegal copying and distribution of copyrighted software, music, and other forms of recorded media as well as providing videotaped pornographic productions

H. Code of conduct
1. *Omerta*, the unwritten code that governs behavior among members of organized Sicilian-American criminal groups, concentrates power in the hands of the crime bosses and also ensures their protection
2. The code imposes two indisputable requirements on all family members: obey your superiors and keep silent
3. Failure to obey the code means death

I. Other organized criminal groups
1. A true criminal organization is able to function independently of any of their members, including their leaders, and have a continuity over time as personnel within the organization change
   a. The James Gang dissolved when Jesse James died, thus it was not a true criminal organization
   b. The Capone Organization is a true criminal organization: it continued after Al Capone was imprisoned and continues to operate in a more modern form in Chicago today

2. In addition to Sicilian-American criminal enterprise, there are other organized criminal groups in the United States, each characterized by some degree of organizational continuity independent of its membership: these groups include the Haitian Mafia, Russian Mafia, Black Mafia, Cuban Mafia, Colombian cartels, various Asian groups, inner-city gangs, outlaw motorcycle gangs, and many others
3. Latino-organized groups are believed to be responsible for the majority of cocaine illegally entering the United States today

J. Transnational organized crime
1. Transnational organized crime is unlawful activity undertaken and supported by organized criminal groups operating across national boundaries
2. Transnational organized crime is seen as a major force in world finance and one of the major challenges of the early twenty-first century
3. The world's major crime clans include the Hong Kong-based Triads, South American cocaine cartels, the Italian Mafia, the Japanese Yakuza, the Russian Mafiya, and West African crime
4. Russian organized crime has grown quickly since the collapse of the Soviet Union and has emerged in the United States and other countries outside the former Soviet sphere of influence
   a. They include many ex-KGB officers, war veterans, underpaid military officers, and former operatives of the Communist Party
   b. Russian organized crime is involved in a variety of activities, including narcotics, prostitution, racketeering, illegal gambling, product diversion and counterfeiting, software and music duplication, and illicit arms sales and smuggling
   c. Currently, Russian organized criminal groups operate out of 17 U.S. cities in 14 states
5. The globalization of crime has required increased coordination of law enforcement efforts throughout the world and forced American law enforcement activities to expand beyond national borders

K. Organized crime and the law
1. The Hobbs Act, a series of statutes passed beginning in 1946, was the first federal legislation specifically aimed at curtailing organized crime activities
   a. The act made it a violation of federal law to engage in any form of criminal behavior that interferes with interstate commerce
   b. It also criminalized interstate or foreign travel in furtherance of criminal activity and made it a crime to use the highways, telephone, or mail in support of activities such as gambling, drug trafficking, loansharking, and other forms of racketeering
2. The most important piece of federal legislation ever passed which specifically targets organized crime activities is RICO, the Racketeer Influenced and Corrupt Organization statute, which was part of the federal Organized Crime Control Act of 1970
   a. RICO brought together under one piece of legislation many activities of American organized crime and increased punishments
   b. RICO did not make racketeering itself illegal but focused on the proceeds from these activities, making it illegal to derive profit from racketeering

c. Punishments provided for under RICO include asset forfeiture, allowing federal officials to seize the proceeds of those involved in racketeering

3. Money laundering
   a. Money laundering, the process by which illegal gains are disguised as legal income, is prohibited by the U.S. Criminal Code
   b. The 1986 federal Money Laundering Control Act requires banks to report to the government all currency transactions in excess of $10,000
   c. The money laundering problem in the United States is increasing, especially after a recent U.S. Supreme Court case made it more difficult to obtain money laundering convictions

IV. Policy Issues: The Control of Organized Crime
   A. Currently, policies to control organized crime focus primarily on criminal aspects of organized crime rather than on the organizational aspects, which may be more useful in formulating future policy
      1. We need to study the social context within which organized crime occurs, as it is an integral part of the social, political, and economic system
      2. To fight organized crime, society must meet the demands of the consumers of organized crime's products and services, and fight corruption in politics and law enforcement
   B. Howard Abadinsky recommends four approaches to the control of organized crime:
      1. Increase the risk of involvement in organized crime by increasing the resources available to law enforcement agencies that are useful in fighting organized crime
      2. Increase law enforcement authority, which will increase the risks of involvement in organized crime
      3. Reduce the economic lure of involvement in organized crime by making legitimate opportunities more readily available
      4. Decrease organized criminal opportunity through decriminalization or legalization of activities from which organized crime draws income
   C. Another option is the strict enforcement of existing laws, which may serve as a strong general deterrent to other potential offenders, although the commitment of organized criminal groups to criminal activities may make them less likely to be deterred by such threats

# Key Concepts

**Asset forfeiture:** The authorized seizure of money, negotiable instruments, securities, or other things of value. In federal antidrug laws, the authorization of judicial representatives to seize all monies, negotiable instruments, securities, or other things of value furnished or intended to be furnished by any person in exchange for a controlled substance, and all proceeds traceable to such an exchange.

**Bank fraud**: Fraud or embezzlement that occurs within or against financial institutions that are insured or regulated by the U.S. government. Financial institution fraud includes commercial loan fraud, check fraud, counterfeit negotiable instruments, mortgage fraud, check kiting, and false credit applications.

**Corporate crime:** A violation of a criminal statute either by a corporate entity or by its executives, employees, or agents acting on behalf of and for the benefit of the corporation, partnership, or other form of business entity.

**Environmental crime**: A violation of the criminal law which, although typically committed by businesses or by business officials, may also be committed by other people or by organizational entities and which damages some protected or otherwise significant aspect of the natural environment.

**Ethnic succession:** The continuing process whereby one immigrant or ethnic group succeeds another by assuming its position in society.

**Kefauver Committee:** The popular name for the federal Special Committee to Investigate Originated Crime in Interstate Commerce, formed in 1951.

**La Cosa Nostra:** Literally, "our thing." A criminal organization of Sicilian origin. Also call *the Mafia, the Outfit*, *the Mob*, *the syndicate*, or simply *the organization*.

**Mafia** See **La Cosa Nostra.**

**Money laundering:** The process of converting illegally earned assets, originating as cash, to one or more alternative forms to conceal such incriminating factors as illegal origin and true ownership.

**Occupational crime:** Any act punishable by law that is committed through opportunity created in the course of an occupation that is legal.

***Omerta*** The informal, unwritten code of organized crime, which demands silence and loyalty, among other things, of family members.

**Organized crime**: The unlawful activities of the members of a highly organized, disciplined association engaged in supplying illegal goods and services, including gambling, prostitution, loan-sharking, narcotics, and labor racketeering.

**Racketeer Influenced and Corrupt Organizations (RICO):** A statute that was part of the federal Organized Crime Control Act of 1970 and that is intended to combat criminal conspiracies.

**Securities fraud:** The theft of money resulting from intentional manipulation of the value of equities, including stocks and bonds. Securities fraud also includes theft from securities accounts and wire fraud.

**Transnational organized crime**: Unlawful activity undertaken and supported by organized criminal groups operating across national boundaries.

**White-collar crime**: Violations of the criminal law committed by a person of respectability and high social status in the course of his or her occupation.

# Additional Lecture Topics

Consider discussing in more detail some of the best known cases of corporate crime. These might include:

A. The conspiracy case involving a number of electrical companies, such as General Electric and Westinghouse. Relate back to neutralization theory while reviewing how the defendants used various techniques of neutralization when explaining their involvement in the conspiracy.
B. The Ford Pinto case, in which Ford executives ignored a fuel rupture problem with Ford Pintos after determining that it would be unprofitable to fix the problem, despite their knowledge that failure to correct the problem with the gas tank would result in death and serious injury to drivers.

Review some of the federal statutes that have been passed to help control environmental crimes. These include, but are not limited to:

- The Clean Air Act, which requires companies to comply with air quality standards established by the Environmental Protection Agency (EPA)
- The Clean Water Act, which provides sanctions to companies that knowingly or negligently discharge pollutants into navigable waters
- The Toxic Substance Control Act, which regulates the manufacture, processing, and distribution of chemicals and toxic substances
- The Superfund (Comprehensive Environmental Response, Compensation, and Liability Act), which requires companies to clean up hazardous waste at contaminated dumping sites

The text discusses RICO, but there were other federal statutes passed in the 1970s and 1980s to help the criminal justice system fight organized crime. Title III of the Omnibus Crime Control and Safe Streets Act (1968) allows federal law enforcement officers to use electronic surveillance devices to listen to conversations among suspected organized criminals (after obtaining a warrant) and to submit into evidence in federal court information obtained through electronic surveillance. The Organized Crime Control Act (1970) has a number of important provisions in addition to RICO. These include the establishment of the witness protection program, witness immunity, and special grand juries to investigate multistate organized crime activities.

# Discussion Questions

These discussion questions are found in the textbook at the end of the chapter. The instructor may want to focus on these questions during the coverage of Chapter 12.

1. What is the difference between white-collar crime and organized crime? What linkages, if any, might exist between the two?

2. What types of white-collar crime has this chapter identified? Is corporate crime a form of white-collar crime? Is occupational crime a form of white-collar crime?

3. Describe a typical organized crime family, as outlined in this chapter. Why does a crime family contain so many different "levels"?

4. What is money laundering? How might money laundering be reduced or prevented? Can you think of any strategies this chapter does not discuss for the reduction of money laundering activities in the United States? If so, what are they?

5. What strategies does this chapter discuss for combating the activities of organized crime? Which seem best to you? Why? Can you think of any other strategies that might be effective? If so, what are they?

# Student Exercises

## Activity #1

Explain how the routine activity approach to explaining crime might be applied to organized crime.

## Activity #2

Obtain a chart showing the organizational structure of a modern legitimate corporation. Compare this to Figure 12.1, which shows the structure of a typical organized crime family. How do the structures differ? What similarities do you see?

# Criminology Today on the Web

### http://www.usdoj.gov/atr

This is the home page of the U.S. Department of Justice Antitrust Division.

### http://www.epa.gov

This is the home page for the U.S. Environmental Protection Agency.

### http://www.occ.treas.gov/moneylaundering2002.pdf

This booklet provides information on money laundering and discusses ways that banks can protect themselves against becoming involved in money laundering schemes.

### http://www.nw3c.org

This is the home page of the National White Collar Crime Center, which provides support services for law enforcement agencies that are involved in fighting economic crime.

### http://www.wccfighter.com

This is the home page for "White Collar Crime Fighter," an online newsletter.

**http://www4.law.cornell.edu/uscode/18/ch96.html**

At this site, read Title 18, Chapter 96 of the U.S. Code, the Racketeer Influenced and Corrupt Organizations Act (RICO).

# Student Study Guide Questions and Answers

## True/False

1. According to Sutherland, it is rare for large corporations to become involved in illegal activities until long after their inception. **(False, p. 404)**

2. Sutherland found that white-collar criminals are more likely to be investigated than other types of offenders. **(False, p. 404)**

3. Tax evasion includes failure to file a tax return at all. **(True, p. 406)**

4. Michael Milken was involved in the savings and loan scandal of the 1980s. **(False, p. 407)**

5. Blue-collar crime involves crimes committed by members of less prestigious occupational groups. **(True, p. 410)**

6. State authority occupational crime is occupation specific. **(True, p. 411)**

7. Corporations can be held criminally responsible for the actions of their officials. **(True, p. 413)**

8. The Union Carbide Corporation liability case centered on the issue of criminal negligence. **(True, p. 413)**

9. According to Sutherland, white-collar crime is motivated by a disparity between corporate goals and legitimate means. **(False, p. 414)**

10. Hirschi and Gottfredson have outlined a theory that is specific to white-collar crime. **(False, p. 414)**

11. White-collar crime is more dangerous than other "common" forms of crime. **(False, p. 415)**

12. John Braithwaite's theory is specific to white-collar crime and does not apply to other forms of criminal behavior. **(False, p. 415)**

13. Braithwaite suggests that corporate officers are motivated to evade the law despite the generally positive relationship that exists between businesses and the government agencies that regulate them. **(False, p. 415)**

14. The Sarbanes-Oxley Act created the Securities Exchange Commission. **(False, p. 416)**

15. Structural reforms to address white-collar crime may include adding members of the public to corporate boards. **(True, p. 417)**

16. Jonathan Wild was famous for running the largest criminal organization in 18th century England. **(True, p. 420)**

17. During the last half-century, organized criminal activity has been dominated by the descendants of Irish-American immigrants. **(False, p. 420)**

18. Most Sicilians who emigrated to the United States had ties to or experience with Mafia organizations in Italy. **(False, p. 421)**

19. The Unione Siciliana was an organization set up as a rival to the American Mafia. **(False, p. 421)**

20. Prohibition elevated street thugs to crime overlords. **(True, p. 422)**

21. One result of Prohibition was police corruption. **(True, p. 422)**

22. According to the Wickersham Commission, Prohibition had a corrupting influence on police in America. **(True, p. 422)**

23. Gang warfare among organized criminal groups was fairly rare during the Prohibition era. **(False, p. 422)**

24. According to the Kefauver Committee, the American Mafia has international linkages that appear most clearly in connection with the narcotics trade. **(True, p. 423)**

25. Within a crime family, *caporegime* are the soldiers. **(False, p. 423)**

26. The Civella mob is headquartered in New Orleans. **(False, p. 424)**

27. Organized crime families may infiltrate legitimate businesses for the purpose of money laundering. **(True, p. 426)**

28. The code of *omerta* functions to ensure the protection of crime bosses. **(True, p. 427)**

29. According to the code of organized crime, a family member may be an informer only if there is no other way to avoid a conviction and prison sentence. **(False, p. 428)**

30. One of the general features of the code of organized crime is to be a "stand-up" guy. **(True, p. 428)**

31. One hallmark of a true criminal organization is that it has a continuity over time as personnel within the organization change. **(True, p. 428)**

32. Organized crime is primarily a national issue. **(False, p. 429)**

33. Many Russian private security firms are fronts for Russian gangsters and organized criminals. **(True, p. 430)**

34. Al Capone was convicted of income tax evasion. **(True, p. 430)**

35. RICO made racketeering illegal. **(False, p. 431)**

36. Asset forfeiture was authorized by the Hobbs Act. **(False, p. 431)**

37. The Bank of Credit and Commerce International was significantly involved in money laundering for drug cartels and terrorist organizations. **(True, p. 432)**

38. Federal statutes such as the Money Laundering Control Act have succeeded in reducing the problem of money laundering in the United States. **(False, p. 432)**

39. According to Gary Potter, to attack organized crime, society must meet the demands of the consumers of organized crime's products and services. **(True, p. 433)**

## Fill in the Blank

40. According to Sutherland, white-collar crime involves crimes committed by a person of __________ social status. **(high, p. 404)**

41. Sutherland claimed that the only real difference between modern-day white-collar criminals and those of the past is that today they are more __________. **(sophisticated, p. 404)**

42. Stealing trade secrets from an individual or business is an example of __________. **(economic espionage, p. 406)**

43. __________ is the unlawful misappropriation for personal use of money, property, or some other item of value entrusted to the offender's care, custody, or control. **(Embezzlement, p. 406)**

44. The early definition of white-collar crime focused on the __________. **(violator, p. 407)**

45. According to Gary Green's typology of occupational crime, __________ occupational crime benefits the employing organization, not the individual employees. **(organizational, p. 411)**

46. A crime committed by an attorney in his capacity as an attorney is an example of a(n) __________ occupational crime. **(professional, p. 411)**

47. __________ crime is a violation of a criminal statute by a corporate entity or by its executives, employees, or agents acting on behalf of and for the benefit of the corporation. **(Corporate, p. 413)**

48. Intentional pollution is an example of a(n) __________ crime. **(environmental, p. 414)**

49. According to Hirschi and Gottfredson, the personal characteristics of most white-collar workers are those that would be expected to produce __________ in behavior. **(conformity, p. 415)**

50. Braithwaite has recommended the implementation of a(n) __________ model as a way of reducing white-collar offending. **(accountability, p. 415)**

51. As an element of an integrated theory of organizational crime, __________ theory would emphasize the way stigmatization can foster criminal subculture formation. **(labeling, p. 415)**

52. The Corporate Fraud Task Force was created by President __________. **(George W. Bush, p. 416)**

53. The 1914 __________ Act prohibited mergers and acquisitions in which the effect may be to create a monopoly. **(Clayton, p. 416)**

54. According to Coleman, providing larger research budgets for regulatory investigators falls into the __________ area of reform. **(enforcement, p. 417)**

55. The elimination of campaign contributions from businesses is an example of the __________ area of white-collar crime reform. **(political, p. 417)**

56. The Italian __________, based in Naples, was infamous for murder and extortion during the 19th century. **(Camorra, p. 420)**

57. __________ refers to the continuing process by which one immigrant group supplants another through assumption of a particular place in society. **(Ethnic succession, p. 420)**

58. Prohibition resulted from the passage of the __________ Amendment to the U.S. Constitution. **(Eighteenth, p. 421)**

59. During Prohibition, organized crime leaders worked to __________ power. **(consolidate, p. 422)**

60. In the case of __________, the convictions of Joseph Bonanno and 26 other well-known organized crime figures were overturned. **(*U.S. v. Bufalino*, p. 423)**

61. According to the President's Crime Commission, there are __________ groups operating as criminal cartels in large cities across the U.S. **(twenty-four, p. 423)**

62. The function of the __________ within a crime family is to collect information for the boss. **(underboss, p. 423)**

63. The function of the __________ within in a crime family are to serve as chiefs of operating units. **(lieutenants/caporegime, p. 423)**

64. A total of __________ of the 24 crime families operate out of New York. **(five, p. 424)**

65. __________ involves lending money at rates significantly higher than legally prescribed limits. **(Loan-sharking, p. 426)**

66. In a pornographic __________ movie, a sex star is actually killed on screen. **(snuff, p. 426)**

67. Al Capone's Chicago Organization currently operates in Chicago as the __________. **(Outfit, p. 428)**

68. The majority of cocaine entering the United States illegally has been handled by __________ organized criminal groups. **(Latino, p. 428)**

69. The __________ Act made it a violation of federal law to engage in any criminal behavior that interferes with interstate commerce. **(Hobbs, p. 431)**

70. __________ is the process by which illegal gains are disguised as legal income. **(Money laundering, p. 431)**

71. The federal Money Laundering Control Act requires banks to report to the government all currency transactions that exceed __________. **($10,000, p. 431)**

## Multiple Choice

72. White-collar crime was originally defined by
    a. Emile Durkheim.
    b. **Edwin Sutherland. (p. 404)**
    c. Richard Quinney.
    d. George Vold.

73. According to Sutherland, __________ percent of corporations were recidivists.
    a. 28
    b. 58
    c. 78
    d. **98 (p. 404)**

74. Martha Stewart was involved in the insider trading scandal involving
    a. Enron.
    b. WorldCom, Inc.
    c. **ImClone. (p. 405)**
    d. Arthur Andersen.

75. __________ is an activity that illegally inhibits competition between companies and within an industry.
    a. Insurance fraud
    b. Insider trading
    c. Embezzlement
    d. **Antitrust violation (p. 406)**

76. Currently, the concept of white-collar crime focuses on the
    a. **nature of the crime. (p. 407)**
    b. person involved.
    c. occupation involved.
    d. work environment.

77. The concept of "upperworld crime" was developed by
    a. Herbert Edelhertz.
    b. Edwin Sutherland.
    c. **Gilbert Geis. (p. 407)**
    d. Gary Green.

78. According to Gary Green's typology of occupational crime, __________ occupational crimes benefit the employing agency.
    a. professional
    b. state authority
    c. **organizational (p. 411)**
    d. individual

79. Employee theft is an example of __________ occupational crime
    a. organizational
    b. **individual (p. 413)**
    c. state authority
    d. professional

80. The fires set in Kuwait oil fields by retreating Iraqi Army troops during the 1991 Gulf War are an example of both ecological terrorism and __________ crime.
    a. occupational
    b. **environmental (p. 414)**
    c. state authority
    d. organizational occupational

81. __________ suggest(s) that white-collar criminals are motivated by the same forces that drive other criminals.
    a. Edwin Sutherland
    b. **Travis Hirschi and Michael Gottfredson (p. 415)**
    c. Gary Green and Gilbert Geis
    d. John Braithwaite

82. Which of the following forces does *not* motivate white-collar criminals, according to Hirschi and Gottfredson?
    a. The avoidance of pain
    b. The pursuit of pleasure
    c. Self-interest
    d. **Danger and excitement (p. 415)**

83. According to Braithwaite, the central explanatory variable in all criminal activity is
    a. self-control.
    b. **inequality. (p. 415)**
    c. learning.
    d. social class.

84. The Securities and Exchange Commission was created by the __________ Act.
    a. Sherman
    b. Sarbanes-Oxley
    c. **Securities Exchange (p. 416)**
    d. Securities

85. __________ occupational criminals are unlikely to be deterred by sanction or threat.
    a. **Professional (p. 417)**
    b. State authority
    c. Organizational
    d. Individual

86. According to Coleman, enforcement reforms include all but which of the following?
    a. Increasing the funding for enforcement agencies that deal with white-collar crime
    b. **Increasing the level of fairness in determining government grants, purchases, and contracts (p. 417)**
    c. Providing larger research budgets for regulatory investigators
    d. Insulating enforcement personnel from undue political influence

87. Changing the process by which corporations are chartered to include control over white collar crime is an example of the __________ area of white-collar crime reform.
    a. ethical
    b. enforcement
    c. **structural (p. 417)**
    d. political

88. Prior to the arrival of Italian immigrants, many of the rackets in New York City were run by __________ gangsters.
    a. Irish
    b. **Jewish (p. 420)**
    c. Hispanic
    d. Asian

89. The key to the transformation of organized crime from "small time" to "big business" was
    a. **Prohibition. (p. 421)**
    b. prostitution.
    c. gambling.
    d. the Kefauver Commission report.

90. Prohibition was repealed by passage of the __________ Amendment to the U.S. Constitution.
    a. Tenth
    b. Eighteenth
    c. **Twenty-first (p. 422)**
    d. Twenty-fourth

91. The St. Valentine's Day massacre established Al Capone as the undisputed ruler of organized crime in
    a. **Chicago. (p. 422)**
    b. New York.
    c. Boston.
    d. the United States.

92. Which of the following was *not* one of the conclusions reached by the Kefauver Committee?
    a. A nationwide crime syndicate exists with influence in many large cities.
    b. The American Mafia has international linkages, especially in narcotics trafficking.
    c. Mafia leaders usually control the most lucrative rackets in their cities.
    d. **Leadership appears to be centered in a single individual, rather than in a group. (p. 423)**

93. The *consigliere* is also known as the
    a. boss.
    b. underboss.
    c. **counselor. (p. 423)**
    d. lieutenant.

94. The __________ are the lowest level of family membership.
    a. **soldiers (p. 423)**
    b. lieutenants.
    c. agents
    d. *consigliere*.

95. Which of the following organized crime groups operates out of Chicago?
    a. **The Carlisi family (p. 424)**
    b. The Scarfo organization
    c. The Marcello gang
    d. The Civella mob

96. __________ involves the intimidation of legitimate businesses through threats of strikes, walkouts, and sabotage.
    a. **Labor union racketeering (p. 426)**
    b. Loan-sharking
    c. Infiltration of legitimate businesses
    d. None of the above

97. The strict unwritten code of conduct of organized crime, which demands silence and loyalty, is known as the
    a. Cosa Nostra.
    b. RICO.
    c. ***omerta.* (p. 427)**
    d. tong.

98. Unlawful activity undertaken and supported by organized criminal groups operating across national boundaries is known as __________ organized crime.
    a. international
    b. intercontinental
    c. **transnational (p. 429)**
    d. overseas

99. Russian organized criminal groups currently operate in __________ states in the United States.
    a. 10
    b. **14 (p. 430)**
    c. 15
    d. 17

100. The __________ Act made it a crime to use the mail in support of activities such as gambling and loan-sharking.
    a. RICO
    b. **Hobbs (p. 431)**
    c. BICI
    d. *Omerta*

101. The single most important piece of federal legislation that specifically targets organized crime activities is
    a. *omerta.*
    b. **RICO. (p. 431)**
    c. the Hobbs Act.
    d. the United States Code.

102. According to Gary Potter, the __________ aspects of organized crime offer the most useful data for formulating future policy.
    a. criminal
    b. **organized (p. 433)**
    c. social
    d. political

103. Which of the following would be an example of increasing the risk of involvement in organized crime?
    a. **Putting more law enforcement officers on the streets (p. 433)**
    b. Passing asset forfeiture statutes
    c. Creating educational programs and scholarships
    d. Legalizing gambling

104. Abadinsky's suggestion that a special good faith exception to the exclusionary rule in prosecutions involving RICO violations be provided falls under which of his approaches to controlling organized crime?
    a. Increasing the risk of involvement in organized crime
    b. **Increasing law enforcement authority (p. 433)**
    c. Reducing the economic lure of involvement
    d. Decreasing opportunity for organized criminal activity

105. Legalizing or decriminalizing illegal drugs falls into which of Howard Abadinsky's approaches to controlling organized crime?
    a. Increasing the risk of involvement in organized crime
    b. Increasing law enforcement authority
    c. Reducing the economic lure of involvement
    d. **Decreasing opportunity for organized criminal activity (p. 433)**

# Word Search Puzzle

| | |
|---|---|
| Bank | Kefauver |
| Braithwaite | Mafia |
| Corporate | Occupational |
| Cosa Nostra | *Omerta* |
| Environmental | Organized |
| Forfeiture | RICO |
| Fraud | Securities fraud |
| Geis | Succession |
| Gottfredson | Sutherland |
| Green | Transnational |
| Hirschi | White collar |

# Crossword Puzzle

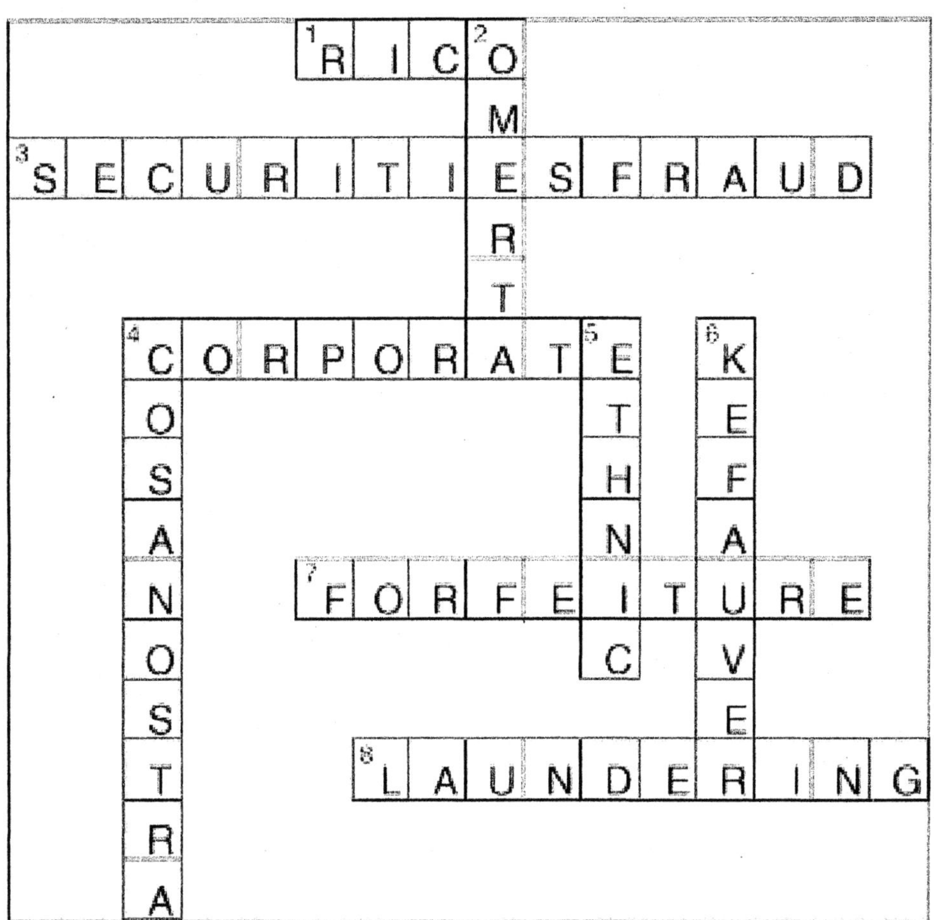


## Across

1. A statute intended to combat criminal conspiracies.
3. The theft of money resulting from intentional manipulation of the value of equities. (2 words)
4. A crime committed by employees acting on behalf of the company.
7. Asset __________ is the authorized seizure of money or other items of value.
8. Money ______ is the process of converting illegally earned cash into other forms to conceal incriminating factors.

## Down

2. The informal, unwritten code of organized crime.
4. A criminal organization of Sicilian origin. (2 words)
5. ______ succession is the process by which one immigrant group succeeds another.
6. The federal committee formed in 1951 to investigate organized crime.

# 13 Drug Abuse and Crime

## Learning Objectives

After reading this chapter, students should be able to:

1. Discuss drug-defined crime and drug-related crimes
2. Define *dangerous drugs* and identify the characteristics of psychoactive substances
3. Describe drug trafficking and government efforts to curtail it
4. Identify the pros and cons of various drug control strategies
5. Explain arguments for and against drug legalization and decriminalization

## Chapter Outline

Introduction
History of Drug Abuse in the United States
  *Extent of Abuse*
  *Young People and Drugs*
  *Costs of Abuse*
Types of Illegal Drugs
  *Stimulants*
  *Depressants*
  *Cannabis*
  *Narcotics*
  *Hallucinogens*
  *Anabolic Steroids*
  *Inhalants*
  *Pharmaceutical Diversion and Designer Drugs*
Drug Trafficking
Drugs and Crime
  *Illegal Drugs and Official Corruption*
Social Policy and Drug Abuse
  *Recent Legislation*
  *Drug-Control Strategies*
  *The National Drug-Control Policy*
  *Policy Consequences*
  *Alternative Drug Policies*

# Chapter Summary

Drugs, and their relationship to crime, is one of the most significant policy issues today. There is a number of sources of data on drug abuse in the United States; this chapter reviews the findings of several recent surveys of both juveniles and adults. The costs of drug abuse are extremely difficult to measure, as they include not only measurable expenditures (law enforcement activities, criminal justice case processing, drug-treatment programs, etc.) but also related costs (illness and death resulting from exposure to controlled substances, drug-related crime, family fragmentation caused by illegal drug use, attitudinal change, etc.). There are seven main categories of controlled substances: stimulants, depressants, cannabis, narcotics, hallucinogens, anabolic steroids, and inhalants. In addition, there is a separate eighth category, dangerous drugs, which refers to broad categories or classes of controlled substances other than cocaine, opiates, and cannabis products.

Stimulants include amphetamines, cocaine, crack, and methamphetamine. These drugs stimulate the central nervous system. Depressants include barbiturates, sedatives, and tranquilizers and may be used both legitimately (to reduce anxiety or elevate mood) or illegitimately. Cannabis, or marijuana, is nonaddictive. Research suggests that it may be used to treat pain and glaucoma, and as a supplement to cancer chemotherapy. Most marijuana used in the United States is either grown in the country or brought in from Mexico. Narcotics such as opium, morphine, heroine, and codeine have both legitimate and illegitimate uses. Frequent users may build up tolerances to the drugs and require ever-increasing doses to obtain the desired effects. Hallucinogens have no official legitimate use. They produce hallucinations and perceptual distortions. Anabolic steroids are used legitimately for weight gain and the treatment of certain disorders, such as arthritis. They may be used illegally by body builders and professional athletes trying to build body bulk or increase strength. Inhalants are volatile substances which depress the central nervous system. They are sometimes considered gateway drugs because they may initiate young people into illicit drug use. Pharmaceutical diversion, primarily of depressants, stimulants, and anabolic steroids, occurs through illegal prescribing by physicians and illegal dispensing by pharmacists. Designer drugs are manufactured by slightly altering the chemical makeup of other illegal or controlled drugs.

Drug trafficking includes the manufacturing, distributing, dispensing, importing, and exporting of a controlled or counterfeit substance. Most cocaine comes into the United States from the Western Hemisphere, especially from South America; it is smuggled in primarily aboard maritime vessels. The Drug Enforcement Agency's heroin signature program tracks heroin trafficking and has found that the majority of heroin in the United States originates in South America.

Drug-defined crimes include violations of laws prohibiting or regulating the possession, use, or distribution of illegal drugs. Drug-related crimes are crimes in which drugs contribute to the offense. There is clear evidence of a strong relationship between drug use and crime. The Arrestee Drug Abuse Monitoring Program attempts to measure the degree to which criminal offenders use controlled substances as a way of understanding the connection between drugs and crime. Drugs are also linked to official corruption; studies of police corruption have found that much illegal police activity was drug-related. Corrections officials may also be involved in drug-related corruption.

The text discusses the history of drug-control policy in the United States, beginning with the 1906 federal Food and Drug Act, which required manufacturers to list their ingredients and specifically targeted mood-altering chemicals. The Comprehensive Drug Abuse Prevention and Control Act, passed in 1970, may be the most comprehensive piece of federal legislation to address controlled substances. The Violent Crime Control and Law Enforcement Act of 1994 also included a number of drug-related provisions. There are five main types of policy initiatives in the fight against illicit drugs. Current policy emphasizes antidrug legislation and strict enforcement. Interdiction is an international drug-control policy that focuses on stopping drugs from entering the country illegally. Crop control involves the eradication of drug crops, both in the United States and abroad. Asset forfeiture allows judicial representatives to seize any items that were involved in drug trafficking or sale. Antidrug education and drug treatment have become extremely popular recently. School-based programs such as D.A.R.E. have increased, although recent research has begun to question the effectiveness of D.A.R.E.-type interventions.

The Office of National Drug Control Policy was established in 1988, with the mission of establishing policies, priorities, and objectives for the national drug-control program. The goals of the program are to reduce illicit drug use, manufacturing, and trafficking; to reduce drug-related crime and violence; and to ameliorate drug-related health consequences.

The war on drugs has been extremely expensive. As a result of the war on drugs, all phases of the criminal justice system have become drug-driven; the civil justice system has also been affected. Rates of imprisonment for drug offenders has increased significantly as a result of strict enforcement and a policy of incarceration.

Alternative drug-control policies are based on the assumption that drug abuse will never be eliminated. Decriminalization involves the reduction of criminal penalties associated with personal possession of a controlled substance. Legalization eliminates the laws and penalties that prohibit the production, sale, distribution, and possession of a controlled substance. There is a variety of arguments for and against legalization of drugs in the United States today.

# Lecture Outline

I. History of Drug Abuse in the United States
   A. The use of illegal drugs affects all segments of society in the United States
      1. Almost all forms of illicit drug use are associated with other forms of criminality, making drugs and their relationship to crime a key policy issue today
      2. The widespread use and abuse of mind- and mood-altering drugs is of relative recent origin
         a. Until the early 1900s, drug abuse was confined primarily to artistic individuals and fringe groups
         b. One exception was the opium dens that were common on the West Coast and that moved across the country as a result of Asian immigration
      3. Psychoactive substances became more commonly accepted during the hippie movement of the late 1960s and early 1970s
      4. Harvard professor Dr. Timothy Leary formed the League of Spiritual Discovery in the mid-1960s, emphasizing the use of LSD and marijuana
   B. Extent of abuse
      1. Discuss the various sources from which current data on drug use are available:

a. The *Monitoring the Future* study conducted by the Institute for Social Research at the University of Michigan
b. The *National Survey on Drug Use and Health* (NSDUH) conducted each year by the Substance Abuse and Mental Health Services Administration (SAMHSA)
c. The *NNICC Report* published by the National Narcotics Intelligence Consumer's Committee and the Drug Enforcement Administration
d. The Arrestee Drug Abuse Monitoring Program quarterly report published by the National Institute of Justice
e. The *Pulse Check: National Trends in Drug Abuse* report published annually by the Office of National Drug Control Policy (ONDCP)

2. Discuss the results of the 2003 NSDUH survey (data released in 2003)
   a. Approximately 19.5 million Americans aged 12 or older were current users of illicit drugs in 2002
   b. Men had higher rates of current illicit drug use than women, but rates of nonmedical psychotherapeutic drug use were similar for men and women
   c. The most commonly used illicit drug in 2002 was marijuana, although approximately 8.8 million Americans use illicit drugs other than (or in addition to) marijuana
   d. The survey also looked specifically at youths between the ages of 12 and 17 and found that approximately 12 percent reported current use of illicit drugs, with marijuana the most commonly used
   e. Individuals aged 18–20 years have the highest rate of illicit drug use, with rates of use declining in each successively older age group; the one exception is in the 60–64-year-old age group
   f. Rates of illicit drug use vary by racial/ethnic group, with the highest rates among the American Indian/Native American population and among persons reporting multiple race
   g. The rate of illicit drug use is higher in metropolitan than in nonmetropolitan areas
   h. Both NSDUH and the *Monitoring the Future* survey show that after an increase in the use of cigarettes, marijuana, and illicit drugs by adolescents in the early 1990s, there has been a leveling or declining trend since 1997
   i. Illicit drug-use rates are highly correlated with education, so that the more education a person receives, the more likely s/he is to discontinue using drugs with age
3. The results of the survey seem to suggest that drug abuse is substantially less of a problem today than it was 20 years ago, although there are some methodological problems associated with the survey
4. Data from the National Crime Victimization Survey suggest that illicit drugs are readily available to teenagers, illustrating another facet of the drug problem in modern American society

C. Young people and drugs: results from the year-2002 *Monitoring the Future* survey of junior high and high school students
   1. Past-year use of any illicit drug by eighth and tenth graders has declined significantly since 1997, although use by seniors (twelfth graders) showed only a small decline
   2. Overall, past year use of cocaine and crack increased from 2001 to 2002
   3. Past year use of heroin year increased for seniors but declined for eighth graders

4. Although the use of inhalants is more prevalent among eighth graders than among students in the other grades, inhalant use decreased among eighth graders from 2001 to 2002
5. The use of MDMA (Ecstasy) decreased among all three grades for the first time in four years

D. Costs of abuse
1. ONDCP estimates that Americans spent $62.4 billion in 2000 to purchase illegal drugs
2. Discuss additional costs associated with drug abuse
   a. Measurable expenditures include law enforcement activities, criminal justice processing, drug-treatment programs, money laundering, and time lost from work as a result of drug involvement
   b. Other costs that are harder to quantify include illness and death resulting from drug use, drug-related crime, damage to families and other relationships, changes in attitudes due to drug-crime fear, lost human potential, and the image of the United States
3. Many cases of AIDS can be traced to intravenous drug use, further increasing the costs of abuse
   a. AIDS is the leading cause of death of black and Hispanic males aged 25–44 and the second-leading cause of death among black women in that age group
   b. ONDCP estimates that in 1995 there were over 52,000 drug-related deaths (not included deaths due to overdose)
4. Another significant cost is lost productivity due to drug abuse

II. Types of Illegal Drugs

A. Introduction
1. Controlled substances are generally grouped according to both pharmacological and legal criteria into seven categories: stimulants, depressants, cannabis, narcotics, hallucinogens, anabolic steroids, and inhalants
2. There is also an additional "catchall" category, dangerous drugs, which includes broad categories or classes of controlled substances other than cocaine, opiates, and cannabis products

B. Stimulants
1. This category includes cocaine, crack cocaine, amphetamines, and methamphetamines
   a. These drugs stimulate the central nervous system, increasing heart rate, blood pressure, and mental activity
   b. Legitimate uses include increased alertness, weight control, reduced fatigue, and topical analgesic
2. Cocaine
   a. Crack cocaine, which is less expensive than the powdered variety, is made by mixing cocaine powder with water and baking soda or ammonia and is usually smoked
   b. Powdered cocaine is inhaled or snorted, or may be mixed with volatile chemicals and freebased
   c. The effects of cocaine include euphoria and a feeling of boundless energy
   d. Prolonged use can cause delusions, hallucinations, weight loss, and overall physical deterioration

3. Amphetamines produce mental alertness and increased concentration and have a number of legitimate medical uses
   a. They may also cause talkativeness and wakefulness, and reduce fatigue
   b. Abuse of amphetamines leads to irritability, overexhaustion, and eventually psychosis and death from cardiac arrest
4. Methamphetamine, which has a stronger effect on the central nervous system than other amphetamines, has recently become popular
   a. It may be ingested in pill form or injected or snorted in powder form
   b. Crystallized methamphetamine may be smoked and is a more powerful form of the drug
   c. Effects include increased heart rate, blood pressure, wakefulness, physical activity, insomnia, decreased appetite, anxiety, paranoia, and violent behavior
   d. It is not physically addictive but may be psychologically addictive

C. Depressants
1. This category includes barbiturates, sedatives, and tranquilizers
2. Legitimate uses include release from anxiety, treatment of psychological problems, and mood elevation
3. Illegitimate users take depressants to produce intoxication, to counter the effects of other drugs, or in the self-treatment of drug withdrawal
4. Abuse of depressants may lead to psychological dependence and addiction

D. Cannabis (marijuana)
1. Marijuana has limited hallucinogenic properties and is nonadddictive
2. Some research suggests that the drug has medical uses, including the treatment of pain, the treatment of glaucoma, and as a way of controlling nausea associated with cancer chemotherapy
3. It is used illegitimately to produce states of euphoria, gaiety, detachment, relaxation, intoxication, and focused awareness
4. Use of marijuana may be accompanied by time distortion, increased sex drive, increased appetite, uncontrollable giddiness, and short-term memory loss

E. Narcotics
1. This category includes opium, morphine, heroin, methadone, codeine, and Dilaudid
2. Legitimate uses include pain relief, antidiarrheal action, and cough suppression
3. They are used illegitimately to produce pleasure, euphoria, a lack of concern, and general feelings of well-being
4. Drugs such as heroin and morphine may be injected under the skin or directly into the bloodstream
5. Frequent users build up a tolerance to these drugs and need ever-increasing doses to induce the desired effects
6. These drugs are addictive and withdrawal symptoms include nervousness, restlessness, severe abdominal pain, watery eyes, nasal discharge, vomiting, diarrhea, weight loss, and pain in the large muscles of the body

F. Hallucinogens
1. This category includes drugs such as LSD, PCP, peyote, and mescaline
2. There are no official legitimate uses for any of these drugs
3. They are used illegally to produce hallucinations, "trips" or "psychedelic experiences"

4. The effects are unpredictable; hallucinations may be pleasant or frightening

G. Anabolic steroids
1. Steroids are used legitimately for weight gain, the treatment of various types of cancer, arthritis, anemia, and connective tissue disorder
2. Some athletes use steroids illegally to gain body bulk and strength

H. Inhalants
1. This category includes a variety of highly volatile substances that may be found in many commonly available products (e.g., lighter fluid, glue, nail polish remover, paint thinner, gasoline)
2. Inhalants have been termed "gateway drugs" – because they are readily available, they are often the first drug tried by young people

I. Pharmaceutical diversion and designer drugs
1. Pharmaceutical diversion occurs through illegal prescribing by physicians and illegal dispensing by pharmacists and their assistants
   a. Practices that compound the problem include "doctor shopping" and visits to multiple physicians to collect more prescriptions
   b. The most commonly diverted drugs include depressants, stimulants, and anabolic steroids
2. Designer drugs are new substances designed by slightly altering the chemical makeup of other illegal or tightly controlled drugs
   a. Many are manufactured in "basement laboratories" operated out of personal homes or apartments
   b. Laws such as the Chemical Diversion and Trafficking Act (CDTA) of 1988 and the Domestic Chemical Diversion Control Act of 1994 have placed a number of essential chemicals used in the production of designer drugs under federal control

III. Drug Trafficking

A. Introduction
1. Drug trafficking includes manufacturing, distributing, dispensing, importing, and exporting (or possession with intent to do the same) of a controlled or counterfeit substance
2. May also include the sale of controlled substances
3. Federal law enforcement agencies focus largely on preventing smuggling and apprehending smugglers

B. Drugs such as cocaine, heroin, and LSD are relatively easy to smuggle into the United States
1. Most cocaine entering the United States originates in South America (Colombia, Ecuador, Peru, Bolivia, etc.)
2. There are several main smuggling routes
   a. Shipment overland from South America through Central America
   b. Direct shipments to United States ports
   c. Flights into the United States on either commercial or private airplanes
   d. Airdrops to vessels waiting offshore
3. The DEA follows heroin trafficking through its heroin signature program (HSP)
   a. The HSP identifies the source of a heroin sample through the laboratory detection of specific chemical characteristics peculiar to a source area
   b. Most heroin in the United States originated in South America; other sources include Asia and Mexico

IV. Drugs and Crime
   A. The Bureau of Justice Statistics distinguishes between two types of crimes associated with drugs
      1. Drug-defined crimes involve the violation of laws prohibiting or regulating the possession, use, or distribution of illegal drugs
      2. Drug-related crimes are not violations of drug laws but are crimes in which drugs contribute to the offense
      3. Illegal drug use is related to crimes against people and property in three major ways:
         a. Drugs can induce violent behavior
         b. The cost of drugs may induce users to commit crimes to support their drug habits
         c. Violence often characterizes relations among participants in the drug-distribution system
   B. The U.S. Department of Justice states that there is considerable evidence of a strong relationship between drug use and crime, which can be summarized in three points:
      1. Drug users report greater involvement in crime and are more likely than nonusers to have criminal records
      2. Persons with criminal records are more likely than those without criminal records to report being drug users
      3. Crimes rise in number as drug use increases
   C. There are several sources of information about drug use among offenders
      1. NIJ's Arrestee Drug Abuse Monitoring Program (ADAM) tracked trends in the prevalence and types of drug use among booked arrestees in urban areas (the program was eliminated recently for lack of funding)
         a. Adam's 2000 annual report showed that two-thirds of adult male arrestees tested positive for drug use, with marijuana the most commonly used drug
         b. The proportion of male adult arrestees testing positive for marijuana was greater than the rate for female adult arrestees
         c. Marijuana was the most commonly used drug among juvenile detainees
      2. The National Crime Victimization Survey reports that approximately one-third of all victims of violent crime believed that their assailants were under the influence of drugs or alcohol at the time of the crime
      3. Self-report studies of jail and prison inmates suggest that many offenders were using drugs before or during the offense for which they were arrested
   D. Illegal drugs and official corruption
      1. Lucrative drug profits also have the potential to corrupt official agents of control, such as the police
      2. The Mollen Commission study of police corruption in New York City reported in 1994 that much illegal police activity was drug-related: activities include robbing drug dealers, selling drugs, and conducting illegal raids to confiscate additional drugs for personal gain
      3. Correctional officers and employees may also be involved in drug-related corruption, such as smuggling drugs into correctional institutions

V. Social Policy and Drug Abuse
   A. The history of drug control policy in the United States
      1. Prior to 1907, all drugs could be bought and sold in the United States without restriction

2. The federal Food and Drug Act, passed in 1906, required manufacturers of "patent medicines" to list ingredients and specifically targeted mood-altering chemicals, although it did not outlaw them
3. The Harrison Act (1914) was the first major piece of federal antidrug legislation
   a. The act required anyone dealing in opium, morphine, heroin, and cocaine, or their derivatives, to register with the federal government and pay an annual tax of $1
   b. Because it only authorized the registration of medical professionals, it effectively outlawed street use of these drugs
   c. By 1920, court rulings severely curtailed the use of heroin for medical purposes, leading to the beginning of complete federal prohibition over at least one major drug
4. Alcohol prohibition
   a. The Eighteenth Amendment to the U.S. Constitution, ratified in 1919, prohibited the manufacture, sale, and transportation of alcoholic beverages
   b. Prohibition was mandated by the 1919 Volsted Act, although support for Prohibition declined rapidly
   c. In 1993, the Twenty-first Amendment, which repealed Prohibition, was ratified
5. The Marijuana Tax Act (1937) outlawed effectively marijuana
6. The Boggs Act (1951) reinforced this and also mandated deletion of heroin from the list of medically useful substances and required its complete removal from all medicines
7. The Narcotic Control Act (1956) increased penalties for drug traffickers and made the sale of heroin to anyone under age 18 a capital offense
8. The Comprehensive Drug Abuse Prevention and Control Act (1970) includes the Controlled Substances Act, which established five schedules that classify psychoactive drugs and outlined penalties for possession of each type of substance
9. The 1988 Anti-Drug Abuse Act substantially increased penalties for recreational drug users, made it more difficult for suspected drug dealers to purchase weapons, and denied various federal benefits to federal drug convicts
10. The 1996 Drug-Induced Rape Prevention Act increased penalties for trafficking in Rohypnol, the "date rape drug"

B. Recent legislation
   1. The Comprehensive Methamphetamine Control Act of 1996 (CMCA) has several important elements:
      a. It contains provisions for the forfeiture and seizure of chemicals used in the manufacture of methamphetamine
      b. It added iodine to the list of chemicals controlled under federal chemical diversion acts
      c. It created new reporting requirements for distributors of products containing certain key chemicals
      d. It increased penalties for the manufacture and possession of equipment used to make controlled substances
   2. The Violent Crime Control and Law Enforcement Act of 1994 contained a number of drug-related provisions, including:

a. Authorizing $1 billion in grant program money to reduce or prevent juvenile drug- and gang-related activity in federally assisted low-income housing areas
b. Authorizing $1.6 billion for direct funding for anticrime efforts (drug treatment, education, jobs, etc.)
c. Allocating drug treatment money for the creation of state and federal programs to treat drug-addicted prisoners
d. Providing $1 billion for drug court programs for nonviolent offenders with substance abuse problems
e. Increasing penalties for drug crimes committed by gang members and for using children to deal drugs near schools and playgrounds
f. Increasing penalties for drug dealing in areas near playgrounds, schools, video arcades, youth centers, and public housing projects
g. Expanding the federal death penalty to include large-scale drug trafficking and mandating life imprisonment for criminals convicted of three drug-related felonies
h. Creating special penalties for drug use and drug trafficking in prison

C. Drug-control strategies have included five main policy initiatives
1. Antidrug legislation and strict enforcement
a. Current policy emphasizes strict enforcement of antidrug abuse laws, focusing particularly on the arrest, prosecution, and incarceration of distributors of controlled substances
b. Other enforcement activities include the seizure and destruction of illegal drugs and clandestine drug laboratories
2. Interdiction is an international drug control policy focusing on stopping drugs from entering the country
a. Agencies involved in interdiction include the FBI, the DEA, the U.S. Customs Service, the U.S. Border Patrol, and the U.S. Coast Guard
b. Interdiction enforcement in the United States is difficult because of gaps in border coverage and instances of corruption in U.S. border agencies
3. Crop control involves the eradication of both domestic and overseas drug crops such as marijuana and coca plants
4. Asset forfeiture allows the criminal justice system to seize money and property that has been used in drug trafficking or manufacture or that was obtained as a result of drug trafficking
5. Antidrug education and drug treatment strategies have become increasingly popular recently
a. Educational programs reach targeted individuals through schools, corporations, and media campaigns
b. There are many school-based programs, such as D.A.R.E., although recent studies have questioned the effectiveness of these types of interventions

D. The national drug control policy
1. In 1988 Congress passed the Anti-Drug Abuse Act, which established the Office of National Drug Control Policy (ONDCP) and endorsed as a national policy goal the creation of a drug-free America
2. The mission of ONDCP is to establish policies, priorities, and objectives for the country's drug-control program
a. Current goals include reduction of illicit drug use, manufacturing and trafficking, reduction of drug-related crime and violence, and amelioration of drug-related health consequences

b. To meet these goals, ONDCP produces and published a National Drug Control Strategy which directs antidrug efforts through the country and establishes a program, budget, and guidelines for cooperation among various agencies
c. The National Drug Control Strategy focuses on prevention, treatment, research, law enforcement, protection of U.S. borders, drug supply reduction, and international cooperation
d. The stated goals or "national priorities" of the strategy include:
(1) Stopping substance use before it starts through education and community action
(2) Healing drug users by getting treatment resources where they are needed
(3) Disrupting the markets by attacking the economic basis of the drug trade
e. The United States continues to focus international drug control efforts on source countries as well
3. The war on drugs has been extremely expensive in financial terms
a. The federal government's proposed drug control budget for fiscal year 2005 is $12.6 billion, an increase of 4.7% over the 2004 budget
b. This does not include state monies spend on the control of illegal drugs and the enforcement of drug laws or the personal and social costs of drug abuse
4. As a result of the drug war, the criminal justice process and much of the civil justice system have become "drug driven"
a. In some jurisdictions, drug cases account for up to two-thirds of all criminal case filings
b. Strict enforcement combined with an emphasis on incarceration has led to very high rates of imprisonment for drug offenders

E. Alternative drug policies
1. Decriminalization and legalization are based on the assumption that drug abuse will never be eliminated
a. Decriminalization reduces criminal penalties associated with personal possession of controlled substances
b. Legalization eliminates the laws and criminal penalties prohibiting the production, sale, distribution, and possession of controlled substances
2. Arguments in favor of legalization include:
a. Drug use is a victimless crime, and drug laws make criminals out of otherwise law-abiding people
b. Keeping drugs illegal keeps the prices high, whereas legalization could lower the price, thus reducing many forms of drug-related crimes
c. Legalizing drugs would reduce other forms of vice (prostitution, pornography, gambling) because many of these crimes are committed in an effort to obtain money to purchase expensive drugs
d. Legalizing drugs would reduce the influence of criminal cartels involved in the production, transportation, and sale of controlled substances
e. The illegal status and associated high costs of drugs victimizes others (family members, property owners in high-drug-use areas, taxpayers) indirectly
f. Legalization would reduce opportunities for official corruption
g. Legalization would allow the government to tax drugs in the same way that alcohol and tobacco are taxed, resulting in increased tax revenues

h. Legalization of drugs would increase control over public health issues related to drug use (e.g., needle sharing) and allow monitoring of drug quality and potency

i. Legalization of controlled substances would allow them to be dispensed under controlled conditions, and people using them injudiciously (e.g., while driving) could still be penalized

3. California and Arizona voters passed resolutions in 1996 legalizing the medical use of marijuana under certain circumstances

   a. The California law permits possession of marijuana for valid medicinal purposes, but buying and selling marijuana is still illegal

   b. Arizona law requires prescribing physicians to write a scientific opinion explaining why the drug is appropriate for the specific patient and requires a supportive second opinion

4. Although other states have also passed various laws and resolutions allowing therapeutic research programs involving marijuana use or asking the federal government to lift its ban on medical use of the drug, federal law enforcement agencies have announced that they will continue to enforce federal antidrug laws prohibiting marijuana possession by citizens of all states

**Show the ABC News program *Medical Marijuana* from the video library.**

5. Arguments against drug legalization include:

   a. Claims that reducing official control over psychoactive substances is immoral and socially irresponsible, and would result in heightened costs to society from drug abuse

   b. Legalization would increase the problems now associated with alcohol abuse (time lost from work, drug-induced criminality, loss of personal self-control, severing of important relationships)

   c. Just because laws are not easily enforceable is no reason to eliminate them

# Key Concepts

**Arrestee Drug Abuse Monitoring (ADAM) Program**: A National Institute of Justice program, which tracks trends in the prevalence and types of drug use among booked arrestees in urban areas.

**Dangerous drug:** A term used by the Drug Enforcement Administration to refer to "broad categories or classes of controlled substances other than cocaine, opiates, and cannabis products." Amphetamines, methamphetamines, PCP (phencyclidine), LSD, methcathinone, and "designer drugs" are all considered to be dangerous drugs.

**Decriminalization (of drugs):** The reduction of criminal penalties associated with the personal possession of a controlled substance.

**Designer drugs**: One of the "new substances designed by slightly altering the chemical makeup of other illegal or tightly controlled drugs."

**Drug-defined crime**: A violation of the laws prohibiting or regulating the possession, use, or distribution of illegal drugs.

**Drug-related crime:** A crime in which drugs contribute to the offense (excluding violations of drug laws).

**Drug trafficking:** Manufacturing, distributing, dispensing, importing, and exporting (or possession with intent to do the same) a controlled substance or a counterfeit substance.

**Heroin signature program (HSP):** A Drug Enforcement Administration program that identifies the geographic source of a heroin sample through the detection of specific chemical characteristics in the sample peculiar to the source area.

**Interdiction:** An international drug control policy that aims to stop drugs from entering the country illegally.

**Legalization (of drugs):** Elimination of the laws and associated criminal penalties that prohibit the production, sale, distribution, and possession of a controlled substance.

**National Survey on Drug Use and Health (NSDUH):** A national survey of illicit drug use among people 12 years of age and older that is conducted annually by the Substance Abuse and Mental Health Services Administration.

**Office of National Drug Control Policy (ONDCP):** A national office charged by Congress with establishing policies, priorities, and objectives for the nation's drug-control program. ONDCP is responsible for developing and disseminating the *National Drug-Control Strategy*.

**Pharmaceutical diversion**: The process by which legitimately manufactured controlled substances are diverted for illicit use.

**Psychoactive substance:** A substance that affects the mind, mental processes, or emotions.

# Additional Lecture Topics

Consider discussing drug use in countries such as the Netherlands, where drugs have been legally obtainable since 1976. The rate of addictions in the Netherlands is low compared to other European countries and the crime rate has decreased significantly since 1976. On the other hand, although Spain decriminalized some drugs and tolerates the use of heroin and cocaine, it still has the highest AIDS death rate in Europe, with approximately 75% of these deaths related to the use of intravenous drugs.

Discuss possible causes of drug abuse. For example, consider whether genetics may play a role in substance abuse; adoption research has found a link between parental alcoholism and the development of alcohol problems among adoptees raised by nonalcoholic adoptive parents. Other theories that may apply include rational choice theory, social learning theory, and subcultural theory.

# Discussion Questions

These discussion questions are found in the textbook at the end of the chapter. The instructor may want to focus on these questions during the coverage of Chapter 13.

1. This book emphasizes a social problems versus social responsibility theme. Which of the social policy approaches to controlling drug abuse discussed in this chapter (if any) appear to be predicated upon a social problems approach? Which (if any) are predicated upon a social responsibility approach? Explain the nature of the relationship.

2. What are some of the costs of illicit drug use in the United States today? Which costs can be more easily reduced than others? How would you reduce the costs of illegal drug use?

3. What is the difference between decriminalization and legalization? Should drug use remain illegal? What do you think of the arguments in favor of legalization? Those against?

4. What is the difference between drug-defined and drug-related crime? Which form of crime is more difficult to address? Why?

5. What is asset forfeiture? How has asset forfeiture been used in the fight against illegal drugs? How have recent U.S. Supreme Court decisions limited federal asset seizures? Do you agree that such limitations were necessary? Why?

# Student Exercises

## Activity #1

Write a short paper discussing the advantages and disadvantages of legalizing marijuana in the United States. Include your personal opinion on the question of legalization and explain why you feel this way.

## Activity 2

Go to the Drug Enforcement Administration Web site (http://www.usdoj.gov/dea) and answer the following questions:

1. What is the "red ribbon campaign," and how did it begin?
2. What is the DEA's Mobile Enforcement Team?

3. Explain the DEA's Demand Reduction Program, including its goals and objectives
4. What was Operation Zorro II, and why was it unique?
5. What was the French Connection?
6. What is the mission of the DEA?

# Criminology Today on the Web

### http://www.usdoj.gov/dea

This is the home page of the Drug Enforcement Administration.

### http://www.dare.com

This is the official Web site for D.A.R.E.

### http://www.nida.nih.gov

This is the home page of the National Institute on Drug Abuse.

### http://www.undcp.org

This is the home page of the United Nations Office on Drugs and Crime.

### http://www.rand.org/multi/dprc

This is the home page for the Drug Policy Research Center at the Rand Institute.

### http://www.DrugWatch.org

This is the Web site for Drug Watch International.

### http://www.ojp.usdoj.gov/bjs/drugs.htm

This Web site provides statistics on drugs and crime from the Bureau of Justice Statistics.

### http://www.samhsa.gov

This is the home page of the Substance Abuse and Mental Health Services Administration.

### http://www.whitehousedrugpolicy.gov

This is the home page of the Office of National Drug Control Policy.

### http://www.lindesmith.org

This is the home page of the Drug Policy Alliance, an organization working to end the war on drugs.

### http://www.mpp.org

This is the home page of the Marijuana Policy Project, a nonprofit organization in the District of Columbia with the goal of providing the marijuana law reform movement with full-time lobbying on the federal level.

**http://www.sadd.org**

This is the home page of Students Against Destructive Decisions, a peer leadership organization dedicated to preventing underage drinking and drug use.

# Student Study Guide Questions and Answers

## True/False

1. During the 19th century, the use of illegal drugs was widespread throughout all levels of society. **(False, p. 441)**

2. The use of illegal drugs in America during the 19th and early 20th centuries was mostly associated with fringe groups. **(True, p. 441)**

3. Men are more likely to abuse nonmedical psychotherapeutic drugs. **(False, p. 442)**

4. In general, rates of illicit drug use decline with age. **(True, p. 443)**

5. Rates of illicit drug use in 2002 were lowest among Hispanics than among any other major racial/ethnic group. **(False, p. 443)**

6. Adults who have not completed high school are more likely to have tried illicit drugs in their lifetime than are college graduates. **(False, p. 443)**

7. The more education a person receives, the more likely that person is to discontinue using drugs with age. **(True, p. 443)**

8. The rate of illicit drug use is correlated with employment status. **(True, p. 443)**

9. According to survey data, drug use is a substantially greater problem today than twenty years ago. **(False, p. 443)**

10. The results of the *National Survey on Drug Use and Health* are extremely accurate. **(False, p. 443)**

11. Students in private schools report a wider availability of drugs than do students in public schools. **(False, p. 444)**

12. Drugs are more available in urban than rural schools. **(False, p. 444)**

13. The *Monitoring the Future* survey provides data primarily on drug abuse among adults. **(False, p. 444)**

14. The cost of enforcing drug laws is a direct cost of illegal drug use. **(True, pp. 446-447)**

15. *Ice*, *crystal*, and *glass* are street names for crystallized methamphetamine. **(True, p. 449)**

16. Depressants are used illegitimately in the self-treatment of drug withdrawal. **(True, p. 449)**

17. Marijuana is nonaddictive. **(True, p. 450)**

18. Most marijuana consumed in the United States is imported from South America. **(False, p. 450)**

19. Narcotics are physically addictive. **(True, p. 450)**

20. Inhalants are an example of a gateway drug. **(True, p. 451)**

21. Most inhalants are easily available. **(True, p. 451)**

22. In colloquial usage, a drug trafficker is a person who sells drugs. **(True, p. 451)**

23. Most cocaine entering the United States is smuggled via commercial airplanes. **(False, p. 452)**

24. According to the DEA, most heroin in the United States originates in Asia. **(False, p. 453)**

25. Committing a violent crime while under the influence of an illegal drug is an example of a drug-related crime. **(True, p. 453)**

26. Drug users are more likely to report involvement in crime than non-users. **(True, p. 453)**

27. According to the ADAM program, arrestee drug use varies significantly by city. **(True, p. 454)**

28. According to the ADAM report, marijuana was the most commonly used drug among juvenile detainees. **(True, p. 455)**

29. The Mollen Commission studied police corruption in New York City. **(True, p. 456)**

30. Only a small percentage of illegal police activity is drug related. **(False, p. 456)**

31. Official corruption due to drugs and drug money extends to corrections officers as well as police officers. **(True, p. 456)**

32. The Narcotic Control Act required the complete removal of heroin from all medicines. **(False, p. 457)**

33. The Controlled Substances Act established five schedules classifying psychoactive drugs on factors such as potential for abuse. **(True, p. 457)**

34. The Anti-Drug Abuse Act denied federal benefits to federal drug convicts. **(True, p. 458)**

35. The Comprehensive Drug Abuse Prevention and Control Act provided funding for drug court programs throughout the country. **(True, p. 459)**

36. Interdiction is an international drug-control policy. **(True, p. 460)**

37. The Office of National Drug Control Policy is responsible for producing a national drug-control strategy. **(True, p. 461)**

38. The national drug-control strategy attempts to stop drug use before it starts by getting treatment resources where they are most needed. **(False, p. 461-464)**

39. International drug control efforts are focused on source countries. **(True, p. 464)**

40. The cost of the "war on drugs" has been decreasing in recent years. **(False, p. 464)**

41. Decriminalization is based on the assumption that drug abuse will never be eliminated. **(True, p. 465)**

42. Decriminalization involves eliminating the laws and criminal penalties associated with the production, sale, distribution, and possession of controlled substances. **(False, p. 465)**

43. Proponents of legalization of controlled substances argue that it would reduce a variety of vice crimes. **(True, p. 465)**

44. The U.S. Supreme Court has prohibited the use of medical marijuana. **(True, p. 467)**

## Fill in the Blank

45. __________ substances were widely accepted during the hippie movement of the 1960s. **(Psychoactive, p. 441)**

46. Dr. Timothy Leary formed the __________ in the 1960s. **(League of Spiritual Discovery, p. 441)**

47. Of those reporting current use of illicit drugs in 2002, approximately __________ percent use marijuana. **(75, p. 442)**

48. Recently, heroin use among eighth graders has __________. **(decreased, p. 444)**

49. Inhalant use is most prevalent among __________ graders. **(eighth, p. 444)**

50. Deaths resulting directly from drug consumption are known as __________ deaths. **(drug induced, p. 446)**

51. __________ are used illegally by people trying to produce feelings of competence and power and a state of excitability. **(Stimulants, p. 448)**

52. Research suggests that __________ can be used in the treatment of glaucoma. **(marijuana, p. 450)**

53. Both morphine and heroin are derived from __________. **(opium, p. 450)**

54. LSD falls into the __________ family of drugs. **(hallucinogen, p. 450)**

55. Visiting numerous physicians to collect large quantities of prescribed medicines is known as __________. **(doctor shopping, p. 451)**

56. Major heroin and cocaine trafficking routes are sometimes called __________. **(pipelines, p. 452)**

57. The most commonly used drug among adult arrestees is __________. **(marijuana, p. 454)**

58. Approximately __________ percent of all murders are committed to obtain drug money. **(five, p. 456)**

59. All drugs could be bought and sold in the United States without restriction prior to the year __________. **(1907, p. 456)**

60. The Pure Food and Drug Act was passed in __________. **(1906, p. 457)**

61. The __________ Act required anyone dealing in drugs such as opium and cocaine to register with the federal government and pay a small annual tax. **(Harrison, p. 457)**

62. The __________ Act mandated Prohibition. **(Volsted, p. 457)**

63. The __________ Act effectively outlawed marijuana. **(Marijuana Tax, p. 457)**

64. The Narcotic Control Act made the sale of __________ to anyone under the age of 18 a capital crime. **(heroin, p. 457)**

65. *Roofies* is a street name for the date rape drug __________. **(Rohypnol, p. 458)**

66. __________ involves the elimination of the laws and associated criminal penalties that prohibit the production, sale, distribution, and possession of controlled substances. **(Legalization, p. 465)**

## Multiple Choice

67. During the late nineteenth century, which of the following people would have been most likely to be abusing drugs (other than opium)?
    a. An upper-class merchant
    b. A servant
    c. **An artist (p. 441)**
    d. A factory worker

68. In 2002, approximately __________ million Americans were current users of cocaine.
    a. one
    b. **two (p. 442)**
    c. three
    d. four

69. In 2002, approximately __________ percent of juveniles between the ages of 12 and 17 were current users of illicit drugs.
    a. **12 (p. 442)**
    b. 22
    c. 32
    d. 42

70. The highest rate of illicit drug use in 2002 was found among persons aged __________ years.
    a. 12–17
    b. **18–20 (p. 442)**
    c. 21–25
    d. 26–29

71. During the early 1990s, illicit drug use among adolescents
    a. **increased significantly. (p. 443)**
    b. increased slightly.
    c. decreased significantly.
    d. decreased slightly.

72. Illicit drug use is highly correlated with
    a. current employment status.
    b. educational status.
    c. **Both a and b (p. 443)**
    d. Neither a nor b

73. Past year use of illicit drugs by __________ graders decreased only slightly, according to the *Monitoring the Future* study.
    a. sixth
    b. eighth
    c. tenth
    d. **twelfth (p. 444)**

74. According to the *Monitoring the Future* study, which of the following statements about high school seniors (twelfth graders) is true?
    a. Past-year use of any illicit drug declined significantly since 1997.
    b. **Cocaine use decreased from 2001to 2002. (pp. 444-445)**
    c. Use of hallucinogens remained stable from 2001to 2002.
    d. There has been a decrease in the use of ecstacy from 2001to 2002.

75. According to the *Monitoring the Future* study, which of the following statements about tenth graders is true?
    a. Past year use of any illicit drug increased significantly since 1997.
    b. Use of inhalants is more prevalent among tenth graders than among students in the other grades studied.
    c. **Past year use of steroids increased from 2001 to 2002. (pp. 444-445)**
    d. Past year use of ecstacy increased from 2001 to 2002.

76. __________ is the leading cause of death of Hispanic men between the ages of 25 and 44.
    a. Drug overdose
    b. Cancer
    c. **AIDS (p. 446)**
    d. Homicide

77. Which of the following is *not* an indirect cost of illegal drug use?
    a. The cost to the criminal justice system of investigating crimes committed for drug money
    b. Lost property values due to drug-related neighborhood crime
    c. **The cost of enforcing drug laws (pp. 446-447)**
    d. The cost of medical care for injures from drug-related child abuse or neglect

78. Crack cocaine is usually
    a. **smoked. (p. 448)**
    b. inhaled.
    c. snorted.
    d. freebased.

79. The __________ category of drugs includes barbiturates, sedatives, and tranquilizers.
    a. stimulant
    b. cannabis
    c. narcotic
    d. **depressant (p. 449)**

80. Which of the following is *not* a narcotic?
    a. Opium
    b. **LSD (p. 450)**
    c. Codeine
    d. Heroin

81. __________ have no official legitimate use.
    a. Narcotics
    b. Depressants
    c. Stimulants
    d. **Hallucinogens (p. 450)**

82. __________ are produced by slightly changing the chemical makeup of illegal or controlled substances.
    a. **Designer drugs (p. 451)**
    b. Inhalants
    c. Hallucinogens
    d. Anabolic steroids

83. Most cocaine entering the United States originates in
    a. **South America. (p. 452)**
    b. Central America.
    c. Asia.
    d. Mexico.

84. The heroin signature program identifies the __________ of a heroin sample.
    a. port of entry
    b. **geographic source area (p. 453)**
    c. manufacturer
    d. place of seizure

85. The Golden Triangle area is located in
    a. South America.
    b. Mexico.
    c. **Southeast Asia (p. 453)**
    d. Southwest Asia.

86. Which of the following is an example of a drug-defined crime?
    a. A drug addict who commits a theft to obtain money to buy drugs
    b. A drug importer who kills a rival drug dealer
    c. **A drug dealer who sells cocaine to a juvenile on the street (p. 453)**
    d. They are all drug-defined crimes.

87. People with criminal records are _________ likely than/as others to report being drug users.
    a. **more (p. 453)**
    b. less
    c. equally
    d. We have no information on this topic.

88. Methamphetamine use among ADAM arrestees appears to be concentrated in the __________ part of the United States.
    a. eastern
    b. southern
    c. midwestern
    d. **western (p. 456)**

89. The Pure Food and Drug Act
    a. restricted the importation and distribution of opium.
    b. **required manufacturers to list their ingredients. (p. 457)**
    c. controlled the sale and possession of marijuana.
    d. outlawed the sale and distribution of medicines containing opium.

90. The Narcotic Control Act was passed in
    a. 1919.
    b. 1937.
    c. 1951.
    d. **1956. (p. 457)**

91. The goal of a "Drug-Free America by 1995" was part of the federal __________ Act
    a. Controlled Substances
    b. **Anti-Drug Abuse (p. 457)**
    c. Comprehensive Drug Abuse Prevention and Control
    d. Violent Crime Control and Law Enforcement

92. Which of the following was *not* one of the provisions of the Comprehensive Methamphetamine Control Act?
    a. It added iodine to the list of chemicals controlled under federal chemical diversion acts.
    b. It created new reporting requirements for distributors of products containing certain key chemicals.
    c. It increased penalties for the manufacture and possession of equipment used to make controlled substances.
    d. **It allocated drug treatment money to create state and federal programs to treat drug-addicted prisoners. (p. 458)**

93. The __________ Act expanded the federal death penalty to include large-scale drug trafficking.
    a. Comprehensive Methamphetamine Control
    b. **Comprehensive Drug Abuse Prevention and Control (p. 459)**
    c. Violent Crime Control and Law Enforcement
    d. Controlled Substances

94. __________ strategies focus on stopping drugs from entering the United States illegally.
    a. Source control
    b. **Interdiction (p. 460)**
    c. Asset forfeiture
    d. Crop control

95. Eradicating cultivated marijuana plants within the United States falls into which of the major drug-control strategies?
    a. Interdiction
    b. **Crop control (p. 460)**
    c. Forfeiture
    d. Antidrug legislation

96. The drug control strategy that authorizes judicial representatives to seize all proceeds traceable to the sale of illegal drugs is known as
    a. crop control.
    b. **forfeiture. (p. 460)**
    c. strict enforcement.
    d. interdiction.

97. Research suggests that D.A.R.E.-type interventions do have a significant effect on __________ use.
    a. marijuana
    b. alcohol
    c. **tobacco (p. 461)**
    d. cocaine

98. Which of the following is *not* an argument in favor of legalization?
    a. Legalization could lower the price of drugs.
    b. Legalization would reduce the opportunity for official corruption.
    c. **Drug laws are enforceable. (p. 465-466)**
    d. Legalization would result in increased tax revenues.

99. California's Proposition 215 legalizes
    a. **the medical use of marijuana. (p. 466)**
    b. the sale and purchase of marijuana.
    c. Both a and b
    d. Neither a nor b

# Word Search Puzzle

```
N X T F C B Z X A A T I J H I S C I U K T C I F R Z D Q D
Z L F V S U B S T A N C E S S I M J H E M P F I N R F G K
O T L D T N W D N Y P A H I Z J Y M Q M H E I A Z Y E Q Z
Q A H U S N K B R C R W Q A B I W Y E D D L D O S C B C F
O O D A H H S X S Q A N J W J H C N W D H I K H F T D U D
G L O L W C U W U R F K E Z U M B A O M C S L A P T D N J
C R N X F L H Q Z O V S A B Y T X V R E F Q P P Q S E B C
B L P Q H C A R R U D K X O J U D C P M C H K E A M S X P
F P M B B L Y G H X R D X S H F S O E H P N P A A K I Q Q
S P G N H V N N G A C T A A W F H A Y J T L N Y Z R G A T
A X Q S A Y V O Y K J B H N E M K N G S Q I C D L V N D F
K C H F J P O I C W H J U O G L K J M P S J R V A C E B K
R A R X J C Y J X G O B O J T E W Y W L R M A L D E R L M
P D L U J R V T V Q D G O L I F R H I K R K Y L B E Y C Q
J A L Q I N Q A R K E M M G F G Q O L H S P W Y F H R A X
R M Z B H F Z L Q I B I Y T B L G U U H H R K Y Q T U J A
F H T I L E G A L I Z A T I O N Y P E S I W N G K A J B R
A E I R N Q L H J D W R R L G A Z Z K V M K N F Y Y A I B
L V B M A T A J R Z U K K B V M R J I Z R M Z H X D W N F
P Q Z I H F E F E A O Y L Q O L I P Q E S G G E W S R B R
B Z N H R H F R A Q J N A V R K R O W T P G G W H Z W Z W
K F N J Z L U I D S A T O O B C S W C C U V C M B F J P U
X C G S P I Z F C I H Y E A M A W Y Y I U B G Y X G X S J
Y L Z W F H F I J K C X N S K S M L X B V M J P I G G L T
W S O V I C I D D R I T P H A R M A C E U T I C A L G E V
Z T Z T U D H Q K O B N I M E T P N K Y A R V E O R I T V
U J G E Y K R E Z J R M G O A T W E M R B N T J O W E T E
Z D I C D D K E V Q T G W Z N I K E I L T X W O W N M L C
L X C T P K W L D Q B P P V I A G F I Y L Q W K I S B L C
P B H B I G Q O Z X L K K W D J C V Q E G T N H W T S J T
```

ADAM
Dangerous
Designer
HSP
Interdiction
Legalization
Pharmaceutical
Substances
Trafficking

## Crossword Puzzle

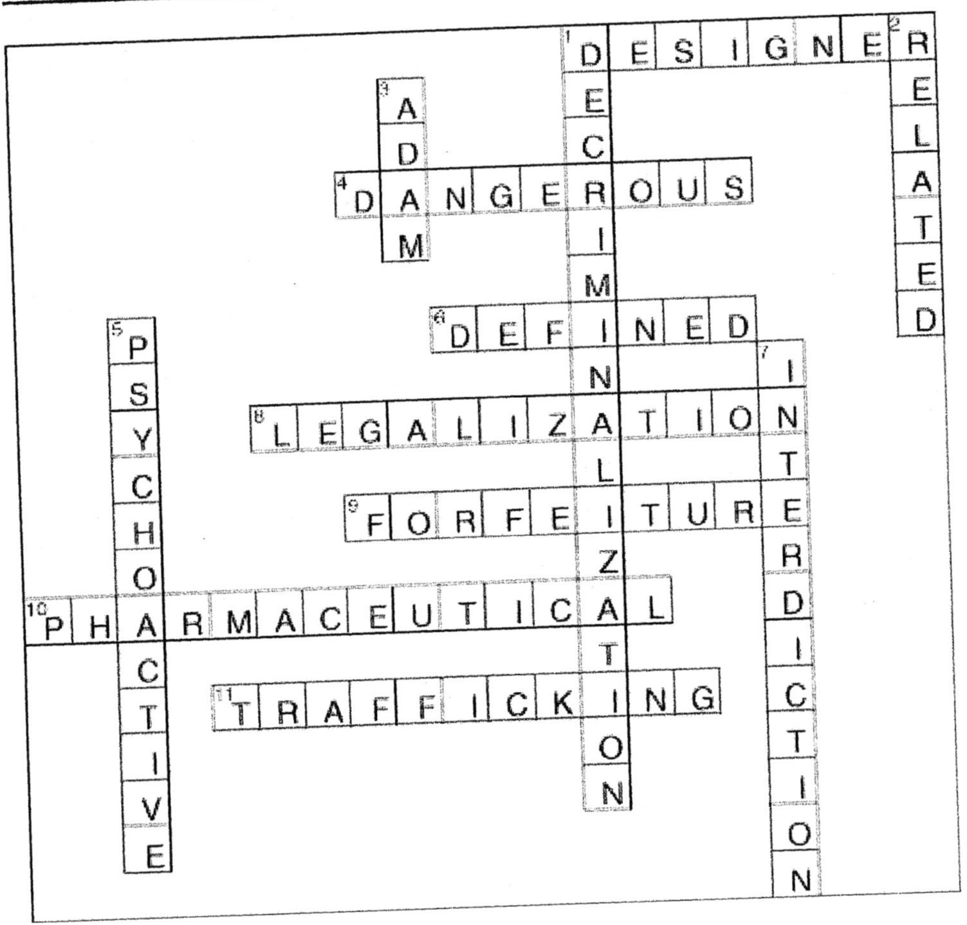


### Across

1. A drug created by slightly altering the chemical makeup of other illegal drugs.
4. A DEA term referring to drugs other than cocaine, opiates, and cannabis products.
6. A drug ________ crime violates the laws prohibiting or regulating the possession, use, or distribution of illegal drugs.
8. Eliminating the laws that prohibit the possession and sale of controlled substances.
9. Asset ________ is the authorized seizure of money or other things of value.
10. ________ diversion involves diverting legitimately manufactured controlled substances for illicit use.
11. Drug ________ involves manufacturing and distributing controlled substances.

### Down

1. Reducing criminal penalties associating with the personal possession of a controlled substance.
2. A drug ________ crime is one in which drugs contribute to the offense.
3. An NIJ program which tracks trends in the prevalence and types of drug use among booked arrestees in urban areas.
5. A substance affecting the mind, mental processes, or emotions.
7. An international drug control policy trying to stop drugs from entering the country illegally.

# 14 Technology and Crime

## Learning Objectives

After reading this chapter, students should be able to:

1. Describe the nature of high-technology and computer crime
2. Describe some high-technology crime countermeasures
3. Explain various computer-security techniques, including data encryption
4. Discuss the nature of a threat analysis and explain how one might be conducted
5. Explain the nature and potential usefulness of DNA technology

## Chapter Outline

Introduction
The Advance of Technology
High Technology and Criminal Opportunity
*Technology and Criminal Mischief*
*Computer Crime and the Law*
A Profile of Computer Criminals
*The History and Nature of Hacking*
*Computer Crime as a Form of White-Collar Crime*
Securing the Internet
Technology in the Fight Against Crime
*DNA Technology*
*Computers as Crime-Fighting Tools*
Combating Computer Crime
*Police Investigation of Computer Crime*
*Dealing with Computer Criminals*
Policy Issues: Personal Freedoms in the Information Age
What the Future Holds

## Chapter Summary

This chapter discusses the links between technology and crime. Technology, which facilitates new forms of criminal behavior, can be used both by criminals and by those who enforce the law. Because of the increasing value of information, high-tech criminals have taken a variety of routes to obtain illegitimate access to computerized information. Some criminals may focus simply on destroying or altering information rather than copying it. Technically, computer crime is defined as any violation of a federal or state computer crime statute. The text discusses several typologies of computer crime. Some authors use the term "cybercrime" to refer to crimes involving the use of computers or the manipulation of digital data. One example of cybercrime is phone phreaking, which involves the illegitimate use of dial-up access codes and other restricted technical information to avoid long-distance charges or to steal cellular telephone numbers and access codes. In addition, some computer crime is malicious rather than being committed for financial gain; this includes the creation and transmission of computer viruses, worms, and other malicious forms of programming code.

Originally, most jurisdictions in the United States attempted to prosecute unauthorized computer access under preexisting property crime statutes. However, today, all states and the federal government have developed computer crime statutes specifically applicable to invasive activities aimed at illegally accessing stored information. There is a variety of federal statutes of relevance to crimes committed with or against computer equipment and software. One of the most controversial has been the Computer Decency Act (CDA), signed into law in 1996, which focused on protecting minors from harmful material on the Internet by making it a crime to knowingly transmit obscene or indecent material to a recipient under the age of 18. However, the ACLU filed suit against the federal government, challenging the constitutionality of the CDA's provisions relating to the transmission of obscene material to minors. After a federal district court ruled that the provisions violated the First Amendment guarantees of free speech, the case was appealed to the U.S. Supreme Court, which upheld the lower court's ruling in the 1997 case of *Reno* v. *ACLU.* Individual state laws are rarely modeled after federal legislation and generally vary greatly among states. Some experts distinguish among several categories of crimes involving computers, including computer crime, computer-related crime, and computer abuse.

Many computer criminals come from the hacker subculture. Hackers and hacker identities are a product of cyberspace, which exists only within electronic networks. The text discusses a typology of hackers that is based on psychological characteristics. In addition, some high-tech crimes are committed by professional criminals who use technology to commit serious crimes, such as the theft of money. The World Wide Web may also be used to facilitate criminal activity, such as the computerized transmission of illegal pornography among pedophiles. Computer crime also shares a number of characteristics with white-collar crime.

The Internet is the world's largest computer network; its growth has encouraged hackers and computer criminals to attack it through the creation and development of programs such as viruses and worms. Because information and property can be transmitted through data networks, cybercriminals are not affected by national boundaries, nor do they have to be anywhere near the location of the victim to commit crimes. However, law enforcement agencies are still affected by geographic boundaries and may still have to deal with the difficulties of international cooperation.

Technology helps both criminals and criminal justice personnel; law enforcement capabilities and criminally useful technologies usually leapfrog each other. Key technology in law enforcement service today includes traffic radar, computer databases of known offenders, machine-based expert systems, cellular communications, electronic eavesdropping, DNA analysis, and less-than-lethal weapons. DNA profiling has become an important tool for criminal justice, and all states have passed legislation requiring convicted offenders to provide samples for DNA databasing.

Computers themselves may serve as tools in the fight against crime. Technologies such as AFIS (automated fingerprint identification systems) and online criminal information services (NCIC, VICAP, etc.) facilitate the work of law enforcement agents. Expert systems that attempt to duplicate the decision-making processes used by skilled investigators may be used in offender profiling. Combating computer crime necessarily involves a realistic threat analysis that identifies organizational perils so that strategies to deal with them can be introduced. One powerful tool is the audit trail. Currently, few police departments have specialized computer crime units or personnel skilled in the investigation of computer crime, and many place a low priority on the investigation of computer crime.

Any effective policy for dealing with computer criminals must recognize various issues associated with personal freedoms and individual rights and must address the issues of deterrence. Sanctions that may be effective in deterring high-tech offenders include confiscating equipment used to commit a computer crime, limiting the offender's use of computers, and restricting the offender's freedom to accept jobs involving computers. One key policy issue is whether the First Amendment's protection of free speech applies to electronic communications. Private groups such as the Electronic Frontier Foundation (EFF) have been formed to focus on the protection of constitutional principles as new communications technologies emerge.

# Lecture Outline

I. Introduction
   A. Discuss the U.S. Supreme Court's reaction to the federal Child Online Protection Act
   B. Review other court decisions that affect federal acts focusing on online pornography

II. The Advent of Technology
   A. Technology and criminology have always been linked
   B. Early forms of technology, such as the telephone, the two-way radio, and the automobile, were used by police as well as by offenders
   C. New technology also facilitates new forms of criminal behavior

III. High Technology and Criminal Opportunity
   A. Introduciton
      1. In the twenty-first century, information may be incredibly valuable
         a. Patents on new products, chemical compositions of new drugs, corporate marketing strategies, and so on are forms of information whose illegitimate access could give competitors unfair advantages
         b. High-tech criminals have several routes of illegitimate access to databases containing computerized information:
            (1) Direct access by employees
            (2) Computer trespass involving remote access to targeted machines
            (3) Electromagnetic field decoders may be used to detect and interpret computer activity from a distance

   c. Computers conforming to the military's TEMPEST security standards are generally secured against passively invasive practices, but most computers in the commercial marketplace do not meet these standards
   d. Hackers, disgruntled employees, and business competitors may destroy or alter data rather than copying information
   e. Computer crime is defined as any violation of a federal or state computer crime statute
2. Typologies of computer crime
   a. David L. Carter developed a four-part classification scheme:
      (1) Crimes in which computers serve as targets
      (2) Crimes in which computers serve as the instrumentality of the crime
      (3) Crimes in which the computer is incidental to other crimes
      (4) Crimes associated with the prevalence of computers
   b. An FBI typology has five main categories:
      (1) Internal computer crimes
      (2) Telecommunications crimes
      (3) Support of criminal enterprises
      (4) Computer-manipulation crimes
      (5) Hardware and software theft
3. Software piracy involves the unauthorized and illegal copying of software programs; various types include
   a. Softlifting
   b. Internet piracy
   c. Software counterfeiting
   d. OEM unbundling
   e. Hard disk loading
   f. Renting
4. Cybercrime refers to crimes that involve the use of computers or the manipulation of digital data
   a. Phone phreaks are cybercriminals who use dial-up access codes and other restricted technical information to avoid long-distance charges or to steal cellular telephone numbers and access codes
   b. Phishing involves using official-looking e-mails to steal valuable information
   c. The Violent Crime Control and Law Enforcement Act of 1994 made it illegal to use interstate telephone lines to further telemarketing fraud

B. Technology and criminal mischief
1. Some computer crime is malicious rather than being committed for financial gain: this includes the creation and transmission of computer viruses, worms, and other malicious forms of programming code
2. A computer virus is a program designed to invade a computer system and to either modify the way the system operates or to alter the information stored in the computer
   a. They can spread from one machine to another via modem, high-speed cable or DSL connections, networks or direct links, or through the exchange of floppy disks or CD-ROMs
   b. Viruses can infect desktops, laptops, and even PDAs and mobile phones
   c. Polymorphic viruses can alter themselves once they have infected a computer

C. Computer crime and the law

1. All states and the federal government have developed computer-crime statutes specifically applicable to invasive activities aimed at illegally accessing stored information
2. Federal laws protect equipment owned by the federal government or a financial institution, or equipment accessed across state lines without prior authorization
   a. The U.S. Criminal Code, Title 18, Section 1030(a) relates to intentional unauthorized access of a computer and specifies punishments
   b. The Cyber Security Enhancement Act of 2002 deals with the creation of sentencing guidelines for computer criminals
   c. The Digital Theft Deterrence and Copyright Damages Improvement Act of 1999 increased the amount of damages that could be awarded in copyright infringement cases (e.g., software piracy)
   d. The No Electronic Theft Act (1997) criminalizes willful infringement of copyrighted works, including by electronic means
   e. The Communications Decency Act (CDA) was passed in 1996 and focused on protecting minors from harmful material on the Internet by making it a crime to knowingly transmit obscene or indecent material to a recipient under the age of 18
      (1) The ACLU filed suit against the federal government, challenging the constitutionality of the CDA's provisions relating to the transmission of obscene material to minors
      (2) In 1996, a federal district court ruled that the provisions violated First Amendment guarantees of free speech
      (3) The case was appealed to the U.S. Supreme Court: in the 1997 case of *Reno* v. *ACLU* the Court upheld the lower court's ruling
3. Individual state laws are rarely modeled after federal legislation and generally vary greatly among states
4. Some experts distinguish among several categories of crimes involving computers:
   a. Computer crime
   b. Computer-related crime: any illegal act for which knowledge of computer technology is involved for its investigation, perpetration, or prosecution
   c. Computer abuse: any incident without color of right associated with computer technology in which a victim suffered or could have suffered loss and/or a perpetrator by intention made or could have made gain

IV. A Profile of Computer Criminals

A. Computer criminals tend to come from the hacker subculture

1. Hackers and hacker identities are a product of cyberspace, which exists only within electronic networks
2. Profile of the average hacker
   a. He is a male between the ages of 16 and 25 who lives in the United States
   b. He is a computer user (not a programmer) who hacks with software written by others
   c. His primary motivation is to gain access to Web sites and computer networks rather than to profit financially

B. The history and nature of hacking

1. Hacking may have begun with the creation of the interstate phone system and direct distance dialing: the audible tones could be duplicated by electronics hobbyists
2. Voice-mail hacking, a new form of illegal telephone access, has recently become popular
3. Voice-mail fraud involves sharing mailbox access codes so that callers to toll-free numbers can leave messages in voice mailboxes and avoid personal long-distance charges
4. Hackers fall into six main groups, based on psychological characteristics:
   a. Pioneers: people fascinated by the evolving technology of telecommunications who explore it without knowing what they will find
   b. Scamps: hackers with a sense of fun who intend no overt harm
   c. Explorers: hackers motivated by their delight in the discoveries associated with breaking into new computer systems
   d. Game players: hackers who enjoy defeating software or system protections and who see hacking itself as a game
   e. Vandals: malicious hackers who deliberately cause damage with no apparent gain for themselves
   f. Addicts: classic computer "nerds" who are addicted to hacking and computer technology
5. Some high-tech crimes are committed by professional criminals who use technology to commit serious crimes, such as the theft of money
6. The World Wide Web may also be used to facilitate criminal activity, such as the computerized transmission of illegal pornography among pedophiles

**Show the ABC News program *Revolution in a Box, Part 2* from the video library**.

C. Computer crime as a form of white-collar crime
1. Some analysts see computer crime as a new form of white-collar crime
2. According to Donn B. Parker, computer criminals and white-collar criminals share several behavior-related issues:
   a. Both are generally committed through nonviolent means, although some may have life-threatening consequences
   b. Access to computers or computer storage media is often needed
   c. Both generally involve information manipulations that create profits or losses
   d. Both can be committed by an individual, several people working in collusion, and/or organizations
3. Other similarities between computer crime and white-collar crime include:
   a. Both are hard to detect and are often discovered accidentally or by customer complaint
   b. The general public sees many of these acts as less serious than crimes involving physical violence
   c. They cost individuals, organizations, and society large amounts of resources
   d. Prevention requires a combination of legal, technical, managerial, security, and audit-monitoring controls

V. Securing the Internet
  A. The United States is becoming a service-oriented information-rich society
    1. The Internet is the world's largest computer network, consisting of tens of thousands of computers linked together, and use a way of making information accessible to millions of people
    2. The growth of the Internet has encouraged hackers and computer criminals to attack it through the creation and development of viruses, worms, etc.
  B. In 1996, President Clinton created the Commission on Critical Infrastructure Protection, which was assigned to assess threats to the nation's computer networks and recommend policies to protect them
    1. As a result of the Commission's report, the National Infrastructure Protection Center (NIPC) was created in 1998 with the mission of serving as the federal government's center for threat assessment, warnings, investigation, and response to threats or attacks against the country's critical infrastructures
    2. NIPC was succeeded by the Information Analysis and Infrastructure Protection Directorate which operates within the Department of Homeland Security
  C. The President's Working Group on Unlawful Conduct on the Internet released a report in 2000
    1. It stated that the Internet provides a new tool for committing crimes; criminal activities may use both the product delivery and communications features of the Internet
    2. Cybercriminals are not affected by national or international boundaries because information and property can be transmitted through communications and data networks
      a. Criminals do not need to be at or near the scene of the crime to defraud victims
      b. Victims and offenders may be located in different countries
      c. However, law enforcement agencies may still have to deal with the difficulties of international cooperation, possibly slowing or even halting investigations
  D. The U.S. Computer Emergency Readiness Team (US-CERT) was established in 2003
    1. It is a partnership between the Department of Homeland Security and the public and private sectors and was created to protect the nation's Internet infrastructure and to coordinate defenses against cyberattacks
    2. US-CERT is also in charge of the National Cyber Alert System

VI. Technology in the Fight Against Crime

**Show the ABC News program *Simpson Defense Makes Opening Statement* from the video library.**

  A. Technology helps both criminals and criminal justice personnel
    1. Criminals are provided with new weapons to commit crimes while the criminal justice system has new tools to fight crime
    2. Key technology in law enforcement service today include traffic radar, computer databases of known offenders, machine-based expert systems,

cellular communications, electronic eavesdropping, DNA analysis, and less-than-lethal weapons

3. Computer-aided dispatch systems are becoming increasingly sophisticated, and other new crime-fighting technologies are constantly being developed

B. DNA technology
1. DNA profiling has resulted in the release of a number of unjustly convicted people and, in some cases, the discovery of the true offender
2. DNA samples can be taken from evidence at the scene of a crime and may provide the evidence necessary to identify a suspect
3. In 1993, the U.S. Supreme Court, in the civil case of *Daubert* v. *Merrell Dow Pharmaceuticals, Inc.*, revised the criteria for the admissibility of scientific evidence by rejecting an earlier standard established in the 1923 case of *Frye* v. *United States*
   a. The *Frye* standard required general acceptance of a test or procedure by the relevant scientific community
   b. In *Daubert*, the Court said that all relevant evidence is admissible unless otherwise provided by the U.S. Constitution, an act of Congress, the Federal Rules of Evidence, or other authority
   c. The Court found that to determine whether any form of scientific evidence is reliable, the factors used are:
      (1) Whether it has been subject to testing
      (2) Whether it has been subject to peer review
      (3) Known or potential rates of error
      (4) The existence of standards controlling application of the techniques involved
4. Several states and the federal government have begun building digitized forensic DNA databases
   a. In 1998, the FBI began operation of the National DNA Index System, which allows public forensic laboratories throughout the United States to exchange and compare DNA profiles electronically
   b. All states have passed legislation requiring convicted offenders to provide samples for DNA databasing and all states have been invited to participate in the system

C. Computers as crime-fighting tools
1. Offenders and the criminal justice system both use computers to keep records
2. Computers connect people: law enforcement professionals and criminologists throughout the United States are linked together through specialized Web sites
3. Innovative computer technologies, such as AFISs (automated fingerprint identification systems) facilitate the work of law enforcement agents
4. Online criminal information and database services may make information accessible to law enforcement agencies at remote sites (e.g., NCIC, VICAP, and METAPOL)
5. PC radios, combinations of police radios and laptop computers, are used by police to obtain information, report incidents, and outwit offenders who use police scanners to keep abreast of enforcement activities
6. Expert systems that attempt to duplicate the decision-making processes used by skilled investigators may be used to develop profiles of serial killers or to make recommendations to investigators attempting to solve problems relating to crime and its commission

VII. Combating Computer Crime
  A. Threat analysis/risk analysis
    1. Threat analysis involves a complete assessment of the kinds of perils facing an organization, including unpredictable natural events, events of human origin, and intentional human intervention
    2. Once threats are identified, strategies to deal with them can be introduced
      a. An audit trail traces and records the activities of computer operators and allows auditors to examine the sequence of events relating to any transaction
      b. It is a powerful tool that can be used in identifying instances of computer crime
    3. In reality, few small businesses, schools, hospitals, and individuals have any real understanding of the need for security in the use of their computers
      a. Little is being done to deter computer crime
      b. Industry has not really improved security, the police are not well equipped to catch electronic thieves, and judges do not hand down the types of sentences that will impress would-be computer criminals
  B. Police investigation of computer crime
    1. Few police departments have the time or the qualified personnel to investigate computer crimes effectively
      a. Some departments have created specialized computer-crime units but they are often poorly funded and understaffed
      b. Most state and local departments have no specialized computer crime units or personnel skilled in the investigation of computer crime
    2. Many departments place a low priority on computer crime
      a. Investigations are complex and demanding, and many departments feel that the time and money could be better allocated elsewhere
      b. Frequently, such investigations cross state lines and involve several telecommunications companies and other services
      c. Investigators who focus on computer crimes may not be promoted as readily as their counterparts in homicide and property crime divisions
      d. Personnel who are skilled in computer applications frequently take jobs with private industries where the pay scales are considerably higher
    3. Most computer crimes go unpunished, prosecutions are too rare to deter, and the punishments if convicted are also not much of a deterrent
    4. In 1992, the FBI formed a National Computer Crime Squad to investigate violations of federal computer crime laws such as the Computer Fraud and Abuse Act of 1984
    5. The U.S. Department of Justice formed the Computer Crime and Intellectual Property Section in 1991 and staffed it with attorneys who focus on issues raised by computer and intellectual property crime
    6. The FBI's network "sniffer," DCS-1000, is a network diagnostic tool that assists in criminal investigations by monitoring and capturing large amounts of Internet traffic
  C. Dealing with computer criminals
    1. Any effective policy must recognize issues associated with personal freedoms and individual rights
    2. Effective policy must also address the issue of deterrence
    3. Sanctions that may be effective in deterring high-tech offenders include:
      a. Confiscating equipment used to commit a computer crime

b. Limiting the offender's use of computers
c. Restricting the offender's freedom to accept jobs involving computers
4. These could be supplemented with a short term of incarceration in a county jail

VIII. Policy Issues: Personal Freedoms in the Information Age
A. The development of telecommunications resources has led to concerns about privacy, free speech, and personal freedoms
1. The Constitution obviously does not address electronic documents and advanced forms of communications facilitated by technologies that did not exist when it was created
2. One key issue is whether the First Amendment's protection of free speech applies to electronic communications
B. The Electronic Frontier Foundation (EFF) was formed in 1990 by a concerned citizens group to help ensure that constitutional principles are protected as new communications technologies emerge

IX. What the Future Holds
A. As new technologies continue to be developed, they will lead to new forms of crime, which will lead to the creation of new and innovative law enforcement efforts
B. Data encryption, the process by which information is encoded to make it unreadable to anyone other than the intended recipients, is an example of techniques that will be commonly used
1. Many forms of encryption are now in use, but most can be broken by using supercomputers to uncover the codes on which they are built
2. Technologies such as clipper (key escrow encryption) may also be used by offenders to make their communications unintelligible to investigators

# Key Concepts

**Audit trail:** A sequential record of computer system activities that enables auditors to reconstruct, review, and examine the sequence of states and activities surrounding each event in one or more related transactions from inception to output of final results back to inception.

**Communications Decency Act:** A federal statute signed into law in 1996, the CDA is Title 5 of the federal Telecommunications Act of 1996 (Public Law 104-104, 110 Stat. 56). The law sought to protect minors from harmful material on the Internet and a portion of the CDA criminalized the knowing transmission of obscene or indecent messages to any recipient under 18 years of age. In 1997, however, in the case of *Reno* v. *ACLU* (521 US 844), the U.S. Supreme Court found the bulk of the CDA to be unconstitutional, ruling that it contravenes First Amendment free speech guarantees.

**Computer abuse:** Any unlawful incident associated with computer technology in which a victim suffered or could have suffered loss, or in which a perpetrator by intention made or could have made gain.

**Computer crime**: Any violation of a federal or state computer crime statute. See also **cybercrime**.

**Computer-related crime:** Any illegal act for which knowledge of computer technology is involved for its perpetration, investigation, or prosecution.

**Computer virus:** A set of computer instructions that propagates copies or versions of itself into computer programs or data when it is executed.

**Cybercrime:** Crime committed with the use of computers or via the manipulation of digital forms of data. See also **computer crime**.

**Cyberspace:** The computer-created matrix of virtual possibilities, including online services, wherein human beings interact with one another and with the technology itself.

**Data encryption:** The process by which information is encoded, making it unreadable to all but its intended recipients.

***Daubert* standard**: A test of scientific acceptability applicable to the gathering of evidence in criminal cases.

**DCS-1000**: A network diagnostic tool that is capable of assisting in criminal investigations by monitoring and capturing large amounts of Internet traffic. Previously called *Carnivore*.

**Digital Theft Deterrence and Copyright Damages Improvement Act:** Passed in 1999, this federal law (Public Law 106-160) attempted to combat software piracy and other forms of digital theft by amending Section 504(c) of the Copyright Act, thereby increasing the amount of damages that could potentially be awarded in cases of copyright infringement.

**DNA fingerprinting:** See **DNA profiling.**

**DNA profiling:** The use of biological residue found at the scene of a crime for genetic comparisons in aiding the identification of criminal suspects.

**Expert systems**: Computer hardware and software that attempt to duplicate the decision-making processes used by skilled investigators in the analysis of evidence and in the recognition of patterns which such evidence might represent.

**Hacker:** A person who uses computers for exploration and exploitation.

**Identity theft:** The unauthorized use of another individual's personal identity to fraudulently obtain money, goods, or services; to avoid the payment of debt; or to avoid criminal prosecution.

**Internet:** The world's largest computer network.

**No Electronic Theft Act:** A 1997 federal law (Public Law 105-147) that criminalizes the willful infringement of copyrighted works, including by electronic means, even when the infringing party derives no direct financial benefit from the infringement (such as when pirated software is freely distributed online). In keeping with requirements of the NETA, the U.S. Sentencing Commission enacted amendments to its guidelines on April 6, 2000, to increase penalties associated with electronic theft.

**Phishing**: Pronounced "fishing." An Internet-based scam to steal valuable information such as credit card numbers, social security numbers, user IDs, and passwords.

**Phone phreak**: A person who uses switched, dialed-access telephone services for exploration and exploitation.

**Software piracy**: The unauthorized and illegal copying of software programs.

**TEMPEST:** A standard developed by the U.S. government that requires that electromagnetic emanations from computers designated as "secure" be below levels that would allow radio receiving equipment to "read" the data being computed.

**Threat analysis:** A complete and thorough assessment of the kinds of perils facing an organization. Also called *risk analysis*.

# Additional Lecture Topics

Consider discussing some of the characteristics of high-tech crimes that distinguish them from "street" crimes. These might include:

- Victim/offender contact: in high-tech crimes, victims and offenders generally do not come into direct contact with each other and may even be thousands of miles apart at the time of the crime.
- The type of property targeted: most property crimes target tangible items, but computer crimes generally focus on intangible property such as information or data.
- The international component: unlike street crimes, computer crimes may involve victims and offenders in different countries.
- The amount of profit: although most street crimes do not involve large profits, high-tech crimes can allow offenders to steal huge amounts.
- The complexity of the crime: computer crimes require offenders to have a much greater level of technical proficiency and skill than do street crimes.

Discuss some of the aspects of computers and computer technology that make them vulnerable to criminal activity. These might include:

- The ease with which anyone with some knowledge of programming can create a program such as a virus or logic bomb and insinuate it into a target computer
- The ease with which people with some knowledge of computers can erase any records of their illicit presence within a computer
- The ease with which computer software may be copied by anyone with even a small amount of skill with computers

# Discussion Questions

These discussion questions are found in the textbook at the end of the chapter. The instructor may want to focus on these questions during the coverage of Chapter 14.

1. This book emphasizes a social problems versus social responsibility theme. Which perspective best explains the involvement of capable individuals in criminal activity necessitating high-tech skills? What is the best way to deal with such criminals?

2. What is the difference between high-tech crime and traditional forms of criminal activity? Will the high-tech crimes of today continue to be the high-tech crimes of tomorrow? Why?

3. What forms of high-tech crime can you imagine which this chapter has not discussed? Describe each briefly.

4. Do you believe that high-tech crimes will eventually surpass the abilities of enforcement agents to prevent or solve them? Why?

5. What different kinds of high-tech offenders can you imagine? What is the best way to deal with each such offender? Give reasons for your answers.

# Student Exercises

## Activity #1

Select three theories that you have discussed in previous chapters and discuss how each of these might explain the actions of high-tech offenders.

## Activity #2

Visit a local, county, or state police department in your area and find out how they handle cases of computer crime.

# Criminology Today on the Web

**http://www.eff.org**
This is the home page of the Electronic Frontier Foundation.

**http://www.polcyb.org/**
This is the home page of the Society for the Policing of Cyberspace.

**http://www.usdoj.gov/criminal/cybercrime/index.html**
This is the home page of the U.S. Department of Justice Criminal Division's Computer Crime and Intellectual Property Section.

**http://www.fraud.org/welcome.htm**
This is the home page of the National Fraud Information Center, which includes information on Internet fraud.

**http://www.fbi.gov/hq/lab/carnivore/carnivore.htm**
This Web site provides information on the FBI's Carnivore Diagnostic Tool.

**http://www.siia.net**
This is the home page of the Software and Information Industry Association.

**http://www.wired.com/news/lovebug**
This Web site provides information on the Love Bug virus.

**http://www.cnn.com/US/9703/cda.scotus**
This CNN site provides information on the case of *Reno* v. *ACLU* and the history of the debate over the Communications Decency Act.

**http://www.cpsr.org**
This is the home page of Computer Professionals for Social Responsibility.

# Student Study Guide Questions and Answers

## True/False

1. The link between technology and criminology has only recently been discovered. **(False, p. 473)**

2. The path of direct access to computer information is generally used by office workers violating positions of trust. **(True, p. 474)**

3. Most computer systems today have security procedures installed to prevent computer trespass. **(False, p. 474)**

4. The first individual criminally prosecuted for creating a computer virus allegedly infected the computer of a former employer. **(True, p. 474)**

5. Cybercrime involves any violation of a federal or state computer crime statute. **(False, p. 475)**

6. According to David Carter, techno-vandalism involves using a computer to commit a crime. **(False, p. 475)**

7. According to David Carter, using one computer to obtain information stored in another computer is an example of a crime associated with the prevalence of computers. **(False, p. 475)**

8. Identity theft is an example of a computer manipulation crime. **(False, p. 475)**

9. According to the Software and Information Industry Association, softlifting involves illegally duplicating and distributing copyrighted software in a form designed to make it appear legitimate. **(False, p. 475)**

10. Software counterfeiting involves making unauthorized copies of copyrighted software available to others electronically over the Internet. **(False, p. 475)**

11. China has extremely low rates of illegal software use. **(False, p. 476)**

12. The responsibility for payment of stolen telephone time may rest with the company from whom the access codes were stolen. **(True, p. 476)**

13. The electronic theft of cellular telephone numbers and access codes is known as phishing. **(False, p. 478)**

14. The creation and transmission of computer viruses is committed for financial gain. **(False, p. 478)**

15. Viruses can spread from one computer to another via high-speed DSL connections. **(True, p. 478)**

16. A PDA may be infected by a computer virus. **(True, p. 479)**

17. Polymorphic viruses have the ability to change themselves after infecting a computer. **(True, p. 479)**

18. The individual who sent the Love Bug computer virus out onto the Internet was eventually convicted of computer hacking. **(False, p. 479)**

19. The Communications Decency Act criminalized the willful infringement of copyrighted works by electronic means. **(False, p. 481)**

20. The computer crime laws of most states contain great variation. **(True, p. 481)**

21. Computer-related crime is defined as the violation of a federal or state computer crime statute. **(False, p. 482)**

22. ]Cyberpunk is the place where computers and people interact with one another. **(False, p. 482)**

23. The average hacker is female. **(False, p. 482)**

24. Most hackers use software that they wrote themselves. **(False, p. 482)**

25. The primary motivation of the average hacker is financial profit. **(False, p. 482)**

26. Phone phreaking is one of the earliest forms of hacking. **(True, p. 484)**

27. Scamps are malicious hackers who intend to damage computer records. **(False, p. 484)**

28. Explorers focus on computer systems that are geographically distant from the hacker's physical location. **(True, p. 484)**

29. Addicts are the classic computer nerds. **(True, p. 484)**

30. Money is only information. **(True, p. 486)**

31. The discovery of computer crime is frequently made by accident. **(True, p. 488)**

32. Cybercriminals do not need to come into direct contact with victims. **(True, p. 489)**

33. The "Spiderman snare" is a discolike strobe light which quickly disorients human targets. **(False, p. 490)**

34. DNA evidence may last for many years. **(True, p. 491)**

35. The case of *Frye v. United States* stated that general acceptance of a test by the scientific community is not a necessary precondition to the admissibility of scientific evidence in court. **(False, p. 492)**

36. The *Daubert* standard deals with the application of the laws requiring convicted offenders to provide DNA samples. **(False, p. 492)**

37. DNA evidence has not yet been used to exonerate defendants sentenced to incarceration. **(False, p. 493)**

38. Computers are used by both offenders and the criminal justice system to keep records. **(True, p. 493)**

39. A PC radio is a combination of a police radio and a laptop computer. **(True, p. 493)**

40. Expert systems such as NCAVC may eventually replace human investigators. **(False, p. 493-494)**

41. Most small businesses today have a clear understanding of the need for security in the use of their computers. **(False, p. 494)**

42. Most police departments today are prepared to effectively investigate computer crimes. **(False, p. 494)**

43. Most local police departments do not have specialized computer crime units. **(True, p. 494)**

44. The best way to deter computer offenders is to incarcerate them. **(False, p. 495)**

45. The U.S. Constitution specifically addresses the issue of electronic documents. **(False, p. 496)**

46. Encryption technology was developed in the 1980s. **(False, p. 497)**

## Fill in the Blank

47. As __________ advances, it facilitates new forms of behavior. **(technology, p. 473)**

48. Computer __________ involves remote access to targeted machines. **(trespass, p. 474)**

49. The TEMPEST program was developed by the U.S. Department of __________. **(Defense, p. 474)**

50. The term used by the computer underground for pirated software is __________. **(Warez, p. 475)**

51. __________ is a form of software piracy that involves purchasing a single licensed copy of software and loading the same copy onto several computers. **(Softlifting, p. 475)**

52. A computer __________ is a program designed to invade a computer system and modify the way it operates or alter the information it stores. **(virus, p. 478)**

53. Early attempts at prosecuting unauthorized computer access used preexisting __________ crime statutes. **(property, p. 479)**

54. The Communications Decency Act was challenged on the grounds that it contravened the __________ Amendment to the U.S. Constitution. **(First, p. 481)**

55. Computer criminals tend to come from __________ subculture. **(hacker, p. 482)**

56. Computer hackers and hacker identities are products of __________. **(cyberspace, p. 482)**

57. Hackers who intend no overt harm but just have a sense of fun are known as __________. **(scamps, p. 484)**

58. __________ see hacking itself as a game. **(Game players, p. 484)**

59. In some jurisdictions, __________ systems involve computers prompting police dispatchers for important information which allows them to distinguish locations within a city. **(CAD/computer aided dispatch, p. 490)**

60. The __________ police were the first national police force in the world to begin routine collection of DNA samples from anyone involved in a serious crime. **(British, p. 492)**

61. __________ allows investigators to use computers to match a suspect's fingerprints against stored records. **(AFIS/automated fingerprint identification systems, p. 493)**

62. The FBI's National Center for the Analysis of Violent Crime is an example of a(n) __________ system. **(expert, p. 493)**

63. __________ involves a complete and thorough assessment of the perils facing an organization. **(Threat analysis, p. 494)**

64. The FBI's National Computer Crime Squad investigates violations of the federal __________ Act. **(Computer Fraud and Abuse, pp. 494-495)**

65. The FBI has created a network "sniffer" known as __________. **(DCS-1000, p. 495)**

66. Data __________ is a process by which data is encoded and made unreadable to all but the intended recipients. **(encryption, p. 497)**

## Multiple Choice

67. The person most likely to invade a computer is a(n)
    a. hacker.
    b. unauthorized user.
    c. **current employee. (p. 474)**
    d. skilled computer amateur.

68. Using a computer to create a database of drug buyers falls within which of David Carter's categories of computer crime?
    a. Crimes in which computers serve as targets
    b. Crimes in which computers serve as the instrumentality of the crime
    c. **Crimes in which the computer is incidental to other crimes (p. 475)**
    d. Crimes associated with the prevalence of computers

69. Phone phreaking is an example of the __________ category of computer crime.
    a. internal computer crime
    b. **telecommunications (p. 475)**
    c. computer manipulation crimes
    d. support of criminal enterprises

70. __________ is/are an example of the "information theft" category of computer crime.
    a. Viruses
    b. Hacking
    c. **Software piracy (p. 475)**
    d. Money laundering

71. According to the Software and Information Industry Association, __________ involves making unauthorized copies of copyrighted software available to others over the Internet.
    a. softlifting
    b. **Internet piracy (p. 475)**
    c. renting
    d. OEM unbundling

72. According to the Software and Information Industry Association, __________ involves selling stand-alone software that was intended to be bundled with specific accompanying hardware.
    a. softlifting
    b. software counterfeiting
    c. renting
    d. **OEM unbundling (p. 475)**

73. The goal of __________ is generally to encourage the end user to purchase hardware from a specific hardware vendor.
    a. **hard disk loading (p. 475)**
    b. renting
    c. OEM unbundling
    d. softlifting

74. Which of the following is *not* an example of a destructive computer program?
    a. A virus
    b. A logic bomb
    c. A Trojan horse
    d. **A Spiderman snare (p. 478)**

75. Which of the following factors is *not* being considered by the U.S. Sentencing Commission in the creation of new sentencing guidelines for computer criminals?
    a. The financial loss caused by the computer crime
    b. The level of planning involved in the crime
    c. The presence or absence of malicious intent on the part of the perpetrator
    d. **The type of technology used in the crime (p. 479)**

76. The __________ Act criminalized the willful infringement of copyrighted works.
    a. **No Electronic Theft (p. 481)**
    b. Communications Decency
    c. Digital Theft Deterrence and Copyright Damages
    d. National Stolen Property

77. __________ is defined as any incident without color of right associated with computer technology in which a victim suffered or could have suffered loss and/or a perpetrator intentionally made or could have made gain.
    a. Computer crime
    b. Computer-related crime
    c. **Computer abuse (p. 482)**
    d. Cybercrime

78. __________ are hackers who are fascinated by the evolving technology of telecommunications and explore it without knowing exactly what they will find.
    a. **Pioneers (p. 484)**
    b. Scamps
    c. Explorers
    d. Addicts

79. __________ are malicious hackers who deliberately cause damage with no apparent gain for themselves.
    a. Explorers
    b. Scamps
    c. Game players
    d. **Vandals (p. 484)**

80. The __________ was created by President Clinton in 1996.
    a. **Commission on Critical Infrastructure Protection (p. 489)**
    b. National Infrastructure Protection Center
    c. President's Working Group on Unlawful Conduct on the Internet
    d. National Cybercrime Training Partnership

81. The Information Analysis and Infrastructure Protection Directorate operates within the
    a. **Department of Homeland Security. (p. 489)**
    b. Department of Justice.
    c. Federal Bureau of Investigation.
    d. National Infrastructure Protection Center.

82. In the case of __________, the U.S. Supreme Court held that for scientific evidence to be admissible in court, the test or procedure must be generally accepted by the relevant scientific community.
    a. ***Frye* v. *United States* (p. 492)**
    b. *Reno* v. *ACLU*
    c. *Daubert* v. *Merrell Dow Pharmaceuticals, Inc.*
    d. None of the above

83. Bulletproof software, which compares a bullet's ballistic characteristics with those stored in a database, was developed by the
    a. FBI.
    b. Police Executive Research Forum.
    c. **Bureau of Alcohol, Tobacco, and Firearms. (p. 493)**
    d. Bureau of Justice Statistics.

84. A(n) __________ records the activities of computer operators surrounding each event in a transaction.
    a. threat analysis
    b. **audit trail (p. 494)**
    c. DNA profile
    d. expert systems analysis

85. DCS-1000 is being challenged on the grounds of
    a. freedom of speech.
    b. First Amendment issues.
    c. **the right to privacy. (p. 495)**
    d. All of the above

86. Which of the following is *not* one of the three sanctions that may be especially effective in deterring high-tech offenders?
    a. Limiting the offender's use of computers
    b. Restricting the offender's freedom to accept jobs which involve computers
    c. Confiscating the equipment used to commit a computer crime
    d. **Providing training in socially acceptable ways to use a computer (p. 495)**

87. Attempts to define computer crimes often result in concerns about the __________ Amendment to the Constitution.
    a. **First (p. 495)**
    b. Fifth
    c. Sixth
    d. Eighth

88. Key escrow encryption is also known as
    a. **clipper. (p. 497)**
    b. threat analysis.
    c. TEMPEST.
    d. DCS-1000.

# Word Search Puzzle

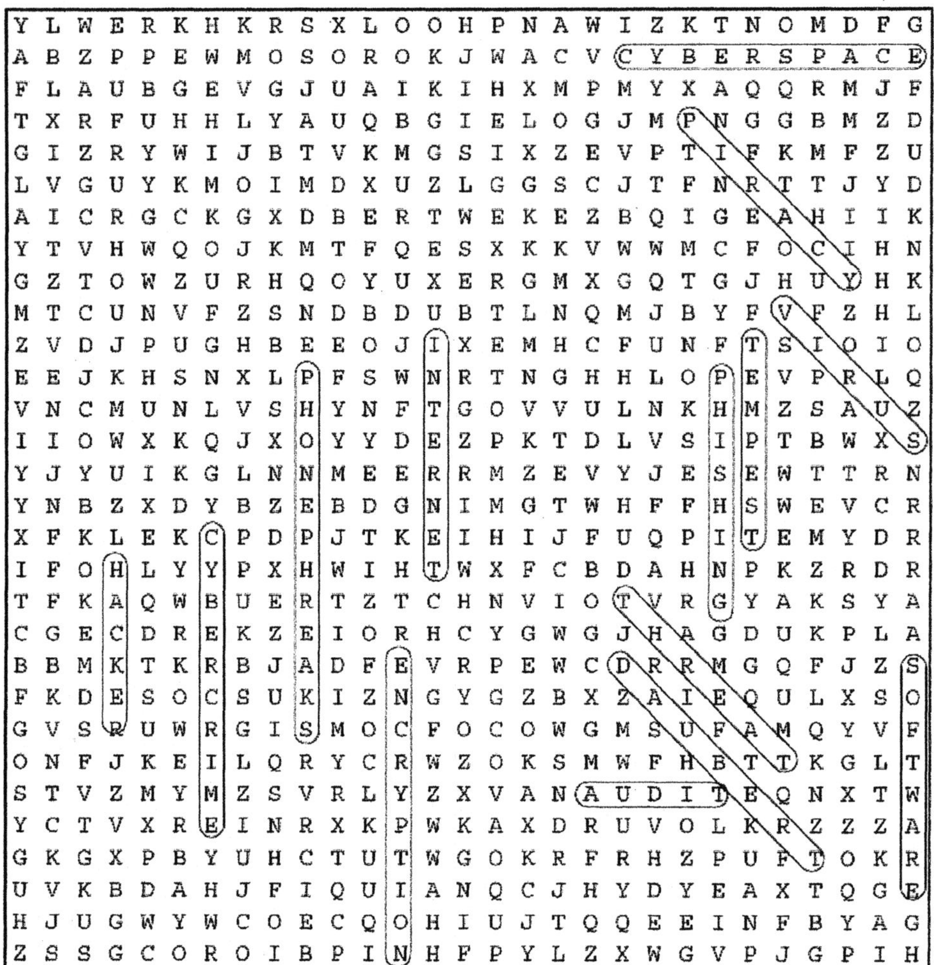

| | |
|---|---|
| Audit | Phishing |
| Cybercrime | Piracy |
| Cyberspace | Phone phreaks |
| Daubert | Software |
| Encryption | TEMPEST |
| Hacker | Threat |
| Internet | Virus |

# Crossword Puzzle

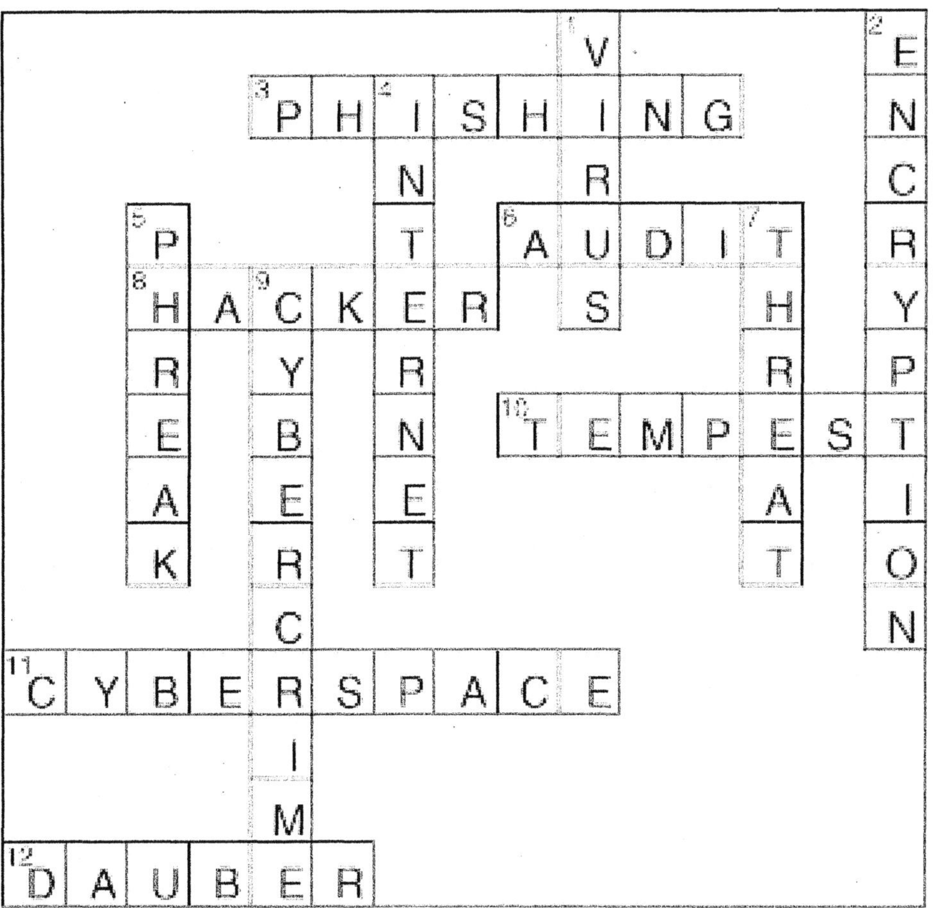

## Across

3. An Internet-based scam to steal valuable information.
6. A(n) _____ trail is a sequential record of computer system activities.
8. A person who uses computers for exploration and exploitation.
10. A government regulating electromagnetic emanations from secure computers.
11. The computer-created matrix of virtual possibilities wherein human beings interact with one another and with the technology itself.
12. The _____ standard is a test of scientific acceptability of evidence gathering in criminal cases.

## Down

1. A set of computer instructions that propagates copies or versions of itself into computer programs.
2. The process by which information is encoded.
4. The world's largest computer network.
5. A phone __________ uses telephone services for exploration and exploitation.
7. _________ analysis is a thorough assessment of the kinds of perils facing an organization.
9. Crime committed with the use of computers or via the manipulation of digital forms of data.

# 15 Criminology and Social Policy

## Learning Objectives

After reading this chapter, students should be able to:

1. Distinguish between the social problems approach and the social responsibility approach to crime control
2. Recognize and understand the different types of crime control strategies
3. Relate various crime control strategies to recent American crime control policy initiatives
4. Describe the history and the current state of the victims' movement in this country

## Chapter Outline

Introduction
Federal Anticrime Initiatives
    *The Hoover Administration*
    *Federal Policy Following World War II*
    *The Reagan and Bush Years*
    *Clinton Administration Initiatives*
    *The Administration of George W. Bush*
Crime Control Philosophies Today
    *Types of Crime Control Strategies*
    *International Policies*
Criminology and Social Policy
The Victims' Movement
    *A History of the Victim*
    *Current Directions in Victims' Rights*
    *Victim-Impact Statements*
    *Victim Restitution*
Can We Solve the Problem of Crime?
    *Symbolism and Public Policy*

# Chapter Summary

Today's public policymakers are faced with a variety of crime-related problems and issues. Public or social policy is a course of action that government takes in an effort to solve a problem or achieve an end. In many cases it appears that crime-fighting policies may be more the result of politics than they are the direct outcome of social science research and data.

Federal involvement in crime began during the Hoover administration, when Hoover established the National Commission on Law Observance and Enforcement (the Wickersham Commission). Hoover's administration developed a wide variety of policy initiatives in the areas of police, courts, and corrections, using experts in a number of criminal justice–related fields; many of his reforms were effective. One key problem with policymaking groups such as the Wickersham Commission was that they failed to include broad representation of racial or ethnic minorities.

After World War II, the United States experienced a period of economic prosperity and lowered crime rates that lasted until the 1960s. During the Kennedy administration, crime and crime control were important political issues. Crime and violence issues were again emphasized during the Johnson administration. Johnson established the President's Commission on Law Enforcement and Administration of Justice, which reported that crime was the inevitable result of poverty, unemployment, low education levels, and other social and economic disadvantages. One result of the Commission's report was the passage of the Omnibus Crime Bill and Safe Streets Act of 1967. Title I of this act created the Law Enforcement Assistance Administration (LEAA), which provided technical and financial assistance to states for the purpose of improving and strengthening law enforcement activities at the local level. President Nixon developed the concept of a "war on crime," emphasizing tough-on-crime policies and reducing interest in the rights of the accused. Nixon commissioned the National Advisory Commission on Criminal Justice Standards and Goals, which called for improved police–community relations and enhanced communications between agencies in the criminal justice system.

President Reagan felt that the choice of a career in crime was not the result of social problems such as poverty or an unhappy childhood but was a conscious and willful choice. He emphasized holding individual offenders responsible for their crimes while reducing the focus on the root causes of crime. In support of this, Congress passed the Comprehensive Crime Control Act of 1984, which included a variety of "get tough" provisions. Reagan also developed the "war on drugs," emphasizing his belief that drugs contributed both directly and indirectly to much of the country's crime problem. He created a new cabinet-level position to coordinate federal drug-fighting efforts. During President George Bush's administration (1989–1993), the war on drugs continued to be funded by federal and state tax dollar.

During his administration, President Clinton was able to influence the development of a number of crime control initiatives already underway. He emphasized gun-control legislation, such as the Brady Handgun Violence Prevention Act. The centerpiece of the Clinton administration crime control legislation was the Violent Crime Control and Law Enforcement Act. It provided massive funding for increased law enforcement and correctional resources, increased control over firearms, expanded the federal death penalty, created drug-free zones, included federal three-strikes provisions, and increased or enhanced penalties for over 70 criminal penalties. It also had several provisions in the areas of victims' rights. Other components of the Act include the Violence Against Women Act.

Three key pieces of legislation have been passed during the administration of President George W. Bush: the USA Patriot Act, the Sarbanes–Oxley Act, and the Homeland Security Act. President Bush is also committed to providing federal funding to faith-based community initiatives.

Currently, there is a two-pronged approach to crime control in the United States: the social responsibility perspective and the social problems perspective. There are three main crime control strategies. Protection/avoidance strategies involve attempts to reduce criminal opportunities in some way; deterrence strategies attempt to reduce the motivation for crime by increasing the perceived certainty, severity, or swiftness of penalties; and nurturant strategies focus on preventing the development of criminality. Although many criminologists feel that a comprehensive crime control strategy would be a balanced mix of all three strategies, politicians and policymakers focus primarily on protection/avoidance and deterrence strategies and generally ignore nurturant strategies. Although many criminologists feel that criminological research is not directly influencing policy and practice, there is evidence that the conceptual use of ideas developed through criminological research has affected policymakers in a broad way.

Victims were a forgotten element of the criminal justice system until the 1960s, when renewed interest in victim issues led to the development of victim compensation laws in all states. Victim–witness assistance programs are designed to provide comfort and assistance to victims of crime and help prevent or alleviate postcrime victimization. Many states now provide for the use of victim impact statements in court; these statements are written documents describing the losses, suffering, and trauma experienced by victims or their survivors. Some states also allow victims to attend and participate in sentencing and parole hearings, and some also allow victims to testify directly at sentencing. Victim restitution involves payment of compensation to the victim by the offender and emphasizes the concept that offenders should be responsible for at least a portion of the financial obligations needed to make the victim whole again.

Currently, many criminologists expect to work closely with politicians and policymakers to develop crime control agendas based on scientific knowledge and criminological theorizing. Many critics feel that the only way to address the issues underlying high crime rates is to implement drastic policy-level changes such as drug legalization, the elimination of guns throughout the country, nightly curfews, and close control of media violence. These reforms may be unlikely because of cultural taboos rooted in citizens' demands for individual freedoms. Because of this, many feel that there may not be a solution to the crime problem. Some even suggest that crime control policies are largely symbolic and that crime will always be a part of our society.

# Lecture Outline

I. Introduction
   A. Discuss the violence surrounding many of the gangsta rappers and the violence contained in many of their lyrics
      1. Some claim that gangsta rap and hip-hop music promote antisocial and violent behavior; others feel that the problems are outside rap music
      2. Supporters suggest that rap may be a method of raising awareness about the increasing problem of black-on-black violence

B. In addition to the issue of media-fed violence, other concerns facing policymakers today include drug trafficking, illicit drug use, gun violence, youth violence, school shootings, overcrowded prisons, high imprisonment rates, and victims' rights

II. Federal Anticrime Initiatives
  A. Introduction
    1. Public policy or social policy is a course of action that the government takes in an effort to solve a problem or to achieve an end
    2. The development of public policy involves five stages:
      a. Identify the problem(s)
      b. Prioritize the problems (agenda setting)
      c. Policy formation
      d. Program implementation
      e. Program evaluation and reassessment
    3. Crime-fighting policies may be more the result of politics than they are the direct outcome of social science research and data
  B. The Hoover administration
    1. President Herbert Hoover's administration was the beginning of federal involvement in crime-control policy
    2. In 1929, Hoover appointed former attorney general George Wickersham to chair the National Commission on Law Observance and Enforcement (also known as the Wickersham Commission)
    3. The commission's mandate was to develop objectives to improve justice system practices and to reinstate law's role in civilized governance
    4. Hoover's administration developed a wide variety of policy initiatives in the areas of police, courts, and corrections, using experts in a number of criminal justice–related fields
    5. One key problem with policymaking groups, including the Wickersham Commission, was that they failed to include broad representation of racial or ethnic minorities; Hoover wanted to avoid having any special interests represented, as he felt that this might produce less than objective results
    6. Many of the Hoover-era reforms were effective
      a. Hoover's administration was the first to give formal policy attention to federal prisons and prisoners
      b. Prison expansion was begun
      c. Federal parole board activities were streamlined and centralized
      d. New federal district court standards were introduced
  C. Federal policy following World War II
    1. After World War II, the United States experienced a period of economic prosperity and lowered crime rates
    2. This ended in the 1960s, when baby boomers reaching their teen years contributed to rising crime rates
    3. Crime and crime control were important political issues during President John F. Kennedy's administration
      a. Federal crime control policies were expanded to address juvenile crime and the rights of indigent defendants to be afforded counsel
      b. Federal anticrime efforts also focused on combating organized crime
    4. During the administration of President Lyndon B. Johnson, crime and violence issues were again paramount

a. Johnson established the President's Commission on Law Enforcement and Administration of Justice as part of his drive toward building "The Great Society"
b. The commission's report was published in 1967 and saw crime as the inevitable result of poverty, unemployment, low education levels, and other social an economic disadvantages
(1) One result was the passage of the Omnibus Crime Bill and Safe Streets Act of 1967
(2) Title I of the Safe Streets Act created the Law Enforcement Assistance Administration, which provided technical and financial assistance to states for the purpose of improving and strengthening law enforcement activities at the local level
c. Crime was much less a reality in 1967 than it is today
(1) Although fear of crime was widespread, the crime rate was less than a third of what it is now
(2) Problems such as carjackings, crack cocaine, drive-by shootings, drug cartels, and gang warfare were unfamiliar

5. During the administration of President Richard M. Nixon, the emphasis became an all-out "war on crime"
a. Interest in the rights of the accused and offenders was reduced as Nixon emphasized mandatory minimum sentences, fewer pretrial releases for multiple offenders, and heavier penalties, and selected judges who were strict on crime
b. Nixon commissioned the 1971 National Advisory Commission on Criminal Justice Standards and Goals, which called for improved police–community relations and enhanced communications between agencies in the criminal justice system

D. The Reagan and Bush years

1. During the administration of President Ronald Reagan, the war on crime moved in new directions
a. One change was an increased focus on holding individual offenders responsible for their crimes while reducing the focus on the underlying causes of crime
(1) In support of this, Congress passed the Comprehensive Crime Control Act of 1984, which mandated new sentencing guidelines for federal offenders, eliminated federal parole, limited the use of the insanity defense for federal defendants, and increased penalties associated with drug dealing
(2) Reagan emphasized that the choice of a career in crime was not the result of social problems such as poverty or an unhappy childhood but was a conscious and willful choice
b. The second change was a focus on drugs and their relationship to crime
(1) Reagan believed that drugs contributed greatly to the crime problem and was greatly opposed to decriminalization or legalization of controlled substances
(2) Congress passed the Anti-Drug Abuse Act (1986), which enacted new federal mandatory minimum sentences for drug offenses
(3) Congress also passed the Omnibus Anti-Drug Abuse Act (1988), which substantially increased penalties for recreational drug users and created a new cabinet-level position to coordinate federal drug-fighting efforts

2. During President George Bush's administration, the war on drugs continued to be funded by federal and state tax dollars
3. However, even with massive spending, the war on drugs appeared to have little immediate impact on the rate of drug crimes, although it did result in overworked criminal justice agencies and extremely overcrowded jails and prisons

E. Clinton administration initiatives
1. During his administration, President William Clinton was able to influence the development of a number of crime control initiatives already underway
   a. The Brady Handgun Violence Prevention Act (1993) called for the initiation of a national background checking system for all potential gun purchasers
   b. The Violent Crime Control and Law Enforcement Act (1994) called for spending billions of dollars on crime prevention, law enforcement, and prison construction, outlawed the sale of certain types of assault weapons, and enhanced federal death penalty provisions
   c. Clinton also backed the Violence Against Women Act (1994), which is part of the Violent Crime Control and Law Enforcement Act
   d. The Hate Crimes Sentencing Enhancement Act (1994), which was also part of the Violent Crime Control and Law Enforcement Act, increased the penalties for hate crimes
2. Gun control legislation
   a. In 1998, Clinton signed a law that applies to all violent criminals and drug felons committing gun crimes and strengthens federal penalties for those using guns during the commission of a crime
      (1) Violent criminals and drug felons who possess a firearm during the commission of a federal crime are to be sentenced to a mandatory minimum sentence of five years in addition to any penalties that apply for the underlying offense
      (2) Offenders who brandish a firearm receive a mandatory minimum sentence of seven years and those who discharge a firearm receive a sentence of at least ten years
   b. In 1994, Clinton signed the Youth Handgun Safety Act, banning the possession of handguns or handgun ammunition by juveniles under 18 and making it a federal offense for adults to transfer handguns to juveniles
   c. In 1998, Clinton announced a general ban on the importation of over 50 nonrecreational modified assault weapons
   d. In 2000, Clinton announced a voluntary partnership between the government and gun manufacturer Smith and Wesson, which was designed to reform the way that guns are designed, distributed, and marketed
   e. The Brady Handgun Violence Prevention Act, or Brady Law, was passed in 1993 and was the centerpiece of the Clinton Administration gun control legislation
      (1) The law provided for a mandatory waiting period before the purchase of a handgun and established a national instant criminal background check system that firearms dealers must contact before the transfer of any firearm
      (2) It requires firearms dealers to register with the federal government and notify law enforcement officials of all handgun purchase applications

(3) The five-day waiting period for handgun purchases was phased out after the national system became fully operational
(4) Proponents of the Brady Law believe that the availability of guns in the United States is a significant factor contributing to the crime problem and statistics from the Bureau of Justice Statistics seem to support this view
(5) However, opponents of the Brady Law, such as the National Rifle Association, claim that it has not reduced crime and that it is unconstitutional

3. Gun control strategies
   a. Public opinion polls suggest that the majority of Americans believe that some form of gun control is needed
   b. There are four fundamental gun control intervention strategies:
      (1) Reducing the number of guns in society
      (2) Reducing the destructiveness of guns
      (3) Changing gun allocation
      (4) Altering the uses or storage of guns
4. The Violent Crime Control and Law Enforcement Act of 1994
   a. This act was passed in response to increasingly hard-nosed voter sentiment about crime and provided massive funding for increased law enforcement and correctional resources
   b. Other key provisions included
      (1) Increased control over firearms
      (2) The creation of drug-free zones
      (3) Authorization of adult treatment of 13-year-olds charged with serious violent crimes
      (4) Enhanced federal penalties for terrorism
      (5) Expansion of the federal death penalty to cover approximately 60 crimes
      (6) Three-strikes provisions: mandatory life imprisonment for offenders convicted of three violent offense felonies or drug offenses
      (7) Increased or enhanced penalties for over 70 criminal penalties
      (8) Designated funding for immigration enforcement
      (9) Increased federal criminal penalties for various types of fraud
   c. The act had several provisions in the areas of victims' rights, including:
      (1) Allowing victims of violent and sex crimes to speak at the sentencing of the assailant
      (2) Requiring sex offenders and child molesters to pay victim restitution
      (3) Prohibiting diversion of victims' funds to other federal programs
5. The Violence Against Women Act (VAWA)
   a. VAWA is a component of the 1994 Violent Crime Control and Law Enforcement Act
   b. VAWA originally focuses on improving interstate enforcement of protection orders, providing effective training for court personnel involved with women's issues and improving the training and collaboration of police and prosecutors with victim service providers
   c. The Violence Against Women Act 2000 was reauthorized by President Clinton

6. Three-strikes legislation
   a. The 1994 Violent Crime Control and Law Enforcement Act includes a three-strikes provision which mandates life imprisonment for offenders convicted of three serious violent felonies and/or serious drug offenses
   b. Three-strikes laws, which are a type of habitual offender statute, are attempts to keep repeat offenders incarcerated
   c. In addition to the federal government, many states have also passed three-strikes legislation
   d. The U.S. Supreme Court has upheld California's three-strikes laws despite claims that it violates the Eighth Amendment
7. Youth violence initiatives
   a. The 1994 Violent Crime Control and Law Enforcement Act targeted gangs and youth violence
      (1) It provided new and stiffer penalties for violent and drug crimes committed by gangs
      (2) It tripled penalties for using children to deal drugs near schools and playgrounds
      (3) It enhanced penalties for all crimes using children and for recruiting and encouraging children to commit a crime
   b. The 1998 Safe Schools/Healthy Students Initiative (SS/HS) focused on helping communities design and implement a comprehensive approach to help fight youth violence
   c. In 1999, the Clinton administration created a National Campaign Against Youth Violence which developed antiviolence activities and highlighted effective youth violence initiatives around the United States

F. The administration of George W. Bush
1. Three key pieces of legislation resulted from the Bush presidency
   a. The USA Patriot Act, passed in response to the terrorist attacks of September 11, 2001
   b. The Sarbanes-Oxley Act, which established new requirements for corporate governance and set stiff criminal penalties for violators (See Chapter 12)
   c. The Homeland Security Act of 2002, which established the cabinet-level Department of Homeland Security
2. The USA Patriot Act
   a. The USA Patriot Act was designed to fight terrorism but also has provisions that apply to other forms of crime
   b. The Act also amends a number of federal statutes and rules, such as the Bank Secrecy Act, the Federal Rules of Criminal Procedure, and the federal Wiretap Statute
   c. Questions have been raised as to whether the Act unfairly expands police powers at the expense of individual rights and civil liberties
3. Faith-based community initiatives
   a. The White House Office of Faith-Based and Community Initiatives provides federal funding to religious organizations and other charitable service groups for community-oriented programs
   b. The Department of Justice passed a rule that these organizations may not use government funds to support inherently religious activities but that they may retain their religious identity

III. Crime Control Philosophies Today
  A. Currently, there is a two-pronged approach to crime control in the United States
    1. The crime control or social responsibility perspective defines crime as an issue of individual responsibility
    2. The social problems perspective, which is based on a public health approach, sees criminals as victims of social problems and poor social conditions
      a. This approach stresses the need to improve the American infrastructure and increase educational and employment opportunities for the disenfranchised
      b. This approach has recently been recast in terms of social epidemiology: the study of social epidemics and diseases of the social order
      c. The social epidemiological approach holds that crime arises from festering conditions promoting social ills and that people caught in such a criminogenic environment may display symptoms of the disease of crime
      d. The epidemiological approach is becoming increasingly popular among crime control policymakers
  B. Types of crime control strategies
    1. The three main crime control strategies differ in terms of strategic focus and are distinguishable from one another by whether the try to block opportunities for crime, change the outcome of the decision-making preceding a criminal act, or change the broad strategic style with which people approach many aspects of their lives
      a. Protection/avoidance strategies involve attempts to reduce criminal opportunities in some way; examples include incapacitating offenders (via incarceration or electronic monitoring), target hardening, and changing routine activities
      b. Deterrence strategies attempt to reduce the motivation for crime by increasing the perceived certainty, severity, or swiftness of penalties; examples include tougher laws, quicker processing of offenders, harsher punishments, and faster imposition of sentences
      c. Nurturant strategies focus on preventing the development of criminality; examples include increased infant and maternal health care, child care for the working poor, training in parenting skills, enhanced public education, and better programs to reduce unwanted pregnancies
    2. Many criminologists feel that a comprehensive crime control strategy would be a balanced mix of all three strategies
    3. Currently, politicians and policymakers are focusing primarily on protection/avoidance and deterrence strategies while ignoring nurturant strategies
  C. International policies
    1. Although social policies may indirectly impact crime rates, the effect may be difficult to see
      a. A key example is China's one-child policy, which has led to a gender imbalance, with boys significantly outnumbering girls
      b. One result of this imbalance is that many men who are unable to marry may band together in criminal gangs, becoming involved in crime, violence, and even terrorism, seriously threatening the country's social order

2. Increasing global conservationism and increased concerns about crime have led a number of countries to enact legislation designed to control crime using deterrence strategies
   a. For example, Britain passed the Criminal Justice and Police Bill in 1994, which returned England to a get-tough crime policy
   b. The bill removed a suspect's right to silence during police questioning, showing a significant shift in British social policy

IV. Criminology and Social Policy
  A. Criminologists are concerned that criminology and criminological research are not influencing policy and practice
    1. There is a pervasive feeling that policymakers and practitioners ignore research findings or even act counter to these findings
    2. Some policymakers and practitioners are unaware of the influence of research on the system
    3. Research funding is changing in scope and nature
  B. However, there is evidence that the conceptual use of ideas developed through criminological research has affected policymakers in a broad way by generally influencing the types of provisions put into place at the state and national level

V. The Victims' Movement
  A. Victims of crime is an area of growing policy concern in the United States
    1. There is a growing view that certain potential victims need special legal protections
    2. Support is increasing for national legislation providing victims with procedural protections similar to those granted individuals accused of committing crimes
  B. A history of the victim
    1. In early times, victims took the law into their own hands, attempted to apprehend offenders, and take retaliation against them
    2. The Code of Hammurabi had many provisions relating to victims, such as requiring many offenders to make restitution
    3. By the Middle Ages, crimes were seen as offenses against society and victims were forgotten, except for their usefulness in providing evidence of a crime and testifying against offenders; justice for the victim was translated into the idea of justice for the state
    4. In the 1960s, renewed interest in victim issues led to the development of compensation laws for victims of violent crimes
      a. Today, all states and the District of Columbia have legislation providing for monetary payments to crime victims, although most programs are underfunded
      b. All states require applicants to meet minimum eligibility requirements, and most set award maximums
      c. A study of the effectiveness of government-sponsored compensation programs in New York and New Jersey found that most victims had negative attitudes toward the programs, because of issues such as delays, inconveniences, restrictive eligibility requirements, and the large number of denied applications

C. Current directions in victims' rights
 1. Problems following from initial victimization are known as postcrime or secondary victimization
 2. Victim-witness assistance programs, designed to provide comfort and assistance to crime victims, have developed throughout the United States
  a. These programs counsel victims, orient them to the criminal justice process, and provide a variety of services, such as transportation to court, child care during court appearances, and referrals
  b. Recommendations from President Reagan's 1982 Task Force on Victims of Crime led to the passage of the 1984 Victims of Crime Act (VOCA), which established the federal Crime Victims Fund to supplement state support of local victims' assistance programs and state victim compensation programs
 3. The Crime Victims' Rights Act was passed by the U.S. Senate in 2004 and is seen as a partial statutory alternative to a constitutional victims' rights amendment
  a. The Act grants a variety of rights to victims of federal crimes and requires federal courts to ensure that the rights are afforded to victims
  b. The Act does not apply to victims of state crimes so it is seen as only a partial solution to addressing victims' needs

D. Victim-impact statements
 1. A victim-impact statement is a written document describing the losses, suffering, and trauma experienced by the victim or the victim's survivors
 2. In jurisdictions using victim-impact statements, judges are supposed to consider them when determining appropriate sanctions
 3. The 1982 Victim and Witness Protection Act requires victim-impact statements to be considered at federal sentencing hearings and makes federal probation officers responsible for creating the statements
 4. Some states also allow victims to attend and participate in sentencing and parole hearings, or to testify directly at sentencing

E. Victim restitution
 1. Restitution involves payment of compensation to the victim by the offender and emphasizes the concept that offenders should be responsible for at least a portion of the financial obligations needed to make the victim whole again
 2. Restitution places responsibility for the process of making the victim whole again on the offender
 3. There are three main types of restitution:
  a. Compensatory fines imposed in addition to other court-ordered punishments which compensate the victim for the actual amount of loss
  b. Double or treble damages, which punish the offender by making him or her pay the victim more than the amount of the original injury
  c. Restitution in lieu of other punishment, which allows the offender to discharge criminal responsibility by compensating the victim
 4. A key problem with many restitution programs is the difficulty associated with actually collecting restitution from offenders, who are often poor, lower class, and not motivated to participate meaningfully in restitution programs

VI. Can We Solve the Problem of Crime?
   A. Introduction
      1. Currently, many criminologists expect to work closely with politicians and policymakers to develop crime control agendas based on scientific knowledge and criminological theorizing
         a. This represents a major change in attitude since the 1950s, when criminologists decried the concept of *Kriminalpolitik* or a criminology-based social policy
         b. Some feel that this is a maturation of the discipline of criminology
      2. Many critics feel that the only way to address the issues underlying high crime rates is to implement drastic policy-level changes, such as drug legalization, the elimination of guns throughout the country, nightly curfews, and close control of media violence
         a. These reforms may be unlikely because of cultural taboos rooted in citizens' demands for individual freedoms
         b. Because of this, many feel that there may not be a solution to the crime problem
      3. Conflicting attitudes about crime and crime control add to the difficulties of creating social policy
   B. Symbolism and public policy
      1. Some suggest that crime control policies are largely symbolic and that crime will always be a part of our society
      2. Many policies supported by the federal government may be symbolic gestures to appease the public rather than attempts to reduce crime
         a. It may not be within the power of the federal government to reduce crime
         b. Changes in political power make it impossible to establish consistent crime control policies
         c. Consistent policies may be inaccurately targeted due to myths created through the presentation of crime by the media
         d. We are unable effectively to conceptualize and define crime: laws may reflect moral conceptions of the political majority, which are always subject to change
         e. It is difficult to measure accurately the extent of crime
      3. Thus, critics of contemporary crime-fighting policies point out that if we do not fully understand what crime is or what causes it, it is impossible to create an effective policy for controlling it
      4. Others suggest the need for increased funding for criminological research

# Key Concepts

**Anti-Drug Abuse Act**: A federal law (Public Law 99-570) enacted in 1986 that established new federal mandatory minimum sentences for drug offenses.

**Brady Handgun Violence Prevention Act:** A federal law (Public Law 103-159) enacted in 1993 and which initiated a national background checking system for all potential gun purchasers.

**Comprehensive Crime Control Act:** A far-reaching federal law (Public Law 98-473) enacted in 1984 that mandated new federal sentencing guidelines, eliminated parole at the federal level, limited the use of the insanity defense in federal criminal courts, and increased federal penalties associated with drug dealing.

**Crime Victims' Rights Act:** A 2004 federal law that establishes statutory rights for victims of federal crimes, and gives victims the necessary legal authority to assert those rights in federal courts.

**Deterrence strategy:** A crime-control strategy that attempts "to diminish motivation for crime by increasing the perceived certainty, severity, or celerity of penalties."

**Habitual offender statute:** A law intended to keep repeat criminal offenders behind bars. These laws sometimes come under the "three strikes and you're out" rubric.

**Hate Crimes Sentencing Enhancement Act:** A federal law (28 U.S.C 994) enacted in 1994 as part of the Violent Crime Control and Law Enforcement Act that required the U.S. Sentencing Commission to increase the penalties for crimes in which the victim was selected "because of [his or her] actual or perceived race, color, religion, national origin, ethnicity, gender, disability, or sexual orientation."

***Kriminalpolitik:*** The political handling of crime. Also, a criminology-based social policy.

**Law Enforcement Assistance Administration (LEAA):** A federal program, established under Title 1 of the Omnibus Crime Control and Safe Streets Act of 1967, designed to provide assistance to police agencies.

**National Advisory Commission on Criminal Justice Standards and Goals:** A federal body commissioned in 1971 by President Richard Nixon to examine the nation's criminal justice system and to set standards and goals to direct the development of the nation's criminal justice agencies.

**Nurturant strategy**: A crime control strategy that attempts "to forestall development of criminality by improving early life experiences and channeling child and adolescent development" in desirable directions.

**Omnibus Anti-Drug Abuse Act:** A federal law (Public Law 100-690) enacted in 1988 which increased federal penalties for recreational drug users and created a new cabinet-level position (known unofficially as the Drug Czar) to coordinate the drug-fighting efforts of the federal government.

**Omnibus Crime Control and Safe Streets Act:** A federal law enacted in 1967 to eliminate the social conditions that create crime and which funded many anticrime initiatives nationwide.

**Postcrime victimization:** Problems that tend to follow from initial victimization. Also called *secondary victimization*.

**Protection/avoidance strategy**: A crime-control strategy that attempts to reduce criminal opportunities by changing people's routine activities, by increasing guardianship, or by incapacitating convicted offenders.

**Public policy;** A course of action that government takes in an effort to solve a problem or to achieve an end.

**Restitution**: A criminal sanction — in particular, the payment of compensation by the offender to the victim.

**Secondary victimization:** See **postcrime victimization.**

**Social epidemiology:** The study of social epidemics and diseases of the social order.

**Three-strikes provision**: A provision of some criminal statutes that mandates life imprisonment for criminals convicted of three violent felonies or serious drug offenses.

**Victim-impact statement:** A written document that describes the losses, suffering, and trauma experienced by the crime victim or by the victim's survivors. In jurisdictions where victim-impact statements are used, judges are expected to consider them in arriving at an appropriate sentence for the offender.

**Victims of Crime Act (VOCA)**: A federal law enacted in 1984 that established the federal Crime Victims Fund. The fund uses monies from fines and forfeitures collected from federal offenders to supplement state support of local victims' assistance programs and state victim compensation programs.

**Victim-witness assistance program**: A program that counsels victims, orients them to the justice process, and provides a variety of other services, such as transportation to court, child care during court appearances, and referrals to social service agencies.

**Violence Against Women Act (VAWA)**: A federal law enacted as a component of the 1994 Violent Crime Control and Law Enforcement Act and intended to address concerns about violence against women. The law focused on improving the interstate enforcement of protection orders, providing effective training for court personnel involved with women's issues, improving the training and collaboration of police and prosecutors with victim service providers, strengthening law enforcement efforts to reduce violence against women, and on efforts to increase services to victims of violence. President Clinton signed the reauthorization of this legislation, known as the Violence Against Women Act 2000, into law on October 28, 2000.

**Violent Crime Control and Law Enforcement Act:** A federal law (Public Law 103-322) enacted in 1994 that authorized spending billions of dollars on crime prevention, law enforcement, and prison construction. It also outlawed the sale of certain types of assault weapons and enhanced federal death penalty provisions.

**Wickersham Commission:** Created by President Herbert Hoover in 1931, and officially known as the *Commission on Law Observance and Enforcement*, the mandate of this commission was to develop "objectives to improve justice system practices and to reinstate law's role in civilized governance." The Commission made recommendations concerning the nation's police forces, and described how to improve policing throughout America.

# Additional Lecture Topics

When discussing victims of crime, review the issue of victims' rights. Today, most states have included a "Victims' Bill of Rights" within their legal codes. These often include rights such as the right to information about the progress of their cases, the right to be present at sentencing hearings, and the right to be present at parole hearings. Information on victims' rights can often be found on the home page of the State Attorney General. For example, the Florida Crime Victims' Bill of Rights can be found at http://myfloridalegal.com/victims.

Consider discussing some of the primary theories of victimization. Topics could include:

- Discussion of some of the early researchers into victimology, such as Hans von Hentig's portrayal of the victim as someone who "shapes and molds the criminal" and Benjamin Mendelson's early typology of victims, which was based on their degree of "guilt" in the perpetration of the crime
- Victim precipitation theory, which suggests that in some cases the victim either actively or passively initiates the encounter that leads to his or her victimization.
- A review of lifestyle theories, which may suggest that some people become victims because their lifestyle places them at greater risk by increasing the possibility of possible exposure to potential offenders
- A review of routine activity theory, which also suggests that how a person lives can affect his or her risk of victimization

Restorative justice emphasizes a reconciliation between the victim and the offender. It often includes the element of victim restitution. Consider discussing restorative justice programs in more detail.

# Discussion Questions

These discussion questions are found in the textbook at the end of the chapter. The instructor may want to focus on these questions during the coverage of Chapter 15.

- This book emphasizes a social problems versus social responsibility theme. What types of anticrime social policies might be based on the social responsibility perspective? The social problems approach? Explain

- What are the major differences between the social problems and the social responsibility approaches? With which do you most closely identify? Why?

- What are the three types of crime control strategies that this chapter describes? Which comes closest to your own philosophy? Why?

- Explain the social epidemiologic approach to reducing crime. In your opinion, is the approach worthwhile? Why?

- If you were in charge of government crime reduction efforts, what steps would you take to control crime in the United States? Why would you choose those particular approaches?

# Student Exercises

## Activity #1

Your instructor will assign you a state. Obtain information on victim compensation in this state, including:

- What are the eligibility requirements?
- What crimes are and are not covered by the state's victim compensation program?
- What expenses are eligible for compensation, and what compensation benefits may be awarded?
- What other sources are available to victims?
- How does a victim go about applying for compensation?
- Is there a right to appeal if compensation is denied? If yes, how does this process work?

## Activity #2

Review the provisions of the Violent Crime Control and Law Enforcement Act of 1994. Identify three provisions that you would consider to be protection/avoidance strategies, three provisions that you would consider to be deterrence strategies, and three provisions that you would consider to be nurturant strategies. Explain your classifications.

# Criminology Today on the Web

### http://www4.law.cornell.edu/uscode/42/ch112.html

This site makes available Title 42, Chapter 112 of the U.S. Code, discussing federal victim compensation and victim assistance.

### http://virlib.ncjrs.org/VictimsOfCrime.asp

At this Web site, publications on victims of crime are available online from the National Criminal Justice Reference Service.

### http://www.musc.edu/cvc

This is the home page of the National Crime Victims Research and Treatment Center, an organization studying the impact of criminal victimization on adults, children, and their families.

### http://www.try-nova.org

This is the home page of the National Organization for Victim Assistance, a private nonprofit organization promoting rights and services for crime victims.

**http://www.ojp.usdoj.gov/ovc**

This is the home page of the Office for Victims of Crime, which was established by the 1984 Victims of Crime Act.

**http://usinfo.state.gov/usa/infousa/laws/majorlaw/gun94.pdf**

This file contains the text of the Violent Crime Control and Law Enforcement Act of 1994.

**http://www.silicon-valley.com/3strikes.html**

This Web site provides information on the California three-strikes law.

**http://www.ncjrs.org/pdffiles/165369.pdf**

This Web site is a link to a National Institute of Justice Research in Brief publication entitled "'Three Strikes and You're Out': A Review of State Legislation," a pdf file available from the National Criminal Justice Reference Service.

**http://www.cjpf.org**

This is the home page of the Criminal Justice Policy Foundation, a private nonprofit educational organization that provides information to the public about issues in federal and state anticrime proposals and promotes solutions to problems facing the criminal justice system.

# Student Study Guide Questions and Answers

## True/False

1. Gangsta rap lyrics appear to promote violent behavior. **(True, p. 505)**

2. The mandate of the Wickersham Commission was to explore the extent to which Prohibition was the basis for general disrespect of the law. **(False, p. 506)**

3. National economic expansion occurred immediately prior to World War II. **(False, p. 507)**

4. Crime rates increased when baby boomers entered their teen years. **(True, p. 507)**

5. The Law Enforcement Assistance Administration's mandate was to improve the federal law enforcement system. **(False, p. 507)**

6. The crime rate in the late 1960s was less than one-third of what it is today. **(True, p. 508)**

7. President Reagan was opposed to the decriminalization of controlled substances. **(True, p. 508)**

8. A "drug zone" city is eligible for federal assistance. **(True, p. 508)**

9. By the end of the George Bush administration, the main result of the war on drugs was severely overcrowded prisons and jails. **(True, p. 509)**

10. The Youth Handgun Safety Act bans the possession of handguns by juveniles under the age of 21. **(False, p. 509)**

11. An individual who did not receive an honorable discharge from the U.S. armed forces may be disapproved for purchasing a handgun under the Brady Law. **(True, p. 509)**

12. The District of Columbia is exempt from the provisions of the Brady Law. **(True, p. 509)**

13. The Brady Law currently requires a five-day waiting period for the purchase of a handgun. **(False, p. 509)**

14. Most crimes committed with handguns are not fatal. **(True, p. 510)**

15. The National Rifle Association is a strong supporter of the Brady Law. **(False, p. 510)**

16. Most Americans are opposed to gun control. **(False, p. 510)**

17. Restricting gun ownership is an example of the gun control intervention strategy of changing gun allocation. **(False, p. 510)**

18. Requiring safety and locking mechanisms on all guns sold is an example of the gun control intervention strategy of changing gun allocation. **(True, p. 512)**

19. Drug courts were not funded by the Violent Crime Control and Law Enforcement Act. **(False, p. 513)**

20. The Violent Crime Control and Law Enforcement Act allows 13-year-olds charged with murder or rape to be treated as adults by the criminal justice system. **(True, p. 513)**

21. Habitual offender statutes are relatively new. **(False, p. 514)**

22. California's three-strikes law has been challenged on Eighth Amendment grounds. **(True, p. 515)**

23. The Sarbanes-Oxley Act focuses on the prevention of terrorism in the United States. **(False, p. 515)**

24. The USA Patriot Act is a stand-alone law. **(False, p. 516)**

25. The social responsibility approach is gaining in popularity among crime-control policy makers. **(False, p. 518)**

26. Increased infant and maternal health care is an example of a deterrence strategy. **(False, p. 518)**

27. Members of the American Society of Criminology feel that the organization has been extremely successful in bringing about significant changes in government policies. **(False, p. 524)**

28. During the Middle Ages, a significant amount of emphasis was placed on the need for justice for the victim. **(False, p. 525)**

29. Victim compensation programs are generally well funded. **(False, p. 525)**

30. Government negligence theory suggests that victims have a right to compensation because the victimization broke the social contract between the victim and society. **(False, p. 525)**

31. Humanitarian theory says victims should be compensated if they are in need. **(False, p. 525)**

32. Social welfare theory is similar to strict liability theory. **(False, p. 525)**

33. Victim-impact statements are used prior to the sentencing of convicted criminal defendants. **(True, p. 529)**

34. Restitution is applied only to adult offenders. **(False, p. 530)**

35. The biggest problem with contemporary restitution programs involves the difficulties associated with collection. **(True, p. 530)**

## Fill in the Blank

36. Social policy is another term for __________ policy. **(public, p. 505)**

37. The fifth stage in the development of public policy is program __________. **(evaluation/reassessment, p. 505)**

38. The administration of President __________ marks the origins of federal crime control policies. **(Herbert Hoover, p. 506)**

39. President Hoover's Commission on Law Enforcement and Observance was also known as the __________ Commission. **(Wickersham, p. 506)**

40. The Comprehensive Crime Control Act placed limitations on the use of the __________ defense in federal court. **(insanity, p. 508)**

41. The __________ Act, passed during the Reagan administration, created new federal mandatory minimums for drug offenses. **(Anti-Drug Abuse, p. 508)**

42. The first federal "Drug Czar" was __________. **(William Bennett, p. 508)**

43. The Brady Handgun Violence Prevention Act was signed into law by President __________. **(Clinton, p. 509)**

44. Under the law signed by President Clinton, an offender who merely possesses a firearm during the commission of a federal crime receives a mandatory minimum sentence of at least __________ years. **(five, p. 509)**

45. The __________ Act established a national instant criminal background check system that firearms dealers contact prior to the transfer of any firearm. **(Brady Handgun Violence Prevention/Brady law, p. 509)**

46. Critics of the Violent Crime Control and Law Enforcement Act claim that it was really a __________ agenda in disguise. **(liberal, p. 512)**

47. According to research by Bryan Vila, __________ crime control strategies are more effective than others in the long run. **(nurturant, p. 515)**

48. Clinton's National Campaign Against Youth Violence attempted to engage the __________ in youth violence prevention. **(private sector, p. 515)**

49. The __________ Act of 2002 created a new cabinet-level department. **(Homeland Security, p. 516)**

50. The policy approach to crime control that sees criminals as victims of social pathology is known as the social __________ perspective. **(problems, p. 517)**

51. Social __________ focuses on the study of diseases of the social order, such as crime. **(epidemiology, p. 518)**

52. The social problems perspective sees crime as a(n) __________. **(disease, p. 518)**

53. Target hardening is an example of the __________ strategy of crime control. **(protection/avoidance, p. 518)**

54. Improving programs to reduce the number of unwanted pregnancies is an example of the __________ strategy of crime control. **(nurturant, p. 518)**

55. China's population control program has led many mothers to abandon or abort baby _________. **(girls, p. 520)**

56. Much recent international legislation has been designed to curb crime through the use of __________ strategies. **(deterrence, p. 524)**

57. According to Joan Petersilia, criminologists who complain that their work is not being used by policymakers generally have a(n) __________ model in mind. **(instrumental use, p. 524)**

58. The Code of Hammurabi required that many offenders make __________ to victims. **(restitution, p. 524)**

59. The __________ theory says that victim compensation is in vogue with the voting public. **(political motives, p. 525)**

60. Postcrime victimization is also known as __________ victimization. **(secondary, p. 526)**

61. The earliest victims' assistance focused on victims of __________. **(rape, p. 526)**

62. The Crime Victims' Rights Act applies to victims of __________ crimes. **(federal, p. 526)**

63. The concept of __________ refers to a criminology-based social policy. **(*Kriminalpolitik*, p. 530)**

64. According to Friedman, reforms that will substantially lower the crime rate are unlikely because of cultural __________. **(taboos, p. 531)**

## Multiple Choice

65. The first stage in developing public policy is
    a. program evaluation.
    b. program implementation.
    c. **problem identification. (p. 505)**
    d. problem prioritization.

66. Crime-fighting policies are probably more the result of
    a. **politics. (p. 506)**
    b. criminological research.
    c. social science data.
    d. immediate opportunities.

67. The expansion of federal crime control policies to address juvenile crime occurred during the __________ administration.
    a. Hoover
    b. **Kennedy (p. 507)**
    c. Johnson
    d. Nixon

68. During the mid-1960s, President Johnson established the __________ to study crime and the criminal justice system in the United States.
    a. **President's Commission on Law Enforcement and the Administration of Justice (p. 507)**
    b. Commission on Law Observance and Enforcement
    c. Kerner Commission
    d. National Advisory Commission on Criminal Justice Standards and Goals

69. The President's Commission on Law Enforcement and the Administration of Justice saw crime as the result of
    a. mental illness.
    b. genetic predispositions.
    c. **social disadvantages. (p. 507)**
    d. All of the above

70. Which of the following does *not* characterize the attitude toward federal crime control efforts during President Nixon's administration?
    a. Mandatory minimum sentences
    b. **Concern for the rights of the accused (p. 508)**
    c. Harsh penalties
    d. Reduction or abolition of parole

71. The move toward swift and certain penalties seen during the Nixon administration best exemplifies the __________ view of criminology.
    a. **classical (p. 508)**
    b. positivist
    c. sociological
    d. conflict

72. In 1971, President Nixon set up the __________ to study methods of crime prevention and examine the criminal justice system.
    a. President's Commission on Law Enforcement and the Administration of Justice
    b. Wickersham Commission
    c. Kerner Commission
    d. **National Advisory Commission on Criminal Justice Standards and Goals (p. 508)**

73. The Comprehensive Crime Control Act was signed into law by President
    a. Nixon.
    b. Carter
    c. **Reagan. (p. 508)**
    d. George Bush.

74. Which of the following acts was part of the Violent Crime Control and Law Enforcement Act?
    a. Brady Handgun Violence Prevention Act
    b. Omnibus Anti-Drug Abuse Act
    c. **Hate Crimes Sentencing Enhancement Act (p. 509)**
    d. Comprehensive Crime Control Act

75. The Hate Crimes Sentencing Enhancement Act became law during the __________ administration.
    a. **Clinton (p. 509)**
    b. George Bush
    c. Reagan
    d. George W. Bush

76. Under the law signed by President Clinton, an offender who brandishes a firearm during the commission of a federal crime receives a mandatory minimum sentence of at least __________ years.
    a. five
    b. **seven (p. 509)**
    c. ten
    d. twelve

77. Under the Brady Law, purchases of handguns may be disapproved for all but which of the following reasons?
    a. The potential buyer is an illegal alien.
    b. The potential buyer has been committed to a mental institution.
    c. The potential buyer was a citizen of the United States but has renounced citizenship.
    d. **The potential buyer is in the process of applying for United States citizenship. (p. 509)**

78. Banning hollow-point ammunition is an example of the gun control intervention strategy of
    a. reducing the number of guns.
    b. **reducing the destructiveness of guns. (p. 512)**
    c. changing gun allocation.
    d. altering the uses or storage of guns.

79. The __________ Act provides college scholarships for students who agree to serve as police officers.
    a. **Violent Crime Control and Law Enforcement (p. 513)**
    b. Violence Against Women
    c. Victims of Crime
    d. Comprehensive Crime Control

80. The __________ is an example of a habitual offender statute.
    a. Brady Law
    b. Violent Crime Control and Law Enforcement Act
    c. **three-strikes law (p. 514)**
    d. Violence Against Women Act

81. Protection/avoidance strategies attempt to
    a. **block opportunities for crime. (p. 518)**
    b. change the outcome of decision making that precedes a crime.
    c. change the strategic style with which people approach aspects of their lives.
    d. improve early life experiences.

82. __________ strategies include infant and maternal health care programs.
    a. **Nurturant (p. 518)**
    b. Protection/avoidance
    c. Deterrence
    d. Social epidemiology

83. Which of the following is an example of a nurturant strategy?
    a. Target hardening
    b. **Providing training in parenting skills (p. 518)**
    c. Speeding up trial court processing and sentence imposition
    d. Incapacitation through the use of electronic monitoring

84. The British Criminal Justice and Police Bill attempts to control crime using __________ strategies
    a. nurturant
    b. social epidemiological
    c. protection/avoidance
    d. **deterrence (p. 524)**

85. During the late Middle Ages, the emphasis was on justice for the
    a. victim.
    b. **state. (p. 525)**
    c. offender.
    d. criminal justice system.

86. The first modern victim compensation statute was adopted by
    a. Great Britain.
    b. the United States of America.
    c. **New Zealand. (p. 525)**
    d. China.

87. The 1965 "Good Samaritan" statute paying compensation to anyone injured while going to the aid of other being victimized by crime was passed in
    a. **New York City. (p. 525)**
    b. California.
    c. the District of Columbia.
    d. Chicago.

88. According to __________ theory, compensation should help to correct social imbalances such as variations in crime risk across the country.
    a. humanitarian
    b. government negligence
    c. political motives
    d. **equal protection (p. 525)**

89. __________ theory holds that compensation programs will encourage more citizens to report crime and result in more effective law enforcement programs.
    a. Humanitarian
    b. **Crime prevention (p. 525)**
    c. Government negligence
    d. Strict liability

90. Which of the following is *not* an example of postcrime victimization?
    a. Fear of retaliation by the offender
    b. Lost time from work
    c. The trauma of testifying
    d. **They are all examples of postcrime victimization. (p. 526)**

91. The offender is directly involved in victim __________ programs.
    a. compensation
    b. **restitution (p. 529)**
    c. impact
    d. assistance

# Word Search Puzzle

H G E C J B P K O D D P R O T E C T I O N Q H L S T C P N
Q D S O V R N I B L O B T T W B K T W M C Q K P C O L A F
T T U J K S N G C B M N N A Q I M G P A E Z I D R Y A E E
S W L T V K E G M J W D W Z Y V G Z Z Z F K K F W C C P P
K R Y H Y P S Q S L P M O S Z H H V T X R N Y T O O U I I
E J P V M B B R L P H A S L L Z Y M N E F T P V V H T D D
N U R T L Q R Q I K W K N E A W J W Z Y Q Y Y C J F A E E
K R I M I N A L P O L I T I K Y H Y M K V J N Z T N B M M
N F Z L M E Y E C Y I K B T D D Y A L T T U Q F K O S I I
F B M J F W R M Q N X C I A F A A V T H H U X F M K I O K
F O A V W A V E S W H N R X C K J O H R R U X I Z H E L L
U A C T U I F X X B L B S A M W T I R E S T I T U T I O N
Q Z X Y K A H A E P C E S M R A M D Z E E B P R I C L G M
O E L Y M X J D U Z C T Q H S B F A O S S V B L M G N Y Y
B X D N H X O E W L N Q O Z F C R N Q T T W S D Z H K C W
D N E F C V K P B X N X S C P Y B C X R R R Y F N E R R E
Z T Z T N H X L C I P J B Q R J R E C I I Q S D K R D B D
U O G H T I U W B L B H V G M K P F B K K Q N K R D F X E
D R M Y O A A Y I O K Z I P P U F R H E E C Q P B R K W Z
F W W U X X N U N N P G U O D P C G U S S S H H E A L B G
U I Y Q Y G Y R Q Y F S C D E X C Y O N U T U R A N T T X
L C W S O D Q L Y S Q J X F T K P G G I K Q K C F S C I N
Q K H E Y A D V H F O V V Z E I A B D D K E J Z G T D Z V
U E Z P D B F K W Q N P I U R C I Z H R M C X U L C F L R
O R G I L J B V Q P X N R I R Y V L F C M E U O E X M J M
C S N B I Y V X N U L R Z A E W R E I V U A X V A T R B R
I H N Y D Q G S F W N U N B N T U L V R W K B L A W B X B
C A B M P D V Y D F H F F D C N U E C A E D Y Q C T W E R
E M E U R I W W Y B Q T C G E V Z I V L Z F I E L V T O G
D V H A B L T X N X Y Z B N B H R K N Z E P Z K C O L S Q

Avoidance
Brady
Deterrence
Epidemiology
*Kriminalpolitik*
LEAA
Nurturant

Protection
Restitution
Three strikes
VOCA
VAWA
Wickersham

# Crossword Puzzle

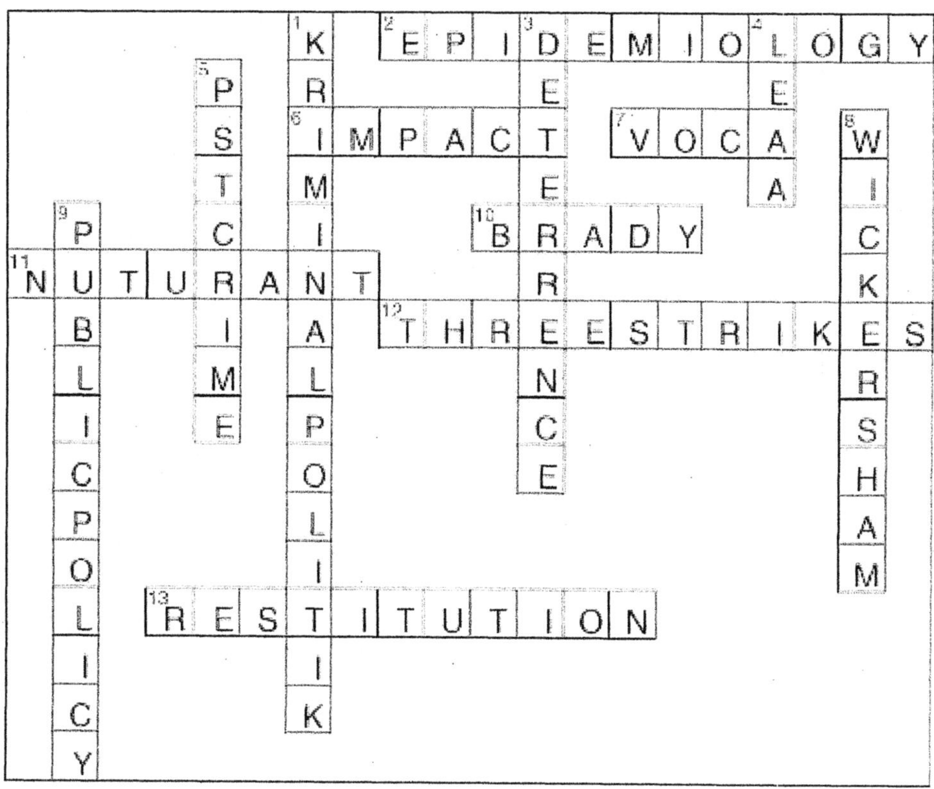

## Across

2. Social __________ is the study of social epidemics and diseases of the social order.
6. A victim __________ describes the victim's losses and suffering as a result of the crime.
7. A 1984 federal law establishing the federal Crime Victims Fund.
10. The _____ law initiated a national background checking system for all potential gun purchasers.
11. Crime control strategies preventing entry into criminality by improving early life experiences.
12. Laws that mandate life imprisonment for criminals convicted of three violent felonies. (2 words)
13. The payment of compensation by the offender to the victim.

## Down

1. The political handling of crime.
3. A crime control strategy that increases the certainty, severity, or swiftness of penalties.
4. A federal program established in 1967 to provide assistance to police agencies.
5. ______ victimization includes problems which tend to follow from the initial victimization.
8. The __________ Commission was created by President Herbert Hoover.
9. Actions the government takes to solve a problem. (2 words)

# 16 Future Directions

## Learning Objectives

After reading this chapter, students should be able to:

1. Discuss future crimes and future studies
2. Identify some techniques for assessing the future
3. Describe the role of the criminological futurist in social policy development
4. Recognize the significance of an integrated theory of crime causation
5. Describe the advantages of a comparative approach to the study of crime and criminals

## Chapter Outline

Introduction
- *Globalization*
- *Comparative Criminology*
- *Techniques of Futures Research*

Future Crimes
- *Terrorism and Technology*

The New Criminologies
- *Theory Integration*

Policies of the Future

## Chapter Summary

People who study the future are known as futurists. Future criminology is the study of likely futures as they relate to crime and its control. There are many groups who study the future; organizations such as the Society of Police Futurists International specifically focus on future crime control policy. Globalization, the increasingly international character of social life, is affecting crime and making it impossible for U.S. policymakers to ignore crime in other countries, especially crime committed by transnational criminal organizations. Transnational crime, which involves unlawful activity undertaken and supported by organized criminal groups operating across national boundaries, is becoming a key challenge to policymakers. The globalization of crime has led to increased interest in comparative criminology or the cross-national study of crime.

Futures research is a multidisciplinary branch of operations research that attempts to facilitate long-range planning based on four elements: forecasting from the past supported by mathematical models; cross-disciplinary treatment of its subject matter; systematic use of expert judgment; and a systems-analytical approach to its problems. Futures research, which requires a futurist perspective, uses seven main techniques: trend extrapolation, cross-impact analysis, the Delphi method, simulations and models, environmental scanning, scenario writing, and strategic assessment. They all provide an appreciation of the risks and opportunities facing those planning for the future. Regardless of the technique, the results are no better than the data used.

Most futurists suggest that although traditional crimes (murder, rape, robbery, etc.) will continue to occur in the future, other new and emergent forms of criminality will increase in number and frequency. New types of criminality predicted by futurists include computer-based and economic crime, identity manipulation, and the increasing involvement of organized crime in toxic and nuclear waste disposal. Georgette Bennett, who helped establish the study of criminal futures as a purposeful endeavor, has predicted a number of areas of coming change, including a decline in street crime and an increase in white-collar and high-technology crimes; increasing involvement of females and the elderly in crime; and safer cities, with an increase in criminal activity in small towns and rural areas. State-sponsored terrorist organizations are also becoming increasingly technologically sophisticated and at least some terrorist organizations are seeking to obtain weapons of mass destruction.

In addition to futures research, new and emerging criminological theories help suggest what criminology will be like in the future. During the 1980s and 1990s, a number of new and dynamic theories were developed, such as postmodernism, feminist criminology, and peacemaking criminology. One new perspective is David Farrington's risk factor prevention paradigm. This paradigm, which emphasizes identifying the key risk factors for offending and implementing prevention methods designed to counteract them, became increasingly influential in criminology during the 1990s.

The 1980s saw an emphasis on theory integration, with the ultimate goal of developing a unified theory of crime causation and prevention. Some theorists have developed theories about theories (meta-theories) which may help merge existing theories. However, there seems to be a consensus that there are too many problems for successful theory integration to occur. An alternative strategy may be a multiple-theory approach, which involves integrating only a few theories at a time. One example of theory integration is Matthew Robinson's integrated systems theory, which works from the assumption that "everything affects everything else."

For policymakers to be able to plan for the future, they need as much information as possible about possible eventualities. The increasingly multicultural and heterogeneous nature of the United States will also affect crime, as it will increase anomie. Diverse heterogeneous societies such as the United States experience constant internal conflict. Disagreement about the law and social norms is common, and offenders tend to deny responsibility and to attempt to avoid capture and conviction. The chapter closes with a list of seven issues that Richter Moore, Jr. suggests are likely to concern crime control planners in the near future.

# Lecture Outline

I. Introduction
  A. Future criminology is the study of likely futures as they relate to crime and its control
    1. Futurists are those who study the future and try to distinguish effectively between multiple impending possibilities, assessing the likelihood of each and making more or less realistic forecasts based on such assessments
    2. Futurists criminologists try to imagine how crime will appear in the near and distant future
    3. There are many groups and individuals who study the future
      a. The World Future Society is a well-known general society that studies the future
      b. Individual futurists who are well known to the general public include Alvin Toffler, John Naisbitt, and Peter F. Drucker
      c. The Society of Police Futurists International conducts research into future crime control policy
    4. Foresight is a government-led program in the United Kingdom that studies the future and has published a report focusing on crimes in the near future
      a. According to Foresight's Crime Prevention Panel, a number of social characteristics will affect future crimes in Great Britain and around the world:
        (i) Individuality and independence: they suggest that as traditional families become less common, traditional limits on antisocial behavior will erode
        (ii) Informational Communication Technology usage: crimes such as electronic theft and fraud will increase, requiring acceptance of digital evidence in court and the need for court personnel and jurors to be educated in relevant technologies
        (iii) Globalization: the increasingly international character of social life is affecting crime, so that local crimes and small-time offenders will be replaced or supplemented by crimes and criminal groups with global scope
      b. The panel states that criminal organizations are adapting to opportunities offered by the Internet and taking advantage of modern technology and the ability to commit crimes that may be virtually unsolvable
  B. Globalization
    1. Globalization is making it impossible for U.S. policymakers to ignore crime in other countries, especially crime committed by transnational criminal organizations
    2. Transnational crime (or transnational organized crime) is unlawful activity undertaken and supported by organized criminal groups operating across national boundaries
    3. Transnational crime has become a key challenge to policymakers today
  C. Comparative criminology
    1. The globalization of crime has led to increased interest in comparative criminology, the study of crime on a cross-national level
      a. Comparative criminologists need to develop increasingly specific theories that are so constructed as to be applicable across more than one culture or nation-state

   b. The globalization of knowledge, which refers to the increase in understanding resulting from a sharing of information between cultures, is playing a significant role in theory formation and in the development of crime control policies
2. Ethnocentrism (culture-centeredness) is an important issue facing comparative criminologists
   a. It interferes with their work in several ways, including how crime statistics are gathered, analyzed, and presented
   b. Researchers need to avoid being ethnocentric, perhaps by realizing that it is common for people to regard familiar things or methods of behavior as more desirable
   c. People are socialized from birth into a particular culture and tend to prefer their culture's values, beliefs, and customs over those of other cultures
3. American criminologists have only recently begun to closely examine crime in other cultures
   a. Difficulties may arise because not all societies are equally open and data-gathering strategies that are accepted in one culture may be taboo in another
   b. It is difficult to compare crime rates of different countries because of differences in how crimes are defined, methods and practices of crime reporting, and various influences on the reporting of statistics

D. Techniques of futures research
1. Futures research is a multidisciplinary branch of operations research that attempts to facilitate long-range planning based on four elements:
   a. Forecasting from the past supported by mathematical models
   b. Cross-disciplinary treatment of its subject matter
   c. Systematic use of expert judgment
   d. A systems-analytical approach to its problems
2. Futures research requires a futurist perspective, which is built around five principles:
   a. The future is determined by a combination of factors, including human choice
   b. There are alternative futures, so that a range of decision and planning choices are always available
   c. We operate within an interdependent and interrelated system so that anything affecting one part of the system will probably affect the entire system
   d. Tomorrow's problems are developing today
   e. We should regularly develop possible responses to potential changes and monitor trends and developments
3. There are seven main techniques of futures research:
   a. Trend extrapolation makes future predictions based on the projection of existing trends
   b. Cross-impact analysis attempts to analyze one trend or event in light of the occurrence or nonoccurrence of a series of related events
   c. The Delphi method involves a set of steps designed to elicit expert opinion until a general consensus is reached:
      (i) Problem identification
      (ii) Development of an expert panel
      (iii) Questions directed at the panel

(iv) Collection and synthesis of responses

d. Simulations and models attempt to replicate the system being studied by reproducing its conditions in a form that can be manipulated to assess possible outcomes

e. Environmental scanning is a targeted effort to collect information systematically to identify future trends or events that could plausibly occur and that might affect the area of interest

f. Scenario writing attempts to assess the likelihood of various possible futures once important trends have been identified

g. Strategic assessment provides an appreciation of the risks and opportunities facing those planning for the future

4. Regardless of the technique used, the results are no better than the data used

II. Future Crimes

A. Although "traditional" crimes will continue to occur in the future, other new and emergent forms of criminality will increase in number and frequency

1. One prediction suggests that socially significant crime in advanced nations will be increasingly economic and computer based

2. Another futurist predicts that the key personnel of criminal organizations in the twenty-first century will be well-educated, sophisticated, computer-literate people who can use current technology to the best advantage

3. Richter H. Moore, Jr. has developed an overview of future crimes

a. He suggests that identity manipulation will be a key element of future criminality

b. Criminal organizations will have their own satellites; satellite communications will coordinate drug trafficking and money laundering operations, and satellite surveillance may alert the organization to law enforcement activity

c. The illegal disposal of toxic materials will become increasing profitable as more hazardous substances are produced

4. Georgette Bennett, who helped establish the study of criminal futures as a purposeful endeavor, has predicted a number of areas of coming change, including

a. A decline in street crime and an increase in white-collar and high-technology crimes

b. Increasing involvement of females and the elderly in crime

c. Safer cities, with an increase in criminal activity in small towns and rural areas

B. Terrorism and technology

1. The technological sophistication of state-sponsored terrorist organizations is increasing

2. International terrorists, like the general public, have access to information that could be used to cripple the United States

3. Despite the 1975 banning of biological weapons, bioterrorism (such as the anthrax letters mailed in the United States in 2001) is a serious issue today

III. The New Criminologies

A. New and emerging criminological theories help provide a picture of what criminology will be like in the future

1. There have been many explanations for crime over the years, but none have been noticeably more effective in explaining, predicting, or controlling crime
   a. Contemporary criminological theorizing is interdisciplinary and conservative in its approach to crime causation
   b. Significant social change, such as an increased aversion to even minor forms of physical force, could create a need for new theoretical formations; our basic understanding of criminal violence may be undergoing major modifications that will require changes in attempts to theorize about its causes
   c. Advances in scientific knowledge, such as the Human Genome Project may also create possibilities for theoretical change
2. L. Edward Wells has made several predictions about the future of criminological theorizing:
   a. Future explanations of crime will be more eclectic and less tied to a single theoretical tradition or discipline
   b. Future explanations of crime will be more comparative and less confined to a single society or single dominant social group
   c. Future explanations of crime will be predominately individualistic and voluntaristic
   d. Future explanations of crime will be more applied and pragmatic in orientation
   e. Future explanations of crime will be more oriented toward explaining white-collar crime
   f. Future explanations of crime will be more biologically oriented
3. During the 1980s and 1990s, a number of new and dynamic theories were developed, such as postmodernism, feminist criminology, and peacemaking criminology
   a. David Farrington's risk factor prevention paradigm emphasizes identifying the key risk factors for offending and implementing prevention methods designed to counteract them
   b. During the 1990s this paradigm has experienced an enormous increase in influence in criminology
   c. It is important because it holds great potential for guiding research, policy, and theoretical development in the future

B. Theory integration
   1. The 1980s saw the development of an emphasis on theory integration, with the ultimate goal of developing a unified theory of crime causation and prevention
   2. Some theorists have developed meta-theories, or theories about theories, which may help to meld together existing theories
   3. However, there seems to be a consensus that there are too many problems for successful integration to occur
      a. Crime is a very complex phenomenon
      b. Theories attempt to explain different pieces of the crime puzzle and cannot be made to address all of its aspects
      c. Theories are based on the assumptions we make about human nature and the way the world functions, and everyone makes different assumptions
   4. One critique of theory integration suggests that the approach leaves gaps between integrated theories and that it falsely suggests that a comprehensive coverage of criminological theory has been achieved

5. Another strategy may be to work toward a multiple-theory approach, integrating only a few theories at a time, possibly providing building blocks of larger and more comprehensive integrated theories in the future

C. Integrated theory: An example
1. Matthew Robinson's integrated systems theory of antisocial behavior attempts to bring together explanations for crime ranging from fundamental chemical and biological influences on criminal behavior to complex forms of social interaction
2. Robinson works from the assumption that everything affects everything else and outlines complex systems interrelationships that influence or produce specific forms of human behavior

IV. Policies of the Future

A. Gene Stephens, a well-known criminological futurist, suggests that the increasingly multicultural and heterogeneous nature of the United States will affect crime
1. Multiculturality and heterogeneity increase anomie, as is seen in previously isolated and homogeneous societies, such as Japan, Denmark, China, and Greece
2. Failure to recognize and plan for diversity can lead to serious crime problems
3. Changing world demographics and politicoeconomic systems may result in low-crime cultures becoming high-crime cultures
4. In homogeneous societies, a tradition of discipline, a belief in the laws, and acceptance of personal responsibility are typically the norm
5. However, diverse societies suffer from constant internal conflict, much of which is focused on acceptable ways of living and working
   a. Disagreement about the law and social norms is common
   b. Lawbreakers tend to deny responsibility and to attempt to avoid capture and conviction
6. The growth of a technological culture in the United States has produced several separate and distinct groups of people: those who are technologically capable, those who are unable to use modern technology, and those who are technologically aware but lack the necessary skills
7. Another reason that crime rates are high in increasingly heterogeneous societies may be the lack of consistent child-care philosophies and child-rearing methods, producing adults who are irresponsible and fail to adhere to legal or other standards of behavior

B. Richter H. Moore, Jr. has identified seven issues likely to concern crime control planners in the near future:
1. New criminal groups
2. Language barriers
3. Distrust of government and the criminal justice system by ethnic communities
4. Greater reliance on community involvement
5. Regulating the marketplace
6. Reducing public demand for drugs and other illegal services
7. Increased focus on treatment of all forms of criminality

## Key Concepts

**Comparative criminologist:** A criminologist involved in the cross-national study of crime.

**Comparative criminology:** The cross-national study of crime.

**Cross-impact analysis:** A technique of futures research that attempts to analyze one trend or event in light of the occurrence or nonoccurrence of a series of related events.

**Delphi Method:** A technique of futures research that uses repetitive questioning of experts to refine predictions.

**Environmental scanning:** "A systematic effort to identify in an elemental way future developments (trends or events) that could plausibly occur over the time horizon of interest" and that might affect one's area of concern.

**Future criminology**: The study of likely futures as they impinge on crime and its control.

**Futures research**: "A multidisciplinary branch of operations research" whose principal aim "is to facilitate long-range planning based on (1) forecasting from the past supported by mathematical models, (2) cross-disciplinary treatment of its subject matter, (3) systematic use of expert judgment, and (4) a systems-analytical approach to its problems."

**Futurist**: One who studies the future.

**Metatheory**: A theory about theories and the theorizing process.

**Scenario writing**: A technique, intended to predict future outcomes, which builds upon environmental scanning by attempting to assess the likelihood of a variety of possible outcomes once important trends have been identified.

**Strategic assessment:** A technique that assesses the risks and opportunities facing those who plan for the future.

**Trend extrapolation:** A technique of futures research that makes future predictions based on the projection of existing trends.

## Additional Lecture Topics

Consider discussing Akers' conceptual absorption theory. In his text *Criminological Theories* (Roxbury Press, 2000), Ronald Akers has argued that theory integration occurs naturally through a process of conceptual absorption. He suggests that many of the concepts that various theorists use to explain offender behavior are often similar or even identical. For example, he suggests that the social bonding concept of attachment, which refers to the extent of a person's relationships with family and friends, also means the extent to which people identify with others as role models, which is basically the same as the social learning theory concept of imitation. Essentially, the difference is in the terms rather than the concepts used. In general, Akers claims that social learning theory concepts are present in all other theories. He does not suggest that common concepts lead automatically to similar propositions about delinquency.

Discuss the comparative findings of national victimization surveys conducted in various countries. For example, compare results of surveys conducted in the United States and in England and Wales, as reported by the Bureau of Justice Statistics in Report NCJ-173402. Other countries that have conducted national victimization surveys include Canada, Switzerland, Holland, and West Germany.

# Discussion Questions

These discussion questions are found in the textbook at the end of the chapter. The instructor may want to focus on these questions during the coverage of Chapter 16.

1. This book emphasizes a social problems versus social responsibility theme. Which perspective do you think will be dominant in twenty-first century crime control planning? Why?

2. Do you believe that it is possible to know the future? What techniques are identified in this chapter for assessing possible futures? Which of these do you think holds the most promise? Why?

3. What is meant by "theory integration"? How might theory integration be achieved in the field of criminology?

4. What is comparative criminology? What are the advantages of a comparative perspective? Are there any disadvantages? If so, what are they?

# Student Exercises

## Activity #1

Your instructor will place you into groups. The text outlines several crime-related issues which may be key issues for policymakers over the next ten years. Each group is to identify three other issues they believe may be of concern. The groups are to compare and contrast the items on their lists. Focus on the wide range of issues present among a fairly homogeneous group.

## Activity #2

Your instructor will place you into groups. Using at least three of the theories you have studied, create an integrated theoretical model of crime causation. Outline the assumptions on which your model is based.

# Criminology Today on the Web

### http://www.wfs.org

This is the home page of the World Future Society.

### http://www.policefuturists.org

This is the home page of the Society of Police Futurists International.

### http://www.foresight.gov.uk/

This is the home page of the UK's government-led Foresight program.

### http://www.fbi.gov/hq/td/fwg/workhome.htm

This is the home page of the FBI's Futures Working Group.

### http://www.futures.hawaii.edu

This is the home page of the Hawaii Research Center for Futures Studies.

### http://www.ryerson.ca/~mjoppe/ResearchProcess/841TheDelphiMethod.htm

This Web site provides a brief explanation of the Delphi Method, including an interactive flowchart.

### http://hops.wharton.upenn.edu/forecast

This is the Wharton School's Forecasting Principles Web site.

# Student Study Guide Questions and Answers

## True/False

1. Futurists primarily focus on how crime will appear in the distant future. **(False, p. 538)**

2. From the present point of view, multiple futures exist. **(True, p. 538)**

3. Assumptions made by futurists are based totally on existing statistics and mathematical analyses of trends. **(False, p. 538)**

4. The journal, *The Futurist*, is published by the World Future Society. **(True, p. 538)**

5. Members of the Society of Police Futurists International apply the principles of futures research to understand the world as it is likely to be in the future. **(True, p. 539)**

6. According to Foresight's Crime Prevention Panel, traditional family forms will decline over the next few decades. **(True, p. 539)**

7. Foresight's Crime Prevention Panel suggests that digital evidence will be increasingly accepted in courts. **(True, p. 539)**

8. According to Foresight's Crime Prevention Panel, local crimes will be replaced by crimes with a global scope. **(True, p. 539)**

9. Ethnocentric individuals generally do not stop to think that people in other parts of the world may have different beliefs and values. **(True, p. 540)**

10. In some societies, the study of crime is taboo. **(True, p. 540)**

11. Information on Chinese crime rates comes primarily from official sources. **(True, p. 540)**

12. Most countries have similar definitional concepts of crime. **(False, p. 541)**

13. American crime rates are the highest in the world today. **(False, p. 541)**

14. According to the futurist perspective, distinct trends and developments cannot be ignored. **(True, p. 542)**

15. Demographic and economic models are sometimes used to predict future criminality. **(True, p. 544)**

16. Environmental scanning provides an appreciation of the risks and opportunities facing those who plan for the future. **(False, p. 544)**

17. Scenario writers focus on predicting a specific future. **(False, p. 544)**

18. Futurist Richter Moore, Jr. suggests that identity theft will be a nexus of future crime. **(True, p. 546)**

19. Futurist Georgette Bennett predicts an increase in street crime. **(False, p. 547)**

20. According to futurist Georgette Bennett, women will become less involved in crime. **(False, p. 547)**

21. The anthrax letters mailed in 2001 is an example of bioterrorism. **(True, p. 547)**

22. Some criminological theories have been significantly more effective than others in explaining, predicting, and controlling crime. **(False, p. 551)**

23. L. Edward Wells suggests that future explanations of crime will be primarily confined to a single society. **(False, p. 551)**

24. L. Edward Wells suggests that in the future, explanations of crime will focus more on explaining juvenile crime. **(False, p. 552)**

25. According to futurist L. Edward Wells, future explanations of crime will more greatly emphasize biological factors. **(True, p. 552)**

26. Macrolevel theories analyze crime at the individual level. **(False, p. 552)**

27. The complexity of crime may make successful theory integration impossible. **(True, p. 553)**

28. In a heterogeneous society, citizens tend to share backgrounds, life experiences, and values. **(False, p. 555)**

29. Heterogeneous societies suffer from constant internal conflict. **(True, p. 555)**

30. The United States is an advanced heterogeneous society. **(True, p. 555)**

31. A lack of consistent child-rearing methods contribute to increasing crime rates in homogeneous societies. **(False, p. 555)**

32. Richter Moore, Jr. suggests that in the future, there will be a greater emphasis on the treatment of criminality. **(True, p. 556)**

## Fill in the Blank

33. The book *Megatrends* was written by futurist __________. **(John Naisbitt, p. 539)**

34. According to Foresight's Crime Prevention Panel, Web sites written in __________ will be the most likely to be targeted. **(English, p. 539)**

35. According to Foresight's Crime Prevention Panel, technology is leading to the growth of a(n) __________ society. **(impersonal, p. 539)**

36. Globalization refers to the increasingly __________ characterization of social life. **(international, p. 539)**

37. The __________ of crime has required law enforcement agencies around the world to cooperate and coordinate their efforts. **(globalization, p. 540)**

38. Comparative criminologists study crime on a(n) __________ level. **(cross-national, p. 540)**

39. According to the __________ perspective, there are alternative futures. **(futurist, p. 542)**

40. __________ makes future predictions based on the projection of existing trends. **(Trend extrapolation, p. 543)**

41. The first step of the Delphi method is __________. **(problem identification, p. 543-544)**

42. __________ is a technique of futures research that builds upon environmental scanning. **(Scenario writing, p. 544)**

43. According to the CIA, the end goal of al-Qaeda is to use __________. **(weapons of mass destruction/WMDs, p. 547)**

44. David Farrington developed the __________ paradigm. **(risk factor prevention, p. 552)**

45. A theory about theories and the theorizing process is known as a(n) __________. **(metatheory, p. 552)**

46. __________ suggested the use of a social support paradigm for theory integration. **(Francis T. Cullen, p. 553)**

47. __________ recently has developed an integrated systems perspective. **(Matthew B. Robinson, p. 553)**

48. Gene Stephens suggests that crime will __________ worldwide in the future. **(increase, p. 554)**

49. According to Gene Stephens, multiculturalism and heterogeneity increase __________. **(anomie, p. 554)**

50. In some __________ societies, offenders who break norms will often punish themselves, even if their transgressions are not publicly discovered. **(homogeneous, p. 555)**

51. __________ was the first country to experience the crime problems associated with anomie. **(The United States, p. 555)**

## Multiple Choice

52. Well-known futurist __________ is the author of *Future Shock*.
    a. **Alvin Toffler (p. 539)**
    b. John Naisbitt
    c. Peter Drucker
    d. William Tafoya

53. The __________ is run by the government of the United Kingdom.
    a. Society of Police Futurists International
    b. World Future Society
    c. **Foresight Program (p. 539)**
    d. None of the above

54. The globalization of crime has led to a resurgence of interest in __________ criminology.
   a. strategic
   b. **comparative (p. 540)**
   c. interdisciplinary
   d. critical

55. __________ countries are more likely to report crime statistics to the United Nations.
   a. Socialist
   b. Communist
   c. **Democratic (p. 541)**
   d. None of the above

56. Futures research facilitates long-range planning based on all but which of the following?
   a. Cross-disciplinary treatment of its subject matter
   b. Systematic use of expert judgment
   c. Forecasting from the past supported by mathematical models
   d. **Evaluations based on public opinion (p. 541)**

57. Which of the following is *not* one of the main techniques of futures research?
   a. The Delphi method
   b. Scenario writing
   c. **Cross-cultural surveys (p. 543)**
   d. Trend extrapolation

58. The technique of futures research that attempts to analyze one trend or event in light of the occurrence or nonoccurrence of a series of related events is known as
   a. trend extrapolation.
   b. the Delphi method.
   c. scenario writing.
   d. **cross-impact analysis. (p. 543)**

59. The technique of futures research that involves a targeted effort to collect as much information as possible in a systematic effort to identify in an elemental way future developments that could plausibly occur over the time horizon of interest is
   a. the Delphi method.
   b. trend extrapolation.
   c. **environmental scanning. (p. 544)**
   d. scenario writing.

60. The technique of futures research that provides an appreciation of the risks and opportunities facing those who plan for the future is
   a. **strategic assessment. (p. 544)**
   b. trend extrapolation.
   c. cross-impact analysis.
   d. simulations and models.

61. The book *Crimewarps* was written by futurist
    a. Richter Moore, Jr.
    b. **Georgette Bennett. (p. 547)**
    c. Peter Drucker.
    d. William Tafoya.

62. According to predictions made by Georgette Bennett, cities will
    a. **become safer. (p. 547)**
    b. become more dangerous.
    c. have relatively stable crime rates.
    d. Bennett did not make any predictions about cities.

63. According to futurist L. Edward Wells, future explanations of crime will be more
    a. eclectic.
    b. comparative.
    c. applied.
    d. **All of the above (p. 551)**

64. A new era of theory building in criminology began in the
    a. 1960s.
    b. 1970s.
    c. **1980s. (p. 552)**
    d. 1990s.

65. Theories concerned with analyzing crime at the individual level are known as
    a. cross-national theories.
    b. **microlevel theories. (p. 550)**
    c. metatheories.
    d. macrolevel theories.

66. Which of the following is *not* typically the norm in a homogeneous society?
    a. A tradition of discipline
    b. A belief in the laws
    c. An acceptance of personal responsibility
    d. **Cultural diversity (p. 555)**

# Word Search Puzzle

```
V D E L P H I L A U K V V D V F K O I C P Q A P N T I W U
Z X C U Y D Z U A U T N F M S K R H H F I P G O B C C A G
T P Z N B A H U P E K V A N G B X P D Q J A N B H D P Z E
P P Y O M S R E G A U G K C I K M J C P O O S D H N I Z R
R L E K W N E D B N R C I N T P E A Y Y Z W D U K F V L J
D L H S C F C I T P U G O H X F S S K M H W W S H C H C X
A F Q N S T K M M I E I G M D U T L I Y T F C N M C M P U
B Q Q O I J C T C T T A C P I B C A T U W I L K O G N F P
V S F D X W W S A A I O V K K J M O F P O V C Q T R G C J
K D F C S K L R L O T G E U T V N R M O S F V Y F K S R T
M F R P A D T O B Y I R M J O B W E N P Y X P L S L O O U
G S Z J S S P L J E B F O N A I S W Y Y A A D M Q I N S B
S E X A K A Y B E I O W K H Z N V J L O U R P K T Z Q S P
S R L W R U X D Q Y W T S J E N F U G G L L A W A U Z I T
G D U T V V B X G Z S H P H K C R U D M O Q W T X P G M A
B G X T J O G J H I M D P V J C P E X L U M Y N I T F P G
O E C M K S E J R W S E Z A R A C Q Q J M I O K S V B A I
J S S M H D E U O X T Y T B B C D H P J V I T F Y W E C A
W N N Q B R T K P S N A M A O T T W Y B A K M B X P L T U
X X E F C U C I V F U W V Q T U G Z B C Z X A T K R Z U R
F Q C E E H F X S F G B D V M H V A V X R I E T C L E J O
U K P P N E Z Y K V H F F L O U E U N T P H Y P S U G I O
E Z V A O S B I H O B A H N Q K B O B D P X J K C F R E M
I N B I O E T Y G X L B A S D D A O R J V V T Z D A X D O
M W D R P Q X Q O L E V I N K X H A A Y E N V U N T C V O
F P P F Q D R T W R G M L I T E V L Z G D D I E V J G I R
U V A W B K V H U B Q F R M T F Y L U C Z Q C Z X P H E E
U P X J N J F F G Q T X D U R K J T Y P W S W M R P F H Y
L O F A Q K H Y Y E U F X Z A W T F P W M R U T A W L K U
I Q O B E P O D K T O Q G V K O W Q A D Q P X Z B Z Y J V
```

Comparative
Cross-impact
Delphi
Extrapolation
Futurist
Levin
Metatheory
Moore
Scenario
Stephens
Strategic
Tafoya

# Crossword Puzzle

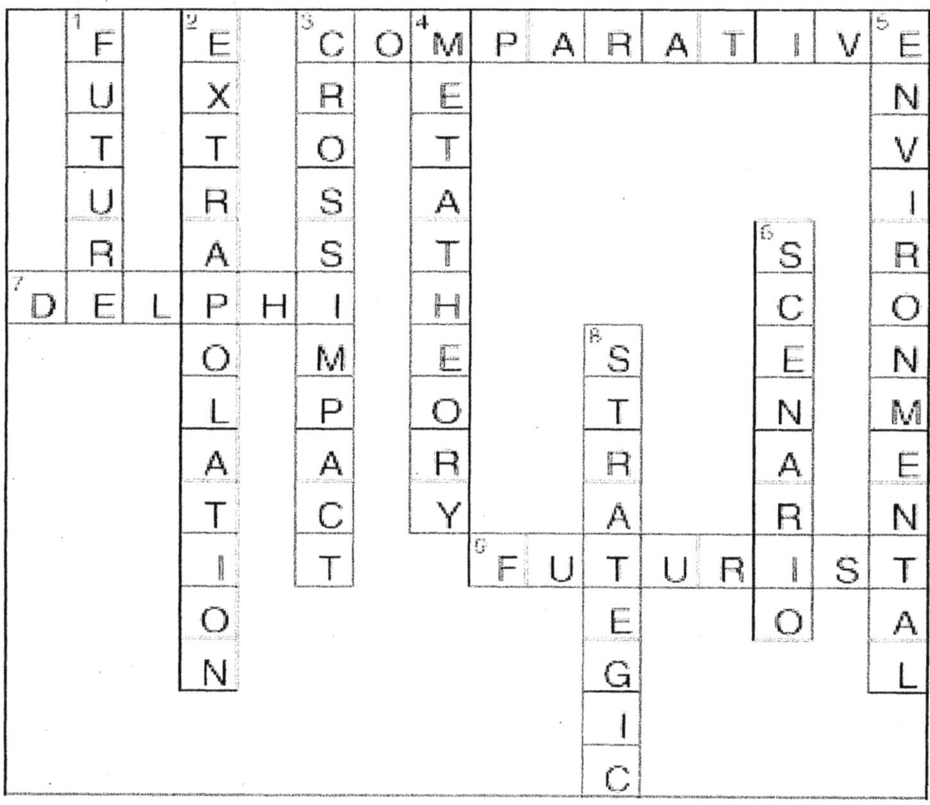

## Across

3. ________ criminology focuses on the cross-national study of crime.
7. The __________ method uses repetitive questioning of experts to refine predictions.
9. One who studies the future.

## Down

1. __________ criminology is the study of likely futures as they impinge on crime and its control.
2. Trend ________ makes future predictions based on the projection of existing trends.
3. ________ analysis attempts to analyze one trend or event in light of the occurrence or nonoccurrence of a series of related events.
4. A theory about theories and the theorizing process.
5. __________ scanning identifies future developments that could occur over a time period of interest.
6. __________ writing attempts to assess the likelihood of a variety of possible outcomes once important trends have been identified.
8. __________ assessment assesses the risks and opportunities facing those who plan for the future.